I RODE WITH STONEWALL

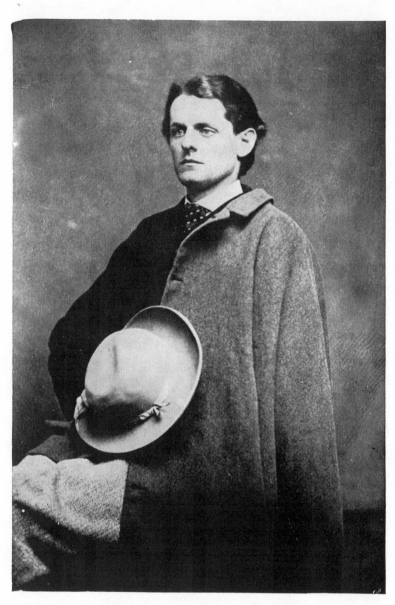

Henry Kyd Douglas shortly after
the close of the War

I RODE
WITH STONEWALL

*Being chiefly the war experiences of the youngest
member of Jackson's staff from the John Brown Raid
to the hanging of Mrs. Surratt*

HENRY KYD DOUGLAS

*And men will tell their children
When all other memories fade
How they fought with Stonewall Jackson
In the old Stonewall Brigade.*

CHAPEL HILL

THE UNIVERSITY OF NORTH CAROLINA PRESS

TO THE MEMORY OF
ANY GOOD SOLDIER WHO DIED IN BATTLE AND IS FORGOTTEN
THIS BOOK IS OFFERED,
AS AN HUMBLE TRIBUTE TO HIS
VALOR AND PATRIOTISM

PREFACE

This book is not a biography nor a history; neither is it a challenge to the military critic. The greater portion of it was written immediately after the close of the war from diaries I had kept and notes I had made and when my recollection was fresh and youthful. It was then laid aside and about thirty-three years have passed over it. At times the manuscript was examined in preparing addresses and articles for magazines, and some of its stories and material have been given to the public in a different form. Other writers, too, have had the benefit of occasional information from these pages, and now and again my recollection is not entirely in harmony with theirs. I was *there*, however, in nearly all I relate.

Now I have been persuaded to rewrite this manuscript with such assistance in the way of correcting errors as the kindred literature of thirty years has given me. I have added somewhat and taken away more freely; and time has mellowed the acerbity of more youthful days. My wounds have healed long ago and have left no hurt. While I cannot "go back on" the boy soldier of '61, whose hair was as black as his coat is now and whose coat was as grey as his hair is now, I remember that in '99 he is wearing glasses, that few of his comrades are left, and that it behooves him to write soberly, discreetly, and fairly.

H. K. D.

April, 1899

ACKNOWLEDGMENTS

As the only living nephew of Henry Kyd Douglas, I inherited all of the original manuscripts, diaries, letters, and photographs that have made the publication of this book possible. About thirty-five years passed before I attempted to have this work published.

In connection with a great deal of the work of preparation and the selection of a publisher I am deeply indebted to and appreciative of the labor given by Mr. Joseph McCord of New York; also, my thanks and appreciation are extended to Miss Ida F. Mongan for her very valuable secretarial and stenographic assistance.

JOHN KYD BECKENBAUGH

Sharpsburg
April, 1940

CONTENTS

ILLUSTRATIONS

I RODE WITH STONEWALL

WAR MAKES A BEGINNING

Born in Shepherdstown, Virginia, I lived in my youth on both sides of the Potomac River. On the Southern side, historic places like Harper's Ferry and Charlestown (present day Charles Town), where John Brown was hung, were familiar to me as my own garden, in Washington County, Maryland. My early acquaintance with the Antietam, Blackford's Ford, and the fields around Sharpsburg was of much service to me at the time of the battles there. For some years before the war I had lived at "Ferry Hill Place," in Maryland and on a hill over against Shepherdstown, where from the gallery of its old house I could look for miles out into Old Virginia. The Potomac, spanned by a convenient bridge, formed no obstacle to constant, friendly communication and represented no hostility between those on opposite sides; and it never occurred to me what it would represent from 1861 to 1865.

John Brown lived for a little while, before his attempted insurrection, at the Kennedy Farm among the hills, about three miles down the river from my father's place, five miles from Harper's Ferry, and near the Antietam Iron Works. He seemed a hermit and only attracted attention because of his apparent eccentricity of manner and life, and went by the name of Isaac Smith. Although, it was reported, he had occasional unknown visitors, I never saw but one person at his humble home, an old Negro woman of most uncomely aspect, who seemed to be his housekeeper and companion.

He professed to be prospecting for minerals, which he said were hidden in these wooded hills. In this as in all other respects his life proved to be a lie.

One wet day, not long before his attack, I was crossing from Shepherdstown, when I found him at the foot of the hill which rises from the river, with an overloaded two-horse wagon. He told me he was hauling miner's tools for prospecting and needed help. I went up home, got my father's carriage horses and their driver, Enoch, and with their aid Mr. Smith's wagon was taken a mile over the hills toward Sharpsburg, his best route home. Being very young, I was much impressed with the grateful simplicity of the venerable actor as we parted in the rain and mud, with many dignified expressions of thanks on his part. I had not a suspicion that he was other than he seemed. But it was not very long until I found out that the rickety wagon contained boxes of "John Brown's pikes" and that I was an innocent *particeps criminis* in their introduction into Maryland. He had brought them from a station on the Baltimore and Ohio Railroad in Virginia, to which they had been shipped from New England.

It is an historical regret that John Brown, *alias* Isaac Smith, had not fallen among a more curious people, who might have watched and made record of his movements. Our people took little notice of him for they did not like him.[1] As he was leading a life of deception, preparatory to crime, he of course did not seek acquaintances or friends. Not a kindly or creditable act is told of his life during these days. With a previous record as a horse thief and a murderer, he was now playing the new role of a conspirator. Full of cunning, with much experience and no little intelligence, cruel, bloodthirsty, and altogether unscrupulous, he seemed singularly ignorant not only of the white people among whom he had camped, but of the characteristics of the race for whom he was about to raise the standard of insurrection. His cause, when the time came, frightened but did not attract the Negroes, and only made them keep quiet and remain the closer to their quarters. Five of them joined him in his

Raid: one of these was killed, and the others deserted him.

There is nothing in all the history of fanaticism, its crimes and follies, so strange and inexplicable as that the people of New England, with all their shrewdness and general sense of justice, should have attempted to lift up the sordid name of that old wretch and, by a political apotheosis, to exalt him among the heroes and benefactors of this land. I can understand why enthusiasts and fanatics in the cause of the abolition of slavery might have sent him to Kansas and aided him with their means to keep that from becoming a slave state; but why they should have sent him money and arms to encourage him to murder the white people of Virginia is beyond my comprehension.

Personally I had no feeling of resentment against the people of the North because of their desire for the emancipation of the slave, for I believed Negro slavery was a curse to the people of the Middle States. As a boy I had determined never to own one. Whether I would have followed the example of shrewd New Englanders in compromising with philanthropy by selling my slaves for a valuable consideration before I became an abolitionist, I will not pretend to say. But I do not think I could have followed that example so far as to drag the banner of freedom into the mire of deception and insurrection that Brown prepared for it and then glory in the falsification of his true character. John Brown closed a life of vice and cruelty by flagrantly violating the laws of God and his country; if "his soul is marching on" it is to be hoped it will confine its wanderings to the people who exalt and glorify it.

I never saw John Brown again until the morning of the 19th of October, 1859, when I witnessed the attack of the United States Marines under Lieutenant Israel Green on the engine house at Harper's Ferry and saw him brought out of it. There were present two men destined to achieve great military distinction. Colonel Robert E. Lee and Lieutenant J. E. B. Stuart. John Brown was wounded, his sons, Watson and Oliver, mortally wounded, and eight others of his party killed; another son, Owen, and four others escaped. Three citizens and some Negroes were killed by Brown's party and a number wounded.[2]

I did not take much notice of Brown after he came out of his "Fort," for I was more interested in Colonel Lewis Washington, whom Brown, after partaking of his hospitality, had taken from his home and family at night and had shut up with him as a hostage. Washington was in the engine house with him when the assault was made and fortunately escaped unhurt. I recall my admiration of his coolness and nonchalance when, walking quietly away from the fort with some excited friends, he took from his pocket a pair of dark-green kid gloves and began pulling them on, and when in reply to the invitation of a friend as he approached "The Wager House" to "take something," he smilingly replied, "Thank you, I will. It seems a month since I've had one." Very soon all the gloom of the occasion had floated away and merriment abounded. Little did anyone suspect what that evil day was hatching!

I saw John Brown again during his trial at Charlestown before Judge Richard Parker and heard Andrew Hunter's great speech for the Commonwealth. Brown's bearing on that occasion was admirable and I was told it had been so during the whole trial, which did not last long. He was convicted and so was John E. Cook (the only man—a misguided dreamer and enthusiast—whose fate aroused any sympathy),[3] and so also three other white men, a free mulatto, and a Negro. The feeling of indignation and bitter criticism aroused in the North by the execution of these criminals filled me with confusion and amazement as to its significance.

A committee of the United States Senate made a long and elaborate investigation of the facts connected with the Brown Raid, and on the 14th June, 1860, reported:

"It was simply an act of lawless ruffians, under the sanction of no public or political authority, distinguishable only from ordinary felonies by the ulterior ends in contemplation by them, and by the fact that money to maintain the expedition, and the large armament they brought with them, had been contributed and furnished by the citizens of other states of the Union, etc."

And yet there are people who would have us believe today that the name of this John Brown of "Osawatomie" is a synonym for martyrdom.

In November, 1860, and before excitement throughout the country over the Brown Raid had subsided, by the suicidal and idiotic division of the Democratic party, Abraham Lincoln was elected President of the United States.[4] All the land seemed full of uneasiness, but I was too young and hopeful to give much attention to gloomy forebodings or prophecies. Having gone to college in the North and to law school in Lexington, Virginia,[5] equally intimate with fellow students on both sides of Mason's and Dixon's line, I did not believe our people would ever take up arms against each other. In those days Virginia boys read *The Federalist* and all the debates of the framers of our government and Constitution. I had no more doubt of the right of a state to secede than I had of the truth of the catechism. Yet I could not make myself believe that there could be a dissolution of the Union; perhaps because I was so much opposed to it. In this hopefulness I went to St. Louis, after the election, to begin the practice of law. I had a winter of leisure for thought; and wisdom came in the spring.

When on the 17th April, 1861, Virginia passed the Ordinance of Secession, I had no doubt of my duty. In a week I was back on the Potomac. When I found my mother sewing on heavy shirts—with a heart doubtless heavier than I knew—I suspected for what and whom they were being made. In a few days I was at Harper's Ferry, a private in the Shepherdstown Company, Company "B," Second Virginia Infantry. Here I had all the experiences of one in the awkward squad, in drill, duty, and discipline.

My first night duty as sentinel was on the canal path along the Potomac; it was a lonely "beat" and gave me little suggestion of the future. Colonel Thomas Jonathan Jackson was in command of the post for about a month after the 27th of April. Then General Joseph E. Johnston arrived and Jackson was placed over four Virginia Regiments, afterwards five —the Second, Fourth, Fifth, Twenty-seventh and Thirty-third—and began to mold them into that brigade which made for themselves and him the name of "Stonewall."

Society was plentiful, for the ranks were filled with the best blood of Virginia; all its classes were there. Mothers and sisters and other dear girls came constantly to Harper's Ferry and there was little difficulty in seeing them. Nothing was serious yet; everything much like a joke. When George Flagg, cleaning barracks, was seen carrying two buckets of scrubbings across the grounds and was guyed for carrying slops, he responded, with assumed dignity, "Slops! This is not slops. It is patriotism!" This was but a sample of the lightheartedness with which all duty was done. The roll of the privates on duty at Harper's Ferry contained many names of families of public distinction in the history of Virginia and the Republic. There were Randolphs, Harrisons, Hunters, Masons, Carters, Conrads, Beverleys, Morgans, Lees, and many, many more, not forgetting that young, gentle and manly George Washington, who afterwards gave me the first sword I ever owned and two years later died a soldier's death at Gettysburg.

General Johnston was opposed to remaining at Harper's Ferry, knowing it was really indefensible and might prove a trap, as it afterwards did to General Julius White. He took all possible care to guard the crossings of the Potomac, east and west. When General Robert Patterson began to demonstrate from Hagerstown to cross the Potomac at Williamsport, General Johnston determined to evacuate Harper's Ferry. I was with the regiment that marched to Shepherdstown to destroy the bridge over the Potomac at that point. I was with the company that set fire to it, and when, in the glare of the burning timbers, I saw the glowing windows in my home on the hill beyond the river and knew my father was a stockholder in the property I was helping to destroy, I realized that war had begun. I knew that I was severing all connection between me and my family and understood the sensation of one, who, sitting aloft on the limb of a tree, cuts it off between

himself and the trunk, and awaits results. Not long after,
when I saw the heavens lighted up over in Maryland one dark
night and knew that the gorgeous bonfire was made from the
material and contents of my father's barn, I saw that I was
advancing rapidly in a knowledge of the meaning of war; and
my soul was filled with revengeful bitterness.

Then my regiment was moved through Martinsburg and
put in camp on a wooded hill, which overlooked Williamsport
beyond the Potomac. There neuralgia seized me and gave me
my first experience of its tortures and I was received in the
family and house of a Union man, Mr. Lemon, and had the
fullest hospitality, without reproach.

While in this camp DeWitt Clinton Rench, a roommate at
college and the most intimate friend I then had, was foully
murdered in Williamsport. He had sent me word that he was
coming over the river to enlist with me as a private in my
company. The day before his intended departure, he was sent
into that town on business for his father. When mounting his
horse to return home, he was set upon by a mob, and turning
upon them to resent their cowardice, he was shot and left dead
upon the ground. No attempt was made to arrest the murderers.[6] A large body of my regiment were wild for revenge—he
had been among them several weeks before—and had it not
been for the vigilance of officers, the gun and torch would have
visited the town of Williamsport to demand the murderers of
Clinton Rench or wreak a cruel vengeance.

General Patterson with his command had been across the
Potomac on his way to Martinsburg to meet Johnston, but in
a few days he recrossed into Maryland. Before the first of
July, Colonel, now Brigadier General,[7] Jackson had come up
and gone into camp near Martinsburg. On the 2nd of July
General Patterson crossed the river and advanced again, and
General Jackson with a regiment and a company or two as
skirmishers went out to meet him and get some practice. It was
only a little "affair at Falling Waters," as General Johnston
called it, and few were hurt. To me it was of memorable importance; for there for the first time I heard the whiz of a
musket ball and the shriek of a cannon shot.

Jackson retired and joined Johnston in the neighborhood of Darkesville. A line of battle was formed to receive Patterson and kept in position for three or four days. But the Federal general did not accept the challenge and was himself too strong to be attacked by Johnston. The Confederate army then withdrew to Winchester, to be nearer to General Pierre G. T. Beauregard. For several weeks there was much chasséing between Patterson and Johnston. Nothing came of it, but the war had made a beginning.

MANASSAS

O<small>N THE</small> 18th of July General Johnston received a message that General Beauregard was about to be attacked and he should go to help him. He went at once, for he had been expecting such a summons. Jackson's brigade took the lead, as it was to do ever after.

We marched as rapidly as the country would permit, seventeen miles to Paris and then early the next morning to Piedmont, six miles, and there took the cars. Other troops did not get along so well. In fact the greater part of our army did not reach Manassas until Saturday, some not until the day of the battle.

It is not my intention nor is it within the scope of this book to give a detailed report of the battle of Bull Run or any other battle to be mentioned. In fact, as the orderly sergeant of a company at Manassas, my personal experience and observation were very limited. On the morning of Sunday, the 21st of July, our brigade was moved from place to place in what seemed to us in the ranks, a meaningless way. I had been quite sick during the night and was horrified at the thought that I might be compelled to fall out; but the distant sound of musketry coming nearer and nearer made me forget my bodily ills and acted as a bracer. Ever after I never felt so sorry for the soldier wounded in battle as for the one too ill to go into it.

It was a beautiful Sunday, but the sacredness of the day was soon forgotten. In Washington General Winfield Scott was anxiously awaiting the result of General Irvin McDowell's skillful plan of battle. General J. E. Johnston had just arrived from the Valley in response to General Beauregard's appeal, "If you will help me, now is the time."

Wavering had been the fortunes of the day, and the hours passed slowly to men who had never tasted battle before. The advantage had been with the Federal army and it seemed to me, as a looker-on, that the day was lost to us. In the early afternoon Jackson hurried to the assistance of the hard-pressed General B. E. Bee, marching through the wounded and stragglers hastening to the rear—not an encouraging sight to brand-new troops. Our brigade was formed along the crest of Henry Hill near the Henry House, the men lying down behind the brow of it, in support of two pieces of artillery. General Jackson was sitting on his horse very near us. General Bee, his brigade being crushed, rode up to him and with the mortification of an heroic soldier reported that the enemy was beating him back.

"Very well, General," replied Jackson.

"But how do you expect to stop them?"

"We'll give them the bayonet!" was the brief answer.

Bee galloped away and General Jackson turned to Lieutenant H. H. Lee of his staff with this message, as it came to Colonel Allan.[1]

"Tell the colonels of this brigade that the enemy are advancing; when their heads are seen above the hill, let the whole line rise, move forward with a shout and trust to the bayonet. I'm tired of this long-range work!"

It was about this time that Jackson was shot in the finger. The storm swept toward us. Bee was back with his brigade but could not stay the onset. His horse was shot under him as he tried to rally and hold his men. At that supreme moment as if by inspiration, he cried out to them in a voice that the rattle of musketry could not drown,

"Look! There is Jackson's brigade standing behind you like a stone wall!"

With these words of baptism as his last, Bee himself fell and died; and from that day left behind him a fame that will follow that of Jackson as a shadow.

It was Bee who gave the name of Stonewall to that Virginia brigade,[2] but it was the men of that brigade who made the name immortal under the leadership of their great commander and gave it to him for all time. As he said on his deathbed, the name belonged to the brigade; but the world has wisely determined that it is necessary to the truth of history and to his own proper description that it should forever be his.

When Bee fell and the command with him fell back, the time and opportunity for our brigade came. Historians have described what it did and accomplished. I confess of that I remember very little; my observation was confined to my own company, and I am sure my vision was not particularly clear. General Jackson said the Second and Fourth Regiments pierced the enemy's center. I have no doubt he knew. I have been surprised that I cannot remember any of my sensations during that turmoil, but I have a vague recollection of personal discomfort and apprehension, followed by intense anxiety for the result of the battle. Since then it has not been difficult for me to understand how much better it is for a war correspondent, in order to describe a battle vividly and graphically, not to be in it at all. I know we went in. My part of the line was driven back at first; then we went in again and fought it through, and found, when the smoke cleared and the roar of artillery died away and the rattle of musketry decreased into scattering shots, that we had won the field and were pursuing the enemy. This is not very historical but it's true.

At the time, I question whether anyone in our brigade but the General knew the good work we had done. He said in a letter to a friend, "You will find when my report shall be published that the First Brigade was to our army what the Imperial Guard was to Napoleon. Through the blessing of God it met the victorious enemy and turned the fortunes of the day."

And yet Jackson afterwards was never enthusiastic over the results of that battle; on the contrary, he said to me once in the Valley that he believed a defeat of our army then had been less disastrous to us. The South was proud, jubilant, self-satisfied; it saw final success of easy attainment. The North, mortified by defeat and stung by ridicule, pulled itself together, raised armies, stirred up its people, and prepared for war in earnest.

Bull Run was not such an awful rout on the part of the Federal army nor such an easy victory on the part of the Confederates as both sides are wont to consider it; nor can an engagement which was fought with about 18,000 men on each side and in which there were less than 500 Union soldiers killed and not more than 400 Confederates be considered a very sanguinary one.[3] But the troops were new and green and there is no ground for harsh criticism.

McDowell and Beauregard determined simultaneously to attack the other's left flank—when flanks were attacked during the war, why was it always the right flank, if successful? McDowell's movement was more dangerous and difficult, but he moved more quickly, and but for the soldierly intuition of Colonel Nathan G. Evans and the admirable disposition of his brigade the surprise might have been a disastrous one. The Confederate army was at once put on the defensive and up to noon was outmarched and outgeneraled, a thing that never occurred again in the many campaigns between the Army of the Potomac and the Army of Northern Virginia. McDowell was hindered by new troops or his tactics were faulty, for when he attempted to execute his well-laid plan piecemeal, it went to pieces. He ought to have hopelessly defeated Beauregard before noon and before Johnston began to get in his work.

It was remarkable how little Jackson's brigade was demoralized or disorganized by the battle. The next morning it seemed ready for another. This was doubtless due to the material in it, and to the steady, cool leader who commanded it. But any experienced soldier would have known by its morale and condition then that whatever of hard duty might be in store for it, it would not falter when the trial came. I remember very well how the men stood the trying camp life during the hot and unhealthy months of August and September. There was disease but no epidemic of consequence; camp life was tedious and monotonous. Furloughs were freely granted in some divisions of the army; few in Jackson's brigade. He refused to take one himself even for a few days; his troops stood it with little grumbling when he refused them, officers or men. His brigade was a good school of war.

From my experience in the army I am convinced that a good officer ought to have been a private. Unlike poets, good officers are made, not born so. There are many things officers do not know who have not served in the ranks; and while they are learning them the service and the troops under their command must suffer. The South did not suffer as much in this regard as the North. Whatever criticisms may be passed on Jefferson Davis, it is certainly true that he was little influenced by politicians in making appointments in the army. Mr. Lincoln, however upright his motives, cannot be relieved of the bitter censure he deserved for the political and disgraceful appointments he imposed upon his troops in the field. Since then, even Mr. Lincoln's error in this respect has been made respectable by President McKinley's appointments in the war with Spain, a responsibility history will not allow him to put off on anyone else, for McKinley himself had once been a soldier and knew what was due to his soldiers.

For several tiresome weeks we were encamped; for a while near Fairfax Court House and then near Centreville. Camp monotony was sometimes broken by little incidents of no moment except the amusement they gave, as when Private Green in the Second Regiment, on guard near the General's tent, was inveigled by Berny Wolfe into a discussion, when on post, as to whether the war would be a long or short one. Green was enticed by Wolfe's apparent earnestness into following him up, after depositing his gun against a tree, until he was reminded of his duty. It was then too late, for the General had seen him and the guardhouse was his portion. Private Green was afterwards sent to the Legislature, but between its sessions he joined the army as a volunteer with a musket. As such he would straggle, always to the front, and was invariably on hand in a battle. He always believed the war would last four or five years, although no one else seemed to think so. He was

an able lawyer and after the war Judge of the Supreme Court of West Virginia.

I was made a Junior Lieutenant of my company in August and was often sent out on night picket duty at sundry places in the direction of Washington. More than one kindly matron unwittingly detracted from my new dignity by telling me that a boy as young as I looked had better stop soldiering and go home to his mother. The picket posts would be occasionally driven in at night by the enemy—they captured all of Green's equipment once and his boots also—but there was not enough of such excitement to make it interesting.

About that time I had my first interview with General Jackson. It was a dark and wet night and I was Lieutenant of the Guard and on duty at his Headquarters. He had been stopped by the sentinel and asked for the countersign; he refused to give it and had me called. He was standing in the rain with his coat off, and quietly asked my authority for demanding the countersign at that hour, when it was not required by his order until after "taps." I replied I did not know of his order, but my authority was Gilham's *Manual.*' He told me quietly and apparently without any annoyance to reinstruct the sentinel and bring Gilham to his tent next morning. I did both and he was very cordial in the morning reception, admitted Gilham's authority, but had a copy of his order given me.

In early November the organization of the Confederate Army in Virginia was changed. General Joseph E. Johnston was assigned to the command of the Department with his Headquarters with the Army of Northern Virginia, which was under the immediate command of General Beauregard. General Jackson was made Major General and sent to command the Army of the Valley, with his Headquarters at Winchester.

This promotion of General Jackson had a doubtful reception. There were those among the officers of rank—not a few —who questioned his ability for a higher command. As one of them put it, "I fear the Government is exchanging our best Brigade Commander for a second or third class Major General." The men in the ranks, however, and the young officers

of his brigade never doubted; from Bull Run to Chancellorsville they never faltered in their faith. While they were broken
up by his leaving them and considered his loss to them irre-
mediable, they never for one moment questioned his fitness for
any position of command and were proud of his promotion.

The General prepared at once to depart for his new assignment, and expressed his willingness to receive any officers of
the brigade that might wish to call on him. A party represent-
ing each regiment and company immediately called to say
good-by. The interview was pleasant, cordial, and brief. As we
took our departure, being the youngest in years and rank I
was the last to shake hands with him. I ventured to remark
that having lately been in the ranks I wished to express the
general grief among the soldiers at parting with him; while he
had all their good wishes for his success in the future, they
hoped he would not forget that the old brigade he left behind
would be ready to march at a moment's notice to his assistance
when he needed them. As I said this a strange brightness came
into his eyes and his mouth closed with more than its usual
tightness. But he held my hand to the door and then said in
his quick way, "I am much obliged to you, Mr. Douglas, for
what you say of the soldiers; and I believe it. I want to take
the brigade with me, but cannot. I shall never forget them. In
battle I shall always want them. I will not be satisfied until I
get them. Good-by."

I left and did not know I should ever see him again. I never
dreamed that after a little while I should be with him on the
march and on the battlefield, when as an invincible soldier
he should be acknowledged by both armies as "the foremost
man of all his time."

It was that day he said to the Reverend Dr. White [5] who
was with him when he received his assignment to the command
of the Valley District, "Had this communication not come
as an order, I should instantly have declined it and continued
in command of my brave old brigade."

The men were so restless and eager to see him once more
before he left, that he consented to see and speak to them in

a body. The brigade on the 4th of November was drawn up in the rear of the Second Regiment's camp in column of regiments closed en masse. Accompanied by several of his staff Jackson rode up to the troops on "Little Sorrel." He glanced for a moment over the silent ranks—they were as silent as if in church—took off his cap, and in his sharp earnest voice spoke to them thus:

"Officers and men of the First Brigade, I am not here to make a speech but simply to say farewell. I first met you at Harper's Ferry in the commencement of the war, and I cannot take leave of you without giving expression to my admiration of your conduct from that day to this, whether on the march, in the bivouac, the tented field, or on the bloody plains of Manassas, where you gained the well-deserved reputation of having decided the fate of the battle. Throughout the broad extent of country over which you have marched, by your respect for the rights and property of citizens, you have shown that you were soldiers not only to defend, but able and willing both to defend and protect. You have already gained a brilliant and deservedly high reputation, throughout the army and the whole Confederacy, and I trust in the future by your own deeds on the field, and by the assistance of the same Kind Providence who has heretofore favored our cause, that you will gain more victories, and add additional lustre to the reputation you now enjoy. You have already gained a proud position in the history of this our second War of Independence. I shall look with great anxiety to your future movements, and I trust whenever I shall hear of the First Brigade on the field of battle it will be of still nobler deeds achieved and higher reputation won."

He paused for an instant. He then rose on his stirrups, threw the reins upon the neck of his horse, and stretching out his gauntleted right hand he concluded in a voice that sent a thrill through all that presence:

"In the army of the Shenandoah you were the First Brigade; in the army of the Potomac you were the First Brigade; in the second corps of this army you are the First Brigade; you are the First Brigade in the affections of your

Stonewall Jackson. Winchester, 1862

General; and I hope by your future deeds and bearing you will be handed down to posterity as the First Brigade in our second War of Independence. Farewell!"

He ended and gently settled into his saddle. As he gathered up the reins slowly with his left hand and turned his horse's head to depart, his old brigade could keep silence no longer and broke the air with one of those wild discordant yells, with which he was afterwards so familiar, and which he once pronounced, "The sweetest music I have ever heard." Unable to bear it calmly, he seized his old cap from his head and waving it to them galloped away; while the noise of their shouting still rang in his ears he disappeared from view and departed for his new field of labor and glory.

The foregoing speech of General Jackson, the only one he ever made during the war, appears in all the memoirs of him, taken from the Richmond *Dispatch* of that time. There was not a newspaper reporter, "war-correspondent," in our army at that time so far as I know—certainly none in Jackson's brigade. In these days when they possess the earth, in peace and war, it may be inconceivable how he carried on his campaigns without them, but he did. He said, "My brigade is not a brigade of newspaper correspondents." I never saw but one reporter in Jackson's army and he lasted about twenty-four hours. In this may be found the secret of his secrecy and the thunderbolt swiftness of his surprises. Within fifteen minutes after the foregoing speech of General Jackson was made, it was carefully written out in my tent by Sergeant T. Harris Towner of my company and myself. We wrote it out from memory, comparing our recollection of every word until we thought it absolutely accurate. I then sent it to the Richmond *Dispatch*, which published it together with the brief description of the scene on November 8, 1861. It is the only report of that speech ever made and therefore its verbiage has never been changed.[6] Sergeant Towner was a good soldier; he was killed at Kernstown.

At Winchester General Jackson found a small and ineffective force. He could not get along without his own brigade, and before the month was out they were with him. They never left him again while he lived and helped to make him, in their belief,

Virginia's greatest son
He that won in all his fights
And never lost a Southern gun.

AT WINCHESTER

NOVEMBER and December, 1861, were spent by General Jackson in organizing and increasing the very inadequate force under his command; he was really a Major General without a division. Shortly after the arrival of his old brigade however, he received several other brigades under Major General W. W. Loring.

Before New Year's General Jackson made several trips to Dam Number Five on the Potomac for the purpose of destroying it and thereby impairing the efficiency of the Chesapeake and Ohio Canal, over which large supplies of coal and military stores were transported to Washington. These trips were only partially successful; but there was no loss and the health of the troops was maintained. Returning home from one of these expeditions, after riding along some distance, the General spied a tree hanging heavy with persimmons, a peculiar fruit of which he was very fond. Dismounting, he was in a short time seated aloft among the branches, in the midst of abundance. He ate in silence and when satisfied started to descend, but found that it was not so easy as the ascent had been. Attempting to swing himself from a limb to the main fork of the tree, he got so completely entangled that he could move neither up nor down and was compelled to call for help. He remained suspended in that attitude until his staff, convulsed with laughter, brought some rails from a fence near by and made a pair of skids to slide him to the earth.

On the 1st day of January, 1862, the army of General Jackson started upon the expedition to Bath and Romney, one that seemed for a while to confirm the impression that General Jackson was crazy. At the time he was greatly blamed by officers, people, and the press. But as years of war passed away, it was seen that General Jackson had only been somewhat in advance of the times; and making raids in winter with much less success than the Bath trip became a common amusement.

The day on which the expedition started was a beautiful one, bright and unusually mild for the time of year. The weather had been pleasant for a week or more and it was not unreasonable to suppose that it would continue so for a week longer—before which time the General knew he could accomplish what he set out to do, namely, drive the Federal troops across the Potomac and out of his Department.

The morning he started on this trip a gentleman of Winchester sent him a bottle of fine old whiskey. It was consigned to the care of one of the staff. As evening came on, it began to grow much colder, and it occurred to the General that a drink of wine—for such he supposed it was—would be very acceptable. Asking for the bottle, he uncorked it, tilted it to his mouth and without stopping to taste, swallowed about as much of that old whiskey as if it had been light domestic wine. If he discovered his mistake he said nothing but handed the bottle to his staff, who, encouraged by the dimensions of the General's drink, soon disposed of all that he had left. In a short while the General complained of being very warm, although it was getting still colder, and unbuttoned his overcoat and some of the buttons on his uniform. The truth is, General Jackson was incipiently tight. He grew more than usually loquacious, discussed various interesting topics and among them the sudden changes of temperature to which the Valley is liable. Dr. Hunter McGuire can give full particulars of this amusing incident.

It was the most dismal and trying night of this terrible expedition. It had been and was still snowing lightly, and the small army was in uncomfortable bivouac. A squad of soldiers in the Stonewall Brigade had built a large fire and some of them were standing and some lying about it wrapped up in their thin and inadequate blankets. The sharp wind was blowing over the hills and through the trees with a mocking whistle, whirling the sparks and smoke in eyes and over prostrate bodies.

A doleful defender, who had been lying down by the fire, with one side to it just long enough to get warm and comfortable, while the other got equally cold and uncomfortable, rose up and, having gathered his flapping blanket around him as well as possible, stood nodding and staggering over the flames. When the sparks set his blanket on fire it exhausted his patience and in the extremity of his disgust he exclaimed,

"I wish the Yankees were in Hell!"

As he yawned this with a sleepy drawl, around the fire there went a drowsy growl of approbation. One individual, William Wintermeyer, however, lying behind a fallen tree, shivering with cold but determined not to get up, muttered, "I don't. Old Jack would follow them there, with our brigade in front!"

There seemed to be some force in the objection, but the gloomy individual continued, "Well, that's so, Bill,—but I wish the Yankees were in Heaven. They're too good for this earth!"

"I don't!" again replied the soldier behind the log, "because Old Jack would follow them there, too, and as it's our turn to go on picket, we wouldn't enjoy ourselves a bit!"

The discomfited soldier threw himself to the ground with a grunt, and all was quiet but the keen wind and crackling flames.

Once during the summer campaign, after I joined his staff, I told the General this story. He exhibited his enjoyment of it by a very hearty laugh, something he seldom indulged in. The General often smiled as other men do, but rarely gave way to audible laughter.

On the same night that the above conversation occurred, the General and his staff occupied a room in a very small log house. They neither felt like talking nor going to bed. While in this charming social state, someone asked if there was no readable book in the party. Sandy Pendleton [1] said he had Charles Lamb, whereupon he was requested by the staff to read the famous essay on roast pig. Being a good reader, Sandy gladly consented. We all know what a charming bit of writing that essay is. As the reader proceeded, the irresistible humor of it elicited smiles and laughter from all but the General. He said nothing but sat looking into the fire, as if unconscious that anything was being read in his presence.

"The wind was raving in turret and tree," but Sandy seemed to have forgotten it until he was suddenly interrupted by General Jackson.

"Captain Pendleton, get your horse and ride to General Winder and tell him, etc."

General Winder was three or four miles distant and one can imagine what a miserable ride Pendleton had on such a night, and in such a country. When he departed no one had the courage to finish the essay.

General Jackson marched directly on Bath, and at his approach the inconsiderable force of the enemy retired, after a little skirmishing, across the Potomac to Hancock, Maryland.

While encamped near Berkeley Springs, if it can be called a camp, I was sent out one night in the direction of Hancock with my company to guard against any curiosity the Yankee cavalry might have to investigate us during the darkness. Some cavalry pickets were in front of us who assured me that there was no danger of such an attempt. I thought it safe, therefore, after throwing some rifle men to the front, to let the men lie down in a field which commanded an advance on either road and go to sleep. It was cloudy but not cold for the season. In the middle of the night I felt moisture on my face, and covering myself from head to foot in a blanket I slept soundly. In the early light I awoke and found myself oppressed with heat. Rising up and throwing off my blanket, I scattered to the air and ground perhaps five inches of snow that had fallen on me.

The scene before me was a weird one. Great logs of men were lying in all directions, covered over with snow and as quiet as graves. Now and then one would break out and look

about him with amazement. Suddenly all were aroused by
the strident voice of Bill Wintermeyer, the wag of the few
nights before, who jumping to his feet, cried out, "Great
Jehosophat! The Resurrection!" After that night I knew what
the Bible means when it speaks of snow as wool,—I often
wished we could make durable blankets out of it—and why
farmers always want a good layer of snow in the winter to
protect their tender wheat from excessive cold.

My breakfast that morning consisted of a piece of beef—
cooked before a fire by using my George Washington sword [2]
as a spit—with hard tack, a tin cup of coffee, and dessert. The
dessert was furnished by a sutler's wagon, captured by the
cavalry. It consisted of a can of peaches into which I poured
a small can of condensed milk and stirred it up with the point
of my useful sword. Peaches and cream in January, and
furnished by the enemy, too!

The next night I was permitted to take that part of my
company into the vacated Berkeley Springs Hotel. It was a
most fashionable summer resort and I had often wanted to see
it, but under different conditions. There was "the banquet
hall deserted"; the men took possession of that and soon had
a fire roaring in the wide chimney. There was the ballroom,
empty, and echoing departed music and merriment and the
soft sound of dancing feet. I took that, but it was most un-
cheerful and cold. A mattress was brought to me and from the
corner where a pile of white lace curtains reached halfway to
the ceiling I drew a great mass of them for covering, but the
more I spread over me the colder I got. I laid aside the lace
curtains and dignity and went in to the banquet hall and laid
down among the men as I had often done before.

Some stores and a few prisoners were taken, but the fruits
of the expedition did not compensate for the sickness and
suffering in our army.

After remaining several days in the vicinity of Bath (Berkeley Springs), the General withdrew his command to Unger's
Store and thence marched to Romney, which the enemy evacuated hurriedly on his approach. Here I was sent on detail as
Judge Advocate of a court-martial in Winchester. Leaving

General Loring and his command at Romney, General Jackson returned to Winchester with the Stonewall Brigade.

The expedition had been conducted in fearful weather. Rain, snow, and storm spent their fury upon the unprotected troops, at one time marching through water, mud, and slush and again over hill and valley of solid ice. Sometimes it was impossible for the men of a regiment to move together over the smooth roads, and limbs were broken as well as guns and swords when a dozen soldiers went down at the same time. Horses fell and were killed. Sometimes a team of four would be struggling on the ice, while the wagon or artillery to which they were attached was pressing upon them, slipping over the glassy surface. The soldiers laughed and swore and compared the trip to those of Hannibal and Napoleon and all others with which their knowledge of ancient and modern history made them familiar.

I think this an appropriate place to introduce several of General Jackson's letters—three of them written before the campaign of 1862 opened, and the other after it had closed. They were addressed to the Honorable Alexander R. Boteler, Representative from the Winchester District in the Confederate Congress and when not in Richmond Colonel and volunteer aide-de-camp on the staff of General Jackson. Colonel Boteler was at all times the General's unconditional friend, one whom he admired greatly, and in whom he evinced great confidence. To this gentleman General Jackson wrote more freely than to anyone else, so far as I am informed, and yet how little information escaped him!

Upon his return from the "Bath Trip," General Jackson, as I have said, left Brigadier General Loring with his command at Romney. This was exceedingly distasteful to that officer and he made known his complaints both personally and through his officers in a most reprehensible manner. The conduct of General Loring on this occasion and that of the War Department led to the resignation of General Jackson and nearly deprived the country of his services.

The complaints of General Loring and his subordinates were not confined to the camp, but were carried by a special committee of his officers to the War Department at Richmond. These representatives to the Government were entirely *ex parte*, for General Jackson made none; indeed, when one of his staff, justly indignant, was about to go to Richmond, the General peremptorily forbade his departure or his taking any action in the matter.

The result was, the Secretary of War ordered General Loring to evacuate Romney and return with his command to the vicinity of Winchester. This order was issued without consultation with General Jackson, and in direct opposition to his known wishes.

Such a pointed violation of military custom and courtesy left General Jackson but one course. Not wishing to embarrass the Government, and having no object but the good of the cause in which he had engaged, he sent in his resignation, and declared his intention of returning to his professor's chair in the Virginia Military Institute.

This caused an exciting scene in the Valley. Civilians, as well as soldiers, instinctively felt that we must not lose the services of General Jackson. The indignation of his troops burst forth in terms of crystallized denunciation. In the parlors of Winchester harsh words escaped between fair lips, little fists were clenched, and bright eyes flashed in anger at the treatment of their General. The regret took a more practical form, and earnest letters were sent to Richmond from prominent citizens, declaring that the resignation of General Jackson would produce a panic throughout the Valley.

Governor John Letcher, Colonel Boteler and others exerted their influence and their energies to prevent the resignation from being accepted. Colonel Boteler wrote to the General on the subject and received in reply the following brief and characteristic note.

Winchester, Febry 5th 1862

Hon. A. R. Boteler;
Dear Sir:
Your letter of the 3rd inst. has been received and I am much obliged for your kindness.

In regard to my resignation, to which you refer, I hold to

the opinion that a man should be in that position where he can be most useful. And I don't see how I can be of any service in the field, so long as that principle which has been applied to me—of undoing at the War Department, what is done in the field—is adhered to.

I trust you will succeed in securing an Engineer Officer for this District, for whoever has command of it will need him.

Very truely your friend,
T. J. JACKSON

After receiving this note, Colonel Boteler, at the urgent solicitation of several gentlemen, determined to go to Winchester and appeal in person to General Jackson to withdraw his resignation. Through him Governor Letcher sent the characteristic message that when the General's resignation arrived at the War Department, as Governor of Virginia and in the name of the Commonwealth, he intended to withdraw it.

Colonel Boteler visited General Jackson and had a prolonged interview with him. The General very feelingly and with eloquent simplicity and directness stated his general views in such cases, and the principle which had influenced him in his course. He seemed calmly resolved, but Colonel Boteler urged the wishes of the people, and finally told General Jackson that Virginia in this great struggle needed the help of all her sons and in her name he appealed to him not to desert her. This last appeal General Jackson could not resist. The resignation was withdrawn and the Pleiad, nearly lost, was saved to our glorious constellation. General Jackson thus in the beginning taught the administration a valuable lesson, and he was never afterward interfered with by orders from the War Department.

A few days afterward the following note was written.

Winchester, Febry 12th 1862

Hon. A. R. Boteler,
Dear Sir:
An official dispatch received this morning informs me that the enemy are in possession of Moorefield. Such is the fruit

of evacuating Romney. Genl. Loring should be cashiered for his course.

Very Truely Yrs
T. J. JACKSON

Just before the evacuation of Winchester at the opening of the Valley Campaign, the General wrote the following very interesting letter.

Winchester, March 3rd 1862

Hon. A. R. Boteler
Dear Sir:
Yours of the 25th ultimo reached me on the evening of the 1st inst., and though Winchester was not evacuated, yet as Mrs. Boteler was in danger of being caught within the lines of the enemy, I wrote to her immediately.

I fear that were I to issue the proclamation of which you speak, that the enemy would soon hear of it and being thus apprised of our weakness would advance on me more rapidly and penetrate our valley farther than he will attempt to do in his present comparative ignorance.

My plan is to put on as bold a front as possible and to use every means in my power to prevent his advance, whilst our reorganization is going on. I fear that the good fruits of the proclamation would not compensate for the inspiriting effect that would be produced upon the invader. What I desire is to hold the country as far as practicable until we are in a condition to advance and then with God's blessing, let us [make] thorough work of it. But let us start right. Let the Legislature pass a law at once that all promotions after the first organization of Companies, Battalions, and Regiments shall be by seniority except for the lowest grade of Company officers. Let Congress pass a law that if any officer is reported for being ignorant of his duties, or for inefficiency, it shall be the duty of the Commanding Officer of the Department to order a Board of Officers, to examine the officer and if their report is unfavorable, that the Commander of the Department shall have authority to approve of the same and the officer shall be dismissed from the service. We should, as far as practicable put a stop to electioneering for office and let the officers feel that after receiving their first commission their promotion will not depend upon personal popularity, but upon qualification for their duty. If you can get these two laws passed you will render more than valuable services to the Country.

In regard to your question as to how many troops I need. You will probably be able to form some idea when I tell you that Banks, who commands about 35,000, has his headquarters at Charlestown. That Kelly who has succeeded Lander, has probably 11,000 with his Headquarters near Paw Paw. Thus you see two Generals whose united force is near 46,000 of troops already organized for three years of the war, opposed to our little force here; but I do not feel discouraged. Let me have what force you can. McClellan as I learn, was at Charlestown on Friday last; there may be something significant in this. You observe then the impossibility of saying how many troops I will require, since it is impossible for me to know how many will invade us. I am delighted to hear you say that *Virginia* is resolved to consecrate all her resources, if necessary, to the defense of Herself. Now we may look for war in earnest. Let the idea of selecting desirable positions for individuals be ignored and let merit be the basis of reward and everything subordinate to the success of our cause. If you were not so invaluable in Richmond I would like to have you here, but you can serve the country better in Richmond than in the field.

I hope that the Indians will come.

I trust that General Lee will be Secretary of War. You ask me for a letter respecting the Valley. I am well satisfied that you can say much more about it than I can, and in much more forcible terms. I have only to say this, that if this Valley is lost, Virginia is lost.

Very Truely Your friend
T. J. Jackson

P.S. I do not understand why it is, that when I ask for an officer whose services are much needed and go so far as to name the person to be commissioned that it is not *done at once*. The enemy are active and industrious, we must be so too if we expect success.

This letter was endorsed in pencil by President Davis:

"To appoint an officer, after the person has been selected, requires a nomination and confirmation, and therefore cannot be '*done at once*.' J. D."

The remarks of General Jackson in regard to a proclama- tion were in answer to a suggestion from Mr. Boteler, that in order to increase his force the General should put forth an address to the people of the Valley, telling them of his inferior- ity to the enemy in numbers, and calling upon them to come forward for the protection of their Valley.

General Jackson never appealed to the people by proclama- tions. He never issued congratulatory orders to his troops, except to set apart a day for thanksgiving and prayer. I remember that about a month before the date of this letter, while on court-martial duty in Winchester, I called upon the General at the request of many officers of the Stonewall Bri- gade and in their name represented to him, that as the term of service of the brigade was about to expire some immediate and effective measure should be adopted to secure a general re-enlistment for the war, and to accomplish so desirable an object it was only necessary for him to issue an address to his old brigade, calling upon them to re-enlist for the war. The General listened attentively to my representation and replied that he did not think the men of that brigade would require such a stimulant; that there were objections to issuing such an address and at any rate he would wait awhile. The address was never issued because it was not necessary; when the term of service expired, the whole brigade, with wonderful unanim- ity re-enlisted for the war.

It will be observed that in the beginning General Jackson was in favor of starting right. It does not appear that he was at all elated by the early successes of the Confederacy; nor did he concur in the opinion which so extensively prevailed in the fall of 1861, that the war would be a short one and our independence easily gained. He regarded with great regret the inactivity, which for a while so seriously injured the South, after the first battle of Manassas. I remember that when someone mentioned in his presence that our cause seemed involved in great gloom and doubt in the spring of 1862, when New Orleans and Fort Donelson passed into the hands of the enemy and General George B. McClellan was within sight of Richmond, the General replied that he saw that the energies of our people were aroused and did not fear the result of these disasters; but he believed that the darkest period in our struggle was immediately after the battle of Manassas in 1861.

The laws which General Jackson thought Congress should pass were afterwards passed, but his plan for getting rid of inefficient officers was not adopted in all its stringency. The General desired to see all our troops subjected to the discipline and organization prescribed for the regular army without delay, but every bill introduced into Congress with that view met with decided opposition from those civilian critics who believed that a volunteer soldier should be subjected to very little discipline and inconvenience.

As the General corresponded regularly with Colonel Porcher Miles of South Carolina, Chairman of the Congressional Committee on Military Affairs, it is not doubtful that he gave him the benefit of many suggestions. Indeed, I am informed that Colonel Miles frequently acknowledged his indebtedness to General Jackson for valuable suggestions, and that the General framed one or two bills that were passed by that body. I do not know that he had anything to do with the Conscript Act, but I know that he had a conscript law of his own, virtually in operation in the Valley, before one was passed by Congress.

It is proper to add that General Jackson's army was not reinforced at that time; and that the army with which he engaged General James Shields at Kernstown on the 23rd of the same month, numbered 2,750 infantry, with, say, 300 cavalry and 18 guns.

"I hope the Indians will come." It had been proposed to send General Jackson a few Indians to be used as scouts and terrifiers. The General believed he could discipline and make them useful and was in favor of having them. He may have been right, although it may well be doubted whether the idea was practicable.

The above letter evinces also the confidence the General had in General Lee at that early date, when our greatest man had made for himself no reputation in the war, when many doubted his ability or his fortune, and when he was holding a position of honorary retirement in Richmond as *quasi* amanuensis to the Secretary of War and President Davis.

"If this Valley is lost, Virginia is lost." In the light of after events this sounds like prophecy, but it was only the expression of military sagacity.

It is appropriate, I think, in this connection to introduce another letter from the General, written to Colonel Boteler after the campaign of 1862 was over. It exhibits the interest he always felt and frequently expressed in the Valley and the Valley people.

> Caroline County, Va.
> Dec. 31st 1862

My dear Colonel.

In reply to my communication to Genl. Lee, respecting the sending of troops to the Valley, he expressed his desire to do so, if he had the troops to spare. As he asked the question whether I thought troops could be wintered there to advantage, I stated that 20,000 could be wintered near Winchester, if entrusted to an enterprising officer. Since then I have heard nothing more from him on the subject. I named the officer to whom the trust might be confided—Genl. Early—. I have repeatedly urged upon Genl. Lee the importance of protecting the Valley and upon more than one occasion have apologised to him from a conviction that I was apparently forgetting my position and encroaching upon the prerogative of my Commanding General. He has always kindly received what I said; but I don't know that much more has been accomplished. I am well satisfied that General Lee desires to protect the Valley.

Since I was relieved from the command of the Valley and assigned to the command of the 2nd Corps of this army, I have felt the liberty of saying to Genl. Lee that the Officer who may be sent to command the Valley District should have the authority of a Department Commander. This is important to the full efficiency of the command. I always shrank from saying so to him when I was in command there; and such a statement from me at a time when I would have derived advantage from such authority might have done more harm than good by giving occasion to suspect that my object was a personal one and thus create prejudice against me which might impair my opportunities for future usefulness.

It is but natural that I should feel a deep and abiding interest in the people of the Valley, where are the homes of so many of my brave soldiers,[3] who have been with me so long and whose self-sacrificing patriotism has been so thoroughly tested. Apart from this the tried loyalty of those who are still there and their many acts of kindness to me personally, taken in connection with what still remains which could be made tributary to our cause, give me a special interest in that section of the State. As you are a member of my Staff, I write to you more freely than I would have further known. You must not think from what I have said to you at any time that I desire to be sent to the Valley, even if it should be made a Department. I would rather remain in a subordinate position as long as the war lasts; provided that my command is kept near my Commanding General. This is my real feeling. When, in the Valley, I spoke to you about securing a Department, my command was so far separated from the Comdg. Genl. as to render it desirable. I have never told you of the difficulties under which I labored last spring in consequence of my limited authority. When I speak of not desiring a separate command it is upon the supposition of the interest of the service not requiring a change of command. I hope that you will soon find it convenient to make me another and a longer visit.

Very Truely Your friend
T. J. JACKSON

This ingenuous and artless letter is worthy of repeated and careful perusal. The noble and manly letter of General Albert Sidney Johnston to Mr. Davis, coming after such severe censures had been heaped upon him and just before the battle of Shiloh in which he fell, will always be regarded as a model of soldierly dignity and unselfishness. The one before us is not less admirable for its simplicity and truth.

In mentioning General Jubal A. Early by name for the command of the Valley District, Jackson plainly testifies his confidence in that able but finally unfortunate officer. Of all the generals who made for themselves a reputation in the Army of Northern Virginia, there were none of General Lee's subordinates, after the death of General Jackson, who possessed the essential qualities of a military commander to a greater extent than Early. With a mind clear, direct, and comprehensive, his opinion was entitled to that respect which it always received from his Commanding General. Quick to decide and almost inflexible in decision, with a boldness to attack that approached rashness and a tenacity in resisting that resembled desperation, he was yet on the field of battle not equal to his own intellect or decision. He moved slowly from point to point, but had he possessed the personal vie and dash of General John B. Gordon, he would have escaped such severe censure in his misfortune.

Moreover, he received with impatience and never acted upon, either advice or suggestion from his subordinates. Arbitrary, cynical, with strong prejudices, he was personally disagreeable; he made few admirers or friends either by his manners or his habits, and those who defend him now do so because they are convinced of his patriotism, of his earnestness, and of his great ability. If he had a tender feeling, he endeavored to conceal it and acted as though he would be ashamed to be detected in doing a kindness; yet many will recall little acts of General Early which prove that his heart was naturally full of loyalty and tenderness.

It will not be possible to make posterity comprehend and appreciate the enormous difficulties with which General Jackson had to contend in the Valley Campaign of 1862. They were only surpassed by those of Early in 1864. Jackson succeeded; Early did not. And in war—success is everything.

History can never know the whole truth. The historian may analyze, investigate, and speculate until he is weary, and knowing the small and uncertain means with which such great results were achieved, he may pronounce it all wonderful; yet his conclusion will fall short of the truth. General Jackson seldom, if ever, complained, and never uselessly and apologetically to those under him, nor to those above him. Determined to deserve good fortune, he never quailed before disaster; but trusting in God, himself, and his army he always commanded success.

I would like in this place to put on record a letter from General Jackson, in reply to one from Colonel Boteler telling the General that the people were beginning to use his name in connection with the next Presidency and facetiously suggesting that he should conduct himself accordingly. But I have not been able to obtain the manuscript of that letter. The General, of course, was very much astonished. He was unwilling to believe that the people were so foolish and declared emphatically that he never would be a candidate for nor accept the office of President. Nor do I believe he ever could have been induced to accept the position. His strategy was military, not political; he had no aspirations for civil honors.

After the return of General Jackson from his "Bath Trip," everything was quiet until the first of March. The enemy then became restless and it was evident that General Jackson could not hold Winchester with the small force under his command. General Loring had been transferred to another part of Virginia, and a portion of his division departed about the same time. All the public stores were removed. And Mrs. Jackson, who had spent the winter with the General, left with them. General N. P. Banks having approached in force, General Jackson and his small army evacuated Winchester on the night of March 11th, and that devoted town passed for the first time into the hands of her enemies.

KERNSTOWN

I CANNOT believe that any other great man ever went down to his grave knowing so little of his fame throughout the world, or of the love his people had for him as General Jackson. He regulated his conduct, personal and military, in accordance with his own ideas of right and wrong; he acknowledged accountability to no one but God and his superior officers.

There could in consequence be very little intimacy between the General and the press. He read newspapers only for the facts they contained, when he read them at all. Their criticisms upon his movements or those of his associates he ignored. After a while he stopped reading them altogether. He was accustomed to ask some member of his staff if there was any important news in those that arrived and if so, to read it to him. The reason, I am sure, why he gave up reading the papers was that he was so modest that their broad compliments embarrassed and annoyed him. People with him, therefore, rarely ever told him what "all the world" was thinking and saying of him and his achievements. No man in the war was the subject of so many newspaper paragraphs that were purely fictitious, and he evidently had a suspicion of that.

One day after dinner the General asked Sandy Pendleton to read him any news in the papers worth hearing. After reading a few telegrams, Pendleton said there was an amusing article taken from the New York *Mercury* which would make him laugh and help to digest his dinner.

"Go on, Captain—let's hear it, if it will make us laugh," said the General.

Pendleton began. "The life and character of the rebel General, Stonewall Jackson." The General was up in an instant and said he didn't want to hear that.

"Hold on, General," said Pendleton, "it is only a parody on the "Lives" which fill the Northern papers; it is entirely unobjectionable and you will enjoy it."

The General took his seat and Pendleton read it in his happy manner. It was clever, satirical, most humorous. Tracing his pedigree from Jack, the Giant-killer, it gave an absurd history of his adventurous boyhood, followed up the development of his peculiar mental and moral traits, and laid special stress upon his force of will and that wonderful abstemiousness which enabled him to live for a fortnight on two crackers and a barrel of whiskey. It was the kind of humor that takes in camp.

The General listened attentively, his expression relaxed. A smile appeared which grew broader as the "Life" continued, kindled into audible delight; and at the end he broke into the heartiest and loudest burst of laughter I ever heard him indulge in. This is the only time I ever heard him listen to what the press had to say about him.

After the evacuation of Winchester on March 12th General Jackson retreated slowly up the Valley as far as Mount Jackson and went into camp. In less than two weeks, being advised that General Banks was sending his army from Winchester, perhaps to reinforce McClellan, and determined to stop that if he could, he started off again down the Valley; making a twenty-five-mile march the first day. The next day, the 23rd, he was off early and did not stop until he ran up against the enemy near Kernstown and prepared for battle. General Jackson had been misinformed by Ashby [1]—almost invariably correct in his information—as to the strength of the enemy. He had less than 3,000 of all arms and it turned out afterwards that Shields had about 6,000 on the field, with reserves at hand.

The battle was joined about two o'clock and it was one of the most stubborn fights of the war on the part of our troops.

In that fight I commanded as lieutenant the color company of the second Virginia Regiment, General Richard B. Garnett's brigade, and saw seven color bearers fall. The Confederates were defeated and driven from the field, but the Federal troops going to McClellan were recalled. It was the pride of General James Shields until his death that he was the only Union General who ever whipped Stonewall Jackson.

The battle was fought until sundown, when General Garnett, commanding the Stonewall Brigade, ordered it to retire, leaving some wounded men on the field. For this order General Garnett was subsequently put under arrest by Jackson and relieved of his command.

Then arose great bitterness of feeling in the old brigade. Garnett had completely won the confidence and affection of its officers and men and their astonishment at his arrest was only equaled by their indignation. General Garnett maintained that he could not have held his position much longer with his weak line and that by falling back he saved some of his soldiers from unprofitable deaths and many from capture. General Jackson never ceased to believe that if the unfortunate order had not been given his troops would have held their position until dark, the battle would have been a drawn one, and the enemy would have retired to Winchester during the night. The officers in the brigade thought General Garnett was right; in fact I do not know an exception to this opinion. General Jackson had great personal regard for Garnett as a man and soldier; but he was so positive in his opinion that he relieved Garnett from command and put General Charles S. Winder in his place.

It may be said that, for once, the officers and the men of General Jackson's old brigade almost unanimously differed with him. Their regret at the loss of General Garnett was so great and their anger at his removal so intense and universal that their conduct amounted almost to insubordination. General Winder was received in sulky and resentful silence, and for nearly three weeks General Jackson was permitted to ride past his old command without hearing a shout. General Garnett asked for a court of inquiry immediately, but as the

active campaign was begun, this request was refused. He was
not restored to duty until after Chickahominy. If General
Jackson thought Garnett had committed a grievous fault,
most grievously did he answer it.

Afterwards, until the death of General Jackson, Garnett
was only seen once by his faithful brigade. On this occasion,
he happened to appear suddenly before them, and as he rode
along the line, with pale face, they greeted him with shouts
of love and remembrance that must have rung in his ears during the rest of his short life.

The next time I saw him was in Richmond. General Jackson was lying dead in the Executive Mansion and General
Garnett had come to look upon his remains. Major Pendleton
and myself met him at the door and led him to the parlor. He
raised the veil which covered the face of the dead and looked at
it long, in silence. "Tears gathered in his heart and rose to his
eyes," as his manly frame trembled with emotion and sorrow.
Forgetting all personal wrongs, that unsullied patriot wept
for the loss that had fallen on his country. In a little while,
taking Pendleton and myself by the arms, he led us to the
window. "You know of the unfortunate breach between General Jackson and myself; I can never forget it, nor cease to
regret it. But I wish here to assure you that no one can lament
his death more sincerely than I do. I believe he did me great injustice, but I believe also he acted from the purest motives.
He is dead. Who can fill his place!"

When the painful interview ended, Pendleton asked him to
be one of the pallbearers in the honorary procession to take
place on the following day, and he willingly consented. A year
after, he fell at Gettysburg, commanding a brigade in Pickett's famous charge, and left behind a blessed memory and
never a doubt as to his flawless courage and unselfish patriotism.

General Winder took command of the brigade about April
1st, and his relations with General Jackson were not any more
pleasant, although he was one of the most brilliant officers in
the army. The two were in some respects, determination and
wilfulness, very much alike; in personal appearance and bear-

ing the exact opposite. In fact, if Jackson was in error with
Garnett, as nine-tenths of all the officers and soldiers who
were at Kernstown then believed, it was but another instance
of what has been often charged, that he was not always in
pleasant accord with officers next in rank to him and was apt
to judge them harshly.

The Army of the Valley remained in the neighborhood of
Mount Jackson until after the middle of April. In the meantime the Northern papers that reached us were celebrating,
all by themselves, the great victory of General Shields over
James Longstreet and Kirby Smith, as they said; and the
Confederacy passed a vote of thanks to Jackson and his little
army.

The Second Virginia Regiment was encamped on Rude's
Hill, two miles South of Mount Jackson. One cold day in the
first quarter of April I was exercising myself and trying to
keep warm by chopping wood for the mess, much to the amuse-
ment of the men of the company who expressed the hope that
I enjoyed the labor as much as they did my awkwardness.
I had about all I wanted of the so-called exercise when someone rode up and handed me a slip of paper. It was from my
Colonel, a copy of an order detailing me for special duty at
General Jackson's Headquarters and directing me to report
to Lieutenant Colonel W. S. H. Baylor, Assistant Inspector
General of his staff. The suggestion had come from Sandy
Pendleton, ever after until his death one of my most intimate
friends. I gladly made the exchange from exercise at a wood-
pile to exercise on horseback—from early boyhood I had been
accustomed to the latter; of woodpile exercise the "little nig-
gers" had the monopoly at home.

I immediately reported to General Jackson's Headquarters.
At dinner I again met the General who received me with quiet
politeness; but I remember my embarrassment, caused by his
considerate desire to put me at my ease. After dinner he returned to his room and I saw him no more that day. The General always kept himself very much apart and, although he
was uniformly polite to all persons who came to see him, he did
not encourage social calls. He was especially considerate to

young officers and privates when duties brought them into his presence.

General Banks was preparing to advance. General Jackson seemed to be busily engaged and kept close quarters. Night came on and I went with some of the staff, although not of them, to a large room in the Rude House. At midnight came a quiet message, "The General wishes to see Lieutenant Boswell"—his engineer officer. Lieutenant James K. Boswell, expecting to ride, dressed himself for it and departed to the General. In a few minutes he returned with the information that the General only wanted to know the distance from Gordonsville to Orange Court House. Fifteen minutes after, the General sent to him again to get the same information in writing. I learned afterwards that occasionally his staff officers were subjected to petty ills of that kind. For a while I was wont to wonder if the General ever slept; but I soon found out that he slept a great deal, often at odd times. If he had just five minutes to spare for that recreation, he could sleep four and a half minutes of it and be wide awake when the five minutes was up. In that he had the advantage of everyone about him; Sandy Pendleton came next.

A week passed during which I was kept busy with Major Baylor, organizing and apportioning recruits and militia, and I saw little of the General. And then we began to move.

At once I was put on staff duty, and got my first taste of its delightful excitement. The General when he moved off directed me to remain behind in communication with Colonel Ashby until he was ready to send forward some message. Ashby, with a small squadron of cavalry, had gone across the North Fork of the Shenandoah between us and Mount Jackson to watch the enemy. I took position near a couple of pieces of artillery under Lieutenant Thomson, unlimbered on Rude's Hill. The hill descended abruptly to a level plain of bottom land which spread itself between it and the river. I had been there but a little while when I observed the Confederate cavalry return and cross the bridge. I knew the Federals were close at hand. In a few minutes a heavy dust announced their approach; a regiment of cavalry in blue, with sabres glistening in the sun, came galloping in column of fours into view, led, apparently, by an officer on a milk-white horse. It was beautiful. Distance lent enchantment to it, as it did on other occasions in my war experience.

"Look! See how splendidly that officer on the white horse manages him!" exclaimed someone.

"By Jove, that's the Colonel!" cried Thomson, Ashby's pet. "Ashby, as I live, leading that Yankee regiment! See they are firing on him, he on them. He won't have time to burn the bridge. Sergeant, load!"

It was Ashby. Relying on the speed of his noble horse, he had remained behind his squadron and kept so close to the enemy that at our distance, over a mile, he seemed to be leading the regiment that was after him. The scene became most exciting, as we saw the smoke of pistols. As they approached the bridge Ashby moved off rapidly to cross and burn it. But the two leading files of his pursuers, catching his purpose, followed him in a spirited chase.

Ashby gained the bridge, drew up his horse as if to apply fire to the prepared pile of combustibles, but the enemy were upon him with drawn sabres. One shot from a horseman at his side cut into his boot, grazed his leg and buried itself in the side of his charger. The next moment, the avenging sword of the master came down upon the enemy and rolled him in the dust. To us, watching afar off, it was a moment of terrible anxiety. Not a word was spoken, not an exclamation. The bridge was not burned, but where was Ashby? Instantly he was seen to emerge from the bridge and follow his troops. Centaur-like, he and his horse came sweeping over the plain. They were soon with us. Having borne his master with unabated spirit until danger was over, Ashby's splendid stallion sank to the ground, dappled with the foam of heat and suffering; his wound was mortal. The big-hearted Cavalier bent over him, stroked his mane, stooped down and gazed affectionately into his eyes, and the excitement of the last hour was swallowed up in his sorrow for his dying companion. Thus the most splendid horseman I ever knew lost the most beautiful war-horse I ever saw.

The enemy took time before they concluded to pursue.

I carried the information Colonel Ashby gave me to General Jackson. The next day we moved on. About the time of setting sun and before we reached Harrisonburg, General Jackson called for me. The sky was covered with heavy clouds and the rain was falling heavily. The General handed me a paper from under his rubber cape and requested me to take it to General Richard S. Ewell. And proceeded to tell me that he was on the other side of the Blue Ridge Mountains, somewhere near Culpeper Court House. While my heart stood still with amazement, he told me the contents of the paper and added that, as it was very important, he did not care to send it by a courier. He wanted it delivered by daylight in the morning.

For a moment I was stampeded, paralyzed. I had never been over a foot of the country and had only a vague idea that Culpeper was somewhere beyond the mountains; but how to get there I could not imagine. Night was upon us; it was raining like the deluge; and I had already ridden to and fro about twenty-five miles that day. But a young man soon rallies and I pulled myself together quickly. I was being weighed in the balance right there and I determined to throw all my weight on the scales.

"General, I will start at once if I can get a horse."

"Take my mare," said generous Kidder Meade [2] of the staff, who had left an arm at Bull Run, "and strike for Stanardsville first."

As I rode away on Meade's spirited dun mare, in reply to my "good night," came the voice of the General—"A successful and pleasant ride!"

It was kindly meant, but it sounded singularly like sarcasm. Forward I went into the night and mud, every minute growing darker and wetter. But all weariness was gone and I felt as fresh as my mottled horse. In a little while I was rounding the base of the Massanutton Mountain where it breaks as abruptly down into the Valley as it rises from it at Strasburg; and the towering mass horrified the night. Then on through McGaheysville and across the South Fork of the Shenandoah

Map of the State of Virginia containing the Counties, Principal Towns, Railroads, Rivers, Canals, & all other Internal Improvements. Published by West and Johnston, Richmond, Va., 1862. Copyright secured by West and Johnston, May 1, 1862.

———

This map originally belonged to Colonel Stapleton Crutchfield of General T. J. Jackson's staff, then passed into the hands of the General himself, who used it in the "Valley Campaign" in 1862 and afterwards until the battle of Sharpsburg, when he gave it to Captain Douglas of his staff. The pencil marks encircled were made by Stonewall Jackson.

to Conrad's Store (now Elkton). Here as I approached the
Blue Ridge I felt almost hopeless in the impenetrable stormy
night. I stopped to make some enquiries and procured a small
bottle of whiskey for an emergency. Then into and up the
black mountain.

Vision was impossible, but fortunately the road was solid
and fairly good and my horse could keep to it. I could reach
out my hand and feel her neck and ears, but could not see
them. My speed was necessarily slackened, not only because
a horse cannot climb a mountain like a goat, but because
safety required some caution. At times I heard the water rush
under us and across the road and tumble in torrents so far
down below that I knew we were traveling on perilous edges.
The ascent seemed very steep and very long. At last we reached
the summit of Swift Run Gap. It was from this summit and
through this gap that Governor Alexander Spotswood and
his knights of the Golden Horseshoe, in 1716, obtained the
white man's first view of the Valley of the Shenandoah. From
the same point I did not partake of their enchantment.

Just here I met a knight of a less romantic order. He was
a belated, bedraggled, drowsy courier plodding his way from
General Ewell to General Jackson. From him I extracted
some useful information as to my route and in return gave
him a pull at my flask. It was vile stuff, but as he seemed to
like it I gave him the bottle and left him on the summit.

The descent was quicker and I soon went plunging into
Stanardsville, having done at least thirty-seven miles on that
blooded mare. Here I tried to get another horse but failed.
My efforts cost me half an hour and then I moved on. Anxiety
for my noble beast added another horror to the night. Just
out of Stanardsville the road forked in the middle of a broad
and shallow stream and of course I took the wrong branch.
Half a mile beyond I aroused the inmates of a cabin and
learned my mistake. Retracing my steps I was soon in front
of a white farm house. A few well-directed shouts brought an
astonished head out of an upper window. I appealed to its
owner for a horse. I fancied I saw him smile satirically as he
declined, but he politely urged me to "come in out of the wet."

I then knew I must play trumps and I said plaintively, "My dear friend, I am an officer of Stonewall Jackson's staff, carrying an important message, and I must have a fresh horse."

"The devil!" was the response I had, and down went the window. But immediately I heard at the back of the house, with rising inflection, "Saul! Saul! Drat that sleepy nigger! There you are—run you woolly head, bring out the big black mare and be quick about it!" He soon appeared with Saul, the horse, and a lantern, and helped to exchange the saddle and bridle. As I climbed from the fence on the mare and was about to ride away he threw the light of the lantern in my face and said in a tender voice, "Good luck. I have a boy, maybe your age, with Stonewall Jackson."

My new beast was as tall as a dromedary and as I steered her through the deep mud she seemed to plough it like a gunboat, and knew just as little about a riding bridle. Madison Court House was not quite fifteen miles, and when we reached it she was worn out. There, fortunately, was a courier station. I exchanged her for a little grey horse. I clattered through the streets of that slumbering town, and was soon in the open country and on another deep mud road. Suddenly my horse slipped, gave a groan and was down and I rolled off into the mire. I jumped up and asked him to do the same, but he never responded and was apparently dead. Taking off the saddle I stood by the roadside in hopeless bewilderment. I looked about me and could see no habitation, no light, nothing. Just then a little imp jumped into the road on the opposite side, with a "Good Lordy, wats dat?" Explanations followed. He was on his way to town for the doctor for "ole missus." He said it was "a mile or mo' from town 'round de road, but catabias 'cross de fiel's not more'n half a mile—not dat." I bribed him with a dollar to hurry to the tavern and tell them to send me another horse, and he disappeared like a rabbit in the dark.

I sat on the fence and waited. The rain was pouring down, I was covered with mud and soaking, my little horse gave no sign of life, the night was passing, and my spirits were sinking rapidly. But the little darkey came, the forerunner of another white horse which soon made its appearance. I was soon mounted and as my little black angel received the dollar and let go my bridle he cried, "Golly. I mos' forgot! I mus' run back after de doctor!"

After nine miles more of spurring and splashing I ran into James City where I changed to a tall gaunt roan that carried me valiantly the eleven miles to Culpeper Court House. As I approached there was a suspicion of light in the direction of dawn and the rain had partially worn itself out. In all directions I heard the drums of an early reveille, and presently encountered a group of men sitting on their horses in the gloaming. I found it was General Dick Taylor, son of General Zachary Taylor of Mexican fame, and his staff. Learning that he was ordered to march and evidently in the wrong direction, I suggested to him that he should not move until he heard from General Ewell, who, he said, was encamped beyond Brandy Station. One of his staff kindly offered me a fresh horse and General Taylor ordered a courier to lead the way and "ride like the devil." This the courier did and so did I; but as I had been doing that thing all night it was no novelty to me. We rushed along like a pair of John Gilpins and, as it never seemed to occur to my guide that I might be nearly worn out, I didn't mention it.

But we soon made the six miles to Brandy Station. After going several miles beyond we drew rein at General Ewell's Headquarters just as I was beginning to be exhausted beyond endurance. The General was just up and I dismounted and handed him the crumpled and saturated dispatch. He read it, and quickly turning to me, said, "You don't say—" The sentence was not finished. Seeing me totter and about to fall, he caught me, led me to his cot, and laid me there; and then the dear, rough, old soldier made the air blue with orders for brandy and coffee and breakfast—not for himself but for me. My ride was done and nature asserted itself by reaction and exhaustion. In less than twenty hours I had ridden about one hundred and five miles, and since I left General Jackson I had passed around the Massanutton, over the Blue Ridge, and through rain and mud and impenetrable night had been under the strain of a cavalry charge for more than eighty miles.

When I revived and had something to eat, the General sent me in his ambulance to Culpeper Court House, where I remained in bed in a hotel for twenty-four hours. Then I began to retrace my steps. It was a weary ride, taking up my horses as I went, and at ten o'clock the second night I rode up to General Jackson's Headquarters near Conrad's Store. It had not ceased to rain for an hour since I left, and except when in bed I had been clad in soaking garments from start to finish.

I went into the General's room to report. It was empty of furniture and on the hearth were some dying coals of a wood fire. He was lying on the floor upon a thin mattress, wrapped in a blanket and asleep. I awoke him and made my report. He listened politely and then with, "Very good. You did get there in time. Good night," he turned over to sleep and I left the room. I will not attempt to describe my surprise and indignation at this cool reception. Refusing to be comforted by the staff, who knew the General better, I threw off my heavy, soggy clothes and retired in grievous disappointment to an uncomfortable bed. A letter that had come through the lines, in a delicate handwriting and with a little gold ring enclosed, did turn my thoughts somewhat in a different direction. After a while youth and tired nature took possession of me and I slept.

The next morning the General sent for me. He was alone, sitting on a campstool, gazing into the fire. He arose, holding in his hand a dispatch which he said he had just received from General Ewell, and then remarked, "Mr. Douglas, Major Baylor leaves me today to take command of the Fifth Regiment of the Stonewall Brigade, and I want to assign you to duty as Assistant Inspector General of my staff." What I said, I do not clearly remember, but my wounded pride was healed. Thus I entered the military family of Stonewall Jackson.

The dispatch I carried that night was an order from General Jackson to General Ewell to put his division in readiness to move toward Swift Run Gap and unite with the Army of the Valley west of the Blue Ridge. That was the initial move in that great game of war now known as Stonewall Jackson's Valley Campaign.

Colonel Baylor, gallant, impetuous officer, charming gentleman, did not long survive his promotion. He fell at Second Manassas August 30th, 1862, while commanding the Stonewall Brigade.

General Ewell moved toward Jackson as ordered and encamped near Stanardsville, east of the Blue Ridge. On the 30th of April, General Jackson sent to him the following order dated from Swift Run Gap:

"General. Please let your command come on this side of the Blue Ridge at once."

This order was endorsed by General Ewell as follows: "Leave the ordnance and Division trains. I will send word at once if anything prevents General Taylor from going. Let Major Green go anyhow. R. S. E."

On that day Ewell crossed the Blue Ridge and moved to Conrad's Store: but Jackson was gone and he occupied the camps in which the dying fires still smouldered. Ewell was surprised and somewhat indignant, for Jackson had not left him an order or an intimation of his future movements—an eccentricity that rumors had partially prepared him for. There is no question that this ignoring of the officers next in rank to him detracted much from his personal popularity with them, especially as he had no individual magnetism to attract them. Thus entered General Ewell into the Army of the Valley, to whose fame and brilliant success he so largely contributed.

On the afternoon of April 30th General Jackson started with his division on that terrible march along the east side of the Shenandoah River to Port Republic. It was only about sixteen miles, but it took him two days and a half to do it. This march and the unwisdom of it was much criticised then as now. Within sight of the enemy's pickets, if they had been enterprising enough to have them along the opposite side of the Shenandoah, over soft and bottomless roads into which horses and wagons and artillery sank, at times almost out of sight, dragged along by main force of horses and men, the

General himself on foot, lifting and pushing among the struggling mass, wet, covered with mud from cap to boots, encouraging soldiers and teamsters by word and example, at the
risk any moment of ruinous attacks from the Federal guns
from opposite bluffs—there is little wonder that many officers
and men in his army thought such a march, under such conditions, was inexcusable rashness, without justifiable emergency. General Banks ought to have scattered and almost
destroyed Jackson's army; it would have been a sorry day
for any Federal general who had given such an opportunity
to Jackson himself. The reason for that desperate movement
was doubtless satisfactory to the General, but it did seem to
many who were with him that he could have crossed the Blue
Ridge through Swift Run Gap by a comparatively solid road,
to Stanardsville and Gordonsville, and thence to Staunton,
just as speedily and as secretly.

Near Port Republic we turned eastward up into the Blue
Ridge and over it through Brown's Gap, and on Saturday
evening went into camp at White Hall. It was the intention of
the General to remain quiet in camp over Sunday, but during
the night word came to him from Staunton that the enemy
was marching rapidly on that place. Early on Sunday the
troops were off via Mechum's River Station, where the General and his staff took the train at once for Staunton. His
troops followed. At Staunton the General found that the report was unfounded. It arose from the fact that when General
Edward Johnson, "Old Alleghany," "Club Johnson," "Old
Blucher," as he was variously and affectionately called by his
troops, was visiting General Jackson, his troops had fallen
back some distance, greatly to the old warrior's disgust.

At Staunton the army was joined by two hundred cadets
from the Virginia Military Institute at Lexington, under
command of General F. H. Smith. The natty appearance of
these youthful soldiers afforded a striking contrast to the
seedy and dilapidated veterans, but before they returned from
McDowell much of the gloss was gone.

After a day of getting ready we started westward, and the
first day came up with General Johnson, who then marched

in advance. There was some skirmishing but the enemy retired
until the afternoon of Thursday, the 8th of May, when they
made a stand on a spur of Bull Pasture Mountain, looking
down upon a little village called McDowell. The Federal troops
were commanded by Generals R. H. Milroy and Robert C.
Schenck. Although there was some preliminary skirmishing,
battle began in earnest about half-past four in the afternoon,
to the surprise of General Jackson, who did not expect an
engagement that day. It was an obstinately contested little
battle of about four hours, when the enemy was routed. The
loss on both sides was heavy for the numbers engaged. Brigadier General Edward Johnson, who had immediate command
of the troops in action, was severely wounded in the ankle.
He was disabled for a year and did not return to active duty
until after the death of General Jackson. He was then promoted and assigned to the command of Jackson's Stonewall
Division.

Jackson's laconic dispatch announcing the result is now
familiar to every one. "God blessed our arms with victory at
McDowell yesterday." The Federal troops made a stiff fight,
such as they might well be proud of.

General Jackson followed the enemy with occasional skirmishing for several days as far as Franklin. He then retraced
his steps by way of McDowell, Lebanon Springs, off to Bridge-
water where he quietly spent Sunday the 18th, and then on
to Harrisonburg. Thence with no delay he moved down the
Valley pike to New Market, crossed to the eastern side of the
Massanutton Mountain and united with General Ewell who
had moved down from near Conrad's Store. There they proceeded to act jointly and to carry out their plans "in Stonewall Jackson's way."

V

GENERAL BANKS

"A portion of the troops passed through Winchester in some confusion, but the column was soon reformed and continued its march in order. . . . My command had not suffered an attack and rout. It had accomplished a 'premeditated' march of nearly 60 miles in the face of the enemy, defeating his plans and giving him battle wherever he was found."—Report of General Banks.

"Send all the troops forward you can immediately. Banks completely routed. Intelligence from various quarters leaves no doubt that the enemy, in great force, is marching upon Washington."—Secretary of War Stanton to the Governor of Massachusetts.

General Jackson: "General, I cannot agree with you. I think General Banks a better officer than his people think he is. I always found he fought well."
General Jeb Stuart: "Well, General, you at least have no cause to complain; indeed it would be ungrateful if you did, for he has been the best commissary and quartermaster you ever had!"—Conversation after Slaughter Mountain.

WHEN General Jackson and General Ewell united, their combined force was about 17,000. The General knew both from information from Generals Lee and Johnston and from his own intuition that it was important that the Federal Government did not send heavy reinforcements from Banks and McDowell to help McClellan in his siege of Richmond. It was his duty and his work to prevent this if possible with his little army, and he determined to try it without delay.

On the 22nd of May he began his march, with Ewell in front, down through the Luray Valley to Front Royal, taking precaution through Ashby to keep his movements veiled from the enemy. This he succeeded in doing with rare success.

In the early afternoon of the next day Ewell struck the pickets of the enemy within sight of and negligently near to Front Royal. They were driven in and the small body of infantry supporting them easily routed. We stopped to form on a hill overlooking the small town of Front Royal and the hurried movement of blue coats and the galloping of horsemen here and there told of the confusion in the enemy's camp. General Jackson, not knowing the force of the enemy there was so small or so unprepared by reinforcements for his approach, was endeavoring to take in the situation before ordering an advance.

I observed, almost immediately, the figure of a woman in white glide swiftly out of town on our right and, after making a little circuit, run rapidly up a ravine in our direction and then disappear from sight. She seemed, when I saw her, to heed neither weeds nor fences, but waved a bonnet as she came on, trying, it was evident, to keep the hill between herself and the village. I called General Jackson's attention to the singular movement just as a dip in the land hid her, and at General Ewell's suggestion, he sent me to meet her and ascertain what she wanted. That was just to my taste and it took only a few minutes for my horse to carry me to meet the romantic maiden whose tall, supple, and graceful figure struck me as soon as I came in sight of her. As I drew near, her speed slackened, and I was startled, momentarily, at hearing her call my name. But I was not much astonished when I saw that the visitor was the well-known Belle Boyd whom I had known from her earliest girlhood. She was just the girl to dare to do this thing.

Nearly exhausted, and with her hand pressed against her heart, she said in gasps, "I knew it must be Stonewall, when I

heard the first gun. Go back quick and tell him that the Yankee force is very small—one regiment of Maryland infantry,
several pieces of artillery and several companies of cavalry.
Tell him I know, for I went through the camps and got it out
of an officer. Tell him to charge right down and he will catch
them all. I must hurry back. Good-by. My love to all the dear
boys—and remember if you meet me in town you haven't seen
me today."

I raised my cap, she kissed her hand and was gone. I delivered her message speedily, and while Jackson was asking
me questions about her—for until then he had never heard
of her—I saw the wave of her white bonnet as she entered the
village and disappeared among its houses.[1]

Very soon the First Maryland Infantry and Major Roberdeau Wheat's Louisiana battalion were rushing down the hill
and into the town. General Jackson with a semi-smile suggested that I had better go with them and see if I could get
any more information from that young lady. It took very
little time to get into Front Royal and clean it out. The pursuit of the retreating Federals was kept up, with cavalry, the
infantry following as quickly as possible. While this was being done I looked for Belle Boyd and found her standing on
the pavement in front of a hotel, talking with some few
Federal officers (prisoners) and some of her acquaintances
in our army. Her cheeks were rosy with excitement and recent
exercise and her eyes all aflame. When I rode up to speak to
her she received me with much surprised cordiality, and as
I stooped from my saddle she pinned a crimson rose to my
uniform, bidding me remember that it was *blood-red* and that
it was her "colors." I left her to join the General.

The pursuit begun was kept up vigorously. There was
much handsome work done by Flournoy's cavalry, with good
results. Another brilliant charge was made by a squadron of
Ashby's cavalry in which two of the best captains in his
command, George F. Sheetz and John Fletcher, were killed
—their great promise had no time to ripen. The Confederate
First Maryland (Colonel Bradley T. Johnson) met the Federal First Maryland (Colonel John R. Kenly) in the conflict,

and the result was most disastrous for the latter. The result of the day's work was about 750 prisoners, chiefly from Kenly's regiment, and about 150 killed and wounded Union soldiers. A great quantity of valuable stores and material of war was taken. The loss of the Confederates was small.

The next day General Jackson moved on toward Middletown. It was soon evident that Banks either was late in getting information of the result at Front Royal or did not appreciate its meaning. He hesitated, delayed, and seemed unwilling to leave Strasburg until convinced that he must do it. His column was struck and cut in two before it had passed Middletown, although General Banks himself and the bulk of his infantry had gone. With the cavalry and the artillery left behind and some little infantry, all sorts of a mixed-up fight ensued. Middletown is five miles from Strasburg and thirteen miles from Winchester. Colonel Oliver R. Funsten of Ashby's cavalry was sent to the right, accompanied by a section of W. T. Poague's battery, to intercept the retreating enemy in the direction of Newtown. The road was literally lined with wagons of all kinds, miles of them. Funsten's and Poague's attack soon created a stampede and the train of quartermaster and commissary stores fell into our hands.

Middletown was the scene of one of Ashby's reckless feats of daring. A regiment of Federal cavalry, coming from Strasburg, halted as it reached Middletown and saw that the way was stopped. There was little hesitation, for the commander decided promptly to go on to Winchester in spite of obstacles. "Forward, trot!" and with gleaming sabres forward they came, boldly and well. General Jackson had gone off to direct Poague in person. Seeing the apparent intention of the Federal cavalry, I directed the officer commanding about one hundred infantry—which General Dick Taylor had considerately sent forward with General Jackson as a kind of bodyguard, with orders to follow and keep up with the General when he moved off to the front so far from his troops—I directed the officer to take these men to a stone fence along the road and prevent if possible the advance of the enemy's cavalry. I didn't want them to get past Middletown, for if they did I apprehended they might do serious damage to Funsten, Poague, and perhaps to the General. Just as these hundred men had reached the fence, the cavalry came thundering by, but a deadly volley stopped their wild career. Some in front, unhurt, galloped off, on their way, but just behind them horses and riders went down in a tangled heap. The rear, unable to check themselves, plunged on, in, over, upon the bleeding pile, a roaring, shrieking, struggling mass of men and horses, crushed, wounded and dying. It was a sickening sight, the worst I had ever seen then, and for a moment I felt a twinge of regret that I had ordered that little line to that bloody work. The extreme rear of cavalry, cut off by the fate of their fellows, turned back in confusion as if to go back to Strasburg.

Just then Ashby rode up, hesitated a moment, looked about him and drew his sabre, glistening like his eye. There was so much action and earnestness about him as he looked after the retreating cavalry that I was impelled to say, "Colonel, surely you're not—" But he was off like a shot. With a touch of spur his black stallion cleared the tottering gate like a hunter, and in a moment, sword in hand, he charged into the demoralized rear of that flying squadron. Such rashness seemed to invite death, but such rashness was his safety. A hundred Confederates stopped, held their breath in speechless anxiety. Having vented his wrath with this outburst, he returned with a squad of prisoners, mounted and dismounted, some soldiers having run to meet and guard him.

General Jackson, coming up, attempted to reprimand him for the useless exposure of a life so valuable to the army, but the rebuke was a failure. The few words were all right as a mild scolding, but somehow his looks and manner seemed to deprive the reprimand of all force.

With all possible promptness we moved on toward Winchester by the pike. The road was encumbered with evidence of the hurry of flight. Wagons broken down, overturned, some with their contents scattered, some sound and untouched, some with good teams, some horseless, sutlers' stores, officers' luggage, knapsacks, Bibles, cards, photographs, songbooks and cooking utensils—a general wreck of military matter.

I was riding with the General and a small party of staff and couriers along the road. He was in good spirits but silent and thoughtful. Once he dismounted and took from an overturned wagon a cracker, hard and not too clean, and attempted to eat it, for he had eaten nothing since early morning. Riding along in a meditative way, thinking over some social movements I intended to execute if Banks let us into Winchester, I was startled when he suddenly called across the road to me. "Mr. Douglas, what do you think of the ladies of Winchester?" A blush mantled my cheek—I believe that is what it is called in novels—before he continued with a quiet smile, "I mean the ladies generally. Don't you think they are a noble set, worth fighting for? I do. They are the truest people in the South." He drew his cap down further over his eyes, moved the "Little Sorrel" into a rather better pace and relapsed into silence, as if he did not expect a reply.

It was after dark when we passed through Newtown, over which a small artillery duel had been fought for several hours. Ashby's cavalry, having given themselves up, in their hunger, to plundering wagons, were so reduced in numbers that they were virtually inefficient. That the defeat of Banks was not his destruction is due to the failure of the cavalry at the critical moment, and General Jackson never ceased to lament and condemn that costly want of discipline.

The General had no thought of going into camp. True, the army had been marching almost daily for weeks, had been up nearly all the night before, had been living for some time on much excitement and very small rations; it was exhausted, broken down, and apparently unfit for battle; but the General was determined to push on that night. Of course no one was surprised for that was already Stonewall's way. The soldiers were tired and weary and grumbled a bit as usual, but they had faith and plodded on, not cheerfully but resignedly. By the sweat of their brow, he was saving their blood.

For some miles from Newtown we rode by the light of burning wagons, to which the enemy set fire when they abandoned them. This bonfire was expensive, but grateful, for it announced to the people of Winchester that Jackson was coming. After passing these, night enveloped us in impenetrable darkness. Footsore and weary, the column moved, Jackson, Ashby, and our staff at its head, and all nodding with hopeless drowsiness—all except Ashby the Black Knight, silent, erect, and wakeful on that coal black stallion. There was Pendleton, whose intense sleepiness took the expression of anger, Lieutenant Colonel S. Crutchfield (descendant of the man who invented sleep) muttering in disgust, "This is uncivilized," Dr. McGuire, meditative as becomes a surgeon, thinking of his home and people in Winchester. Suddenly a sharp volley of musketry, flashing almost in our faces, sounded an alarum on the night and awakened us. We were ambuscaded by a party of the enemy's rear guard, perhaps a score, who had let our cavalry scouts pass and had hidden themselves behind a stone fence. They fired and fled. They must have been terribly scared for not a man was hit. Such an escape was miraculous.

One would suppose that little incident was enough to satisfy the General that he, his chief of cavalry, and his staff, all asleep, were not in their proper place as advance guard. The staff had reached that conclusion on previous occasions, but their opinion lacked weight in convincing the General. We moved on as before and again met a reception somewhat similar, at a greater distance. Result, a horse wounded this time. Even the General seemed satisfied now and concluded not to impose upon Providence any further. He sent a small party of infantry in advance and put an end to the bushwhacking by killing several of the next party that tried it. Then the enemy deployed some skirmishers, and there was rather harmless firing now and then which served to delay our march until we reached Kernstown.

Whenever the column stopped for a minute, the sleepy officers and men would throw themselves on the ground. And thus, skirmishing and halting, marching while sleeping, the night wore away, and within a few hours of daylight we halted within two miles of Winchester. Jackson, Ashby, and the staff

halted and fastened their horses to the fences. The little cavalcade was greatly reduced. Several of the staff had fallen asleep
and had been left by the wayside; couriers, sent off, had not
returned. The General and Ashby to keep awake were walking, separately, up and down the pike, passing each other like
silent sentinels, absorbed in their own thoughts.

At this hour one of the Brigade Commanders, Colonel Samuel Fulkerson, an excellent officer and a great favorite with
the General—whose eyes filled with tears when he heard of
his death at Cold Harbor—came up. He represented the sad
condition of his men, so exhausted that each time the brigade
halted and moved on a large percentage of them were left
asleep in fence corners. He suggested that it would be better
to wait until daylight. The General listened patiently to this
reasonable suggestion and then replied, "Colonel, I do not
believe you can feel more for your men than I do. This is very
hard on them, but by this night march I hope to save many
valuable lives. I want to get possession of the hills of Winchester before daylight." Then after a moment's reflection he
continued, "Colonel, you may rest your command for two
hours. I will go on with my old brigade." But the General
changed his mind, and when dawn came the command had not
moved since his interview with Colonel Fulkerson. General
Banks had taken possession of the range of hills referred to
by the General and was prepared to fight.

Jackson and Ashby mounted their horses, and orders were
sent along the line to close up and get ready for attack. I will
not attempt to describe the battle which followed. The Stonewall Brigade opened the engagement, and a handsome charge
drove the enemy from their first position. While arrangements were being made for still further advance, I conducted
the General, at his request, to General Dick Taylor's brigade.
The soldiers we passed, having been ordered to observe silence,
took off their hats in silent salute; he did the same. But they
watched him carefully and earnestly, looked up into his face,
scanned his features, his expression, as if they were trying to
read, "what the signs of promise are." Riding up to General

Taylor, he said, "General, can your brigade charge a battery?"

"It can try."

"Very good; it must do it then. Move it forward."

Only this and nothing more. Jackson rode back; Taylor, a worthy son of General Zack Taylor, followed with his command. But as the General was returning, the troops could not stand the restraint of that unnatural silence any longer, and regardless of the proximity of the enemy they let forth in one of their deafening yells. Old Jack smiled and passed on. But soon the enemy's artillery sent a shower of shells in acknowledgment of the salute. While under that fire, the General rode along quietly, with his chin thrown out as usual and his cap close over his eyes, in apparent unconcern. I was wondering if this unconsciousness of the "deadly imminent" shot flying through the air was simply indifference to danger, or the action of nerve and will-power; and this may have caused me, involuntarily, to imitate his bearing. The situation seemed to strike a little Irishman of the ranks as amusing, for he cried out, "Be jabers, have your eye on Auld Jack. I'll wager you he thinks them blatherin' bangs are singin' birds. And," with a chuckle, "look at yon officer behint him, imitatin' the Ginril and tryin' to look as bauld as himself." I dodged the next shell.

General Taylor threw his brigade into line where directed, and it moved forward in gallant style. I have rarely seen a more beautiful charge. This full brigade, with a line of glistening bayonets bright in that morning sun, its formation straight and compact, its tread quick and easy as it pushed on through the clover and up the hill, was a sight to delight a veteran. The battery was not taken, because it did not wait. It departed and its infantry support was quickly driven after it.

General Ewell on the Front Royal road with equal success had driven the enemy before him toward the town.

Shortly afterwards followed some sharp fighting but no general engagement. General Jackson and a few of his staff were sitting mounted on the crest of a hill overlooking Winchester. He paid little attention to the line of skirmishers advancing against us, but was watching the movement of troops and artillery in and about town. He was evidently surprised, as if he was expecting something else, and turning to me quickly he said, "Order forward the whole line, the battle's won." Soon the men of Taylor and of Winder came sweeping past and as they did the General cried out, "Very good! Now let's holler!" That is the very language the Professor used. He raised his old grey cap, his staff took up the cheer, and soon from the advancing line rose and swelled a deafening roar, which borne on the wind over Winchester told her imprisoned people that deliverance was at hand. A panic seized the enemy and the retreat became a rout.

Galloping down the hill, the General and staff went into town with the skirmishers, and Winchester—the "Bandy Ball of the Confederacy" as one of her fair daughters named her —that day was again in the hands of her friends.

It was Sunday—was Jackson always to fight on Sunday? —but church bells were silent. The streets were lined with people, but not on their way to the sanctuaries; they had come to meet their own troops, who soon forgot their fatigue in the joy of their reception. Windows and doors, closed for months, were thrown open; there were merry voices and bright faces. For a moment, but only for a moment, the dead and wounded on the field seemed forgotten. Then a missing face here and there sent relatives scurrying to the battlefield. But the flames from burning buildings, set on fire by General Banks because they contained useful stores, soon began to shoot up wildly into the sky and heavy columns of black smoke threw a pall over the town. Terrible as it looked it only heightened the excitement and the enthusiasm of the populace. The reception of General Jackson cannot be described. There were tears and smiles, like rain and sunshine; lips that spoke blessings, and quivering lips that could not speak at all; men, women, and children all joining in the strange welcome. They ignored the sufferings they had gone through and their own fortitude, their losses, their anxieties, but they convinced him surely that they were "worth fighting for."

But he could not stop. He was not a man of words, and such devotion was enough to overwhelm him. Breaking away as quickly as he could, he pushed forward with his troops. The only order he seemed to give was, "Push on to the Potomac." He kept up the chase with his infantry for five miles and then was forced to rest his troops—even their energy and endurance had a limit. Again the cavalry failed him. Banks' army, defeated, scattered, only needed some command to push it and demand surrender. That was the duty of the cavalry, and they were not there. Had they done their duty as well as the infantry, Banks' army would have ceased to exist that day. He might have escaped, but he would not have sent that comic message to Washington that his army had "retired in good order across the Potomac." Banks was a humorist. General Jackson and his army entered Winchester Sunday morning, May the 25th. The next day the army rested, and by order of the General the chaplains held services in their regiments at 4:00 P.M. It was Sunday, *nunc pro tunc.*

Among those who fell in that battle was Lieutenant C. Marshall Barton of Winchester, with the Newtown Artillery. Looking over a scrapbook which he kept in 1855, when a cadet at the Institute at Lexington, I found a satire upon the faculty. Major Jackson was then one of them. The satire is more pointed than skillful, and very severe on some of the professors. Toward "Hickory," as he called Major Jackson, he was more mild—in fact, spoke of him as perhaps no other cadet would.

> *Like some wild beast that ranged the forest wild,*
> *So rude, uncouth, so purely nature's child*
> *Is Hickory; and yet methinks I see*
> *The stamp of genius on his brow and he*
> *With his wild glance and keen but quiet eye*
> *Fills my heart with love for him who bears*
> *His honors meekly and who wears*
> *The laurels of a hero.*

Barton lived just long enough to see Hickory well on his way to earn the laurels of a hero.

In striking contrast to Banks' report to his government was General Jackson's report to his, written in the Taylor Hotel.

Winchester May 26. 1862

Genl. S. Cooper
Adjutant General
General:
During the last three days, God has blessed our arms with brilliant success. On Friday the Federals at Front Royal were routed and one section of artillery in addition to many prisoners captured. On Saturday Banks' main column while retreating from Strasburg to Winchester was pierced, the rear part retreating toward Strasburg. On Sunday the other part was routed at this place. At last accounts Brig. Genl. Geo. H. Steuart was pursuing with cavalry and capturing the fugitives. A large amount of medical, ordnance and other stores have fallen into our hands.

T. J. JACKSON
Maj. Genl. Comdg.

On reaching Winchester I had been informed that Major J. H. Whittlesey, Fifth United States Cavalry, who had married the daughter of General Archie Fauntleroy, was at the house of his father-in-law, too ill to be moved when General Banks retired so rapidly, and would like to see me. Although I had no acquaintance with Major Whittlesey, I called at once, and he surrendered to me. I took his parole until I could see him again. I spoke to General Jackson about it and asked that he be allowed to remain where he was while we were in town. After a few days when the army started up the Valley, I was permitted to inform Major Whittlesey, that he could remain and "go at large" under a proper parole which he gave, and he was left in Winchester. After I was shot and captured at Gettysburg, he kindly wrote me an earnest letter with permission to use it with the War Department to obtain a parole; but it was not so successful.

VI

TO THE POTOMAC AND BACK

G ENERAL JACKSON was a bold leader, probably the boldest the war produced. Indeed, sometimes the temerity of his attack secured success. But he mingled with his boldness great prudence and judgment. He never went so far into danger that he could not get out again. And while we do not doubt that the unprecedented and unexpected boldness of his movements sometimes won an easy victory, we may not say that he rushed blindly into success, or that he did not see his way clear because all seemed dark to those about him. If he played war as poker, he knew exactly when to bluff, and against whom; consequently he was never beaten.

Although General Jackson was not thought by those who knew him best to be a good judge of character generally, yet his opinion of the generals opposing him was always wonderfully correct. I was sometimes led to believe that he was better acquainted with the amount of nerve and military ability possessed by the Federal officers he had to contend with than with those of his own subordinates. By watching their actions he even learned their strong points and their weaknesses. If they set traps for him, he would drive straight into them, but it was only to break out again and catch the trappers.

After General Banks had been driven out of Winchester, General Jackson established his Headquarters at the Taylor Hotel for several days. About midnight of the 27th Captain Pendleton was awakened by an orderly, who reported that a gentleman, just arrived, requested an interview on business of pressing importance. Being accustomed to receive such sensational messages, Pendleton with a growl directed the orderly to bring him in, as he had "no idea of getting up for anything short of battle or fire." When the gentleman was brought in, his grey hairs, intelligence, and dignity of manner soon convinced us that he was no sensationalist. Without preface he said that he had that day ridden a great distance to give some information which he thought valuable: that the sudden expulsion of General Banks from the Valley had produced the impression in Washington that General Jackson's army was large enough to cross the Potomac and sweep over Maryland, if not to take the Federal Capital; that General McDowell, who was near Fredericksburg with the head of his column and supposed to be marching on Richmond, had been ordered to march against Jackson; that General Shields with the advance, numbering 10,000, was making forced marches and that he supposed McDowell was following with the rest of his army; that General Shields was already within a day's march of Front Royal, and that he, the reporter, had passed the column at a point which he mentioned and had not stopped riding until he arrived at Winchester a few moments before.

His report was listened to with attention, for he manifestly spoke what he believed to be the truth. Pendleton thanked the gentleman for his intelligence, and directed that he should be furnished with a bed. After he had retired, it was decided not to disturb the General until daylight, when it was supposed he would act upon the information if he believed it. We knew that if General Shields reached Front Royal before we left Winchester, he would be nearer to Strasburg than we and might cut off our retreat up the Valley. It was supposed that General John C. Frémont in the west had received orders to co-operate with McDowell and that he was, or soon would be, marching for the same point by way of Moorefield and Wardensville. If they should succeed in their object, the situation of the Confederate army would be precarious. Surrounded by such an overwhelming force as McDowell, Frémont, and Banks might concentrate against it, nothing would be left to us but capture or destruction. Such being the danger, we believed that in the morning the General would issue an order for a retrograde movement. But he took a different view of the situation. He heard the report that had been brought and satisfied himself by an interview with the gentleman. Immediately afterwards, to our astonishment, he announced his intention of proceeding to Harper's Ferry and directed Pendleton to have the troops put in motion. We often had such occasions to think the General was "crazy," but afterwards felt obliged to confess there was some method in his madness.

However, to Harper's Ferry we marched, leaving only a Provost Guard at Winchester. The General was determined that, if President Lincoln was already so badly scared as to get up such a formidable combination for his suppression, he would make him still more uneasy by threatening the Capital. Since he had turned McDowell from his march on Richmond, he wished to draw him as far from that line as possible.

Winder's brigade had a small skirmish with the enemy at Charlestown and drove them back to Bolivar Heights and Harper's Ferry. General Jackson then moved his whole army in sight of their position and made the necessary dispositions for an assault.

Great was the commotion among the newspapers, and varied their speculations with regard to the situation. The Richmond press, not satisfied with the defeat of Banks and altogether ignorant of the strength of General Jackson's army, announced that he had crossed into Maryland.

The journals of the North hurled dreadful anathemas against Stonewall Jackson and mysteriously hinted at avenging anacondas already surrounding him and ready at a given signal to crush him. But he who loosened the tongues of these editors and prophets was altogether unconscious of the threats of his enemies or the plaudits of his friends. No one of us supposed that General Jackson had any idea of trying to take Harper's Ferry by assault, or that he went there with the expectation of being able to take it at all.[1] If he had captured the place he could not have held it, and the valuable stores there would have been of little use to him, for he could not have taken them away.

Indeed, he had already captured from General Banks more supplies, quartermaster, commissary, ordnance, and medical, than he had transportation for. But he wished to monopolize the attention of Washington and thus prevent McClellan from being reinforced. General Jackson was maneuvering for the relief of Richmond.

The following letter was received on the 29th or 30th of May, while General Jackson was in Charlestown at the house of one of his staff, Major Wells J. Hawks.

> Hd. Qrs: Dept. North: Va.
> May 27th 1862

Genl.

I congratulate you upon new victories and new titles to the thanks of the country and of the army.

If you can threaten Baltimore and Washington, do so. It may produce an important diversion.

McClellan is near and McDowell reported advancing from Fredericksburg.

Your movements depend, of course, upon the enemy's strength remaining in your neighborhood. Upon that depends the practicability of your advancing to the Potomac and even crossing it. I know of no hostile force to prevent either.

> Most Respectfully
> Your obt. Servant
> J. E. JOHNSTON
> General

Time will be gained and saved by addressing me always instead of the government. J. E. J.

It will be observed that General Johnston's wishes had been anticipated so far as they were practicable.

It appears from this note that General Johnston had no idea what a commotion the movements of General Jackson had produced in the camps of the enemy, that he did not anticipate such results as followed them in the combinations for the destruction of the Army of the Valley District. For clear military judgment and capacity to comprehend and take advantage of what is loosely termed "the situation," General Johnston was not surpassed by any general in either army. Yet, in this instance, he hardly expected that Jackson's advance would be so effectual as to divert the march of General McDowell from Richmond and neutralize the strength (including Frémont) of upwards of 50,000 troops. Perhaps he knew that McDowell was too good a soldier to be thus misled; but he did not know the military incapacity of Mr. Lincoln and Secretary of War Edward M. Stanton.

General Jackson had been communicating directly with General Samuel Cooper at the War Department and not with General Johnston. While it is probable that General Jackson was directed to regulate his movements so as to retain in the Valley as many of the enemy as possible, no plan of campaign was suggested to him, and all details were left to his own judgment and discretion.

It now remained for General Jackson to extricate himself as quickly as possible from the dangerous position he was in. At once his surpassing will and genius were called into service, and it was from here to Port Republic that they displayed themselves most effectually. Having remained before Harper's Ferry as long as he thought prudent—everyone else thought it very imprudent to go there in the first place— General Jackson on the 30th gave the order to retire to Winchester. He had no time to lose and every hour was valuable. Crutchfield quoted gloomily, "*quem Deus vult perdere, prius dementat.*"

The rain fell all day. At Halltown the General informed Colonel A. R. Boteler, Member of Congress from the District and at the time with Headquarters, that he wished him to go to Richmond at once. He told him that General John A. Dix, in his front, was being reinforced by the Baltimore and Ohio Railroad, that General Banks at Williamsport was being reinforced from Pennsylvania, that General Shields was advancing on Front Royal and General Frémont on Wardensville, and that thus, altogether, he was being encompassed by

50,000 or 60,000 troops. He requested Colonel Boteler to urge the War Department to send him 15,000 men without delay. At that time General Jackson's force was not over 13,000 infantry and Ashby's cavalry. Colonel Boteler went to Richmond, and some troops were sent to the Valley, but after the work there was done.

When we were about leaving the front of Harper's Ferry, the question was very generally asked—how are we going to get out of this difficulty?

Facilis descensus Averno [*Harper's Ferry*]

.   .   .   .

Sed revocare gradum, superasque evadere ad auras,
Hoc opus, hic labor est.

Had the time come to verify the prediction of a Federal surgeon—"if Stonewall Jackson ever gets so completely surrounded that he cannot march or fight his way out he will take wings unto himself and his army and fly out"? History has already told how General Jackson solved the difficulty.

During the afternoon and night of the 30th the army arrived at Winchester, with the exception of the Stonewall Brigade, under General Winder, which had been left on Loudoun Heights and in the vicinity of Charlestown. Long after the command reached Winchester we could hear the heavy guns of the enemy on Bolivar Heights, still shelling the empty woods on their front; and I doubt not the telegraph wires were heated by urgent messages for troops and the mails laden with the shrewd speculations of newspaper correspondents with regard to the forces, intentions, and probable fate of Stonewall Jackson.

VII

UP THE VALLEY

AUDACITY, audacity, always audacity." This quality Danton thought was the key to success. We may couple with it a remark attributed to General Jackson. "Mystery—mystery is the secret of success." His was not the mystery of speech; it was the mystery of action. General Jackson came and went; his enemies knew not whence he came, nor his friends whither he was gone. He moved, but gave no reason for his movement. He never looked to his subordinates for advice and it was seldom volunteered. His plans were his own and he took the responsibility.

On this occasion the people of Winchester were not so much astonished at his noisy coming, as they were at his quiet going. They retired at night to safe slumbers and pleasant dreams; when they arose in the morning they found that Winchester was evacuated: General Jackson, his army, his prisoners and captured stores were all gone. The "Bandy Ball" was changing hands again.

On the 31st of May, slowly and sullenly the Army of the Valley moved towards Strasburg. General Jackson sent one of his staff, Captain Jed Hotchkiss, to direct General Winder, who was yet in the vicinity of Harper's Ferry, to join the rest of the army with his brigade. He told him that Winchester might be occupied by the enemy before he passed it, and if so he must avoid it as he might deem best, and, further, that the army would wait for him at Strasburg, eighteen miles from Winchester.

The venerable gentleman who gave us the warning that night was correct in nearly all he said; the enemy were rapidly closing in upon us from all sides. Shields, with the advance of McDowell's corps, had arrived at Front Royal and had driven out one of our regiments, capturing part of it. It was confidently reported that he was advancing from that place upon Strasburg. Frémont had passed Wardensville and was moving to form a junction with Shields. But neither Frémont nor Shields seemed to know the activity of the soldiers they were dealing with or to appreciate the advantage of their position. They had heard that General Jackson was storming away at Harper's Ferry, and acted as if they believed he was still there, in happy ignorance of their combination for his overthrow. They doubtless thought that he was already secured and that there was no particular reason why they should make haste to count the spoils.

General Jackson marched during the 31st steadily and slowly upon Strasburg. Various rumors were brought to us during the day that the town was in possession of the enemy, at one time of Shields and the next of Frémont; but upon our arrival late in the afternoon we found it unoccupied. The little command, weary and footsore, bivouacked for the night and sank to the ground where they halted. Some, before they went to sleep, made a hasty supper of the captured stores; many were too tired to eat. The Stonewall Brigade was still on the road. From Loudoun Heights and Charlestown to a point between Kernstown and Newtown—a distance of thirty-five miles—they made a continuous march and going into camp about midnight rested until morning. It was one of those forced marches which all of General Jackson's army were sometimes called upon to endure, and which won for them the appropriate name of "Foot Cavalry."

When the morning of the 1st of June broke over the three armies, encamped not very far apart, if any of the three Commanding Generals expressed astonishment at the position of affairs, it certainly was not General Jackson. The junction of the Federal armies, upon which depended the fate of Jackson, had not been effected as yet. And with a rebel army of unknown and fabulous size between them it is difficult to tell which was the more at a loss to know what to do—General Shields or General Frémont. Their hesitation very soon made their doubts apparent. They had been sent to shear the wolf —how was it to be done? They took a day to consider; while they were thus occupied General Jackson remained in Strasburg, resting his tired troops and waiting for Winder to come up. The brigade arrived shortly after noon and the men threw themselves in the road and went to sleep. In that desperate state of reckless indifference which it was impossible to describe and which no one can understand who has not traveled in a state of anxiety for days, without sleep, rest, or food, these gallant men did not trouble themselves with useless speculations regarding the complication of affairs. They left such matters to their General, and the opinion of all may be inferred from the expression of one I overheard, "Old Jack got us into this fix, and with the blessing of God he will get us out."

Many who have wondered at General Jackson's success might have learned one of the secrets of it if they had been with him at Strasburg. His army was brave, well-disciplined; that was not it. They had unbounded confidence in their leader and he in them; that was it.

"Stonewall Jackson's men will follow him to the devil and he knows it," said a Federal officer who had been taken prisoner.

General Lee was the great Chieftain of the army; they were proud of him. They admired General Joseph E. Johnston; but they loved "Old Jack." He was as a father to them, sometimes stern and exacting; they were his children, sometimes sullen but always obedient. During the day a small skirmish and artillery duel took place between some of General Ewell's troops and the advance of General Frémont. It was soon over, and the day passed quietly but slowly and anxiously away. Night came at length and General Jackson moved out of Strasburg and up the Valley pike unmolested and unpursued.

About midnight the staff regaled themselves at Woodstock with a heterogeneous supper, furnished by the different sutler

stores of General Banks. There were probably too many delicacies of inconsistent qualities to suit the taste of a *bon vivant*,
but we had no one with us to make objections. It was indeed
a sumptuous table: cake and pickled lobsters, cheese, canned
peaches, piccolomini and candy, coffee, ale, and condensed
milk. It was a feast the like of which was seldom vouchsafed
to Confederate soldiers, and with inexpressible thanks we
drank the health of General Banks. Not knowing from the
dark situation of affairs how soon we and our possessions
might fall into the hands of the enemy, we determined to place
a great portion of these viands beyond the possibility of re-
capture.

After the dyspeptic supper we betook ourselves to such rest
as it and the constant arrival of couriers would admit of. But
hardly had we got asleep when we were called upon to rise and
get in the saddle. The General was up and impatient, and the
rumbling of the wagons told us that the army was in motion.
Of course a thousand different obstacles impeded the movement of the train and consequently of the troops. One brigade
divided another, and generals and colonels were wandering
through the mass in search of their commands. The clouded
brow and closed lips of General Jackson were ominous: he
was becoming impatient at the delay. Quickly and sharply
he hurried his staff in every direction while, stern and watchful, he rode along the tangled line. Quartermasters and line
officers knew his looks forboded no good and exerted all their
energies to move the mass of men, horses, and wagons.

The General rode up to an officer whose brigade had been
divided into two or three parts. "Colonel, why do you not get
your brigade together, keep it together and move on?"

"It's impossible, General; I can't do it."

"Don't say it's impossible. Turn your command over to
the next officer. If he can't do it, I'll find someone who can, if
I have to take him from the ranks."

Soon a different state of things showed the effect of the
indomitable will of this man. The trains moved off without
unnecessary stoppages, under the controlling influence of

Major John A. Harman, Chief Quartermaster, who seemed to understand the management of teamsters and wagons as well as the General did that of soldiers.

Several miles on our right, by a road parallel to the one we were traveling, General Frémont was moving with his command, still hoping to get in advance of General Jackson and at some place farther up the Valley to form a junction with General Shields. The latter officer was moving on our left up through the Luray Valley and beyond the Shenandoah River and Massanutton Mountain. A body of cavalry and some infantry employed themselves in making occasional demonstrations in our rear, but were kept in check by the vigilant Ashby.

As the evening approached the heavens grew black with clouds. The troops knew that their cheerless bivouac would be pitched on the storm-drenched ground, but as they marched they laughed and whistled and sang, and the burden of their song was, "Let the wide world wag as it will; we will be gay and happy still."

The rain began to fall. The General and staff were about a mile in advance of the leading brigade. We had dismounted and were preparing to take shelter from the coming torrent when a courier dashed up with a flourish and handed a note to the General. It was from Colonel Ashby saying that the enemy were pressing him and unless he was supported with infantry he might lose some of his artillery. "To horse!" said the General briefly, and mounting we started. The storm burst forth in fury. Few of the staff had overcoats or gum blankets with them. We were three miles at least from Colonel Ashby and the General wanted to be there at once. We went at a rushing pace, dashing through the mud and the flooded roads. The troops made way and endeavored through the driving rain to raise their usual shout. They looked at "Old Jack" with his hat in his hand replying to their salute by getting his head drenched in the shower and wondered "what has broke loose now?"

By the time we were all thoroughly wet we met Ashby riding calmly and slowly along the road, encased in innumerable

gum blankets and capes, and as unconcerned as if there was
not an enemy within fifty miles. In reply to a question from
the General, the Colonel replied that the enemy had evidently
stopped for the night, as they had not made their appearance
for several hours. The General handed him the dispatch which
had caused our rapid ride. The Colonel read it and with a
smile replied that the enemy were pressing him closely when
that note was sent off, about eight o'clock in the morning, and
he had been surprised that no notice had been taken of it. He
had, however, succeeded in repulsing them and had no further
difficulty with them during the day. At once our anxiety for
Ashby's artillery was changed into indignation against that
infernal courier. It appeared afterwards that he had been
victimized by a rascally fellow who had carried the dispatch
all day and had at last entrusted it to this unsuspecting courier for delivery. We waited impatiently to see the explosion of
the General's wrath. But he quietly turned around and after
contemplating for a moment, first himself and then his staff,
naïvely remarked, "A water haul!" This was the only commentary he made, and with a bow to Colonel Ashby we rode
away through the ceaseless rain. The troops were put into
camp for the night and were soon erecting "quaint and curious" shelters against the storm and tossing their jokes around
the blazing camp fires. Pendleton—who knew every good
house at which to stop in the Valley—had determined that the
General should make his Headquarters at the house of an old
gentleman near Mount Jackson. The General on this occasion made no objection to Sandy's selection. Fastening our
horses to the fence we entered a small enclosed porch in front
of the house and found there an athletic specimen of an
infantry soldier. He was seated upon a bench and looked as
if he regarded us as intruders. He was nearly bare-footed,
his coat was thrown open, and his pantaloons were tattered
and torn. Now the General after he was completely soaked
had thrown a gum cape over his shoulders, and by it the marks
of rank upon his sleeves and collar were concealed.

"I say, Mister," drawled the straggler, "what *calvary* do
you belong to?"

"I don't belong to the cavalry," replied the General innocently.

"Don't, eh! Must be couriers for some general or other."

The General smiled and one of the staff stepped forward and presented him. The tramp was speechless, and the General passed into the house. The old soldier pulled his ventilated hat fiercely over his eyes, gave a jerk at his tattered trousers, seized his gun, and moving rapidly away he uttered his parting soliloquy: "Well! If I didn't put my foot into it that time, may I be d——!"

The rain stopped for a while. A large cheerful fire blazed upon the hearth. Our wet uniforms were soon smoking and drying before the blaze. A little bottle was passed around, and with it in our midst we concurred in the opinion of Medical Director McGuire, that getting wet was not always fatal. A bountiful supper filled up the measure of our content and the soothing tobacco smoke restored natural good humor.

The next morning we were very early up and off. After making the usual day's march without incident we pitched tents and established Headquarters in an open field. Ashby called and took supper with us. He was in a placid good humor. He had that day received his appointment as Brigadier General, and it was hoped that as commander of a brigade, he would expose his person less recklessly than he had done while a colonel and prove a better disciplinarian. Ashby looked upon all men under him as influenced by his own enthusiastic earnestness. He said that his men did not know how to maneuver in line or in column, but on the field of battle they knew his voice and never hesitated to obey it. This was true; but it was equally true that the number present to hear and obey his call was often unpardonably small. We saw the effect of this system at Winchester when his cavalry failed him at the time their service would have been most valuable in following up and capturing a routed army.

On this afternoon Pendleton remarked to General Ashby that, hereafter, he hoped he would not find occasion to expose himself as he had previously done, for he could not expect to escape death very long if he continued in his present course. Ashby replied that he did not concur with the general opinion on the subject. He was not afraid of balls that were shot directly at him for they always missed their mark. He only feared those random shots which always hit someone for whom they were not intended. Within the next forty-eight hours the fatal bullet did find him, and the knightly Ashby lives only in fame.

The clouds grew heavy again, the scattering drops of rain began to fall. The owner of a large house in the immediate neighborhood came to Headquarters and requested the General to go over with him. But General Jackson declined his invitation and said that he was even now too comfortably fixed with a tent, while his men were bivouacking in the woods without shelter of any kind except what they could carry on their backs. But the storm selected the General for special vengeance. When the tents were pitched he had directed that his be placed upon a beautiful green spot in the hollow. Having lost much sleep he retired early. While he slept the waters descended from the hills on either side, collected into a stream, and swept through his tent. "How the floods clapped their hands" as they rushed in upon him and routed him from his slumbers, and, having tossed his hat and boots about in vain endeavor to get them from the tent, went on their way. The next morning the General appeared wet and wearied. As the staff had been provoked when the kind invitation to go to a neighboring house had been declined—for on that campaign each staff officer made it his special care to administer to the General's comfort and protect his health in every way possible—we were not a little amused and perhaps a little gratified at seeing the general wreck and demoralization in his tent. All through it the water was still flowing and various small articles of apparel and furniture were floating about like little boats. As it continued to rain during the day the army did not march. Yet it was not without some difficulty that the General was prevailed upon to go into New Market and establish his Headquarters in a house.

While here a correspondent of a New York paper sought an interview with General Jackson. Contrary to his usual practice the General granted the interview. The correspondent was evidently a sharper and like most of that class he was apt to be sharp at the wrong time. He began by expressing his gratification at meeting with Stonewall Jackson, etc.; but being admonished by the General's frown that he cared little for such things he changed his tactics. He said that being well mounted he could have escaped from Front Royal had he not been suddenly attracted by a conspicuous display of gallantry on the part of some Confederate cavalry. When the Federal troops, he explained, were endeavoring to leave the town of Front Royal, he saw a company or two of cavalry, about 75 or 100 in number, prepare to charge them; and he stopped to see the result. The Maryland regiment of infantry (Federal) had just gotten outside of the town when the charge was made upon them. He was amazed at the rashness of the officer who was leading. On they came with a resounding yell, and he was so bewildered with wonder and admiration at the magnificence of the charge that he forgot his own danger. He remained spellbound on the spot; and when he was aroused he was a prisoner. The General was much amused, and to our surprise, ordered his release as a noncombatant. The incorrigible Yankee at once made an additional request for his horse, which he said was somewhere in the cavalry. He was told that he might take him if he could find him. But having his doubts about the prudence of roaming through Ashby's camp in search of a horse he took his departure.

The next copy of his paper contained a full account of his capture and adventures and a comical description of the appearance and manners of Stonewall Jackson. He was the forerunner of the line of war correspondents who became so conspicuous in the Union armies and are now so abundant, enterprising, and dangerous, on the outskirts of all wars: men whose personal courage is often equal to their conceit, but who do not hesitate to attempt to make or mar the reputation of generals and admirals according to their fancy.

DEATH OF ASHBY

Saw ye the veterans—
Hearts that had known
Never a quail of fear,
Never a groan,—
Sob mid the fight they win,
Tears their stern eyes within
Ashby, our Paladin,
Ashby is gone! [1]

THE sun from its rising to its setting does not shine upon a more blessed spot than the Valley of Virginia. From the beautiful bank of the River of Swans, the historic Potomac, to where the noble and solemn mountains of the old State send down their streamlets to form the Shenandoah and the James, are countless evidences of the generosity with which Providence has dealt with this royal region. The Blue Ridge on the east, the Alleghanies on the west seem to enclose this favorite Valley in a magnificent frame. The odd Massanutton is thrown up in the midst of it, with peculiar effect, so that the rich and fertile garden may offer equal attractions to the artist and the agriculturist. From Jefferson's Rock at Harper's Ferry—to stand upon which, said Thomas Jefferson, was worth a trip across the Atlantic—to the Natural Bridge the traveler may wander over picturesque mountains, by splendid rivers and clear rivulets, through stately groves and broad green fields, each richest of its kind and unsur-

passed in all this great continent. But as it was beautiful and
bountiful it attracted destruction, for it was the great or
chief storehouse of the Army of Virginia. "If this Valley is
lost, Virginia is lost," said Jackson, and the Confederacy
could not survive Virginia. A broad land that blossomed as
the rose when the war began, it was a scene of deserted home-
steads, smouldering ruins, wasted fields, shattered groves, and
general desolation when General Philip Sheridan had done
with it. Now that the war is over, it will in time rise again,
but it will be difficult to convince the future historian that
such wholesale destruction was not useless and barbarous.

It was a lovely Valley to do battle for, a decorated death-
bed for the cavalier and hero; and here Turner Ashby died.
The Valley loved him and loves him yet. During the war he
had never left her for a single day. He had watched over her
without ceasing. He had made memorable her hills and
streams; and the people along the hills still weep for him,
and the forests echo their lamentations.

On the 5th of June General Jackson passed through Harrisonburg with the advance of his column and turned eastward toward Port Republic and the Blue Ridge. On the 6th
Headquarters were established at the hospitable residence of
Mr. Kemper beyond Port Republic, a small village situated at
the junction of the Middle Branch and South Branch as they
flow together and form the South Fork of the Shenandoah
River. The South Branch is fordable at any point; the Middle Branch, having been increased by the waters of the North
Branch higher up the stream, is deep, and was spanned by
an old but substantial bridge across which ran the road from
Port Republic to Harrisonburg. The troops were encamped
on the north side of the Middle Branch, Jackson's old division just opposite Port Republic, and the division of General
Ewell at Cross Keys, several miles nearer Harrisonburg. General Ashby with a rear guard was still at Harrisonburg.

In the afternoon of the 6th Frémont closed in cautiously
upon Harrisonburg, and took possession, Ashby retiring.
General Bayard with his horse and infantry support followed
Ashby, his immediate advance being under Colonel (Sir?)

Percy Wyndham,[2] a soldier of fortune from over the sea who had entered the Federal service. Ashby retired, watchful and provokingly tenacious. Then Wyndham determined to attack with a charge and led it. His troops were not so belligerent. He made the charge very much alone, as he ascertained when his horse was shot under him and he was a prisoner. He was captured by a cavalryman who was out in front of his command, Holmes Conrad of Winchester, afterwards Major and Assistant Adjutant General on the staff of Major General T. L. Rosser and lately Solicitor General of the United States.

In this little affair Ashby took a number of prisoners, and sent Colonel Wyndham to General Jackson's Headquarters. I met Wyndham on the way and heard with amusement of the comical meeting between him and Major Bob Wheat of the Louisiana Tigers. Wheat was sitting on the fence when Wyndham passed by and, recognizing him, he yelled out his name and, springing into the road, greeted him with loud welcome as a prisoner. Wyndham was still an adventurer, caring little on what side he fought; but Wheat was fighting for a cause in which his whole soul was enlisted and for which he afterwards gave up his life.

I returned with Wyndham to Headquarters. He was in a most resentful mood toward his own troops and repeated to me what he had said to Major Wheat, that they started in the charge with him and then deserted him in the most cowardly manner. He was not an attractive-looking warrior and looked like what he was, a soldier of fortune.

The skirmishing continued after the capture of Wyndham with no material results. As the sun was going down, Ashby, desirous of catching a party of the enemy who were in his front, ready to follow if he retired and retreat if he advanced, requested General Ewell to furnish him with several regiments of infantry. The First Maryland, Colonel Bradley T. Johnson, and Colonel John Letcher's Virginia Regiment were sent to him. Skirmishing soon began, and the Federals, having been reinforced with infantry, drove the Confederate skirmish line back upon its support. Just then Ashby had his horse shot under him—the same, by the way, upon which Jackson was wounded at Bull Run. Thus suddenly dismounted, he placed himself at the head of the Virginia regiment, which was wavering under the hot fire, and waving his sword in the air moved forward and called upon them to follow him. At the same time General Ewell rode up and ordered the First Maryland to charge. The order was handsomely obeyed and in a few minutes the enemy was driven from the field.

But Ashby was dead, shot through the heart. He never spoke, but calmly breathed his last in the arms of Lieutenant Jim Thomson, who loved him as only a fearless young soldier can love his hero, and whose love was fully rewarded by Ashby's love for him. Dear, impulsive, generous Thomson, who never afterwards mentioned Ashby's name without a sigh—he went too at the very last. He fell at the head of a regiment of cavalry leading a charge at High Bridge when the end of the war was in sight, and now sleeps near Ashby's side in the Stonewall Cemetery at Winchester.

In this little fight Lieutenant Colonel Thomas L. Kane of the Pennsylvania "Bucktails" and some of his battalion were captured, the Colonel being wounded. In a conversation at the time with Captain James R. Herbert, who commanded the Maryland skirmishers, Colonel Kane said:

"I have today saved the life of one of the most gallant soldiers in either army—General Ashby—a man I admire as much as you do. His figure is familiar to me for I have seen him often enough in our front. He was today within fifty yards of my skirmishers, sitting on his horse, unconscious of the danger he was in. I saw three of them raise their guns to fire, but I succeeded in stopping two of them and struck up the gun of the third as it went off. Ashby is too brave to die in that way."

Unknown to Colonel Kane, Ashby was dead and he was pronouncing his first eulogy. Afterwards Kane remarked to a gentleman who was writing on the war, "Deal justly with the memory of Ashby. He must have been a noble fellow, a brave soldier, and a gentleman."

I saw Colonel Kane and met him once again after the war. I was at the Legislature in Harrisburg, trying to get an appropriation to remove the Confederate dead from Gettysburg. He happened to be there and, in company with another admirable and generous soldier, General John F. Hartranft, then Auditor General of the State, offered to go with me before the proper committees of the Senate and House. They supported my application earnestly, Colonel Kane with so much impetuous feeling that he seemed to make it a matter of personal patriotism. He had not recovered from his wound and that gave emphasis to his words. It gave me great pleasure to be able to tell him what Ashby's comrades thought of his eulogy at Cross Keys.

General Jackson was sitting in his room in a private interview with Colonel Wyndham when a messenger arrived announcing the death of Ashby. Throughout Headquarters there was a gloomy shadow and almost voiceless grief. It was the first heavy personal loss that had befallen the Army of the Valley, and there was no useless attempt to give expression to it. Colonel Wyndham was at once dismissed, and the General locked the door of his room. What transpired there, how he wrestled with his sorrow, no one will ever know. If he found comfort in his grief at the sudden taking off of his invaluable ally, he never spoke of it to anyone.

The body of General Ashby was taken to Charlottesville by his Assistant Adjutant General, Captain Sturgis Davis, for burial. Uncontrollable was the grief of his troopers, a sad parting, as their knightly chief, covered by a military pall, was carried from their midst. He the invincible and, as they had learned to believe, the invulnerable, was wounded and conquered and dead. His own place could not be and was never filled. Their captured foes, standing by as the hearse passed along the road, as if in sympathy for their bereavement and in respect for their great enemy, stood in respectful silence and many of them with uncovered heads.

General Ashby was a man of striking personal appearance, about five feet ten inches tall, with a well-proportioned figure, graceful and compact, black eyes, black hair, and a flowing black beard. His complexion was of the darkest brunette, so dark that a Federal scout whom he once shot with a pistol declared he had been shot by a Negro. His face was placid not stern; even his smile was shadowed with a tinge of melancholy. Some who knew him well said it was because he had never recovered from the death of his brother, Richard, killed early in the war. His face did not flush in battle or under excitement; only the melancholy passed away and his countenance, alive, determined, was still calm. He often smiled, rarely laughed. His eye was gentle, peaceful; in battle it did not sparkle fitfully but burned steadily beneath his dark brows. His was a face that any likeness of must be a caricature, the kind that cannot be photographed. Riding his black stallion, he looked like a knight of the olden time; galloping over the field on his favorite war horse, his white one, eager, watchful, he was fascinating, inspiring. Altogether he was the most picturesque horseman ever seen in the Shenandoah Valley—he seemed to have been left over by the Knights of the Golden Horseshoe.

General Ashby in his brief career of one year had not the same opportunity to show what his ability as a cavalry officer was as to exhibit his personal attractiveness and strength of character. As a captain he was without a superior, popular, exacting. As a colonel with an independent command he was active, vigilant, energetic, never at rest. It was said of him that he evidently had made a contract with President Davis to fight the Yankees every day for the term of one year from the 1st of January, 1862. If so, he kept his promise to the day of his death. Indeed in one of his letters to his friend, Colonel A. R. Boteler, he said he had made thirty fights in twenty-eight days.

The statements of Ashby with regard to the strength and position of the enemy were generally singularly accurate: once, at Kernstown, he was deceived. His idea of the superior patriotism of the volunteer and that he should not be subjected to very much starch and drill, made him a poor disciplinarian and caused the only failures he ever made. It was believed that he was awakening to the necessity of better discipline among his cavalry and that he would have made a better brigadier general than colonel. His service to the army was invaluable, but had he been as full of discipline as he was of leadership his successes would have been more fruitful and his reputation still greater. Yet it should be remembered that he had little time for instruction of any kind. From the beginning his only drill ground was the field of battle and his daily conflicts and marches occupied all his time and thoughts. He was compelled to organize his troops while on the gallop.

General Jackson thus spoke of him: "An official report is not an appropriate place for more than a passing notice of the distinguished dead, but the close relations which General Ashby bore to my command, for most of the previous twelve months, will justify me in saying that as a partisan officer I never knew his superior. His daring was proverbial, his power of endurance almost incredible, his tone of character heroic, and his sagacity almost intuitive in divining the purposes and movements of the enemy."

In October, 1866, General Ashby's remains were removed from Charlottesville and on the 25th of that month were buried in the Stonewall Cemetery at Winchester with many services and ceremonies, in the presence of a great concourse of people. There they now rest in the Valley of Virginia "amid the proudest monuments of his glory."

> *There, through the coming ages,*
> *When his sword is rust,*
> *And his deeds in classic pages;*
> *Mindful of her trust,*
> *Shall Virginia, bending lowly,*
> *Still a ceaseless vigil holy*
> *Keep above his dust.*[3]

CROSS KEYS AND PORT REPUBLIC

ASHBY was dead, but Jackson and his grey legions were apparently confident and defiant, and the more aggressive because of Ashby's death. In the two days of fight that followed there seemed no little revenge in their attacks. Frémont and Shields, rather priding themselves that they had driven Jackson up the Valley and from point to point so easily, thought it not difficult to pen him up and then to do what they were continually doing by telegraph, "bag" him —they seemed to like that effective word.

General Jackson's Headquarters were, as I have said, at Mr. Kemper's house, beyond and south of Port Republic and separated from his troops by that little town and the Middle Branch, across which was a traveler's bridge. Shortly after midnight on the morning of the 8th of June, it was reported that Shields was advancing along the same road that Jackson had marched in the spring from Conrad's Store to Port Republic. The intention of this was evident—to get possession of the bridge at Port Republic and prevent Jackson's escape from Frémont. In accordance with instructions from General Jackson, I sent a squadron of cavalry in the direction of the enemy, with orders to go until they met their pickets and report the locality by courier, to drive in the pickets, ascertain the position of the leading column and promptly report any important information. I mention the particulars of these instructions because their disobedience very nearly resulted in irreparable disaster. No report was received during the night. The morning was Sunday, bright, warm, calm, and peaceful. The absolute quiet of it, after so many of noisy activity was unnatural, but it was most welcome. Orders were sent out that the troops would spend the day in camp and their chaplains hold services.

Between seven and eight o'clock, while the General and a few of his staff were walking in front of the house, enjoying the morning away from the hum of camp and watching the horses grazing over the green lot, a courier rode up with a report that the enemy, cavalry, artillery, and infantry, were at the Lewis House, three miles distant. He was very indefinite and was sent back. He was not out of sight when a lieutenant of cavalry arrived and said the enemy were in sight of Port Republic. And just then a quick discharge of cannon indicated that the little town was being shelled. Then there was hustling for horses. My horse was saddled and fastened to the fence, for I intended to ride. The greatest anxiety was to get the General off, and I offered him my horse, running with an orderly to get his, farthest off, of course, in the field. But the General waited and was soon mounted. Pendleton, being ready, followed, and I was delayed a little getting my horse. Few of the staff got off in time. If any other crossed the bridge in that John Gilpin race with the General but Pendleton, I do not remember him. I was the last to get over, and I passed in front of Colonel S. Sprigg Carroll's cavalry as they rode up out of the water and made my rush for the bridge. I could see into their faces plainly and they greeted me with sundry pistol shots.

I joined the General on a hill overlooking the bridge. Just then the company of cavalry which had accelerated my passage over the river came up to the mouth of the bridge. The General, supposing them, I fancy, to be his company of couriers, called to them loudly and sharply not to stop there, but to come over immediately, waving to them at the same time. I told him they were Yankees, but to our mutual surprise they wheeled and rode off. As they did so, a piece of artillery came up at a gallop, was unlimbered quickly and trained upon us on our side of the bridge. Just then a gun of Poague's battery came into position near us on the hill. General Jackson, mistaken again or encouraged by the success of his order to the cavalry, rose in his stirrups and called out loudly, "Bring that gun over here!" I undertook to correct him again, but the gun itself did it more effectually. There was a flash and a discharge, and the earth flying about us convinced him. The General directed me to ride rapidly for the first regiment I could get (he had sent Pendleton to put Taliaferro under arms), to bring it quickly and "take that piece." I met Fulkerson with the Thirty-seventh Virginia infantry. Poague had opened on the enemy with his gun and speedily demoralized it. Fulkerson rushed his men with a yell across the bridge, poured a volley into the cannoniers, who fled, and captured the piece; and then proceeded to clear the town with his rifles.

A company of infantry under Captain S. J. C. Moore of the Second Virginia, detached and on guard duty with the trains, had prevented the enemy from advancing toward the General's Headquarters. When Carroll's cavalry first appeared and caused a stampede of quartermaster and other trains, Captain Moore's company held its position. He prevented the enemy from getting beyond him, and when Fulkerson charged across the bridge Moore assumed the offensive and did much to speed Carroll's retreat.

By this time three batteries, including Poague's, supported by Winder's brigade, had taken position on the range of hills commanding Port Republic and the river road opposite, on which General E. B. Tyler was advancing. They opened upon Carroll's retreat and made it a stampede. When the head of Tyler's infantry came in sight, they took effective aim at it. The column showed temporary obstinacy and marched on steadily, but only for a short distance. It was stunned, riddled, and scattered, and soon disappeared in the distance or among the adjacent hills.

I have been a little precise in describing this incident of the morning of June 8th because of the confusion arising from the discrepancies in the reports of officers—from General Jackson's, written in the following winter, to Captain

Poague's unofficial account. As I have said, the staff were
scattered, some of them, unable to get through, going a
short distance on the road to Staunton. Colonel Crutchfield
and Lieutenant Edward Willis, being in bed, tried to join
the General but fell into the hands of the enemy, and Dr.
McGuire barely escaped a similar fate. Pendleton and I
were the only ones who were "in it" with the General. Crutchfield, however, in the confusion of the melee caused by Fulkerson and Poague's gun, escaped while crossing the river.
Willis was taken five miles to the rear and placed under
guard in a house. There he met a sympathizing young lady,
whose anti-Union sentiments he soon discovered. He had not
been well, and it occurred to him that he might just as well
be worse—an idea which the young lady heartily encouraged.
She reported his condition and administered potions to him,
awful gruels and bitter tea, but he steadily became worse.
To all appearances alarmed, she kept surgeons away from
him and almost made him ill in reality by the concoctions
she invented and made him taste, to her amusement if not
his. The next day came on the battle of Port Republic; when
the rout came, the retreat was too rapid to include him and
he was left behind. His strength returned marvellously and
we soon met him returning to us on a captured horse, with
its owner sitting quietly behind him.

The attack of Colonel (afterwards Brevet Major General) S. S. Carroll on Port Republic was not a success; for
this he was much censured. The affair led to bitter crimination and recrimination between him and Brigadier General
Tyler. (Later on, when I was wounded and in prison, General Tyler treated me with the greatest courtesy and was my
personal friend until he died; [1] and I met General Sprigg
Carroll, after the war. When I was a candidate for Congress
he voted for me, saying General W. S. Hancock was the first
Democrat he ever voted for and I would be the last. I was,
for he did not long survive.) [2] At first I think Colonel Carroll
was censured more severely than he deserved. It is not probable he knew where General Jackson's Headquarters were,
or that the bridge was so entirely undefended. Still he made

several serious mistakes. He should not have halted before he crossed the stream; in war, he who hesitates is lost. Had he seized the bridge at once, as he did later, he could have separated our army from its commander, perhaps have captured him, and could easily have burned the bridge before relief came. Frémont could not have whipped Ewell with that army, it is true, but Jackson and his wagon train would have been at the mercy of the enemy. And then who would have been the hero of the hour in the North, McClellan or Carroll? To what dizzy height might the latter not have risen!

When Carroll got over the shallow stream, he ought to have burned the bridge at once. He could have done it, even then, and it was his manifest duty. Colonel Carroll said afterwards that he was distinctly ordered before going to Port Republic not to burn the bridge; and it was intimated from other sources that its destruction would not have suited Frémont, for he did not desire to have General Jackson turned over to him for his sole enjoyment. He had heard of the man who, in vulgar parlance, "bit off more than he could chew."

When Frémont heard what he supposed was Shields' attack upon our position at Port Republic, he advanced against Ewell, and very soon the battle was in earnest. Ewell's position was a good one, and he did not hesitate because of Frémont's superior force. He fought his battle well and with his small division defeated Frémont with heavy loss to him. General Frémont did not fight his battle so well, or his troops were not equal to it. It was a conflict which never received the attention it deserved in the series of engagements which made up that Valley Campaign. It was another Sunday fight, which ended with the day, and the moon that shone over the Valley that night threw her rays upon the wounded soldiers and not far off upon their mothers and sisters going to church to pray for them. The result of the battle confirmed the wholesome belief of the old soldiers that the side that inaugurated a battle on Sunday, lost it.

General Frémont repulsed, General Shields checked and not

in sight, it was believed General Jackson would take advantage of the night and slip out of the trap with his prisoners
and stores. But the General seemed to like traps and, at any
rate, was not yet satisfied with the risks he had run and the
blows he had inflicted. He directed his quartermaster, Major
Harman, to bring up all the wagons, over the river, that the
troops might cook rations. Even "Old John" was astonished
at this order, and the rest of the staff, confounded. Pendleton, McGuire, Crutchfield, Boswell, and all present exchanged looks and smiles, as Pendleton said "crazy again."
We were getting used to this kind of aberration, but this did
seem rather an extra piece of temerity. Nevertheless, the
wagons came up. Frémont and Shields must have seen the
campfires and been confused accordingly. The night was
beautiful, after the eventful day, and we retired taking
much thought for the morrow.

At "early dawn," a pet phrase of the General's, we were
in the saddle; all was quiet. We rode to the front, and all the
wagons had gone. Looking over the river and up into the
Blue Ridge, we saw the long white train, moving on its ser-
pentine way to the top of the mountain. Harman was in
command of that imposing column, and no one was more
equal to such a task, although it must be said he possessed
as little of Job's special virtue as any man in the army.

General Jackson's intention was very soon made plain.
Before the sun had risen, or Frémont either, our army had
crossed into Port Republic and from there upon a temporary
bridge of wagons over the South Branch on its way to measure strength with Shields' unwhipped army, and to settle
the account left open since Kernstown. About two miles
below Port Republic, the skirmishers from Winder and Tyler
became engaged, and after the usual preliminaries, the lines
went at each other. The result was a hot fight continued
for several hours with great vigor and varying success, as
was announced by alternate "Rebel yells" and "Yankee
cheers." For the only time in my life I saw a regiment, from
Ohio I believe, change front to rear on first company, under
fire, and with admirable precision. I knew then, that it would

be no easy matter to defeat an army of such troops. The fighting of both armies was obstinate, the gallantry of officers conspicuous, and the loss among them unusually heavy. Finally the Federals began to retire, then to retreat, and then the rout was complete; the pursuit of them was continued for about five miles and prisoners and guns were captured from them. The fight was a very different one from that of the day before, and Jackson found he had met men of like mettle to his own. He did not accomplish his double purpose of whipping Shields and then going back after Frémont. Although the force he had engaged was something larger than Tyler's, he found his hands full, and sent word to General Isaac R. Trimble to burn the bridge and join him.

The fact is, Jackson went into the fight impetuously and was disappointed. Had he waited to get his troops up and into formation, his victory would have been easier and his loss less. Tyler always afterward took much credit to himself for that fight against Jackson and Ewell, and his little army deserved it.

That morning when Frémont was aroused by the sound of artillery and knew what it meant, he moved forward in line of battle. But only Trimble with a little cavalry was in his front and they gave way with little resistance. Frémont moved cautiously after them toward the bridge, but before he reached it a pillar of fire and smoke notified him that it was being destroyed. Judging from his previous conduct I can't help the suspicion that he was gratified. Arriving upon the banks of the river with his glittering line of bayonets, he witnessed the fighting and defeat of his allies on the other side, helpless, if desirous to aid them.

If baffled and made ridiculous, Major General Frémont was at least in a position where he could give vent to his rage. He threw shells among our ambulance corps while they were relieving the suffering of the wounded of both armies, and killed some men and horses. In one instance a piece of shell tore through an ambulance in which a wounded Confederate and a wounded Union soldier were riding side by side; the Union soldier was killed, the Confederate escaped. The next day, as was usual, was one of incessant rain. General Shields sent a note to General Jackson requesting permission to care for his wounded and bury his dead. The General replied that the wounded were being cared for and the dead were being buried; and then called his attention to the unsoldierly conduct of General Frémont's command. General Shields, a soldier and a gentleman, must have felt the rebuke, coming from one who always directed that the wounded of the enemy should be cared for as his own.

This was the last act of that strategic combination of Federal generals, which was "to bag Jackson" and his pestiferous little army. The Chiefs at Washington and the Northern people could hardly wait until it was done, and the loyal press was prepared with suitable accounts of the extinguishment of that fiery comet, whose flight was continually threatening the destruction of the Union. Disappointment and astonishment exceeded all powers of editorial speech, and newspapers confessed their inability to cope with the occasion. In Richmond, on the other hand, the people and press were intoxicated with their enthusiasm over successive victories. How was it with Jackson? At the close of the battle of Port Republic, he rode to General Ewell and laying his hand gently on his arm said, "General, he who does not see the hand of God in this is blind, Sir, blind!"

Immediately after he sent this message to Richmond:

Near Port Republic June 9th
Through God's blessing, the enemy near Port Republic was this day routed, with the loss of six pieces of his artillery.

T. J. JACKSON
Maj. Genl. Comdg.

Up to this time General Jackson had been denied strategic ability of any distinction, although critics agreed that orders explicitly, exacting the same from his subordinates, as an executive officer he had no equal in the war. Obeying moving with marvelous speed and secrecy, with energy without limit and a will that stiffened with opposition, it was conceded he was the man of all others to execute and drive to ultimate success any plan that Johnston or Lee might originate. The Valley Campaign generally dispelled this misconception of Jackson, although there were still some who held to the opinion that, in spite of his remarkable executive capacity, he lacked the comprehensiveness which is required to handle large armies on a broad field. His own rank and file, however, never doubted. Afterwards when he was put to the test, when he hurled his augmented corps against McClellan, when he whirled it around Pope and struck him on all sides, when at Sharpsburg and Fredericksburg he rose higher and higher, and when finally at Chancellorsville he ended his career by the most brilliant movement of his life, military critics ceased to place any limit to his ability.

The campaign just ended was Jackson's masterpiece. The more it is studied and its difficulties comprehended, the greater will be its rank among military successes. The battle of McDowell was fought on the 8th of May, the battle of Port Republic on the 9th of June. In this one month Jackson and his little army became immortal in military history. In that time he had defeated four separate armies. He had relieved Staunton of Milroy and Schenck, had driven Banks beyond the borders of Virginia, had held McDowell with 35,000 troops from going to join McClellan, had defeated Banks, Frémont, and Shields in turn, had broken into pieces their triple combination, and had driven the Federal Administration in Washington to the verge of nervous prostration. In thirty days his army had marched nearly four hundred miles, skirmishing almost daily, fought five battles, defeated four armies, two of which were completely routed, captured about twenty pieces of artillery, some four thousand prisoners, and immense quantity of stores of all kinds, and had done all this with a loss of less than one thousand killed, wounded, and missing. Surely a more brilliant record cannot be found in the history of the world, and General Jackson

might well say this was accomplished "through God's blessing."

In this campaign, greatly resembling the Italian Campaign of Napoleon, General Jackson was not merely executing the plans of his superiors. He was told what Johnston
and Lee wished, but in strategy it was his campaign only.
He took the responsibility. He dared and won. He appealed
to Richmond for reinforcements he did not get, and at one
time Ewell was about to be taken from him. With what he
had he fought the good fight.

On the 20th of May, the day before General Jackson
crossed from the Shenandoah into the Page Valley to unite
with Ewell for his descent upon Banks, General Ewell suddenly appeared at our Headquarters with ill-humor on his
face.

"General Ewell, I'm glad to see you. Get off!" cried Old
Jack to him.

"You will not be so glad, when I tell you what brought
me," said Old Dick.

"What—are the Yankees after you?"

"Worse than that. I am ordered to join General Johnston," quietly answered General Ewell as he dismounted.
They retired to an adjacent grove and General Ewell produced his order. Jackson ceased to smile and his face became
grave and cold. The order was a blow to him and compliance
with it ruined all his hopes and prospects of success. He
hesitated only a moment. He had a few words with General
Ewell, told him he could not spare him, suspended the order,
and directed him to be ready to move the next morning.
General Ewell had not yet fought a single battle with Jackson. Then began their military comradeship. Together they
entered upon that Valley Campaign in which Ewell won
that brilliant fame, second only to that of Jackson.

As I have said the campaign was closed at Port Republic
"with a clap of thunder," and if Colonel Crozet [3] who fought
under Napoleon said it was "extra-Napoleonic," he was not
far from the truth.

For this succession of victories, Jackson issued the following order for thanksgiving and prayer: "The Major General Commanding invites you to observe tomorrow evening, June 14th, from 3 o'clock P.M., as a season of thanksgiving, by a suspension of all military exercises and by holding divine service in the several regiments." In his official report he says this was "for the purpose of rendering thanks to God for having crowned our arms with success and to implore his continued favor."

X

COLD HARBOR

THE battle of Seven Pines (Fair Oaks) had been fought with unimportant success on the part of the Confederates, not enough certainly to compensate for the disabling of General Joseph E. Johnston and the loss of so many brave men.

Richmond was still besieged and McClellan had drawn so close that the tall steeples of the Confederate Capitol reflected the light of the morning sun almost within sight of the Federal camp. People of the city were accustomed to the daily sound of artillery at no great distance, but her fair daughters gave no signs of alarm or want of confidence in the success of their grey-clad defenders. There were the faithful wife of Ulysses and the weeping but undaunted Andromache, with their patience, hope, and courage. And besides, there were those whose indifference to the dangers which encompassed them took the form of gayety and revelry, which at times was not only reckless but unseemly—except that it put to shame any timid man who dared to doubt.

A few days after the battle of Port Republic our army remained bivouacked at the mouth of Brown's Gap in the Blue Ridge, and as it rained during those days the troops suffered greatly. The Federal commanders were evidently very much puzzled to know whether General Jackson was really quiet and at Brown's Gap and, if so, what it portended. They were afraid to move forward and did not like to go backward.

On the 12th of June, General Jackson recrossed the South Branch and encamped several miles south of Port Republic in the vicinity of Weyer's Cave. On the same day Colonel Thomas T. Munford of the cavalry drove in the Federal outposts and entered Harrisonburg; Frémont was in retreat and seemed to have left with a haste that indicated demoralization. General Shields had retired toward Luray, and Frémont kept on until he reached the vicinity of Mount Jackson. We had some days of much needed rest in our new camp. I had often heard of Weyer's Cave and had some curiosity to go into it. I suggested to one of the staff that we do so. He promptly replied, "No, thanks. Chances are that we will get under ground soon enough and I have greater curiosity to know what I'll see then, than I have in regard to Weyer's Cave." I began to think as he did and did not go; very few soldiers went into it, perhaps for the same reason. The place is now called the Grottoes, but it has been entirely eclipsed by the greater glories of the Luray Caverns, then undiscovered.

On the 15th General W. H. C. Whiting, sent up from Richmond by General Lee after giving all the publicity possible to the movement so that it might reach the enemy, arrived at Staunton with Law's and Hood's brigades and part of Lawton's. Why Staunton, except as part of the game of bluff, no one could tell, for as it turned out no one but Jackson knew. Whiting certainly did not, and being a quick-tempered, as well as an excellent officer, he expressed his disgust very freely at being kept in the dark.

On the 16th General Whiting himself appeared at Headquarters and had an interview with the General. I fancy he departed not much the wiser. We, of the staff, began to look for the advent of Whiting's division and wondered how long it would be until we were in Winchester. Soon after dark the General, having directed that the troops should move at "early dawn," started for Staunton with General Whiting. But, as it afterwards turned out, he had gone to meet Colonel Munford by special appointment that night at Mount Crawford, secretly, to give him personal instructions as to his movements in following Frémont and in permitting the latter to get suitable information of the General's intentions. The information was evidently to be doctored. Result: Banks telegraphed a few days afterwards that Jackson was about to move against him with heavy force.

On that same day General Lee wrote to General Jackson that, as McClellan was being strengthened, he had better come to Richmond to unite with him as soon as possible and let Frémont go, after misleading him as much with plausible information as possible. General Lee added, "if you agree with me, the sooner you make arrangements to do so the better." This letter was received by General Jackson on the 17th, after he had made all necessary arrangements in anticipation of General Lee. "*If you agree with me*"—what stronger evidence can we have of General Lee's implicit reliance upon Jackson's judgment than that in such an emergency he should have been willing to subordinate his judgment to it!

At daylight on the 17th of June, Jackson's army was in motion and on its way "somewhere." The staff began to suspect its destination, but kept its own counsel. General Jackson had disappeared and some of us reported to General Ewell for duty. He said with grim humor that he was only commanding a division, marching under orders, but he didn't know where, and that at that time he had more staff than he had any use for. He expressed a suspicion that Jackson was in the vicinity of Richmond. So we went off, a staff in pursuit of a General, and took things easy while we could. The columns, having crossed the Blue Ridge by Jaman's and Rockfish gaps, went winding along in the sunny Valley toward Richmond.

At noon the next day we detected the General as he stepped from the cars at Mechum's River. He came from the direction of Staunton. He had no instructions to give and did not trouble himself to ask the whereabouts of anybody. He had his trunk put on the train, remained about fifteen minutes, and shaking hands all round and saying good-by as earnestly as if he was off for Europe, he departed and gave no sign. Those of us left looked at each other and then gave vent to our suppressed merriment. "What the devil is he up to now?" one said, and we all thought. An inquisitive old fellow at Charlottesville thought he'd find out, and finding verbal tactics ineffectual, he bluntly asked,

"General, where *are* you going?"

"Can you keep a secret? Yes? Ah, so can I," was the answer he got.

Left very much alone, Jackson's young staff—they were nearly all young men—did not go through the green fields and valleys of Albemarle and Louisa without seeing many of their lighted parlors, in which they were always welcomed by bright and pretty girls and merry music. The genial Boswell, he who was killed when Jackson fell at Chancellorsville, was the best of companions—many a rapid gallop with Ned Willis, impulsive Georgian, soon "dead on the field of glory"—and Sandy Pendleton, the best beloved, now sleeping in Lexington by Jackson's side as it were—the witty, droll, most handsome Crutchfield, dead too—and McGuire, always pleasant, ever faithful, who still lives, with much professional work and honor.[1] They and several others all enjoyed that little holiday and made the most of it, seeking new Desdemonas at the close of each day. Major Dabney was with the General, which was just as well, for he was too old, and too reverend, and too unelastic to fit in such a crowd.[2]

We overtook the General at Gordonsville on Saturday, where he was awaiting the arrival of the advance of his troops and put somewhat in doubt by vague rumors of threatening movements of McDowell. He was comfortably fixed in a hospitable house but was ready to go on. We only saw him at dinner, after which he took Dr. McGuire and departed, telling us to follow on Monday. Sunday we gave more to society than the sanctuary, and Monday morning, with uncovered heads, we returned the salute of white handkerchiefs waved by white hands and rode away.

At Fredericks Hall we again found traces of the General, but were informed that he had taken his departure at one o'clock the night before, without explanation and with only a courier to guide him. Our informants looked surprised be-

cause we were not amazed at such eccentricity, and we smiled at their surprise.

The next day we continued the chase, and near Beaver Dam Depot came upon the General. It was afternoon and he was in bed, and not a very refreshing or creditable sight met us. The General must have been on a rollicking frolic. His wet and muddy uniform was being dried by the fire and the appearance of his ponderous boots indicated that he might have been wading all night through mud and mire. No one seemed to know where he had been or what doing. It transpired in time that when he left Fredericks Hall so mysteriously he had gone to Richmond and to General Lee's Headquarters, and that he had returned to Beaver Dam just before we found him. He had traveled as a "Colonel" and carried a pass from General Whiting for "one officer to go to Richmond." It will always seem to the average soldier that this was carrying mystery to an extreme length. He did not get along without some trouble with his own troops. Being stopped at an outpost, he asked permission to pass as a "Colonel" with important information, but was very bluntly informed by the corporal that he could not go through that picket without a pass if he was President Davis. At another post the General asked a sentinel:

"What company is this?"

"Company D, Southern Army," said the noncommittal picket.

The General continued to ask questions, the sentinel to evade them. Then the sentinel began,

"What Company do *you* belong to?"

"Don't ask me any questions," sharply said the General.

"Then why the devil do you ask so many yourself?" retorted the soldier. Just then a corporal came up and whispered, "That's old Jack."

The General passed on, saying, "Is it necessary to know who I am?"

"Not more than I already know," was the reply that followed him.

I never afterwards heard the General allude to that night ride or his trip to General Lee's Headquarters.

The next morning, June 25th, the march was continued to Ashland where we spent a night. Here Major Jasper Whiting reported to General Jackson for duty on his staff as one familiar with the country over which we were to fight and march. He was of invaluable service and soon gained the General's confidence and personal regard.

On the 26th we moved in the direction of Hanover Court House and Hundley's Corner. The General pointed out the birthplace of Henry Clay as we passed it and made a few brief, admiring comments on that great statesman. With the exception of a little cavalry skirmishing and some opposition at the crossing of Totopotomoy Creek, our march that day was untroubled. On this day, however, the battles for the relief of Richmond were begun by A. P. Hill and James Longstreet at Mechanicsville. We remained bivouacked for the night at Hundley's Corner.

General Jackson has been criticized, with some severity, for failing to co-operate with Generals Longstreet and Hill at Mechanicsville and thus detracting from the completeness of that success. The criticism, at first view, seems justified, but further examination will show that those whose faith in Jackson's invariable promptness and reliability caused them to refuse to believe that he could not have been derelict, or that there was not some good cause for his delay, were not far wrong. In the first place General Jackson should not have been assigned to that extremely hazardous and pivotal duty that day. He knew nothing about the country—with which every other General of high rank was doubtless familiar—and had not time to take his bearings and learn the topography, so entirely different from that of the Valley—in fact he must have entirely underestimated the difficulties of the country before him. A staff officer assigned to him, although as capable and intelligent as Whiting, could not supply his want of knowledge in this respect.

It is evident that when General Jackson declined the suggestion of General Longstreet to give himself at least another day to make the march before him, he could not have known the topographical and other embarrassments he would have to contend with. The fact is, he was moving in the dark. Then too, the Army of the Valley had been marching and fighting since early spring and was worn out, and there was some complaint that their supplies in this movement were not promptly furnished. Here again, as had happened before, and happened more than once afterwards, his staff was not large enough, and it was impossible for them to do the work required of them. The General's Chief of Staff, Major Dabney, an excellent officer in camp, was not equal to this occasion in the field. With no previous training, he had not been in the army more than three months and had no experience to fit him for the demands of his position. While he did his duty faithfully, he could not be of any service to the General in such an emergency; and as for training a staff to its duties, he knew nothing about it. He resigned within two weeks because of ill health, and Sandy Pendleton again was at the head, as in fact he always was. One thing is certain, no one on the march that day with Jackson saw any letup in his unceasing push.

On the morning of the 27th we moved forward, cautiously and slowly, pushing back the enemy gradually. A junction was formed with A. P. Hill and pleasant greetings exchanged. General D. H. Hill reported with his division and was thenceforth under the command of General Jackson, his brother-in-law. The troops marched and assembled for the battle of Cold Harbor. Longstreet and A. P. Hill had been fighting for some time vigorously, but it was late in the afternoon when Jackson's command got actively to work and the general battle became fast and furious.

"Mr. Boswell, ride over to General Lee and tell him I have closed upon the flank of the enemy and will open the attack at once," was General Jackson's message as he went in. For some time we had heard the thunder of artillery in the direction of Richmond. General Lee, too, had been waiting anxiously to hear from Jackson's corps and, it is said, officers and men in other parts of the army had begun to doubt whether Stonewall Jackson had really come from the Shenandoah Valley.

While the General was directing the movements of his divisions and personally seeing to the formation of his line, he passed by the battalion known as "The Louisiana Tigers" commanded by Major Bob Wheat. By his brave, reckless, and generally loose men and their gallant, big-hearted commander, General Jackson was regarded with superstitious reverence. No two men could be more unlike than "Old Jack" and Bob Wheat, but the latter's affection for his General was akin to adoration. I never passed his command that he did not stop and ask me how "The Old General" was, sometimes half a dozen times a day, and generally adding, "God bless him!"

This day Major Wheat, looking like a mounted Falstaff, was on horseback as the General passed his battalion. When the General approached he rode up to him, with uncovered head, and almost bluntly said, "General, we are about to get into a hot fight and it is likely many of us may be killed. I want to ask you for myself and my Louisianians not to expose yourself so unnecessarily as you often do. What will become of us, down here in these swamps, if anything happens to you, and what will become of the country! General, let us do the fighting. Just let me tell them that you promised me not to expose yourself and then they'll fight like—er—ah—Tigers!" As he spoke he looked up frankly into Jackson's face, who was listening attentively.

Then suddenly, taking Wheat's hand and shaking it, Jackson said, "Much obliged to you, Major. I will try not to go into danger, unnecessarily. But Major, you will be in greater danger than I, and I hope you will not get hurt. Each of us has his duty to perform, without regard to consequences; we must perform it and trust in Providence." They separated and as the General rode away he said, "Just like Major Wheat. He thinks of the safety of others, too brave ever to think of himself."

They never met again. Within an hour or two Wheat fell, mortally wounded, in a charge of his battalion. When dying he asked to be buried on the battlefield. With his last breath he asked if Stonewall was unhurt and then attempted the little prayer he had learned at his mother's knee and often repeated. May that prayer throw an atoning splendor over the earthly record of Roberdeau Wheat.

General Lee was waiting to hear from Jackson when Boswell rode up with his message. In a few minutes the deep, reverberating sound of artillery came heavily on the air, at first slowly, then with increasing fierceness. In the crowded steeples of Richmond where men and women had gathered to watch the distant signs of a struggle fraught with such vital consequences to them, the welcome sound was heard from a new direction and not understood. When some one said, "Those are Stonewall Jackson's guns," all hearts and eyes grew full, and no more fervent prayers were ever spoken from the chancels beneath them than those unspoken ones that went to Heaven that day from those lofty spires.

On the battlefield where Longstreet's doughty men were confronting a stubborn foe and A. P. Hill, as usual, was doing his share of the fighting, soldiers heard the cannonade and were encouraged in their hot work. Soon came to them a sharper and more earnest clamor, and there was such a rattle and roar of musketry as I never heard before or after. A staff officer dashed along Longstreet's wearied lines, crying out, "Stonewall's at them!" and was answered with yell after yell of joy, which added a strange sound to the din of battle. The battle was on in earnest; skirmishing died away and was succeeded by the crash of line meeting line.

General Jackson mounted his gaunt sorrel (not "Little Sorrel") and leaving his position moved more to the front. At that moment someone handed him a lemon—a fruit of which he was specially fond. Immediately a small piece was bitten out of it and slowly and unsparingly he began to extract its flavor and its juice. From that moment until darkness ended the battle, that lemon scarcely left his lips except to be used as a baton to emphasize an order. He listened to Yankee shout or Rebel yell, to the sound of musketry advancing or receding, to all the signs of promise or apprehension, but he never for an instant lost his interest in that lemon and even spoke of its excellence. His face, nevertheless, was calm and granite-

like. His blue eye was restful and cold, except when now and
then it gave, for a moment, an ominous flash. His right hand
lay open and flat on his thigh, but now and then was raised
into the air as was his habit—a gesture which the troops
learned to believe was as significant as the extended arm of
Aaron. But the lemon was not abandoned.

The moment came when it was taken from his mouth with
an impatient jerk. A wild yell came from the battlefield which
attracted his attention. Pendleton came up and said it was
from the Stonewall Brigade, for he had just seen Winder
taking them in. He drew the lemon away abruptly and said,
"We shall soon have good news from that charge. Yes, they
are driving the enemy!" and he lifted up his yellow banner,
as if in triumph. When I last saw that lemon, it was torn open
and exhausted and thrown away, but the day was over and
the battle was won.

I spoke of the occasional flashes in the eyes of the General
—ominous of a storm brewing. The battle had been raging
for hours with no definite results. Night was approaching, the
enemy were yielding, but the field was not yet won. Fitz-John
Porter was making one of the most splendid fights in the history of the Army of the Potomac and showed no signs of retreat. General Jackson was chafing under the obstinate resistance. At that moment a staff officer arrived from General
John B. Hood, saying his brigade was being seriously annoyed by a certain battery which prevented his advance. The
lemon was forgotten for a moment. "Captain, tell General
Hood I will have that battery silenced at once." Then with
aroused energy, to me, "Bring up several batteries to assist
Pelham and tell them to drive that battery away or destroy
it." Then before I got away, he rose in his stirrups and, turning to Pendleton, he said fiercely. "Ride to General Ewell and
direct him, if the enemy do not retire before dusk, he must
sweep them from that hill with the bayonet!"

"That's the order!" shouted Jeb Stuart, waving his plumed
hat in the air. "Let one of my staff go with Pendleton, for
that order must not miscarry."

The battle grew louder. The sun was down and night was

settling on the bloody scene. There was a momentary lull, and
then—

> *At once there rose so wild a yell*
> *Within that dark and narrow dell*
> *As all the fiends from Heaven that fell*
> *Had pealed the banner-cry of Hell.*

"There goes Old Dick!" broke from us all. Yes, it was
Ewell's last grand charge at Cold Harbor. Soon the sound of
musketry and of shouting receded and died away over the
hill. Ewell had obeyed the order. The noise of battle was
hushed, that battery had been silenced, the enemy swept from
that hill; and soldiers wandering in darkness over the field
in search of fallen comrades told each other that Richmond
was saved.

MALVERN HILL

I AM ONLY relating the little things of the Seven Days' Battle about Richmond, leaving the weightier matters to the historians and the biographers of Lee and McClellan.

The battle of Cold Harbor was fought on the 27th of June, 1862. General Jackson, having sent Ewell toward the White House, remained almost stationary with the rest of his corps during the 28th and 29th. He had much difficulty that night, however, in repairing Grapevine Bridge. When this was done, causing a delay much to be regretted, he crossed the Chickahominy and united with General John B. Magruder. Before daylight on the 30th he directed Magruder to push out his skirmishers and ascertain if the enemy were in his front saying he was confident they were gone. The order was obeyed with some hesitation, and it was found that the fortifications of the enemy were empty. During the day he pressed on past Savage's Station, where he found and seized a large hospital and a valuable quantity of stores, to White Oak Swamp, where Crutchfield with his artillery had a spirited duel with the enemy.

On McClellan's retreat part of his route lay almost within the Confederate lines, and there is one point at which he expected to be intercepted. It is said by a foreigner who was on his staff at this time that as he approached this point he sent out frequent couriers and officers to see if the road was not occupied by the enemy, and made arrangements for a fight if necessary. When informed that the road was clear, he at first discredited it and, when satisfied of the truth, he said with a relieved voice, "Well, someone has blundered—but it is not Lee."

McClellan was right. Someone had blundered, and to the blunder McClellan owed his escape. But what was the blunder? General Lee's plan for the battle of the 30th at Frayser's Farm seems to have been as brilliant as ever, and if it had been as well-executed as designed it would have been fatal to McClellan's army. Perhaps it took too great chances and expected too much clock-like precision from too many generals. One thing is certain, General Lee was not supported by the action of his subordinates, as his strategy demanded. General Jackson has not escaped criticism, and he does not seem to have been his very self. There were things, it is true, he could not overcome. He was in the saddle continuously and seemed never to let up. Tired out with work he certainly was and so were his troops. But no one who rode with him on the 29th and 30th can recall a moment when he rested. But after reading the criticism on both sides, A. P. Hill's and W. B. Franklin's, and giving due credit to all explanations, the impression still remains, that if he had been up to the Stonewall standard that he had established in the Valley and kept to ever after the 30th day of June, he would have found the way to do more effective service that bloody day, and it would have been a sad one for the Army of the Potomac.

On the afternoon of July 1st General Jackson, in the advance, arrived in front of Malvern Hill, upon which the Federal army was advantageously posted. Then followed another fearful and sanguinary battle. I have always felt that it was a criminal blunder. It certainly was a field of useless slaughter, and it certainly was not a Confederate success. General Lee was right in making the attack. He had never had a chance at McClellan's army with his united. He had it here and he wanted to destroy it, if possible. He was too aggressive to let the opportunity pass, and Jackson was in the same vein. But the battle was fought by detachments against an enemy well-posted and ready for the fight. On the part of the Confederate commanders it was not a well-fought battle—let historians and military critics fix the blame where it belongs. The troops fought well as ever, gallantly, but they were uselessly sacrificed. The Federal troops also fought heroically and were well held in hand by their officers. Up to this time General McClellan had managed his retreat with such military skill that no subsequent criticism can detract from it; and at Malvern Hill as at other places he was ably seconded by his chief subordinates.

The Confederates were repulsed at Malvern Hill and McClellan has been criticized for not following up the repulse. If he had done so, he would have been badly beaten, for Longstreet and A. P. Hill had not been in the fight. General D. H. Hill and his troops did the most conspicuous work at Malvern Hill and deserve the chief credit.

During the introductory preparations for the battle General Jackson, nearly a mile in rear of his line, was sitting on the roadside with his back against a tree, writing a note. Troops were passing and raising a cloud of dust which attracted the attention of the enemy, and a shell from a Parrott gun [1] struck the column in front of us and exploded. Five or six men were killed or wounded, and dust was thrown over the General and his paper. Without raising his head he shook the paper to relieve it and proceeded with his note. (He did not repeat the witticism of Junot, who under similar circumstances thanked the enemy for sanding the ink—perhaps because he was using a pencil.) When the message was finished and folded, he arose, gave explicit instructions that the dead be carried out of sight and the wounded cared for, and rode off to the front.

Before long, the battle was at red heat. Generals Lee, Jackson, and Ewell with their staffs were in the rear of Jackson's line, on their horses, and concealed by a strip of wood. A staff officer came up hurriedly and reported that some of our guns were being badly used up by the enemy's fire. The General prepared to go in person to see about it when General Lee protested, saying that Crutchfield was there and would know what to do. Although General Jackson generally considered a suggestion of General Lee equivalent to an order, he did not on occasions like this. He at once started off, taking Pendleton and myself. As soon as we rode in view we became the object of the enemy's pointed attentions. First came a shell, striking near us and ricochetting over our heads with a shriek, then a round shot which passed between the General and Pendleton (we were riding single file), and next, with better aim, a shell which struck right in front of the General, exploded, and threw a shower of dirt over the whole party, while the General's horse squatted to the ground with fright. The situation was getting *painfully* monotonous, and yet the General paid no attention and rode on "into the jaws of death." He got little farther, for a staff officer came up like a charge of cavalry and with a salute said, "General, General Lee presents his compliments and directs that you return at once." The General quietly turned and obeyed the order. Courage is a good thing, but there are times, thought General Lee, when one might have too much of it.

Night, dark and dismal, settled upon the battlefield of Malvern Hill, its thousands dead and wounded. The rain began to fall on the cruel scene and beat out the torches of brave fellows hunting their wounded companions in the dark. The howling of the storm, the cry of the wounded and groans of the dying, the glare of the torch upon the faces of the dead or into the shining eyes of the speechless wounded, looking up in hope of relief, the ground slippery with a mixture of mud and blood, all in the dark, hopeless, starless night; surely it was a gruesome picture of war in its most horrid shape.

At all Headquarters it was a most uncomfortable night. Pickets reported that the enemy was strengthening his position, and general officers expressed freely their opinion that he would advance against us in the morning. General Jackson received these reports and opinions with incredulity and apparent impatience, and directing that his skirmish line should be advanced at daylight said curtly, "The enemy will be gone in the morning!" He gave hope to those who struggled to believe but still doubted. In the morning the enemy was gone.

The next day was one of incessant rain, and the army remained in bivouac. The dead of both armies were buried and the wounded cared for as well as circumstances would permit. During the day General Lee held a council of war, at which were Generals Longstreet, Jackson, and Jeb Stuart. President Davis was also present and took part in the conference. After it had ended, the doors were thrown open and the staff mingled with the generals in social conversation. I was then introduced to Mr. Davis, a dignified, gracious, and impressive gentleman. Very soon, Major Charles Marshall of General Lee's staff came in with a silver flask, which had been presented to him by General George A. McCall, United States Army, captured two days before, and which contained some excellent old whiskey. Drawing off the cap he handed it to the President, who touched it very lightly. General Lee declined, saying he would not deprive some younger officer of a drink which he would better appreciate. General Longstreet took a good, soldierly swig of it. General Jackson declined and also General Stuart, who said, laughingly, he knew General McCall would not give away good whiskey unless he had drugged it and wanted to poison somebody. General Stuart's suggestion, however, did not deter the staff from trying it, and the flask was emptied in short order.

During the 3rd General Jackson moved from the vicinity of Malvern Hill toward Harrison's Landing, following General Stuart, but owing to the condition of the roads did not get very far. When we went into camp at sunset, the General was not in very good humor and ordered that we move at "early dawn" and that we should have breakfast early enough for Headquarters to be in the saddle by that time. We, of the staff, never could convince the General that if the army did move at daylight there was no reason why he should always be at the head of the column at that hour. He was incorrigible in that and in other matters involving ease and comfort. Crutchfield, fond of luxury and ease, always stoutly maintained that there ought to be an international law prohibiting marching or fighting before 8 A.M. or after sundown, before April 1st or after December 1st, but this theory did not prevent him from being one of the best and promptest officers in the service until he was killed.

It is a singular thing that General Jackson, while living, never had a staff member killed or wounded until Chancellorsville, where he fell, and as he never spared them nor himself it was often remarked upon. After the protection of his presence and his prayers had been withdrawn, death played havoc with them. J. K. Boswell fell with him at Chancellorsville, and S. Crutchfield was wounded and disabled for a year. General E. F. Paxton was killed the next day. Colonel W. S. H. Baylor and Colonel Edward Willis were killed after they left his staff, and also J. R. Jones. A. H. Jackson, Colonel A. S. Pendleton, Marshall and Crutchfield followed them in turn. Captain J. G. Morrison, the General's brother-in-law, was wounded and maimed, and I carried a Federal bullet in my body from Gettysburg until after the war.

At the very earliest dawn on the 4th of July, "Jim" [2] came into the room where some of us were sleeping and announced that breakfast was ready and the General enquiring for us. I was up and dressed as if to catch a comet and met the General just coming from his room. He asked if the guides he had ordered sent to General Ewell at daylight were gone and was told they were still asleep. He soon had them galloping on the way, breakfastless. The General's temper was beginning to effervesce. He asked for the staff, and they were not. I was about to propose that we breakfast without waiting when the General turned on Jim quickly and ordered him to put everything into the wagon at once and have it on the road in ten minutes, remarking, "If my staff will not get up, they must go without their breakfast; let's ride!" Why, pray, should the General and I go without breakfast? What the wisdom of this vicarious suffering for the sins of sleepy staff officers? I saw none in it then. I see none in it now. Jim, however, obeyed the General with grotesque gravity and alacrity; he had had his breakfast.

Just as the grass had received the last drop of hot coffee and the chest the last smoking biscuit, Major Dabney, disordered in general appearance, came upon the scene and tried to save something for himself from the wreck, but Jim skillfully thwarted his efforts and pitched things about in all directions.[3] If Captain Pendleton must go without breakfast, Jim was not disposed to tarry for anyone else. By the time the General and myself were mounted, the wagon was in the road, and as I looked I saw the staff appear one after another, shaking their fists at the departing breakfast and showering upon it all kinds of inverted blessings. As we went on our way silently, the General praying and I fasting, I wondered if Mark Tapley [4] would have found such a joke any more jolly than I did. We found General Ewell in bed and General Jackson visited upon him some of his bad humor, and then directed me to go at once and put General Ewell's division in motion. I departed willingly and found Colonel J. A. Walker, commanding the First Brigade, at breakfast. I told him "Old Jack" was on the rampage that morning and that he must move as soon as he gave me some breakfast. I related my discomfiture and got an excellent meal while his brigade was moving out. I immediately began to look upon the whole thing as an excellent joke and, soon after, I joined the General with his grim and funereal staff and entertained them pleasantly in describing Walker's breakfast. I must have done it stupidly, however, for they apparently didn't see the humor of it. The General and staff broke their fast at General Stuart's about one o'clock and I joined them in it.

We remained in the vicinity of Harrison's Landing for several days. General Lee made no serious demonstration against the enemy. It was rumored in camp that General Jackson wished to attack, but the fact is he concurred in the conclusion General Lee had come to—that it was impracticable. The soldiers heard the rumor, and they were not elated at the prospect of an attack. Experience is not lost upon the rank and file, and they generally got a correct idea of the situation; they even anticipated movements that were afterwards ordered by their general. On the battlefield, too, they took in the perils of a situation, and that is doubtless the reason why veteran troops gave away and became panicstricken at times, while fresh volunteers who did not see the danger remained on the field and kept fighting. Old troops often know when they are whipped; new ones often do not and are ignorant of the dangers which lurk in flank and rear. More than once have battles, nearly lost by veterans, been restored by the intrepid obstinacy of new soldiers.

While at Harrison's Landing General Jackson suggested both to General Lee and the administration at Richmond that 40,000 troops should be sent to the Shenandoah Valley to clear it of the enemy, move toward Maryland and threaten Washington, and that this force should move as lightly and rapidly as possible. He wished General Lee to take command of the expedition, but said he was willing to serve in it under Longstreet or Ewell or one of the Hills, if the Government preferred any one of them to himself. At the time Richmond declined to adopt the suggestion, and until finding out more certainly what McClellan intended to do it would have been extremely hazardous to weaken the forces defending the Confederate Capital. Whether the movement could have accomplished as much or more than the one adopted very little later against Pope—when Jackson was again put in front— may be a matter of military speculation.

One morning during these days I was riding with the General along his advanced line, as was his custom daily, when he expressed a desire to get some blackberries which were abundant in a neighboring field along the side of a hill. Our pickets were along the crest of the hill, partially protected by a rail fence, and on this particular morning there was a deal of spiteful firing between them and those of the enemy. Being a place of danger, it was there, of course, that the blackberries were most abundant and the very place of all others that the General preferred to pick them. I think I mentioned classically that it was at just such a place that Proserpine, picking flowers or berries of some kind, was "mined." He did not seem to take in the veiled suggestion but went on picking and eating with great calmness, although, like Falstaff's reasons, the bullets seemed to be "as plentiful as blackberries." After a little he paused and turning to me, with a large, shining berry poised between his thumb and finger, enquired maladroitly in what part of the body I would prefer being shot. I replied that primarily I'd prefer being hit in the clothes but if it was made a question of body, I'd prefer any place to my face or joints, handing him at the same time as if indifferent to the situation a couple of luscious berries. He said he had the old-fashioned horror of being shot in the back and so great was his prejudice on the subject that he had often found himself turning his face in the direction from which the bullets came. Just then our horses put a stop to this foolishness. They had become restless and, a bullet striking a sapling near their heads, they began to snort. With a vague remark about getting his horse killed the General left his feast. We mounted and rode off, nor did I "cast one longing, lingering look behind."

The General continued his ride along the lines. It was found that the picket lines of General Robert Toombs' brigade were not connected on the right or left but were swinging in the air, contrary to Jackson's explicit orders and to his surprise. It could be said of Jackson what Abbott [5] says of Napoleon: "It was his principle to give his directions not merely so that they might be understood, but so that by no possibility could they be misunderstood." The General rode at once to General Toombs' Headquarters and found this gallant but not very military officer lying under the shade of a small fly-tent at full length—for it was a very warm day. He routed him out and found that he had entrusted his orders to a staff officer who in turn had left it to the detailed officer. General Toombs thought it must be all right, while General Jackson was of the decided opinion it was all wrong. He directed General Toombs with some sharpness to go at once, in person, and make the necessary connection and then turned and rode away. I recalled the fact that a few years before I had seen Professor Jackson at Lexington, Virginia, pursuing the "noiseless tenor of his way," instructing a class of mischievous cadets in natural philosophy and almost unknown beyond the limits of that town, and that a few days after I had seen Robert Toombs of Georgia in the Senate at Washington holding the attention of that chamber while he made a great speech in favor of the acquisition of Cuba. *"Tempora mutantur et nos mutamur in illis."*

The 6th of July was a very warm day. The General had returned from his morning ride to the front and was trying to make himself comfortable. Headquarters were in bivouac. He seated himself at the foot of a large tree to take a nap—he could always go to sleep when he had nothing else to do. After a very short rest he aroused himself and asked me if I had a novel. I did not have one, nor did any of the staff, as all books had been left in the vicinity of Mechanicsville with the wagons. He said he had not read a novel for a long time before the war. Hugh McGuire, a clerk at Headquarters, afterwards Captain in T. L. Rosser's Cavalry Brigade, handed me a yellow-back novel of the sensational type, saying he had picked it up on the battlefield. It looked like literary trash, and it was —sensational and full of wood cuts. I handed it to the General, who looked at it with a smile, seated himself again at the foot of the tree, and began to read it. He gave his whole attention to it, as if it was a duty not to give it up, and waded on through it. Now and then his features would relax and smile, but did not take his eyes from the book. He did not speak a word but kept on until he had finished it; fortunately, it was a small paper volume of large print. He then returned it with thanks, saying it had been a long time since he had read a novel and it would be a long time until he read another. This was the only book not strictly military or religious that I ever saw him attempt to read in the army.

On the 8th of July the Army of Northern Virginia began to move back to the vicinity of Richmond. When Jackson's command started he and his staff remained behind until some time after the rest of the army had gone. It was after dark when he started and about midnight when he reached his Headquarters. He was riding along at ten or eleven o'clock with his drowsy staff, nodding on "Little Sorrel," as was his custom, and trusting to that intelligent beast not to give him a fall. More than once did we see his head nod and drop on his breast and his body sway a little to one side or the other, expecting to see him get a tumble; but he never got it. On this occasion our sleepy cavalcade at different times passed small squads of soldiers in fence corners before blazing fires, roasting green corn and eating it. Passing one of these, our staggering leader was observed by one of those thirsty stragglers, who was evidently delighted at the sight of a drunken cavalryman. Perhaps encouraged with the hope of a drink ahead, the ragged Reb jumped up from his fire and, brandishing a roasting-ear in his hand, sprang into the road and to the head of the General's horse, with, "Hello! I say, old fellow, where the devil did you get your licker?"

The General suddenly woke up and said, "Dr. McGuire, did you speak to me? Captain Pendleton, did you? Somebody did," and reined up his horse.

The soldier got a look at him and took in the situation; he saw whom he had thus spoken to. "Good God! it's Old Jack!" he cried, and with several bounds and a flying leap he had cleared the road, was over the fence, and disappeared in the dark.

As soon as the staff could recover from their laughter, McGuire explained the situation to the General, who was much amused. He immediately rode up to the fence, dismounted, and took half an hour's nap. Then he roused himself, said he felt better, and we went on to Headquarters.

AT RICHMOND

GENERAL JACKSON's command arrived in the vicinity of Richmond on the 10th of July and encamped on the road from Richmond to Mechanicsville, about two and a half miles from the former. Headquarter tents were pitched in a yard in front of a gentleman's house, the General having declined to go into the occupied residence. His stay near the Confederate Capital was brief and quiet. During these five or six days he confined himself very closely to his tent, attending to his official duties and endeavoring to get his corps in its normal state of organization and efficiency after the demoralizing effect of its long campaign from Kernstown to Harrison's Landing.

He might have been lionized in Richmond as no one else had ever been, but that did not accord with his tastes, and the simplicity of his character made him shrink from it. His worth had a worthy rival in his modesty. He received many visitors from Richmond of all ranks and condition and treated them cordially by giving them as much time as he could, but he kept away from the city. He visited Richmond only twice, once to attend church and once after dark on official business. He was at that time the favorite of the army and the people, but his style and manners were unchanged and his Headquarters was maintained in all its Valley simplicity.

While encamped there an appreciative lady from lower Virginia sent him a straw hat—the work of her own hands. It was a grateful offering, gratefully received, but I am sure this kind woman would have joined in the laughter had she

seen the comical figure the General presented when he tried
it on. Its effect was like malicious magic, and under its trans-
formation our General, never an Apollo, became a caricature.
He looked into a mirror to see himself; one glance was enough
and he did not "stand and gaze." He handed it to Jim to put
away carefully, and Jim took it with mock gravity and carried it off daintily. The General never asked for it again and
it disappeared. A staff with any respect for its own respecta-
bility could never have submitted to such headgear on its
chief.

On one of these days the General received the only reprimand given him during the war. Accompanied by a courier,
he started to visit the several division encampments, and on
his way he discovered a short path across a plowed field and
took it. But a lion met him in the path. In the middle of the
field he encountered the proprietor, who greeted him with,
"What the devil are you riding across my field for?" Without
waiting for a reply, he brandished his cane in the air and with
an embellishment of miscellaneous oaths he broke into a rustic
tirade. The General had attempted in vain to explain, to the
amusement of the courier at what he afterwards called "that
stunnin' charge on Old Jack!" This increased the voluble
indignation of the irate farmer. When he asked the General
what command he belonged to, he told him and began to
apologize. The doughty countryman, realizing whom he had
been berating, was startled but not discomfited. He apologized for his language but told the General frankly that he
deserved a scolding for setting his troops such a bad example
which they would only too readily follow, and raising his hat
went on his way. The next day the General pointed out the
field on passing and said with a smile, "There I received the
severest lecture I ever had and it will make me more careful
hereafter."

While at Richmond Major R. L. Dabney, Adjutant General, resigned and went home. He had been in the army and
on the staff about three months. Again and until August,
when Major E. F. Paxton was appointed, Captain Pendleton
became Chief of Staff.

General Jackson visited Richmond on Sunday and asked McGuire, Pendleton, and myself to go to church with him. Almost unknown in Richmond, and unobserved because of his simplicity, the hero of the Shenandoah rode quietly through the streets of the Capital to the sanctuary. Many persons whose great desire was to get a glimpse of him looked at him as he quietly passed and knew him not. He went straight to the Presbyterian Church (the Reverend Dr. Moses D. Hoge),[1] or rather to the corner nearest it. Putting the horses in charge of an orderly, we entered the church and were conducted to a side pew. The services had begun and no one seemed to notice the presence of the General until they were ended. As the benediction was pronounced, glances, whisperings soon becoming audible, a gentle excitement, and rising confusion indicated that he had been discovered. The people declined the invitation of open doors and pushed forward toward the pew, from which the General was trying to make his escape. For awhile he was cut off and surrounded and could not cut his way out; there was no relief in sight. The staff were run over and squeezed into a corner and otherwise disregarded, and were very little stars on the solar splendor of our Chief. But in the end we came to his rescue and got him out. Pretty girls then tried to be polite to us but it was too late; we would have none of it! But as we reached the open and drew a breath of relief, a lady, evidently an old friend, came up, seized the General by the arm, and hurried him down the street. He made no outcry nor sign of resistance, and when we reached the horses we halted and waited for him. He returned in about fifteen minutes, apologized for keeping us waiting, and we rode slowly back to camp.

The next time General Jackson entered Richmond it was in solemn state to a mourning people, amid the tolling of bells.

> *Sad and slow*
> *As fits an universal woe,*
> *Did the long, long procession go,*

when amid the lamentation of a nation and its armies he was "to glorious burial slowly borne."

XIII

SLAUGHTER MOUNTAIN

U<small>NDER</small> orders from General Lee, General Jackson left his camp at Richmond for Gordonsville about the 14th of July. General John Pope, Commander of the Army of Virginia, was gathering his forces for an advance from the vicinity of Washington. He had settled himself "in the saddle" and from that contracted Headquarters had fulminated his celebrated proclamation in the shape of a general order, for which he was afterwards ridiculed by the pen and punished by the sword. Believing that Jackson was not likely to be scared by so much military fustian, General Lee sent him to look after this advancing Hannibal. The General went on in advance and we were soon far ahead of troops and wagon trains on the road to Ashland.

About sundown of the first day, we were driven temporarily into a blacksmith shop for shelter from a rain storm, and from there sent out to seek shelter for the night. We found it in a most hospitable house where a plentiful supper, good rooms, and pleasant beds were made doubly enjoyable by the easy and sincere hospitality of host and hostess. The next morning we were in Ashland early and had sundry invitations to breakfast. The General seemed in excellent humor and unusually talkative. While waiting for breakfast he sat in the parlor, amused himself and others as well by his attempts to be playful with a prattling little girl who was running about the room, and then again listened with most respectful attention to a young lady who was at the piano, giving us such songs

and instrumental music as she thought to our taste. Now the
General had the least possible knowledge of music and, as was
said of him, he had so little of it in his soul, that he was necessarily "fit for treason, strategy and spoils." Still it was a
matter of amazement to his staff, when he said with much
politeness to the young lady, "Miss ————, won't you play
a piece of music they call 'Dixie'? I heard it a few days ago
and it was, I thought, very beautiful."

The young lady was nonplussed and answered, "Why, General, I just sang it a few minutes ago—it is about our oldest
war song."

"Ah, indeed, I didn't know it."

He had heard it a thousand times. Perhaps he thought he
would startle the young lady with his knowledge of music: if
so, he succeeded.

At noon, July the 18th, we reached Louisa Court House,
and on the 19th our destination at Gordonsville. A day or
two afterward a young gentleman, with smooth face, clear-
cut, handsome features, bright steady eye, slender body, fairly
tall and well carried, firm mouth and quiet manner, appeared
at Headquarters and presented himself to General Jackson,
with this note from General Jeb Stuart, dated July 19:

"The bearer, John S. Mosby, late first Lieutenant, 1st Virginia Cavalry, is en route, to scout beyond the enemy's lines
toward Manassas and Fairfax. He is bold, daring, intelligent and discreet. The information he may obtain and trans-
mit to you may be relied upon and I have no doubt he will
soon give additional proofs of his value. Did you receive the
volume of "Napoleon and his Maxims," I sent you through
General Winder's orderly?"

Thus enters upon the scene Colonel Mosby, the Partisan
Leader, whose record from that day until the end of the war
forms an interesting chapter in the history of the Army of
Northern Virginia.

About this time Jackson's command occupied three different camps extending from Green Spring to Orange Court
House. His attention and that of his staff was given to the

reorganization of his corps and getting it in shape for active operations. Our Headquarters was kept well supplied by our neighbors. The General's simplicity of diet did not obtain through all his Headquarters and it was well it did not: for otherwise the many delicacies that were sent to camp for his special eating would have been wasted, but they were not. The General governed his appetite with severity. He liked a great many things he did not eat, and ate some things he did not like. He was not a hearty eater, although at times he had a good appetite. Whatever might be the variety before him he generally selected one or two things only for his meal and ate of them abundantly. He seemed to know what agreed with him, and often puzzled others by his selections. I knew him to make a very hearty dinner of raspberries, milk and bread. He was, therefore, at times a great disappointment to hospitable housewives, who, after skillfully providing various handiworks of choice food for his enjoyment, looked on regretfully when he selected one or two simple things and declined all the rest. He did not accept invitations to dinner, when he could politely avoid it, and the majority of those he went to he was led into by members of his staff, who did not believe that good food affected their official usefulness. They felt compelled at times to accept invitations, and they induced him to go in order not to seem unappreciative of the courtesy. Pendleton was much given to these admirable devices and the General never liked to disoblige him, and McGuire was not much more innocent. In fact the staff always knew a good thing when they saw it in the shape of a dinner and recognized it afar off.

I once asked the General why he was so simple in his diet; he replied that he had been a dyspeptic for nearly twenty years. He said it had caused him great suffering in body and mind and that he had never forgotten its horrors. On another occasion when I expressed my surprise that a man in Richmond had committed suicide, driven to it by dyspepsia, he said he could understand that and thought if a man could be driven to suicide from any cause, it might be from dyspepsia.

General Jackson was soon reinforced by the arrival of A. P.

Hill's division and he seemed to become restless for the war path. Having received information that a part of General Pope's army was encamped at Culpeper Court House, Jackson determined to try to strike it before it could be reinforced. He believed that the possession of that point would enable him to prevent a concentration of Pope's somewhat scattered forces. The fact is, he was getting impatient to try conclusions with General Pope. When that General's celebrated order from his "Headquarters in the saddle" was read by Pendleton to Jackson, he did not utter the questionable joke about it that is sometimes attributed to him, that he "could whip any man who didn't know his Headquarters from his hindquarters," but he gave a quiet smile and a frown, as if to say, "there is grim work ahead."

General Jackson moved out from camp on the 7th of August and on the 8th crossed the Rapidan at Barnett's Ford, driving back some cavalry but making a discouragingly slow day's march. After a good day's march on the 9th, with his army wearied and somewhat scattered, battle was rather suddenly joined in the afternoon near Cedar Run and Slaughter Mountain about eight miles from Culpeper, and soon became a hot fight.

From the beginning it was a well-contested field. The Federal troops under the command of General N. P. Banks fought with great courage and obstinacy. General Pope had telegraphed to Washington the rumor of Jackson's advance, saying he was "going to the front to see." But on that day he neither came, saw, nor conquered. The enemy attacked with such vigor that at first they had a decided success and for a time the result was in doubt. General Jackson had not waited for A. P. Hill, but having sent out his orders, he trusted to their prompt compliance by his subordinates and struck at once with what troops he had at hand. It was said of him, there, that he marched into the battle by the flank and commenced the fight with the first file of fours. He certainly took a very great risk, trusting to gain an advantage by promptness and impetuosity. As it was, our line was broken several times before the arrival of A. P. Hill.

On one of these occasions the attention of the General was called to a young officer who was endeavoring to rally some of the demoralized troops and displaying conspicuous gallantry. Not a week before this young aide-de-camp, Lieutenant J. G. Morrison, a brother of Mrs. Jackson, had arrived at Headquarters fresh from the Virginia Military Institute at Lexington and this was his first experience on the battlefield. His bearing was fearless and chivalric. He was riding one of the General's horses, which, shot in the jaw, was rearing and plunging, sprinkling both his rider and himself with blood. It was suggested to the General that he had better call that youth in or his career would be a short one, but he replied that his example would not be lost upon the troops and he would learn more discretion after a battle or two. He would not permit him to be recalled. Morrison escaped that day but after the General's death he was badly wounded twice and came out of the army with the loss of a foot.

On the arrival of A. P. Hill's division, our line was restored and ready for a general advance. On the left was a North Carolina brigade that had done the state much service, commanded by an able and gallant officer who afterwards fell at Sharpsburg. General L. O'B. Branch, when in Congress, was an orator of great force, and on this occasion, while waiting orders, he took occasion to give his troops the benefit of it, by making them a speech. It was a dangerous experiment, for I do not believe any general ever made a speech to his troops on the eve of battle who did not do more harm than good. But no harm was done on this occasion for General Jackson hearing of this delay and the cause of it, started with an unfathomable smile and galloped to the spot. As he reached the right of the brigade he took off his hat, rode rapidly along the line looking the men steadily in their faces as he passed along. When he reached their commander, he said curtly, "Push forward, General, push forward!" and then moved to the front. The effect was instantaneous: this was an eloquence the men understood. Forward with quick step and then quicker went the whole line after their illustrious leader and then with an irresistible yell they charged over the field, their wild yell mingling with the rattle of their musketry. Several officers rushed up to Jackson and almost forced him to the rear, but the charging line swept past him with a shout and kept on.

Off on the right at the same time was heard the welcome sound of Ewell's cannon and rifles, moving with victory to the front. The field was then soon won, and that was the beginning of Pope's eclipse. The troops of Jackson bivouacked for the night on the field of battle. The loss on both sides was unusually heavy for the length of the contest and the numbers engaged. In the death of General Charles S. Winder, of the Stonewall Brigade, the army was deprived of one of its most promising officers. He had been ill for several days, and that morning, at the suggestion of Dr. McGuire, our Medical Director, General Jackson sent me to say to General Winder that he had better turn over his command to the next officer in rank and make himself comfortable at the rear until he was in better condition. General Winder, receiving General Jackson's message rather as a suggestion than an order, refused to adopt it and said he would not leave his brigade on the eve of a battle. He rode forward with me and we met the General coming toward the rear. He greeted Winder cordially and repeated what he had instructed me to tell him, but Winder was inflexible. Seeing this, General Jackson remarked, "Well, General, I will stick to my order as to the brigade; if you will not go to the rear, you will take command of the Division." They shook hands, Jackson going to the front, Winder back to his division. I do not think they had a chance to speak to each other again, for Winder fell early in the action.

General Winder was handsome and attractive in person, graceful on horseback or off, polished in address, dignified and courteous in manner, with a will as inflexible as that of Jackson himself. At first their relations were not very cordial and each certainly underrated the other; in many things, they were too much alike to fit exactly. But General Jackson said of him at the last, when he had found of what stuff Winder was made—"richly endowed with those qualities of mind and

person which fit an officer for command and which attract the
admiration and excite the enthusiasm of troops, he was rapidly rising to the front rank of his profession." He was the
most brilliant of the many valuable officers Maryland gave
to the Confederacy, and I have no doubt that had he lived he
would have been the commander of a corps before the war
ended. But he was one of the victims to the position of Commander of the Stonewall Brigade. After General Jackson's
promotion, no general of that brigade ever lived long enough
to secure further promotion: none ever escaped wounds or
death long enough to be made a Major General.

It was in this battle that Major Snowden Andrews of the
artillery, also from Maryland, received one of those fearful
wounds from which recovery is thought to be an impossibility.
Struck by a piece of shell he was disemboweled and his ab-
dominal viscera rolled in the dust where he fell: he was left
without hope. Dr. McGuire, passing and seeing him, stopped
to say he was grieved to see he could not be any help to him.

"Yes, that's what you fellows all say," said Andrews.

Stung a little by this, McGuire, who greatly liked him,
sprang to the ground to do what he could. He washed off and
restored his viscera to their proper place, stimulated him,
sewed him up, gave him all the benefit of his skill and sent
him to a hospital. Meeting McGuire a few minutes afterwards
I said, "McGuire, is Snowden Andrews mortally wounded?"

"Well—if the good Lord will let the rest of the world take
care of itself for a time and devote his attention exclusively to
Andrews, he may be able to pull him through, but no one else
can!"

Snowden Andrews still lives.[1] Just a year afterwards I
helped to take him from the field, when he was desperately
wounded, before daylight, in our fight with Milroy, near Jordan Springs; he got through the war and may be often seen
on the streets in Baltimore, with just as positive opinions on
all subjects as ever.

Just before the attack of Branch that I have spoken of
General Jackson sent me to General Ewell with the order for

him to move forward and attack. After remaining a little while to explain to him the situation on our left, where our people were hotly engaged and needed his co-operation, I started to return over the field as I had come. When I had gone half way, I found myself in a dilemma. The enemy's skirmishers cut off my further progress. Not knowing the country, I concluded to return to Ewell, but some of the enemy's pickets or skirmishers had cut off my retreat. A line of them was also coming on from the front. Toward the rear I saw no Confederates at all, only a very repulsive fence, which seemed grown up with bushes and impassable for my horse. Scattering shots falling and whizzing about me warned me to be up and doing. Having no choice, I made a rush for the fence; my horse urged with the spur and apparently frantic with fright, did not hesitate, but making a desperate leap he landed on the other side and threw a shower of ploughed dirt into the air. After the battle, when we were riding to the rear, and the staff were guying me not a little about the "big jump" I had told them of, to the General's quiet amusement, I persuaded them to go a little out of the way to see the evidences of it. The General consented and when he had looked at the place, he turned in the saddle and said. "Gentlemen, the evidence is conclusive—that—Douglas was very badly scared!" Then, with what was almost a chuckle, he ambled off to Headquarters.

On the next day, the 10th, satisfied that the enemy had been heavily reinforced, Jackson made no demonstration, but bivouacked on the field ready to receive any attack that might be made. It was a miserable day and one of a deal of unpleasant work for me, going over the battlefield and doing such duty as falls upon an Assistant Inspector General on such occasions. I was, for some reason, impressed more deeply with the horrors of a battlefield, on a day of rain, after a bloody fight, than ever before or after, not excepting Malvern Hill. And yet in all the gloom and misery there would be an occasional display of unaccountable levity. In a barn were lying two badly wounded soldiers, one in blue, the other in grey.

"Johnny, where are you shot?" asked the one in blue.

"Lost my leg—where are you?"

"Ah, you're in a devil of a fix for dancing. I've only lost my arm," said the blue one.

"I'm sorry for you, Yank. You'll never be able to put your arms around your sweetheart again." And then after a moment he asked, "What did you come down here for anyway, fighting us?"

"For the old flag," was the proud response.

"Well, take your darned old flag and go home with it. We don't want it," was "Johnny's" last shot.

On the same day, those two brilliant cavalry commanders of opposing forces, General Jeb Stuart and General George D. Bayard met on the field and had a chat about many pleasant times they had together before the war.

On the night of the 11th General Jackson withdrew and went back to his encampment in the vicinity of Orange Court House.

XIV

SECOND MANASSAS

I N A few days General Longstreet arrived at Gordonsville
with a portion of his corps. General Jackson immediately
reported to him as senior in rank and tendered him the command. This General Longstreet declined because General Lee
would soon be there and General Jackson knew the situation
better than he did. The relations between Longstreet and
Jackson were always very cordial during the life of the latter.
It was only after the death of both Lee and Jackson that
Longstreet seemed to change his opinion of the ability of both
the others and to recognize their inferiority to himself. It is
likely he is too late to affect the verdict of history on this matter.

In a few more days General Lee arrived. General Jackson
went to the train to meet him, but did not mention it on his
return to Headquarters. On the contrary, he took the young
aide-de-camp who went with him to task for mentioning General Lee's arrival at dinner, saying that it was not necessary
for couriers and servants and soldiers to know of it, and staff
officers should make it a point to keep to themselves all special
information they might obtain on such matters.

While we were in camp, the staff were much amused when
one of them overheard Brigadier General Isaac R. Trimble,
as gallant a man as ever drew a sword, say to General Jackson one day, laughingly, "General, before this war is over I
intend to be a Major General or a corpse." The General said
nothing, but did not forget it. Within a fortnight, having oc-

casion to send a brigade at night on a hazardous expedition, he selected that general's. He performed the duty assigned him most successfully; as he was not made a corpse, General Jackson had him at once made a Major General.

The march against Pope began on the 18th of August. The first obstacle we met was a most unmilitary one, although it might have scented the battle from afar. The leading regiment was turned aside from the big road into a field by a pole-cat, and the troops that followed, long after they knew the cause for it, followed the same course. Needless to add that the soldiers afterwards called that little beast, "one of Pope's scouts."

Unfortunately General Lee's army did not cross the Rapidan until the 20th. If it had been ready to move with Jackson on the 18th the issue would have been made with Pope ten days earlier than it was: whether results would have been better it is of course difficult to say. Leaving Culpeper Court House on our left, the head of the army passed Brandy Station and came to the Rappahannock River at Beverly's Ford. The enemy being well posted on the opposite bank, some unimportant artillery skirmishing took place, and our army moved off to the left up the stream, meeting the enemy at several points, until Jackson's corps reached a point opposite Warrenton Springs. It seemed then that the enemy were recovering somewhat from their confusion and gaining confidence in their ability to dispute our crossing successfully.

The bridge had been burned and torn down, and General Jackson went to work to rebuild it. He set the example in his own person, until he was completely drenched by the falling rain and covered with mud from head to foot; and his example had the desired effect on his troops, who, wading in water up to their waists without murmuring, lifted heavy logs and replaced fallen timbers until the work seemed to progress by magic. The brigades that had been thrown across the river were recalled and if passage at that point had been intended, it was abandoned. The enemy soon made their appearance and lined the opposite hills with cannon; then followed the noisiest artillery duel I ever witnessed. It accomplished little and was not expected to accomplish much. It took two days to exhaust this artillery fusillade.

While Early's brigade was on the north side of the Rappahannock, a Negro servant belonging to one of the officers captured and brought into camp a German soldier. Trusting to find a friend in his dark skin, the German confided to the Negro his fear of being taken prisoner. The servant volunteered to set him right but, with great pride, led him to where his battery was and turned him over to his master. The young and good-looking prisoner, of marked intelligence, was much disgusted at being betrayed by one of a race he was fighting to set free. He was taken to General Jackson and very soon admitted to one of the staff that he was on his way to Warrenton to see a "lady friend," which his blushes translated to mean a sweetheart. He expressed great desire to see General Jackson and when he found he had been standing near him all the while, he uncovered and saluted with a dignified bow, saying that a lady he knew treasured as her most cherished souvenir a bracelet made of the tail of the General's horse.

Attached to the staff as special orderly was a youth of thirteen years, named Charley Randolph. He was from Warrenton and a brother of Captain (when killed, Colonel) Randolph of the Black Horse Cavalry whose company was then on duty with the General at Headquarters. His youthful manliness in deportment, his reliability, modesty, sweetness of disposition, and extraordinary courage soon endeared him to everyone. The first time he was ever under fire he was riding with me, calling himself "assistant aide-de-camp," and although he heard plenty of bullets he seemed to act with absolute *abandon* and gave no sign of fear or timidity. He frequently accompanied the General when he went riding and often carried messages in camp. He soon became well-known to the troops, who looked upon him as something of a mascot. In Maryland, riding on his bay pony by the side of or near the General, he was often supposed to be his son, and his serious little face and manner were attributed to his sire. Always good-humored, he was never hilarious. On one occasion, however, during the artillery duel at Warrenton Springs, a courier became so frightened at the explosion of a shell very near us that he struck spurs into his horse and ran away; this was too much for Charley, who, holding his sides and screaming with laughter, ran up to the General, not able to speak, and pointed out the demoralized courier disappearing over the hill.

Charley so distinguished himself at Sharpsburg by riding among the stragglers with his little pistol and turning them back, that his conduct was conspicuous. On the same field, dismounting to secure a better bridle from a dead horse than the one he had, he was struck by a spent piece of shell and toppled over, but with little injury. General Jackson was so pleased with his conduct that he called General Lee's attention to him and spoke of his gallantry and the good service he had done that day. Charley sat on his pony covered with blushes, which became as scarlet when the Commanding General bowed gravely toward him and expressed his gratification that "my young kinsman" had merited such commendation.

At the close of the campaign of 1862 General Jackson sent him to the Military Institute at Lexington, saying he ought to be at school and not in the army. It was a hard thing for Charley, but he obeyed. I saw him there in April, 1864, a cadet longing for the field. In the following June, when the corps of cadets under Colonel Scott Shipp marched down the Valley to join General Breckinridge and oppose General Franz Sigel, Charley went with them. It was a cruel necessity to send these boys to battle, but in the battle at New Market they did excellent service; but Charley Randolph went down with a serious wound in the head. He was taken back to Lexington and I never saw him afterwards.

Jackson's Headquarters were near Jefferson on the 24th. The Rappahannock could not be crossed at Sulphur Springs and a new move must be made. A council of war was held at the General's Headquarters that afternoon. It was a curious scene. A table was placed almost in the middle of a field, with not even a tree within hearing. General Lee sat at the table on which was spread a map. General Longstreet sat on his right, General Stuart on his left, and General Jackson stood opposite him; these four and no more. A group of staff officers were lounging on the grass of an adjacent knoll. The consultation was a very brief one. As it closed I was called by General Jackson and I heard the only sentence of that consultation that I ever heard reported. It was uttered by the secretive Jackson and it was—"I will be moving within an hour."

I was sent by the General to put his divisions in motion and to concentrate them upon Jefferson, and during that afternoon there was quick cooking of rations and getting the corps in readiness to cross the river.

At the same time Stuart's bugle called the troopers of that incomparable cavalryman to the saddle. Since his raid around the rear of McClellan, he had been as conspicuous among cavalry leaders as Jackson was in the infantry. On this occasion he was to sweep, like the flight of eagles, around the flank of Pope and come down with a rush upon his rear at Catlett's Station. This bold stroke was directed at the very center of the Federal Army on the night of the 22nd while a heavy rain storm was at its height. General Pope's headquarter wagon was captured and plundered with others of a large train. Stuart burned what wagons he could in the storm, and while the Federal army was looking at the flames of this destruction in their midst, he disappeared with his horsemen in the darkness and returned to his own people, with such plunder as he could carry off.

Stuart came galloping up next morning to where Jackson was sitting on a fence and to everybody's amusement unrolled from behind his saddle and displayed a beautiful blue uniform coat, inside of which was a tag with the name of its owner "John Pope, Major General." Our Cavalryman was in one of his jolly humors. He dismounted, and repeating to us what we knew, that a week or two before he was surprised in a house he was visiting by some Federal cavalry, and in his hasty flight left his hat and plume to the enemy, he said he had a proposition to make to General Pope. Taking a piece of paper, he wrote a communication about as follows:

Headquarters, Cavalry, etc.

Major Genl. John Pope
Commanding, etc.

General.

You have my hat and plume. I have your best coat. I have the honor to propose a cartel for a fair exchange of the prisoners.

Very Respectfully

J. E. B. STUART
Maj. Genl. C.S.A.

This note amused General Jackson greatly. He was very fond of Stuart, and Stuart could always amuse him. The communication was sent through the lines; whether it amused the Federal General may depend upon the time it reached him. There are times when humor is not humorous—to the other man.

On the 25th the column of General Jackson moved on after its silent leader and asked no questions. Citizens complained that we were again leaving them to the enemy. The army knew that was not "Stonewall Jackson's way," but that was all they did know; while the General thought it could do no harm if that report did reach the enemy. Turning to the right at Amissville, we moved further up the Rappahannock and crossed that river at a hidden and difficult ford, from which ascended a steep and rocky pass to the broad plain beyond. A regiment could have defended it, but it was not even watched by a cavalry vidette, although the right wing of Pope's army rested at Waterloo Bridge not three miles off.

We marched near and seemed almost to touch the right flank of the Federal army. The column dragged its slow length along, through roads and fields and wood, veiled from the enemy by Stuart's cavalry, until it reached the small town of Salem. It had made a very long and tiresome day's march— one of the hardest it ever made—and here Jackson rested his weary troops for the night.

At early dawn we were off again, the General in the lead. We went through Thoroughfare Gap, which was undefended,

General J. E. B. Stuart

Henry Kyd Douglas in 1862, taken in Winchester
just before his promotion to Captain of Company B

and thence, swinging around the flank, to the rear of the
Federal army at Gainesville. The march had been a rapid one
and the soldiers were weary, faint, and footsore, but they
seemed to feel that the emergency demanded this excessive effort on their part. They were hungry as well as tired, but
this confiding army bore the trial with as little complaint as
could be expected from mortal men. Never in the history of
warfare has an army shown more devotion to duty and the
wishes of one man, than the followers of Jackson exhibited
during these days. The sun went down but Jackson did not
halt.

A little while after dark a regiment of cavalry passed our
plodding infantry, in the direction of Bristoe Station. At the
invitation of the officer in command, Colonel Thomas T. Munford, I joined him, for I was in need of a fresh horse and
another pistol. A charge was made upon the place, the Federal guard of cavalry put to flight with a few prisoners, and I
got a horse and a pair of pistols. Instantly a train of cars,
loaded with stores, came dashing past. The dismounted cavalry poured an ineffective volley into it, but it rushed on its
way and bore the alarm to Manassas Junction. In a few minutes more the advance of the infantry, their weariness forgotten in the excitement, came up at double time, and were more
successful in their attempt to stop two trains which came
steaming into the station about the same time. They had no
stores of any value and were subsequently burned. The prisoners taken were from New York and occupied their leisure in
damning General Pope. During a pause one of them cried
out, "What sort of man is your Stonewall Jackson anyway;
are his soldiers made of gutta-percha, or do they run on
wheels?"

It was after nine o'clock at night when we got entire possession of Bristoe Station; yet, before midnight General Jackson sent General Stuart with some cavalry and General Trimble with his brigade to take possession of Manassas Junction,
the great depot of supplies. The work was quickly and well
done; before daylight Trimble took the works at Manassas
with little loss. It was for this success he was made Major Gen-

eral. The valuable stores captured were far in excess of what
any Confederate ever conceived to be in existence. Famished
soldiers, appeasing the hunger that had tormented them, declared that they would not have believed there were so many
rations in the world, and that as a Commissary, Pope was
even superior to Banks.

On the morning of the 27th, leaving Ewell at Bristoe Station, General Jackson moved with the rest of his command to
Manassas Junction. In the afternoon Ewell was attacked by
General Hooker, whom he repulsed for a while, and then retired and joined Jackson. Having distributed to the troops
such stores as they could carry, for we had no wagon trains,
Jackson, after dark, ordered all the rest, trains, commissary
buildings, etc., to be burned. Then, with the divisions of Ewell,
Hill, and Taliaferro (commanding Jackson's division), he
marched by different routes to the neighborhood of the field
of Bull Run. The appearance of the marching columns was
novel and amusing. Commissary, quartermaster, and sutler
stores, enough for an army and a campaign, were carried
along on the backs of soldiers wearied with excessive marching
the days before. Here one fellow was bending beneath the
weight of a score of boxes of cigars, smoking and joking as he
went, another with as many boxes of canned fruits, another
with coffee enough for a winter's encampment, or perhaps with
a long string of shoes hung around his neck, like beads. It
was a martial masquerade by night.

On the morning of the 28th Jackson put his command in
position near Sudley's Church. He was not seeking battle but
rest; but it was the duty of the enemy to force the fight before
Jackson could get breath or reinforcements. It was not, however, until late in the afternoon that an attack was made on
our people. A tough fight, lasting several hours, followed. The
enemy was repulsed but not before he had punished us severely. We lost a number of men and the loss of valuable officers was unusually heavy. The doughty Ewell, one of the
ablest division commanders the Confederacy had, was disabled
for a year and his efficiency permanently impaired by the loss

of a leg. He was never the same old ironsides again. Taliaferro and other valuable officers were badly wounded.

It is not my purpose to attempt a description of the series of battles known as the Second Battle of Manassas. This work is not serious enough for that.

On the morning of the 29th the position of General Jackson was perilous in the extreme. His corps was strongly posted, fronting the main position of the enemy, with its back towards its anxiously awaited friends. The position was independent but not defiant; not inviting but not avoiding an engagement. General Pope's policy was, of course, to attack at once. The morning saw some sharp fighting, and about noon General Longstreet, having forced his way through Thoroughfare Gap, came up on the right of our field with his command. His arrival was not only unknown to the enemy but unknown to the officers and men of Jackson.

Early in the afternoon Pope arrived and assumed command. He must have been engaged in "studying the lines of retreat" of the enemy. He had ordered his generals to bring Jackson "to a stand": this was done. He had notified Washington the day before that he was arranging to "bag Jackson" on the morrow. This was his intention now: did he do it?

The heaviest fighting was in the afternoon. Time and again the heavy lines of the enemy rolled against us, like roaring waves of the sea, but they were broken and thrown back. Each attack was weaker, each repulse more difficult—the Federals dispirited, the Confederates worn out. It was a fearfully long day. Jackson's staff was unusually small, several being absent, the invaluable Pendleton among them, and upon those who remained the labor was unceasing. On that day I acted in every capacity from Assistant Adjutant General to courier, and our Medical Director was most effective as an aide-de-camp. For the first time in my life I understood what was meant by "Joshua's sun standing still on Gideon," for it would not go down. No one knows how long sixty seconds are, nor how much time can be crowded into an hour, nor what is meant by "leaden wings" unless he has been under the fire of a desperate battle, holding on, as it were by his teeth, hour after hour, minute after minute, waiting for a turning or praying that the great red sun, blazing and motionless overhead, would go down.

Late in the afternoon I had occasion to visit A. P. Hill. The last two attacks had been directed particularly against him and the last of the two barely repulsed. One of his brigades was out of ammunition, and details were out on the field collecting cartridges from the boxes of the dead and wounded— friend and foe. He requested me to ride to General Jackson and explain the situation and say if he was attacked again, he would do the best he could, but could hardly hope for success. Such a message from a fighter like Hill was weighty with apprehension. I quickly found the General and delivered the message. It seemed to deepen the shadow on his face, and the silence of the group about him was oppressive; but he answered promptly and sharply, "Tell him if they attack him again he must beat them." As I started off, he followed. We soon met General Hill on the way to General Jackson and he repeated his fears. The General said calmly, "General, your men have done nobly; if you are attacked again you will beat the enemy back."

A rattle of musketry broke along Hill's front. "Here it comes," he said and galloped off, Jackson calling after him, "I'll expect you to beat them."

The attack was fierce and soon over. The Rebel yell seemed to follow and bury itself among the enemy in the wood, and we knew the result. A staff officer rode up, "General Hill presents his compliments and says the attack of the enemy was repulsed."

"Tell him I knew he would do it," answered Jackson with a smile. On this field, a year before, he had been named "Stonewall"; on this day he was confirming the title. This ended Jackson's fighting for the day.

Longstreet had also been somewhat engaged during the afternoon. It was Hood who entered into the fight and his troops, who, Jackson said at Cold Harbor, were "soldiers indeed," quickly showed that they merited the distinction. The easy success of Hood and the readiness of Longstreet to go in with all his command, indicate clearly what would have happened to General Fitz-John Porter, if he had made the attack he was cashiered for not making. Longstreet would have repulsed him, routed his corps and assuming the offensive would have—as General Lee said—probably made the next day's battle unnecessary.

The army of General Lee was reunited, and during the night the line was reformed and ammunition distributed among the troops. Saturday morning, the 30th, was clear and warm. The stillness seemed unnatural—or was it the calm repose of the thousands dead, the resigned silence of the thousands living. Later an occasional picket shot disturbed the peace, and the marching and countermarching of the enemy were seen and reported. General Lee remained impatiently on the defensive, for he believed in offensive strategy and bold tactics. General Jackson was not more aggressive than General Lee. For some reason General Jackson did not believe the battle would be renewed. Perhaps he believed that if Pope expected to win, he ought to attack early to get the advantage of his victory by daylight. But it is just as likely Pope thought it wiser to attack late, that, if defeated, he might escape in the dark. Results rather sustained Pope. At any rate the morning passed away in inaction.

In the afternoon, about three o'clock, General Jackson, some distance in rear of his line, was sitting on the ground with his back against an old strawstack writing a note to General Lee in words like these: "Notwithstanding the threatening movements of the enemy, I am still of the opinion expressed this morning that he does not intend to attack us. If he does"—and here the note ends. A single gun was fired and General Jackson got up hastily and handing me the unfinished note said, "That's the signal for a general attack." All mounting, we rode rapidly to the front to the position occupied by his old division, under General William E. Starke, against which he expected the chief assault to be made. Before reaching the line, the crash of artillery and musketry told us the battle was joined in earnest.

Just then the General's horse, a little bay captured the

day before, stopped and refused to go forward against his old friends. Spurs could not overcome his loyalty or cowardice. Quickly dismounting, the General said, "Let's trade horses; ride rapidly to General Longstreet and ask him for a division." He gave to someone else a message for General Lee to the same effect. He climbed into my saddle by stirrups one third too long for him, while I mounted his horse by stirrups equally too short for me.

As the General disappeared in the wood, I started in the direction of General Longstreet. The wretched beast, at once, ran off with me and I do not believe the war furnished an instance of an order being carried with such velocity. The sight of it, however, was more ludicrous than heroic. The stirrups were of no use to me and I had been happier on the horse's bare back. But away we went like a shot, over bushes and ditches and fallen trees and dead horses, along the rear of S. D. Lee's and Crutchfield's artillery, amid bursting shells, which made my horse more frantic and my situation on him more precarious. The distance was soon done. I found General Longstreet on the left front of his line, watching the attack and making his dispositions. The attack was entirely against Jackson's wing and principally against Starke's division. To General Jackson's message, Longstreet replied, "Certainly, but before the division can reach him, that attack will be broken by artillery." He hurried off a staff officer for D. R. Jones' division, and just then two batteries came galloping up the hill. He requested me while waiting for Jones' division to direct the placing and firing of one of them.

The position taken by these batteries, being still more on the flank of the enemy than Crutchfield's and S. D. Lee's, was a favorable one. They were soon at work, sending a storm of shell through the thickets into the front and flank of the assaulting column. The diversion was most timely. The enemy had rushed through the destructive fire up to the very bank of the railway, where Starke's division, out of ammunition, were hurling rocks and clubs upon them. This attack of artillery did its work effectively. The assaulting line halted, was thrown into confusion, and then fled. In their place came an-

other line, with the same disastrous result. And then again a
splendid column of attack, compact and determined, came
grandly up to their endeavor. Longstreet's artillery, well in
position, with that of Lee and Crutchfield awaited the angry
onset. When the blue line was within proper range, these
hoarse hounds of war were unleashed and the destruction they
did was fearful. Deep rents were torn in the enemy's ranks,
their colors went down, one after another. The charge was
turned into a retreat and they soon broke over the field in a
wild rout. The avenging shot and shell scattered the fleeing
mass and their flight became a panic. And now Jackson ordered his thin line to advance, and revived by success they
became the pursuers and added their destructive fire to that
of the artillery.

As the enemy's attack was broken, Jones' division arrived
on the hill occupied by Longstreet and moved against the retreating foe. I had joined General Jackson as soon as I saw
Jones' division would not be needed. General Longstreet advanced his whole line to the attack, and a little while after a
staff officer came from him to General Jackson, congratulat-
ing him and offering troops.

"Tell General Longstreet," Jackson said with a smile, "that
I am obliged to him but I don't need them now; if he gets
hard pressed I'll send him reinforcements." Perhaps he knew
where he could get them; I didn't. The pursuit was continued
long after dark, driving the enemy across Bull Run to Centreville, and it was ten o'clock before it was entirely ended for
the night. Colonel Baylor,[1] commanding the Stonewall Brigade, who left the General's staff the day I joined it, was
killed. General Field had been killed the day before and Trimble wounded. The loss of officers and men was very heavy.

While returning from the pursuit, all minds occupied by
the events of the day, its victory and its many victims, one
of the staff, either Paxton or McGuire, remarked, with an outburst, "General, this victory has been won by the determined
valor of our soldiers by plain, hard fighting."

"Don't forget, it has been won by the help of God."

In the same spirit, on the 2nd of September, President Davis in sending to Congress two dispatches of General Lee announcing the results, said, "It will be seen that God has again extended His shield over our patriotic army and has blessed the cause of the Confederacy with a second signal victory, on the field already memorable by the gallant achievement of our troops."

Of different tone was General Pope's dispatch to Major General H. W. Halleck on the night of the 30th. "The enemy is badly whipped and we shall do well enough. Do not be uneasy. We will hold our own here." Pope certainly had the courage of his mendacity.

On our return we came where the dead and wounded were lying thick. The General noticed a disabled soldier trying to climb up the railway embankment, where the fight had been so hot. He rode up to the soldier and asked if he was wounded. "Yes, General, but have we whipped 'em?" Answering him in the affirmative and dismounting as he did so, he approached the soldier and asked him to what regiment he belonged. "I belong to the Fourth Virginia, your old brigade, General. I have been wounded four times but never before as bad as this. I hope I will soon be able to follow you again."

An examination showed that the wound was a deep one in the flesh of the thigh, from which the pale soldier was suffering greatly. The General went to his side, placed a hand upon his burning head and in a low and husky voice said, "You are worthy of the old brigade and I hope with God's blessing, you will soon be well enough to return to it." He then directed several of the staff to carry the man to a more comfortable place and Dr. McGuire to give him what relief he could. He sent a courier for an ambulance to take him to a hospital. The grateful soldier tried to speak but could not; sobs choked him and tears ran from his eyes over his ashen cheeks: words would not come and he submitted to everything in silence. But the General understood.

The next day, Sunday, was one of incessant rain: the heavens weep over every bloody battlefield. The enemy were strongly posted upon the heights of Centreville. The day was spent by our people in burying the dead, caring for the wounded, collecting arms and ammunition. It was noticeable in how much better condition were the Confederate dead, who had been lying on the field for several days, than were those of the Union army. The latter were nearly all discolored, some black, some much decayed, while the Confederates were but little affected by the exposure. It created speculative comment, of course not kindly to our foes, but it was not difficult to guess the real cause. The Federal troops were well cared for, well fed, fat, and in good physical condition; upon them decay and decomposition made quick work. The Confederates had little flesh upon them, no fat, nothing to decay. The difference was so marked that in places the lines of battle could be distinguished by the color of the dead. The horrors of war are innumerable.

General Jackson visited several Federal hospitals during the day, and when his presence was known there was great curiosity to see him; wounded soldiers climbed over each other to get a glimpse of him. The sight was a kind of souvenir they wanted to take home.

During the day General Lee met with a painful accident. He was dismounted and talking to a group of people, standing near a tree. His grey horse, "Traveler," was near him, no one holding him. Something startled the horse and he gave a slight jump. General Lee, thinking he might get away, sprang quickly to catch him, slipped on the wet ground, and fell to the earth heavily upon his hands. Both hands were injured, one badly sprained, the other with several bones broken. The accident was a very painful one and I was occupied part of an hour pouring water gently on them until the keenness of the pain somewhat subsided. He bore it calmly and quietly, regretting what he called his awkwardness. The accident itself was especially unfortunate at that time. He was not able to mount his horse and an ambulance was sent for. He carried one of his hands in a sling for some time and was not able to ride on horseback for about two weeks. I remember noticing that day as I stood by him, pouring the water from canteens on his hands, what beautiful hands and feet he had and what a perfect figure: all parts of the handsomest man I ever saw.

General Lee was determined Pope should not stop at Centreville. In the afternoon Jackson's wing was put in motion, crossed Bull Run near Sudley's Church for a flank movement, and after a march of about fifteen miles to the Little River turnpike, encamped for the night. The next morning, the 1st of September, we moved along the pike, passed Chantilly and went in the direction of Fairfax Court House. In the afternoon we came in collision with the enemy, who made a spirited attack on us at Ox Hill, near the almost destroyed village of Germantown, where a short and severe engagement took place. It was fought in a thunderstorm and was most confusing and embarrassing, for at times it was impossible to tell the thunder from the artillery. A staff officer had a hard time. It was a beastly, comfortless conflict. Dark clouds rode overhead, like squadrons of horse, shook their black manes, and discharged their angry volleys upon quarreling mortals. The lightning interchanged continuous flashes with those of musketry in the gloomy woods; guns and ammunition became wet and useless. Peals of thunder, roar of artillery, rattle of musketry—night came down on the scene, made it more infernal for a while, and then put an end to the diabolical battle.

In that battle General Phil Kearny, the bravest of the brave, and General I. I. Stevens were killed. Kearny rode into our lines in the confusion, was called upon to surrender, defiantly tried to escape, and was shot. Jackson had known Kearny in Mexico. No two men were more unlike in all personal qualifications, yet both had that touch of martial genius which made them akin. General Jackson when he heard of Kearny's death, directed that his body, sword, and all his personal belongings be brought to his Headquarters at Chantilly. The next morning General Kearny's body was sent through the lines to his friends with everything on it that he wore when captured—I think in General Jackson's ambulance. I accompanied the ambulance to the place where we opened communication with the enemy. My impression is that a staff officer of General Lee—perhaps Major W. H. Taylor, his Adjutant General—was present. The ambulance was re-turned later.

The next day General Pope withdrew from Fairfax Court House and retired to the fortifications of Washington. We have seen with what pomp and gasconade General Pope began his campaign against Lee.

Before retiring finally to Washington he wrote from Cen-treville to Washington: "Aug. 31. I should like to know whether you feel secure about Washington should this army be destroyed. I shall fight it as long as a man will stand up to the work."

And the next day he retreated to the fortifications of the Capital and removed his Headquarters from the saddle.

THROUGH MARYLAND

THE series of contests which made up the Second Battle of Manassas being ended and Pope confounded, General Lee turned his face northward. The Confederacy for the first time assumed the offensive. Whether the policy was a good one has led to discussion. The temptation was great and there are many good reasons in support of Lee's determination, although it did not take long to find out that if he expected his decimated legions to be speedily filled up by the sons of Maryland he was doomed to disappointment.

On the 3rd of September, the advance of the army, Jackson's wing, encamped in the vicinity of Dranesville. Explicit instructions were sent to each of the division commanders, fixing the hour for starting in the morning, so that the whole corps might be on the march soon after daylight.

When morning came General A. P. Hill, who was to go in advance, was half an hour late, and delayed the whole command. General Jackson requested me to compare watches with him—he offered me his own—and then directed me to find General Hill, get his time, and if the watches were alike, to instruct him to turn over his command to Brigadier General Branch. I found General Hill's command just moving out. His anger flashed out at the order I gave him; he galloped forward with me and at once protested to General Jackson in very dramatic manner and language. The General stopped him with stern abruptness, placed him under arrest, and ordered him to the rear. In this General Jackson was thoroughly justified. Several times since he left Richmond, at Slaughter Mountain and in crossing the Rapidan, General Hill had exhibited provoking want of promptness in spite of orders and it became necessary for the General to teach him one lesson at least. The personal breach begun that day never healed; although it never seemed to impair the high estimation in which General Jackson held Hill otherwise, as a division commander.

On the death of Jackson, Hill was promoted to the rank of Lieutenant General and assigned to the command of the Third Corps, made up of divisions from the First and Second Corps. He was killed on the 2nd of April, 1865, the day Grant broke the Confederate lines at Petersburg. As a division commander he had few equals. He was quick, bold, skillful, and tenacious when the battle had begun; as at Mechanicsville he did his work dashingly and well. In the Second Corps he gained his chief glory and deserved the reputation he had. It cannot be said he added to it when he commanded a corps. Perhaps, like Ewell, who was probably his only superior as a division Commander, after Jackson too much was expected of him.

On the 4th the army encamped in the vicinity of Leesburg. On the 5th we crossed the Potomac at White's Ford, a few miles below Leesburg, and started forward in the direction of Frederick, Maryland. The passage of the river by the troops marching in fours, well closed up, shouting, laughing, singing, with a brass band in front playing "Maryland, My Maryland," was an inspiriting scene. The Marylanders were especially wild in their enthusiasm: and one of them, Captain (and afterwards Colonel and then after the war Reverend) E. V. "Lige" White, whose home was near there, threw himself from his horse, among a group of mothers and daughters, and kissed such a lot of them in five minutes, that I venture to say the record was never broken—until Hobson [1] appeared.

On that march that day a patriotic citizen presented General Jackson with a horse. She could hardly be called a typical "war horse, that snuffed the battle from afar," but she was a strong-sinewed, powerful, grey mare, more suitable for artillery than the saddle; but as "Little Sorrel" had been, tempo-

rarily, stolen a few days before, he accepted the gift gratefully.

There was a surfeit of enthusiasm all about us—except for
enlisting. That night when we went into camp, the General
sent for a farmer on whose ground we were and said as there
was no wood convenient, his troops would be obliged to take
some rails for cooking rations. "Burn away," said the farmer,
"that's what rails are for when there's no other wood about."

The next morning when ready to start, the General called
for his new horse, and then found out what a Trojan gift she
was. He mounted her and she seemed stupid about starting.
He touched her with a spur, and then with distended nostrils
and flashing eyes she rose on her hind feet into the air and
went backward, horse and rider, to the ground. The General
was stunned, bruised, and injured in the back. He lay upon
the ground for more than half an hour before he was sufficiently recovered to be removed. He never mounted the brute
again, but Morrison and myself took occasion at times to give
her a taste of army life and try both her speed and her wind.
The General was placed in an ambulance in which he rode
during the day, having turned over his command to his
brother-in-law, General D. H. Hill. He enjoined upon his
staff, however, to see that citizens were not unnecessarily interfered with, and no injury to private property was permitted.
Lee and Jackson were both being carried in ambulances.

On the morning of the 6th of September, General Jackson's
command—with the exception of his old division, which went
on through Frederick City and encamped on the Emmittsburg road—went into camp about Monocacy Junction on the
Baltimore and Ohio Railroad, about three miles short of
Frederick. There Generals Lee, Longstreet, Jackson, and for
a time Jeb Stuart established their several Headquarters in
Best's Grove, near one another; none of them went into Frederick that day. As soon as the tents were pitched people—especially ladies—began to flock from town, either to get speech
with or to see the four generals: it was a quartet well worth
seeing. Both General Lee and General Jackson, feeling bad

and with many things to attend to, kept close to their tents and generally declined to see people. General Longstreet was much more sociable, and Stuart was ready to see and talk to every good-looking woman.

My mother, who had driven to Frederick to see me, was, however, received very cordially by General Jackson and equally so by Generals Lee, Longstreet, and Stuart, each with their individual and very different manner. As I had at first requested my mother not to ask me to tell General Lee of her desire to see him, as he was much occupied and was declining to see people, she apologized for asking for him. Thereupon he, with merry gravity, apologized to her for me and was afraid I had fallen off in good manners since I had left her for the army; but he added (and the words were for her remembrance and not for mine), "but, Mrs. Douglas, it is the only time I ever knew your son to fail in the performance of his duty, as General Jackson can testify." General Lee was only making a mother happy.

General Jackson said very little, but that little was of his kind, and he urged my mother to remain and spend the day with me. But she declined and left with her little party, for each of whom that visit was long to be remembered.

Later, in the afternoon, the General was called to General Lee's tent. En route he met an open carriage containing two bright Baltimore girls, who at sight of him sprang from the carriage, rushed up to him, one took his hand, the other threw her arms around him, and talked with the wildest enthusiasm, both at the same time, until he seemed simply miserable. In a minute or two their fireworks were expended, and jumping into their carriage, they were driven away happy and delighted; he stood for a moment cap in hand, bowing, speechless, paralyzed, and then went to General Lee's. When he got back to his tent, safe, he did not venture out again until late in the evening.

Still suffering from his hurt, the General would not ride or go out of camp. He did not go to church Sunday morning, but at night he asked Morrison and myself to go to church with him. He rode in an ambulance, we on horseback. Just

after we started he asked me if I had a pass for the party.
Upon my replying that I did not think he needed a pass to go
through his own army, he referred to an order from General
Lee and directed me to go back and get one from his Adjutant General. And this is the pass we traveled on:

Hd. Qrs. Valley District
Sept. 7. 1862

Guards and Pickets
    Pass Maj. Genl. T. J. Jackson and two staff officers and
attendants to Frederick to church, to return tonight.
By Command of
Major Genl. Jackson
E. F. Paxton
A. A. Genl.

There being no service in the Presbyterian Church, I took
him to hear my old friend Dr. Zacharias of the Reformed
Church. As usual, the General went to sleep at the beginning
of the sermon, and a very sound slumber it was. His cap,
which he held in his hand on his lap, dropped to the floor, and
his head dropped upon his breast, the prayer of the Congregation did not awaken him, and only the voice of the choir and
the deep tones of the organ broke his sleep.[2] The Doctor was
afterwards credited with much loyalty and courage because
he prayed for the President of the United States in the presence of Stonewall Jackson. Well, the General didn't hear it;
but if he had I've no doubt he would have joined in it heartily.
    On the 8th General Lee issued an address "To the people
of Maryland." It was prepared by Colonel Charles Marshall
of his staff, then as now a citizen of Baltimore.[3] It was dignified, in good temper and in keeping with the character of
General Lee. Its tone may be gathered from the following
closing sentences: "No restraint upon your free will is intended. No intimidation will be allowed. This army will respect your choice whatever it may be; and while the Southern
people will rejoice to welcome you to your natural position

among them, they will only welcome you when you come of
your own free will."

On the 9th General Lee issued an order directing General
Jackson to move next morning, cross the Potomac near
Sharpsburg and envelop Harper's Ferry. General McLaws
was to march on Harper's Ferry via Middletown and seize
Maryland Heights, and Walker to cross the Potomac below
Harper's Ferry and occupy Loudoun Heights.

At daylight on Wednesday, the 10th, Jackson was in motion. About sunrise he and his staff rode into Frederick, but
early as it was, there were many people in the streets. He
asked his engineer for a map of Chambersburg and enquired
of the people the distances to sundry places and about various
roads. And then the citizens put their heads together and
reasoned out his purposes; the staff didn't try it, they had
been educated. Reticent as he was, however, when it was necessary to take any member of his staff into his confidence, he
did not hesitate to do so. Now through Maryland, where I
was well acquainted with roads and people, it was my turn
to be entrusted with the knowledge of his purpose. I did not
then know of General Lee's order. After asking me whether
I was familiar with the roads in Washington County and the
fords of the Potomac between Harper's Ferry and Williamsport—we had ridden aside and were alone—he said he was
ordered to take Harper's Ferry and would cross the Potomac
either at Williamsport or Shepherdstown or perhaps between
them, depending upon the movements of the enemy in Martinsburg.

The General was anxious, before leaving Frederick, to see
the Reverend Dr. Ross, the Presbyterian clergyman and a
personal friend, and I took him to his house. The Doctor was
not up yet and the General would not allow me to disturb him
by ringing the door bell, but he wrote a brief note and left
it with a manservant on the pavement to deliver to him. We
then went by the most direct route through Mill Street to the
head of the column. As for Barbara Frietchie, we did not pass
her house. There was such an old woman in Frederick, in
her ninety-sixth year and bedridden. She never saw Stonewall

Jackson and he never saw her. I was with him every minute
while he was in the town, and nothing like the patriotic incident so graphically described by Mr. Whittier in his poem
ever occurred. The venerable poet held on to the fiction with
such tenacity for years after, that he seemed to resent the
truth about it. If he had known that the real sentiments of
the old lady had the flavor of disloyalty and that had she
waved a flag on that occasion, it would not have been the
"Stars and Stripes," his fervid desire to make her immortal
would have cooled off more quickly and he would not have
been so anxious for that poem to live.[4]

The General, his staff, and escort were generally half a
mile in advance of his column on the march that day, and
the officer in command of the escort, who was a mile and more
in front of us, was ordered to permit no one to pass to the
front. We thus approached each town or village unannounced.
In Middletown two very pretty girls with ribbons of red, white
and blue in their hair and small Union flags in their hands,
came out of their house as we passed, ran to the curb-stone,
and laughingly waved their colors defiantly in the face of the
General. He bowed and lifted his cap and with a quiet smile
said to his staff, "We evidently have no friends in this town."
The young girls, abashed, turned away and lowered their
tiny battle-flags. That is about the way he would have treated
Barbara Frietchie!

We crossed South Mountain at Turner's Gap and encamped for the night near Boonsboro. The General dismounted at the house of Mr. John Murdock about a mile from
the village and ordered the Headquarter tents to be erected
in a field across the road. I then (by the way, against his advice) rode with a courier into the village to get some information about the fords of the Potomac and incidentally to
see some friends. But I was interfered with. Lieutenant A. D.
Payne with a small squad of the Black Horse Cavalry—the
escort I spoke of—had gone on through the town in the direction of Hagerstown, and Colonel S. Bassett French of the
staff of Governor Letcher, and at the time with General Jackson as volunteer aide-de-camp, in their wake. Colonel French

had stopped at and gone into the United States Hotel on the corner of Main Street and the road which leads to Sharpsburg. I rode leisurely down the street and when we reached that corner we heard the clatter of unseen cavalry coming up the other street, and in a moment a company of the enemy were facing us and proceeded to make war on us. We retired with rapidity and did not stand upon the order of our going; in fact we went at once. A squad of the enemy escorted us. I tried a couple of Parthian shots at them with my trusty revolvers, and in response they shot a hole through my new hat, which, with the beautiful plume a lady in Frederick had placed there, was rolled in the dust. I wanted to stop and get it, but thought better of it.

At the end of the town as we rode up an incline to the top of a hill, I discovered just on the other side General Jackson, walking slowly toward us, leading his horse, swinging his hat and alone. At the signal of alarm, he mounted and galloped to the rear. Just then T. W. Latimer, of the First Virginia Cavalry, joined us, passing the General, and there was but one thing to do. The enemy was slowing up, as if in hesitation, and we turned upon them and, with a cry to unseen troops, charged them. Suspecting trouble they fled. Payne at the other end of town had heard the firing and rushed to the rescue with his usual vigor. One of the enemy was killed, several wounded and their horses captured as well as themselves. I joined Payne and followed for several miles. When we came back to town Colonel French emerged from the hotel. His supper and whatever else he had ordered had been interrupted by the "blamed Yankees," and a friendly contraband had quickly escorted him to the Stygian darkness of a coal cellar for safekeeping. He gave the colored brother a ten dollar Confederate note in gratitude which he may have yet as a souvenir of the war.

I recovered my hat and plume and with it a handsome cap supposed to be that of the Captain of the Federal Cavalry Company, Captain Schaumberg, who had twenty-one men with him, as afterwards reported. I also got General Jackson's gloves which he had dropped when he mounted so suddenly and rode off. When I reached Headquarters the General, with an I-told-you-so air, congratulated me on my escape and my fast horse; but when I, in response, produced the gloves he had dropped in his flight, he saw the "retort courteous" and with a smile retired to his tent.[5]

The next morning the march was continued. I had gone into Boonsboro to take breakfast with the same military adviser and, of course, to ask her again about the fords of the Potomac. When not doing that I was engaged in buying a new horse—my black horse, "Ashby"—from a patriot of uncertain proclivities, who would not take either greenbacks or Confederate money for the valuable animal, but insisted upon having the price of him in Hagerstown Bank notes or gold. My friend Dr. O. J. Smith, at whose house I breakfasted, furnished me the money that was acceptable by a check on that bank. As the column passed through town, with the General and staff at the head, Miss Rose ———, my military adviser, tall, straight, graceful, eyes flashing enthusiasm, ran to the curbstone, drew one of my pistols from its holster, and presenting it in mimic salute, cried with her silvery voice, "A Maryland girl's welcome to Stonewall Jackson." The General with uncovered head rode by and all the envious staff saluted. General Jackson evidently put a meaning in the situation, for one of his aides came galloping back with an order for me to remain where I was and close up the column as it passed. But as I had previously known that the General wished me at the head of the column for the reasons he had given, I mounted my horse and rode to the front.

Jim, the General's servant, had overtaken me and was riding with me. The faithful fellow has become historical by reason of his association with General Jackson, to whom his devotion was a kind of superstition. He became important and was aware of it and never denied an anecdote told of him, however incredible, if the General was in it. He was a handsome mulatto, in the prime of life, well-made and with excellent manners, but perhaps altogether true only to the General. He was a great admirer of the General's temperance views, although they did not apply to himself, for he was fond of liquor and was, it was said, somewhat addicted to cards and a quiet little game.

It was about this time that Jim announced he could always tell the condition of the military atmosphere by the General's devotions: that he didn't mind his daily prayers, but when he got up in the night to pray, "Then I begin to cook rations and pack up for there will be hell to pay in the morning."

He would politely answer all questions with regard to the General's habits and peculiarities of life, but not so much with strict regard to truth as to make his master a very mysterious personage and to magnify his own value to him. Once, he remarked, he was asked to drink General Jackson's health so frequently, that the "hospitality of the people was too many for Jeems." On that occasion he came charging along the road, galloped into camp with his hat on the back of his head and his face suffused with the red cast of liquor. But he was put out of sight, and the General never heard of it, for the staff always screened him.

When the General died Jim's honest grief was almost inconsolable. He then attached himself to Pendleton, but when he fell also Jim seemed to break down. He grew sad and went home on a short furlough, saying he would come back and join some one of the "old staff," Jackson's own. But he was taken ill and died in Lexington and lies buried in that historic town.

On that afternoon, the 11th, we recrossed the Potomac at Williamsport, the bands playing and the soldiers singing, "Carry me back to Ole Virginny, to the old Virginny shore." While sitting on horseback at the opening in the bluff, superintending the movement of the troops, I was approached by two ladies in black and a gentleman. One of the ladies knew me and wanted to enquire if I could ascertain the fate of her husband, who was supposed to have been killed at Slaughter Mountain in command of a regiment. He was conspicuous for his height and person, but his body had never been found and he was not a prisoner. I felt sorry for her grief and promised to get all the information I could for her. She did not know that I was the most intimate friend of that DeWitt

Clinton Rench, who was stoned and shot to death in that town,
a year and a half before, and that her husband was a spectator
of that murder and might have saved the life of the noble
fellow he knew so well. But I did what I could to get the information she wanted, but nothing has ever come to light as
to his mysterious disappearance. As I have said I was over
the field the day after the battle of Cedar Mountain, saw all
the prisoners, and looked to the burial of the dead, but no such
conspicuous dead officer was ever reported to me.

We advanced on Martinsburg by two roads and General
Jackson went into camp about four miles west of that town.
General Julius White and his troops having withdrawn to
Harper's Ferry during the night, General Jackson entered
Martinsburg the next morning. Here his own people gave
him a reception which reminded him of Winchester. We remember when Napoleon, then the conqueror at Marengo, visited the school at Ecouen [6] there was such a scene of devotion
and homage that he exclaimed, "This is the height of happiness; these are the most delightful moments of my life."
General Jackson was not dramatic, but he could not have
hardened himself, if he would, against the effect of such enthusiasm as he met with.

He went to the Everett House for a few hours and there
the crowds began to gather, both sexes, and of all ages and
social conditions. But, saying that he must communicate with
General Lee, he took refuge in the parlor and had the door
locked and the windows on the street closed. But his security
was of short duration. Soon voices were calling him at the
windows and rattling the shutters; he wrote and gave no
heed to the appealing sounds.

The enthusiasts sought such consolation as was at hand
and gathering about his horse were about to despoil the unsuspecting beast of mane and tail. They were soon stopped
by a sentinel, but not before they had obtained little locks of
hair for bracelets and the like. Little did these innocents know
that after all they were not robbing Jackson's war-horse—for
the "Little Sorrel" had been stolen for a time some days before—but that they were doing homage to a commonplace

horse, that had been lent to him by that gruff soldier and woman-hater, General William E. Jones.

But the horse did not satisfy them. Some boys, urged on by the ladies, managed to open the shutters of one of the windows; then with a rush little maiden noses and cherry lips were pressed against the clouded panes of glass, and little twinkling-stars of eyes tried to pierce the gloom of that forbidden room in search of their hero. They called out "Dear, dear General," and managing to force up the window a little way they threw red and white roses all about him. Soon a smile broke over his face, for there is a point beyond which to resist the pleadings of woman is not a virtue. At any rate his dispatch was finished and, giving it to me with very definite instructions for a courier, he said, "Now admit the ladies."

They came and swarmed about him. They all tried to get his hands at once as if he had as many as Briareus. They all talked at once with the disjointed eloquence of a devotion that scorned all coherent language. Blushing, bowing, almost speechless, he stood in the midst of this remarkable scene, saying, "Thank you, thank you, you're very kind."

They were saying everything and asking everything. One little girl who had pushed her way in, was saying, "Oh, can't Papa come home just till tomorrow, please Sir?" and a boy not much larger, "Ain't I big enough to be a soldier?" There were daughters and mothers and sweethearts of his soldiers, and he was too tender at heart to resist them. And when a rosy-cheeked little girl reached both her chubby hands up to his coat and begged him for a button for a breastpin he cut one off and gave it to her. It was a fatal letdown: in a twinkling half the buttons on his coat were gone, and boys, taking advantage of the pressure, robbed his coat tails of their buttons. Another young lady wanted his autograph in her album— with malice prepense she had it with her—and he wrote it. Of course they all wanted autographs, although this was the only album. On sheets of foolscap paper he wrote that modest "T. J. Jackson" and distributed it among them. He seemed to have given away entirely. But when one woman, more venturous, hinted for a lock of hair—of which he had no superabundant supply—he drew the line and put an end to the interview. He declined innumerable invitations to dinner and a little after noon disappeared, and it was said he went to dine with a plain old man and his wife, in one of the back streets, whose son was a private in the General's old brigade.

But these attentions did not delay the General, for on the afternoon he was off again and bivouacked on the banks of the Opequon. On the 13th the march was continued, and early in the afternoon the army closed in upon Harper's Ferry and encamped in the vicinity of Halltown, two miles from the enemy on Bolivar Heights. Colonel Dixon S. Miles was in command of the Federal troops at Harper's Ferry. General Lafayette McLaws, of our army, was moving against Maryland Heights across the Potomac, and General John G. Walker had taken possession of Loudoun Heights across the Shenandoah River. Harper's Ferry was environed.

Major A. S. Pendleton, Assistant Adjutant General, who had been absent, sick, since before the battles of Second Manasses, reported to the General for duty, and we were all glad to have him back.

On that afternoon General A. P. Hill, who had been under arrest since crossing the Potomac, sent for me, and requested me to say to General Jackson that it was evident a battle was at hand and he did not wish any one else to command his division in an engagement, that he asked to be restored to it until the battle or battles were over, when he would report himself under arrest. He added that, as I had carried the order which took his command from him, he hoped I would interest myself promptly in his restoration to it. This I did gladly and with alacrity. I gave the message as forcibly as I could and ventured to add that no one could command Hill's division as well as he could. The General could not refuse a request to be permitted to fight. He directed me to go to General Hill at once, direct him to take command of his division, and then notify General Branch of this order. Hill was soon in the saddle, and we may look out for his work at Harper's Ferry and Sharpsburg.

General Longstreet had moved on through Boonsboro to

the vicinity of Hagerstown as if to threaten an invasion of
Pennsylvania. But in the morning of the same day—the 13th
—General McClellan had come, by an accident never yet explained, into possession of the marching order of General Lee,
now briefly called "The Lost Order," which directed the movements of all the divisions of the Confederate army. This order
notified General McClellan of the division of Lee's army and
of the intention to capture Harper's Ferry. From that moment the Confederate army was in imminent peril. The plans
of the Federal Commander were quickly and skillfully made:
they threatened the destruction of the Confederate army.
Tardy execution and most culpable slowness or incapacity
somewhere prevented General McClellan from reaping the
results his fortunate find put in his power. He ought to have
driven Lee out of Maryland in pieces. This he did not do.

The 14th was Sunday, and it was spent in opening communication with McLaws and Walker and in placing all the
commands in position for tough work the next day. When all
this was done it was too late in the afternoon to do anything
further. From the news Jackson received it was evident that
the military complications were losing their simplicity and
what Jackson had to do must be done speedily. He was impatient at the delay. Hill gained a foothold with little resistance that afternoon well up on the enemy's left and put some
artillery in a favorable position; and Jackson gave orders
for an early attack in the morning. I am not aware that General Jackson made any demand for the surrender of the garrison and do not believe he did. Nor did he to my knowledge
have any communication with the enemy in regard to non-
combatants. He knew that at that time all delay was dangerous.

As soon as dark came and all was quiet, I notified Pendleton that I would be absent until midnight and rode out of
camp. I was on my freshest horse and made my way rapidly
for Shepherdstown, about eleven miles. There I crossed the
Potomac at Blackford's or Boteler's Ford below the Dam, went
up the towpath for a mile, crossed the Chesapeake and Ohio
Canal and was soon at "Ferry Hill Place," my home, not quite

three miles from Sharpsburg. Hiding my horse behind the house, I spent several hours with my father and mother and sister and then returned the same way to Headquarters. I dismounted, entered my tent a little before 3 A.M. and, the night being far spent, I threw myself on the bed without undressing.

XVI

HARPER'S FERRY AND SHARPSBURG

I HAD no sleep that night. At three o'clock General Jackson sent for me and directed me to go at once to his old division, and direct General D. R. Jones who was commanding it to move forward his skirmishers at daylight toward Bolivar Heights, to open on it with his artillery, and make as imposing a demonstration as possible; and also directed me to remain and see that the order was vigorously executed. General Jones occupied the left of our line, with his left near the Potomac, General A. P. Hill the right, with his right resting on the Shenandoah, and General Ewell the center.

I knew, of course, that General Jackson did not expect Jones to attack seriously the steep bluffs of Bolivar, but that he desired a very decided demonstration. But Jones carried out his order strictly and in the early morning filled the air with a din of war that echoed along the Potomac and reverberated in multiplied repetitions against the rocks of Maryland Heights. It seemed a very transparent feint but it had its effect, for I soon discovered a column of Federal troops hastening to the defense of those unscalable heights. Almost simultaneously the guns of McLaws and Walker opened fire, and then in a few minutes I saw the battle flags of A. P. Hill coming over the hills beyond Bolivar; Harper's Ferry was doomed.

I rode rapidly back to the General, and just as I joined him at a little church or school house on the Halltown turnpike a white flag went up on Bolivar Heights and all firing ceased. I took a courier and rode up the pike and through the lines. Seeing a body of horsemen approach, I was informed it was General Julius White and his staff and that of Colonel Dixon S. Miles, who had just been killed by a shell. I introduced myself to General White, and he said he wished to see General Jackson in regard to the surrender of his troops. At that moment General Hill rode up from the direction of his command, and I conducted them to General Jackson.

General Hill rode with General White; I was riding with Colonel Miles' Assistant Adjutant General, who remarked to me that if Miles had not been killed, there would not have been a surrender without a fight. At the same time I took occasion to note the appearance of General White. There was nothing strikingly military about his looks, but he was mounted on a handsome black horse, was handsomely uniformed, with an untarnished sabre, immaculate gloves and boots, and had a staff fittingly equipped. He must have been somewhat astonished to find in General Jackson the worst-dressed, worst mounted, most faded and dingy-looking general he had ever seen anyone surrender to, with a staff, not much for looks or equipment.

The interview was a brief one. General White asked for terms of surrender; General Jackson replied that the surrender must be unconditional. General White then surrendered and General Jackson turned him over to General Hill, with instructions to arrange the terms: they were very liberal, the same that were afterwards given to General Lee by General Grant. The fruits of the surrender were 12,520 prisoners, 13,000 arms, 73 pieces of artillery equipage, and various kinds of military stores.

The memory of Colonel Miles has been harshly dealt with by his own people. He has been charged with cowardice and treachery at Harper's Ferry. He died with his face to the foe and he should not be called a coward. Worse yet is the charge of treachery, for the crime is worse. It was said he had communicated with Jackson and had surrendered according to agreement. Such a charge is like stoning the dead. As closely as I was associated with General Jackson in this movement, I never had a suspicion of such an arrangement; no member of the staff ever heard of it; no one in our army believed it. Everything that Jackson did was inconsistent with it. Colonel Miles may not have been equal to the situation, perhaps was not, but he was no traitor. The surrender was a deep mortification to the Union; the charge against Miles could only make that greater.

Immediately upon the surrender of Harper's Ferry, General Jackson sent a message to General Lee announcing the result. By the same courier, I sent a card to my father, which I find among his papers. On this card was written: "Sept 15. '62—Dear Father: Harper's Ferry has surrendered. Nobody hurt on our side. H. K. D." To be with Jackson was to take lessons in brevity.

Having sent off his dispatch, the General with a portion of his staff rode up into Bolivar and down into Harper's Ferry. The road from Bolivar to Harper's Ferry was lined with Union soldiers curious to see Stonewall Jackson. Many of them saluted as he passed and he invariably returned the salute. I heard one of them say as he passed: "Boys, he's not much for looks, but if we'd had him we wouldn't have been caught in this trap"; and there was an echo of endorsement around the candid soldier.

An officer, well mounted and with all the indications of newness, rode up to me and began conversation. He was an officer of artillery who said his battery had only arrived a day or two before, and he had only been in the service about a week. He was not in a happy mood and ended by presenting me his pistol, which he said he would probably have no more use for and would like to present to a staff officer of Jackson. I observed that while he was talking he never took his eyes from the General, but looked at him as if he was studying the art of war. His pistol was a handsome one and I carried it with the one that General Jackson gave me on the field of Second Manassas until they were both stolen from my holsters on the day I passed through Hagerstown, en route to Gettysburg.

When we reached Harper's Ferry, I recognized on the
street the tall and erect form of Colonel William P. Maulsby,
the commander of a Maryland regiment. I dismounted and
went up to him to ask if I could do anything for him, but he
declined to recognize me and walked away. The Colonel was
such a constitutional belligerent, and a surrender without a
fight was so mortifying and irritating to him, that it made him
repudiate his own invariable politeness. After the war I knew
him for many years and often met him at the bar, where he
was uniformly courteous and kind to me. Toward the end of
his professional career he had a case of his own against another member of the bar. He asked me to appear for him in
the trial of the cause, making it a condition, however, without
which he did not wish my services, that I should let him pay
me such a fee as I should charge a client, not a lawyer, for the
same services. When he died he was the oldest member of
the Maryland Bar, noted for his ability, his astuteness, his
indomitable persistence, his eccentricity and the social manners of an ascetic Chesterfield.

When the General returned to Headquarters, he again became impatient for action and issued an order to his troops
to cook rations and be ready to move. He had given all the
time to the contemplation of his glorious and bloodless victory
that he had to spare, and wanted to "push forward" somewhere. We believed that General Lee was withdrawing toward
the Potomac with a view to crossing into Virginia. The General received a letter from General Lee which Major Pendleton told me was an order for him to march to Shepherdstown
and cover the crossing of Longstreet and others. Pendleton
added that General Jackson had replied, that he could cross
the river and join General Lee at Sharpsburg. In fact, I was
present when Jackson sent off his reply to General Lee, but
do not know its contents. Whether General Jackson's suggestion made General Lee change his mind as to leaving Maryland without a battle, or whether General Lee sent his message
to Jackson before he knew of the surrender of Harper's
Ferry can only be conjectured. I do not think General Lee
wanted to leave Maryland without a fight, for he was always

ready to fight; and I feel confident Jackson did not want him to do so.

General Lee has been liberally criticized for fighting the battle of Sharpsburg with the Potomac behind him, and many opinions have been quoted to show that it involved too great a risk. It was a daring thing to do and in violation of a general principle of war. If disaster had followed, Lee's army might have been destroyed. Napoleon criticized Wellington for making a fight at St. John (Waterloo) because retreat after a defeat would have been impossible. Napoleon himself was censured for making the same error, or a worse one, at Lobau (Aspern—Essling). But battles are not fought, nor fields selected entirely upon strict military principles. Napoleon and Wellington and Lee were familiar with these and disregarded them where occasion demanded. Wellington won at Waterloo. Napoleon has given good reasons for crossing the swollen Danube to give battle to a superior force under the command of the illustrious Archduke Charles. General Lee had both military and political reasons equally imperative for hazarding a battle at Antietam, desperately bold as his determination may seem. General Lee knew that if he retreated into Virginia General McClellan must follow him with an army that much more inspirited; and McClellan's army did not fight well at Sharpsburg. He knew that the longer McClellan had to organize his army the better he would make it. In his address to the people of Maryland General Lee had almost pledged his army not to give up that state without a struggle; and if he could win on Maryland soil, it would be of incalculable benefit to his army and the cause of the South, and so imperil the safety of Washington as to make any result for our good probable. Whatever his reasons, he determined to stake his little army of about 35,000 against McClellan's 87,000 and take the chances.

On Monday night, September 15th, leaving A. P. Hill with his division in front of Harper's Ferry to complete all the details of the surrender—the paroling of prisoners, collection and removal of captured arms, stores, etc.—and directing me to remain with General Hill until after midnight, General

Jackson marched with the rest of his command to Shepherdstown, crossed the Potomac about daylight with his divisions
and General Walker's, and proceeded to Sharpsburg, three
miles farther, to join Lee and Longstreet. The Federal army
was already drawn up in line on the east side of Antietam
Creek. The Confederates present occupied an irregular range
of hills skirting the northern edge of Sharpsburg.

Leaving General Hill very early on the morning of the
16th and passing my home to which I had made the visit two
nights before, I joined General Jackson on what is now Cemetery Hill, where he was in conversation with Generals Lee and
Longstreet. As I approached some soldiers who were loafing
near, I overheard an animated and amusing conversation as
to whether Stonewall Jackson had arrived or not. One insisted
he had arrived while another repeated a report that he was
"over in Virginny, somewhere, up to something lively, I'll be
bound." One of them expressed his determination to ask me
about it and, approaching me, did so.

I told him Jackson had arrived and said, "That's he, talking to your General, 'Old Pete'—the man with the big boots
on."

"Is it? Well, bless my eyes! Thankee, Captain." And returning to his squad, flourishing his tattered tile, he exclaimed,
"Boys, it's all right!"

Near where General Lee was standing was a clump of trees.
During or after the war, the trees were cut away and a large
rock discovered. Rumor soon gave to this bowlder the name
of "Lee's Rock," and when the land was cleared away for
the present National Cemetery this rock was left standing
for historic reasons. But, as usual, fame brought trouble
and envy. People who visited the Cemetery were curious to
see the rock upon which Lee had stood, viewing the progress
of the battle. This souvenir of Lee was most obnoxious to
the extremely loyal (who I need hardly say had *not* been in
the battle) and its removal was demanded. Bitter complaint
was made to the Trustees, a mixed body of soldiers and politicians, and the debate therein grew warm and men lost their
tempers. The conservative members protested against such

narrowness and rather liked the idea of having it there as a historical memento, but the ultraists declared that no such relic of rebellion ought to stand amid the graves of the Union dead. The latter prevailed and Lee's Rock was broken up: dug up, scattered, obliterated. We Rebels looked on, while the fury seethed, in silent amusement, and when it was all over, revealed the truth that Lee never saw that rock; if he had seen it he could not have climbed up on it; if he had done that he could not have seen anything on the outside of the trees; and under any circumstances the front line of battle was no place for the Commanding General of an army, with all the battle raging a mile and more off to the left and out of sight. But those were the early days of reconstruction and now the writer of these pages is one of the battlefield commission, who are placing over the field markers to denote the points where Maryland troops on both sides fought and who are erecting a monument to commemorate the valor of the Maryland troops of both armies.

On that morning the General was invited to breakfast at the house of a gentleman, Mr. Grove, in Sharpsburg, where Generals Longstreet and Stuart were stopping. He was too busy getting his command in position to accept; whereupon Miss Julia, a daughter of the house, sent a delightful breakfast to him by one of General Longstreet's servants. The General received it gratefully and asked what young lady had sent it.

"I dunno, General, but it was the fair one."

"Well, as she has sent me my breakfast to the field, I will call her Miss Fairfield," and evidently amused at this little conceit, he took a pencil and wrote the following note.

Sharpsburg Sept 16. 1862

Miss Fairfield

I have received the nice breakfast, for which I am indebted to your kindness. Please accept my grateful appreciation of your hospitality.

Very Sincerely Yours

T. J. Jackson

Thus the General appears in a new character. Every now and then in the war, a little gleam of this kind, breaking through the heavy seriousness which enveloped these years of his life like little streaks of sunshine seen through the rift in a cloud, prepared those who knew of them for those tender evidences of sentiment which Mrs. Jackson has given us in her domestic memoir of her husband. This note has become well-known. I have seen it spread upon satin and nicely framed, doing duty at bazaars and fairs for "Confederate Homes," since the war. During the war it was lithographed in Baltimore, and five hundred dollars were realized from the sale of those lithographs for the use of Confederate hospitals.

Tuesday, the 16th, passed away with little excitement except some heavy skirmishing in the afternoon. Being quite ill and worn out, I was directed by General Jackson, early in the day, to go home and report to my mother until the next morning at dawn, unless he should send for me, which he promised to do when battle became imminent. There I found Brigadier General W. H. F. (Rooney) Lee—son of General Lee—who had been painfully injured by the fall of his horse, submitting to such ministrations as my mother and sister could give him, and several other disabled Confederate officers. One of whom, seeing me enter the parlor unhurt and with rather more freedom of manner than he thought becoming in a stranger, suggested to me pointedly I had better join my command; and immediately afterwards looked as if he would have a hemorrhage when my sister came in and I put my arm around her. He and I served on the same staff for a while, after Jackson's death, but I never let him forget the time he ordered me out of my father's house.

After supper, or later, rumors began to come in, and finding myself restless and impatient, I started for Headquarters. But riding made me ill, and, stopping near Sharpsburg, I rode into a little wood, tied my horse to the fence, and slept under a tree. I was up and in the saddle before daylight and as I started for the front met a courier coming for me.

I found General Jackson with General Lee. At the suggestion of the latter, General Jackson directed me to ascertain the position of all the artillery which would be engaged, to refamiliarize myself with all the roads leading to and from their positions to Sharpsburg and the rear, so as to direct in what manner to get ammunition, to take off disabled guns or caissons and bring up new ones, and to get any reports that needed attention; and for this purpose to visit them as frequently as possible. He relieved me from personal duty with himself for the day.

With me it was a fearful day—one I am not likely ever to forget. With two hundred pieces of artillery turned against us and pouring a continuous fire with fearful accuracy upon our guns as well as our line of battle, I need not explain that I had more work than play, more danger than glory before me. But I was fighting at my own front door. My first horse, "Ashby," in his first battle, between fright and excitement was exhausted in a few hours; another and then another became necessary. The day was hot, the battle terrific while it lasted, the suspense racking, the anxiety intense. Mars was striking with iron and fire, time moving with leaden heel. At last, about noon, trying to dismount, I fainted on the field; but the battle around Dunker Church was nearly over and there was a lull in the storm of guns. I soon recovered and in an hour or two with the aid of food and brandy was all right for the time.

I will not attempt to describe this marvelous battle: history has given much attention to it in all its details. Longstreet was in the center, stretching an arm out to Burnside's Bridge. On his left was D. H. Hill, and further on the extreme left was Jackson. It was Jackson's fight, with the Dunker Church as his center, although Hill, with a "Bloody Lane," had his full share of it. Longstreet's troops were sent to Jackson, too, and there were no unfought soldiers, no spectators, no reserves in the Army of Northern Virginia that memorable day. Every regiment had its taste of battle and blood. Lee was not on the left at all; as usual he trusted to General Jackson to fight his own battle.

In the heat of the fight I met General Lawton of Georgia,

commanding one of Jackson's divisions, being carried to the rear, badly wounded. He, too, was taken to my father's house, where he found that attention which his services and gallantry merited. He survived and became distinguished in civil life, and when sent as a United States Minister abroad,[1] he did not fail on a proper occasion to send his greetings and remembrances over the sea to those who still live in "the big, red house on the hill."

During the forenoon I had been to visit the artillery on our extreme right and returned by the road from Burnside's Bridge to Sharpsburg. I was crossing the main street of the town, a short distance in rear of the center, when I saw a young lady, Miss Savilla Miller, whom I knew, standing in the porch of her father's house, as if unconscious of the danger she was in. At that time the firing was very heavy, and ever and anon a shell would explode over the town or in the streets, breaking windows, knocking down chimneys, perforating houses and roofs. Otherwise the village was quiet and deserted, as if it was given up to ruin. It gave one an odd sensation to witness it. Knowing the great danger to which Miss Savilla was exposed, I rode up to protest and ask her to leave.

"I will remain here as long as our army is between me and the Yankees," she replied with a calm voice, although there was excitement in her face. "Won't you have a glass of water?"

Before I had time to answer, she was gone with pitcher to the well and in an instant she was back again with a glass in her hand. As she approached me, for I had not dismounted, a shell with a shriek in its flight came over the hill, passed just over us down the street and exploded not far off. My horse, "Ashby," sank so low in his fright that my foot nearly touched the curb, some cowardly stragglers on the other side of the street, trying to hide behind a low porch, pressed closer to the foundations of the house, but over the face of the heroic girl only a faint shadow passed. She poured out the cooling drink and handed it to me without a word of fear or comment. Repeating my warning, I lifted my hat and went on my way to Dunker Church. She remained at her post all day. When a cannon shot and then a shell passed through the house from the gable, she took refuge for a little while in the cellar; but when the battle ended, she was still holding the fort.

Nearly two years afterwards when Early's army was on its way to Washington, I had the pleasure of taking the Commanding General, and Generals Breckinridge, Gordon, and Ramseur, with their staffs, to call on the only person who in the battle of Sharpsburg was never driven back a foot.

About that time a different scene was taking place on the continuation of that same street a little south of the town. There, on a knoll on the right side of the pike going outward, in front of a little wood, now gone, General Lee had his Headquarters during the engagement, and commanding officers were notified where he could be found. Straggling and wounded soldiers would now and then pass along the turnpike toward the Potomac. One of these, a seedy, sulky-looking patriot with a scowl upon his face, was stopped by General Lee and asked where he was going.

"Goin' to the rear," he grimly responded.

"Leave your comrades and your flag at such a time?"

"Look'ee here, General, I've been stunted by a bung and I'm a leetle the durndest demoralized Reb you ever seen!"

"Let him go," said the General, and the doleful soldier tramped on his way.

Another scene, still different, might have been seen that day on the opposite side of the Antietam. A dilapidated North Carolinian was being escorted to the rear with some other prisoners. His dress was decidedly negligee, his bearing equally nonchalant, his manner very droll. He afforded much amusement to his guard.

"To what command do you belong?"

"Belong to Old Stonewall, more'n anybody else."

Thus being quizzed he came to a park of artillery, where were a lot of guns. The dull-looking "Tar Heel" stepped out of the road to examine the guns, which seemed to interest him very much, and he read aloud "U. S." on each gun.

"Well, what now, Johnny Reb?" said one of his good-natured escort.

"I say, Mister—you-all has got most as many of these U. S. guns as we'uns has," was the unexpected reply.

There was a shout all around, as the discomfited guard hurried "Johnny" to the rear.

From early morning the battle had been a desperate one, the fighting principally in front of Jackson, and nearly altogether in front of Jackson and D. H. Hill, although the whole army present had been engaged. A. P. Hill had not yet arrived from Harper's Ferry. At noon there was a lull, and the battle seemed to be wearing itself out. The doughty Sumner had sent Sedgwick in with his fresh division, with success at the first onset, followed by defeat. The skillful Franklin arrived with his hardy corps. "Baldy" Smith tried his luck and was repulsed. Then Sumner refused to let Franklin attack, McClellan sustained Sumner, and the battle around Dunker Church and on our left was over. History tells what a bloody one it had been. On the Federal side, General Mansfield was dead, Richardson mortally wounded, Hooker, Crawford, and Hartsuff wounded. With us, Starke was killed, Jones and A. R. Lawton wounded, with tremendous loss among their field officers.

But the fighting was not over yet. Since early morning General Ambrose E. Burnside with a corps of 13,000 men had been lying on the opposite side of the Antietam, looking for an opportunity to get across a bridge, which is now—is it sarcasm?—called Burnside's Bridge. Why the bridge? It was no pass of Thermopylae. Go look at it and tell me if you don't think Burnside and his corps might have executed a hop, skip, and jump and landed on the other side. One thing is certain, they might have waded it that day without getting their waist belts wet in any place.

"What puzzles me," said an officer of the United States Army to me years after, "is how did Burnside keep his troops from breaking over."

Toombs with his few troops was watching and Jones (D. R.) had his little division of 2,500—at least those who had not been sent to Jackson. Not getting over until one o'clock, Burnside did not advance until three.

I was with General Jackson at General Lee's Headquarters when the advance began. A. P. Hill was coming, but not yet at hand. When Burnside's advance was reported, General Lee asked General Jackson to send to a point in front of the enemy several guns of an absolutely reliable battery. The General sent for Graham's section of Poague's Rockbridge Artillery. It soon came up and went sweeping by at a trot. In the ranks of that noble band was Robert E. Lee, Jr., as a private, and as he passed, black with the grime and powder of a long day's fight, he stopped for a moment to salute his illustrious father and then, hat in hand, rushed after his gun. The son of the Commander-in-Chief a private in the ranks! Would that have been possible in the Union Army?

As I went to put the guns in the position indicated, I saw Burnside's heavy line move up the hill. At that moment he had almost as many troops as Lee had in his whole line of battle; to drive back the thin line of Jones was playing war. They pressed on past Sharpsburg and on toward Lee's line of retreat. Graham's guns tore holes in their ranks, but did not stay them. Just then A. P. Hill in his red and picturesque battle shirt, with 2,500 of his men, who had marched seventeen miles that day and waded the Potomac River, appeared upon the scene. He recognized the situation and without waiting for the rest of the division and without a breathing spell he threw his column into lines and moved against the enemy, taking no note of their numbers. The men rose to the occasion and at that supreme moment forgot all their woes. Three brigades of "The Light Division" threw themselves upon Burnside's splendid corps. The blue line paused, stopped, hesitated, and hesitating was lost. Jones rallied on Hill and they drove Burnside back to the Antietam and the protection of his heavy guns so rapidly that Hill's other brigades could not catch up and get a share in the fighting. Hill struck the last blow and the battle was ended. For the day, McClellan's grand army was beaten.

In the address General A. P. Hill issued to the "Soldiers of the Light Division" on the 24th of September, he may be pardoned for this compliment to them. "You have done well and

I am pleased with you. You have fought in every battle from Mechanicsville to Shepherdstown and no one can say that the Light Division was ever broken. You held the left at Manassas and saved the day. You saved the day at Sharpsburg and Shepherdstown." And it may be said that every brigade that fought at Dunker Church or Bloody Lane, merited an equal compliment. A Northern critic, with some bitterness toward General McClellan has said that the battle of Antietam on the Union side was the grandest failure of the war. This may be well disputed and confuted. However on the Confederate side, Sharpsburg was unquestionably the best fought battle of the war.

The night after the battle of Sharpsburg was a fearful one. Not a soldier, I venture to say, slept half an hour. Nearly all of them were wandering over the field, looking for their wounded comrades, and some of them, doubtless, plundering the dead bodies of the enemy left on the field. Half of Lee's army were hunting the other half.

A Georgia soldier found upon the body of a Federal soldier a small shaving glass of wood, unpainted, with a slide over its face. It perhaps had cost ten cents. He took possession of it and carried it through the war with him, finding it easy to carry and very convenient. Twenty years after the war, he sent it to me, saying he had discovered my name on it, and it had just occurred to him I might like to have it. That glass had something of a career. In the Valley Campaign a soldier gave it to me, saying he had "captured it" on one of the fields. I found it most useful, for then as now I shaved every day and never wore any whiskers. I deplored its loss in the battles around Richmond, when it must have fallen into the hands of the enemy. I have it now. It has almost faded into mouldy glass and is of no use; but it reposes among other relics of the war.

That night General Jackson had his Headquarters in a grassy enclosure in front of the residence of Captain David Smith, and just across a field from where Antietam Station of the Norfolk and Western Railroad now is. I do not think even the General had a tent; the staff rested under the trees on the grass. About midnight General Jeb Stuart made his appearance and informed General Jackson that there was a high knoll or hill, a little to the front and left of our extreme left, that afforded a dangerous opportunity for the enemy. The hill had been occupied during the day by a small party of Stuart's cavalry, accompanied by a gun or two; but when the battle was over it was thought too hazardous to keep these troops there and they were withdrawn further to the rear. He believed that if McClellan took possession of that hill during the night and planted some heavy guns upon it, he could so enfilade our line of battle from the left flank as to make its position untenable. General Jackson seemed impressed with the information and sent me at once to get fifty men, with officers, from General Early, who was lying in front of Dunker Church, and more if found to be necessary, and occupy that hill.

On my way to Early I went off the pike and was compelled to go through a field in the rear of Dunker Church, over which, to and fro, the pendulum of battle had swung several times that day. It was a dreadful scene, a veritable field of blood. The dead and dying lay as thick over it as harvest sheaves. The pitiable cries for water and appeals for help were much more horrible to listen to than the deadliest sounds of battle. Silent were the dead, and motionless. But here and there were raised stiffened arms; heads made a last effort to lift themselves from the ground; prayers were mingled with oaths, the oaths of delirium; men were wriggling over the earth; and midnight hid all distinction between the blue and the grey. My horse trembled under me in terror, looking down at the ground, sniffing the scent of blood, stepping falteringly as a horse will over or by the side of human flesh; afraid to stand still, hesitating to go on, his animal instinct shuddering at this cruel human mystery. Once his foot slid into a little shallow filled with blood and spurted a little stream on his legs and my boots. I had had a surfeit of blood that day and I couldn't stand this. I dismounted and giving the reins to my courier I started on foot into the wood of Dunker Church.

The opposing lines of battle, resting on their arms, were

lying almost within a stone's throw, one of the other. I communicated my instructions to General Early in tones scarcely audible; several officers were sent along his thin line—it seemed like a parody on a line of battle—and in a whisper sent the fifty men to the rear.

As we approached our destination it was reported to me that the hill was occupied by a squad of the enemy. A scout was sent out and preparations made to take the hill with the bayonet, but it was only stumps of trees, cut high, that blocked the way. We entered and took possession. General Jackson had said he would have me relieved in a few hours, but the garish sun had risen and was throwing its merciless searchlight on the debris of that ghastly battlefield when he made his appearance in person and took a careful, critical view of all the surroundings.

That hill attracted much more attention after the battle than it did at the time, and its importance to the Federal army was appreciated when it was too late. General William B. Franklin says that in the afternoon, when General Mc-Clellan visited that part of the field, he pointed the hill out to him and proposed that it should be occupied by artillery early the next morning. So the military intuition of Stuart anticipated the military judgment of Franklin. To this proposition McClellan assented, but he changed his mind during the night and countermanded the order. Jackson had been there, and Franklin could not have taken the hill without a fight.

A few years ago I went over the field with Generals Franklin and W. F. Smith. General Franklin showed me where he sat on his horse when he pointed out the hill to McClellan and impressed him with the importance of occupying it. It was odd and interesting to listen to the information then given me by the venerable General Franklin, trusted friend of McClellan, supplemented by the comments of "Baldy" Smith in regard to the events of that memorable day, when, a stripling, I rode over the field with General Jackson.

It is apropos to recall here the visit of General McClellan to Sharpsburg on the 30th of May, 1885, the first and only time he ever visited it after the battle of Antietam. Having been asked to deliver the annual address on that Decoration Day, I invited him to be my guest at Hagerstown, and he came with his son (now in Congress),[2] his brother, Colonel Wright of his old staff, and several others. We had a most interesting day on the field. It was much of a reunion, and for the first time a large delegation of men who wore the grey came over the Potomac and marched in review past the Federal General, as he stood on the rostrum at the Cemetery, hat in hand, greeting them and responding to their salutes with all the frankness and ease which distinguished him as a soldier and a gentleman. He made an admirable address and his reference to "that splendid man and soldier Robert Lee," with whom he had served "in the land of the Montezumas," made the old Confederates uncover in memory of their great leader and filled them with personal liking for his manly and chivalric opponent.

On that day I heard, for the first time, from General McClellan that when he fought the battle of Sharpsburg he had not been assigned to the command of that army—although he had several times, in person, before leaving Washington, applied for such an order. He further stated that he firmly believed that if he had been defeated in the battle he would have been tried, cashiered, and perhaps shot. He repeated the statement that evening at a dinner given to him and his party by ex-Governor William T. Hamilton;[3] and also the further curious statement that when the Antietam National Cemetery was dedicated on the 17th of September, 1867, he was not asked to take any part in the ceremonies and was not even invited to be present. Hamlet and the Prince of Denmark left out with a vengeance!

At dinner one day, Colonel Wright told a story of the Army of the Potomac, in repeating which I am not conscious of any indelicacy in mentioning the name of a lady. It was told in the presence of General McClellan. There was a report in the Army of the Potomac—whether true or not matters not in this connection—that General McClellan and General A. P. Hill were both in love with the beautiful Miss Nellie Marcy, daughter of General Marcy,[4] when they were at West Point, that she smiled on both these gallant gentlemen, for they were equally attractive, but that in the end she married McClellan. It so happened that in all McClellan's campaigns around Richmond (as well as at Sharpsburg), Hill was always to the fore, and it seemed that whether struck in the front, flank, or rear, especially early in the morning, it was by A. P. Hill. McClellan's soldiers began to get tired of this sort of thing, and attributed it to spite and vengeance on the part of Hill. Early one gloomy morning, before the sun had appeared, there were shots of artillery and rattle of musketry which told of a spirited attack. Hill was at it again. The long roll was beaten, there was commotion and confusion and a rush to arms, in the midst of which one hardened old veteran unrolled himself from his blanket and in an inimitable tone of weariness and disgust, cried out, "My God, Nelly, why didn't you marry him!"

As the laughter went round the table General McClellan joined with a smile and said, "Fiction no doubt, but surely no one could have married a more gallant soldier than A. P. Hill."

Before leaving, General McClellan said he intended to prepare a special article on the Antietam campaign and would return in September on a visit to me, in order to go over and examine carefully the whole field. He never executed his purpose. Within a few months I stood at his open grave at Trenton where I noticed General Joseph E. Johnston standing between Generals W. S. Hancock and W. B. Franklin.

XVII

BUNKER HILL

THE appearance of General Jackson on the morning of the 18th indicated that he was ready for another fight and not in the mood to leave Maryland without it. It has been said that he was in favor of attacking the enemy the next day, saying, when told of the sad plight his own troops were in with their decimated ranks, that the enemy were doubtless worse. I am not able to affirm this from my own knowledge, but I have never been able to accept the statement that the night before he had joined with other subordinate officers in recommending that the army recross into Virginia and that they were overruled by General Lee. If so, it was the first time in their joint career that Lee ever wished to make an aggressive movement that Jackson did not concur. He never consented to retreat unless he could give a stunning back-hand blow to the enemy. True, no one had seen as much of the battle as Jackson, no other General had witnessed such terrific fighting or knew better of the destruction of life and the exhausted, fearful condition of the troops. He might well have been forgiven for advising a retreat that night. If he did, he kept his apprehensions so strictly to himself, in his words, his manner, and his actions, that no one of his staff, I venture to say, ever suspected them. He seemed ready for fight at the drop of a hat.

The day passed away and the enemy made no sign: he, too, seemed to be surfeited with battle. I am not able to agree with Colonel William Allan, that General McClellan acted wisely in refusing to attack. It seems to me he made a grave error when the day before he listened to General E. Sumner and refused to let Franklin renew the assault with his troops and those who were coming to help him, either by making an assault on Jackson's frazzled front, or by moving simultaneously with Burnside along the Boonsboro road directly on Sharpsburg. I cannot see how such a movement, with fair fighting, could have failed. The next morning he had fresh troops at hand. Fitz-John Porter had not been engaged; he could put in line, against Lee, an army much larger in proportion than the one he commanded the day before; he had Sykes' fine division to take the initiative; and it seems to me that if ever there was a time it was then when McClellan should have put his fate "to the touch, to win or lose it all." As General Palfrey says of the day before, if Lee had been in McClellan's place, with Jackson and Longstreet and the Hills, the Army of Northern Virginia would have ceased to exist that day.

On the night of the 18th the Confederate army crossed into Virginia at Blackford's Ford, even taking its debris with it, all its wagons and guns, useless wagons, disabled guns, everything. If a scavenger had gone over the field the next day, he would have found nothing worth carrying off. General Lee watched this crossing, lasting through the night, and gave directions to facilitate it. General Jackson on horseback spent much of his time in the middle of the river, urging everything and everybody to push on. But the genius of this retreat was really Major John A. Harmon, Jackson's Quartermaster, big-bodied, big-voiced, untiring, fearless of man or devil, who would have ordered Jackson himself out of his way if necessary to obey Jackson's orders. But the man who carried Jackson's army on his shoulders from Swift Run Gap to Port Republic on that terrible march of the first of May perhaps thought a little thing like this was only a picnic.

When the next day the Army of the Potomac swarmed down through Sharpsburg and over three miles to the bank of the river, war was brought home with terrible earnestness to my family. Long before that, as I have said, the barn was a black mass of ruins, and its bare stone walls, still standing, told the story of its early destruction. Now in a night, as it were, a beautiful farm was laid waste, its fences disappeared up to the doors of the mansion house, artillery parks filled the wheat fields; corn and fodder and hay soon became contraband of war. In front of the house, which from its high eminence looked over into Virginia, were rifle pits; and several rifled cannon, with their angry muzzles pointing across the Potomac, decorated the lawn. My father, mother, and sister were prisoners in their own house, without the freedom from danger which prisoners usually enjoy. Unfortunately, there were two sons in the Confederacy and the sufferings of those at home must be vicarious; there are harder things to endure than battles and wounds. To invade his house at pleasure and search it as a whim, to enter the chambers of his wife and daughter, looking through the contents of bureaus and wardrobes and pitching beds upon the floor with bayonets, using brutal language to all the inmates—this was scarcely the way to improve the loyalty of the man of the house.

One stormy night in October one of the shutters toward Virginia blew open—they were, by orders, kept shut at night —and my mother, going at midnight to a sick room, passed it with a candle. The sentinel on the river gave the alarm, and the next morning my father was arrested for giving signals to the enemy. He was at once taken from his home, leaving his family absolutely unprotected, and marched on foot to the Headquarters of General Fitz-John Porter on his own farm. He requested an interview with the General, but that was declined and he was turned over to the Provost Guard. Was General Porter so conscious at that time that his own loyalty was under suspicion, that he did not dare do otherwise than permit this cruel wrong upon a white-haired, unoffending civilian? I prefer now to believe his statement that he knew nothing of the arrest and that he was never informed that my father wished to see him or was at his Headquarters. But a few months afterwards the poisoned chalice was commended to his own lips and he underwent the infinitely greater shame of being cashiered by his own Government for disloyalty. My father was hurried on that same day to Berlin below

Harper's Ferry, where he was kept for three days, sleeping at night in the open air without any covering but his cloak, until one of his guard gave him a blanket to lie upon. He was then taken before General Burnside—he of Burnside's Bridge—and the oath of allegiance was offered him as the price of his release. He declined it and was sent to Fort McHenry without further parley.

In the meantime, a scene more pleasant to dwell upon was transpiring. When my father disappeared, no one knew whither, my young sister and a still younger brother, with a female relative, started on the hunt for him. They first went to Harper's Ferry, but could hear no news of him. Night came on and they enquired for the Headquarters of the Commanding officer. They went where directed, with no little trepidation and distrust, and were soon in the presence of Major General Henry W. Slocum, soldier and statesman.[1] A man of battles, who had given hard knocks to the enemy in the field and had received them, *he* could not have been otherwise than tender to these children. Night came and he gave up his own room to the two ladies and saw to it that they were treated with every possible courtesy and consideration. He instantly made enquiries and ascertained that the prisoner had been taken through Harper's Ferry to Berlin and thence to Fort McHenry. He could not do much, but he did that little like a gentleman. I met him for the first time in 1872 and had the pleasure of telling him of our grateful remembrance of his kindness; and when he died his passing cast a deep shadow over this household.

My father was in Fort McHenry six weeks, at first for a time in a horse stable and then in more comfortable quarters. The Provost Marshall—who had always treated this prisoner kindly—took the matter in hand and finding that no charges had ever been preferred against him, had him released. But imprisonment had done its fatal work. His constitution was broken, and he was never well and strong again. He lived to see the war ended, and then he died.

On the 27th of November, 1862, General Fitz-John Porter was arraigned before a court-martial of which General David

Hunter, conspicuous during the war in so many unenviable ways, was president. They lost no time in the trial, although it was midwinter, and were goaded to indecent speed by a letter from Secretary of War Stanton dated January 5, 1863. On the 23rd of January, the court found General Porter guilty of disobedience of orders at the Second Battle of Manassas, and he was accordingly cashiered and dismissed from the service. We shall hear of General Hunter again in similar congenial occupations; it was very generally believed, and was doubtless true, that he was selected for this "bad eminence" because he was a Virginian with special hatred of his native state and therefore a fit tool for a tyrant like Stanton.

Years after the war the persistent appeals of General Porter for justice and a rehearing became too earnest to be resisted. General Grant was induced to look into the record and, satisfied that Porter had been unjustly convicted, he recommended that his case be reheard. On the 12th of April, 1878, an order was issued from the Headquarters appointing a Board of Revision, consisting of Generals Schofield, Terry, and Getty. They sat at Governor's Island and took their time in making an exhaustive examination. Necessarily the location and movements of Jackson's command in that battle or battles were most important, and I had letters from both Colonel Asa Bird Gardner, the Judge Advocate General, and General Porter, making enquiries as to my knowledge.

As I have heretofore stated, General Jackson's staff at Second Manassas was very small and only one or two of these were left. On the 8th of October I was summoned before the Board by the Government, and gave the testimony and prepared the map which will be found in the record. The red line on that map shows that if Porter had attempted to execute the order he was cashiered for not executing, he would first have had to deal with "old Jubal Early," who never shunned a fight, and by the time he was solidly in it with him, he would have had Longstreet on his flank with such blows that there would have been, in all probability, no next day's battle. After giving my evidence I saw and met General Porter for the first time. I have rarely seen him since but often have heard from him. The action of that Board in recommending that the sentence of the Hunter court-martial be set aside and that Porter be restored to the army, and the further action of Congress thereon, are now a part of history.

The ax was falling at the root of more than one tree. We know what was done with Fitz-John Porter, who saved the army of the Potomac at Richmond. We know that "Baldy" Smith, who saved it at Antietam, subsequently incurred the dislike of General Grant and fared little better. But these two friends of McClellan survived longer than he did. He, the only man in that army who could have put it in shape to make the fight it did at Sharpsburg, was, as soon as it was politic, summarily removed from its command and the blunderer at Burnside's Bridge was put in his place. It is on occasions like this that respectful language will not answer the purpose of a chronicler.

Having recrossed the Potomac without any loss, General Lee directed his chief of artillery, General W. N. Pendleton, to station a line of guns on the Virginia bluffs, and sent him a support of infantry. Somebody blundered again or was grossly negligent. It would have been no difficult matter to defend that ford from passage, but in the evening the Federal skirmishers crossed over, drove away our unprepared line, ascended the hills and captured so many of Pendleton's artillery that he reported they were all captured—they really captured four pieces. The next morning Porter sent Sykes across with his division of regulars and other troops and they soon had a fight on their hands. The affair disgusted General Jackson beyond words. He took the matter in his own hands and his staff were little out of the saddle that night. He had A. P. Hill on hand the next morning as soon as Sykes was there; that meant no child's play. A brief but hot fight ensued but it was soon ended, and the enemy were driven across the river. The loss in only one regiment was very heavy, the One hundred and eighteenth Pennsylvania (Corn Exchange Regiment); in killed, drowned, and wounded it is said its loss was one third of its aggregate. The dash across the river was daring and admirable: the result a failure. During the fight I was in the rear of Hill's line and was so worn out that I had dismounted and was lying stretched out on the ground. I noticed a round shot from one of the heavy guns over the river, rolling along the ground in a direct line with me. It indicated no haste, but I quickly rolled out of the way and let it pass. When just beyond me it struck a decayed stump of a tree, shattered it into bits and ricochetted into the air, I saw I would have been but a small meal for that fiery beast. More than one soldier in the war lost a foot or an arm by trying to stop a cannon ball which was apparently spent.

This interruption being disposed of, General Jackson moved his command to Tabler's Mills, on the Opequon Creek, halfway between Shepherdstown and Williamsport, so that he could keep an eye on either ford of the Potomac. After several days he went to the vicinity of Martinsburg. On the first evening we had Headquarters at the edge of a wood, with a green sloping field to the front. It was a cold, damp evening, unpleasantly suggestive of autumn; we were chilly and our wagons had not yet arrived. A gentleman of the neighborhood called and invited the General to make his house Headquarters. This being politely declined, he persuaded the General to go with his staff and take supper with him. Before supper was announced the hospitable host appeared with a decanter of whiskey and glasses, apologized for the state of the weather, and deferentially suggested that the General or some of his staff might be disposed to take an appetizer either straight or with water.

"Have you any white sugar?" smilingly broke in the General. It was instantly forthcoming.

"Come, gentlemen, let's take a drink!" was the General's startling announcement.

Major Paxton declined because he never drank; I, because I had a headache and rather a long ride before me after supper and spirits always aggravate my headaches. The General walked to the table, under the guidance of his Medical Director, who of course doubled the prescription, and with a skill and ease which seemed in shocking contrast to his reputation, mixed a stiff toddy and drank it off. He set down the glass and was complimenting the host upon its flavor and purity although not old, when General D. H. Hill entered. After inviting him to taste a glass of that whiskey and water, the General again said to me,

"Mr. Douglas, you will find it very nice."

Repeating my reasons for declining I added, "Besides, General, I do not like the taste of spirituous liquors."

Suddenly turning from where he was standing with General Hill, he said quietly, but with a distinct seriousness, "In that I differ with you and most men. I like the taste of all spirituous liquors. I can sip whiskey or brandy with a spoon with the same pleasure the most delicious coffee or cordial would give you. I am the fondest man of liquor in this army and if I had indulged my appetite I would have been a drunkard. But liquors are not good for me. I question whether they are much good to anyone. At any rate I rarely touch them." This was the only time I ever saw him take a drink of spirits. He took one by mistake, as I have said, on the Bath trip. I saw him several times take a glass of wine, not often. Some gentlemen of Frederick presented his Headquarters with several baskets of claret; it was on the table daily, but he rarely tasted it.

After remaining near Martinsburg about a week, we moved nearer to Winchester and the rest of the army, and General Jackson established his Headquarters near Bunker Hill on the lawn of Mr. Boyd. Here he rested, and his army also, gaining strength and new vigor, repleting the thin ranks by the accession of stragglers and wounded men returning to duty. General Jackson gave much attention to such important duties of camp and called into requisition the activity of his whole staff. It was a blessed surcease of marching and of fighting, and General Lee and his lieutenants took every possible advantage of it. Little did the enemy know how absolutely necessary such a respite was for the reorganization, the existence of the Army of Northern Virginia. This October gave the Confederacy a new lease of life.

As I have said, the army was reorganized. It was divided into two corps, the first under Longstreet and the second under

Jackson, both of whom were promoted to Lieutenant General, to take precedence according to previous rank. D. H. Hill's division was added to the Second Corps, giving Jackson four divisions and about one hundred and twenty-five guns.

During our encampment at Martinsburg and Bunker Hill details were sent out to tear up the Baltimore and Ohio Railroad from Hedgesville to Halltown—Harper's Ferry was occupied by the enemy. Being an Inspector General on the General's staff, this kind of work kept me very busy, to see that what was done was well done, the ties burned, the rails bent by fire and warped out of all use, small culverts, bridges, and water tanks destroyed, as well as all telegraphic lines over a long line of country. One morning after I had made a careful and tiresome inspection of the whole destruction, General Jackson received a message from General Lee asking him to report to him as to what had been done in that particular. General Jackson said he must make the examination in person so as to make a personal report, for while my report was satisfactory to him, it might not be to General Lee. He would make the examination that day and as I had been over the ground the day before he would not ask me to go, but would take one staff officer and a couple of couriers. The General and party returned late and tired; and both General Lee and himself were satisfied. After all it was a waste of time and energy, for when we left we were hardly beyond the sound of a steam whistle before the road was filling the air with the noise and smoke of countless trains. In those days the Baltimore and Ohio seemed to keep a lot of extra railroad tracks and other equipment lying around loose for just such an emergency. Four times during the war I saw the futility of trying to stop them.

About this time I asked leave of absence for a day to go to Shepherdstown and hear what I could from my home. With a warning from the General to do nothing rash the leave was willingly granted, and I was told to take a courier. It was a bright and quiet morning when I reached Shepherdstown and I immediately rode to the river cliffs opposite my father's residence. From there just over the Potomac on an equal eminence I saw rifle pits on the lawn and a piece or two of light artillery, and soldiers in blue lying sunning themselves on the stone wall and in possession generally. I saw my father come out of the house and walk down toward the burned barn. It was not a cheerful sight and turning away I rode down to the high road and thence into the Potomac to water my horse. As I did so several cavalrymen rode in on the other side, and, after saluting, invited me jestingly to "come over."

"I will meet you halfway," was my reply.

We were soon out of the water and dismounted. Six or eight of them got into the ferry boat, which they had over there; my courier and myself tried our fortune in a leaky skiff, having given our horses to a little "nigger," who was fishing, to hold. The courier rowed and we soon met the enemy's man of war in the middle of the stream, where the boat's men were holding it steady with poles when we grappled it. After a few inconsequent sentences, the captain of the gunboat (a Sergeant by the way) said,

"I see you are a staff officer."

"Yes," replied my courier with an outburst, "and a beastly piece of business it is for a man to get this near home and not be able to see his father and mother!"

What possessed the rash courier—evidently a diplomat in disguise—I cannot imagine, for I had no idea of revealing my identity.

"Ah!" with a low whistle cried the Sergeant. "You're Captain Douglas of Stonewall Jackson's staff and the son of the old gentleman on the hill."

This I admitted and he at once invited me to go over and visit my home. I declined, saying they had no right to ask me, and as they were not officers their safeguard would amount to nothing if I was arrested. They protested their officers were in Sharpsburg at a dinner. Not a commissioned officer being present in camp, they'd pledge me their honor to return me safely, and then as I still hesitated one bluff fellow roared out, "I wouldn't give a d—— for a Union that can be broken up by a man seeing his mother!"

That settled it and four stout arms lifted me into the

boat. We started for Maryland, my courier following, as he grimly said, "to see fair play." A crowd of at least fifty met us on the bank of the river and great was their curiosity, equally great their cordiality. I refused to leave the ship to go up home, and the Sergeant sent a cavalryman at breakneck speed to announce my arrival and that I was holding a reception for my family. In the meantime I was plied with all sorts of questions about Jackson, his looks, his habits, his manners, his piety, etc.

Very soon my mother was seen descending the hill, but father, being under parole not to leave the premises, could not come without permission. My mother came to me, pale, trembling, breathless—thinking I was a prisoner and she the victim of a cruel joke. As she came across the canal and over the towpath, the hilarious cavalrymen were almost hushed and taking my courier with them they passed her with uncovered heads and went and sat on the banks of the canal out of hearing. Marvellous delicacy; a strange family meeting. My mother's alarm and anxiety were too great for long endurance, for she would not believe they would let me go. Her kiss chided my rashness, and the interview was brief. A few words about the family and that was all. She seemed ashamed of her impatience to have me go and yet she could not help it. She left and as she went up the bank the boys came streaming down, and still she could not believe, for she tarried on the towpath.

The men gathered about me. I tried to thank them but did not know how—sometimes words are so stupid. I wrote my name on slips of paper with the date and told them if caught and in prison to send that paper to Jackson's Headquarters; he'd honor it.

"Then," said one jolly fellow, "I'd rather have it than a life insurance policy."

As I got into my skiff the Sergeant said, "Captain, while I'm here I'll keep an eye on your home and do what I can for your people. Good-by." As my courier rowed me off, I stood in the skiff with my hat in my hand and on the bank were "my friends—the enemy" with uncovered heads. On the stone wall above stood my father, but he made no sign. On the canal bank

was my mother; relieved at last, she waved her damp handker-
chief with a tremulous flutter and burying her face in it hurried away.

When I reached camp, the sun was near its setting and I
was very hungry. I informed General Jackson of my adventure. At first a quick reprimand began for disobedience of his
order, then with less tartness the suggestion that I might have
been detained, imprisoned, tried as a spy ("I was in uniform,"
I interposed), then a semi-demand that I must not do such a
thing again, the severity losing force. When I broke in—
"General, I couldn't help it," and with some heat, "Stonewall
Jackson wouldn't have refused to see his mother under such
circumstances"—he was routed. He rose from his chair with
some mild remark about a "lame excuse," but as he went into
his tent I failed to discover the faintest trace of indignation
or reproach lingering around the back of his neck.

So far as I know the Sergeant was as good as his word. His
Captain endorsed his promise and while the company remained at "Ferry Hill Place," my father's family was never
molested.[2] Unfortunately in a few weeks this cavalry went
hence and were replaced by a different set. Then it was that
my father was arrested and the indignities I have spoken of
began. I have no reason to believe that my curious visit home
had anything to do with his subsequent treatment. None of
that little squad of cavalry ever turned up. I did want to capture just one of them that I might send him to his mother with
the compliments of mine.

About this time we had some social variety in a visit to General Jackson from Colonel Garnet Wolseley of the British
Army, later its Commander in Chief.[3] He came to Bunker Hill,
escorted, I believe, by Colonel Bradley T. Johnson, an excellent selection for an entertaining companion, and brought
with him the Honorable Francis Lawley,[4] special correspondent of the London *Times*, afterwards I believe an M.P., and
Mr. Henry Vizetelly,[5] special correspondent of the London
Illustrated News, who became afterwards more distinguished
as Sir Henry Vizetelly, as decorated by the Emperor of Ger-
many. These gentlemen have at various times given an account

of their visit to Headquarters and their impressions of General Jackson.

I took them in and presented them to him, and I still retain a vivid recollection of the shadow of surprise which passed over their faces when, after greeting them cordially and asking them to be seated, he made a "scoop" for their hats and landed them all in a little pile on a camp table by his side. As I left the tent he was branching off into enquiries about certain places in Europe where he had visited. The interview was not a long one and when the Englishmen came out, they expressed themselves very much gratified at the courtesy and consideration they had received.

I never saw General Wolseley again, but we were to see something at Headquarters of both Mr. Lawley and Mr. Vizetelly, who were always welcome and always most entertaining. I had more than one gallop with Mr. Lawley, who evidently thought a horse an excellent thing for locomotion, and while he seemed to wobble around somewhat in the saddle, Britisher-like he managed to stay there, let the horse select what gait he would. The artistic Vizetelly believed however with David that "a horse is a vain thing for safety," and took his enjoyment otherwise. He was a man of infinite humor, but he did not like to be called "Count Fosco," as he sometimes was, and as he had much facility with both pen and pencil he held young swords in check.

During these days General J. E. B. Stuart took it into his head, or General Lee put it there, to make another raid around McClellan. Noting the preparations and suspecting their purpose, I offered to go with Stuart as an aide for the expedition. Thinking my acquaintance in Maryland might be of service to him in his wanderings, he willingly assented. General Jackson at first consented but subsequently declined to let me go, saying he might have use for my knowledge of that part of Virginia and the Potomac before I got back. He did not, of course, forget to express his surprise that I had found out that Stuart was to make the movement, as it had been kept secret until the hour of starting. This ride of Stuart and his six hundred is history now; how he crossed the Potomac at

McCoy's Ford above Williamsport at daylight on the 10th of October and sweeping around the country—through Clear-Spring, Chambersburg, Emmittsburg, near Frederick—"circumventing Little Mac," gathering horses and information for 125 miles, and crossed again into Virginia on the afternoon of the 12th to the tune of "Old Joe, get out of the wilderness." It was his second venture of the kind with the Army of the Potomac and he was again brilliantly successful.

As soon, however, as Stuart had safely crossed the Potomac and his command was out of danger, he left them to move along more leisurely with their impedimenta and he hurried on to report to General Lee. In a day or two he appeared at our Headquarters, approaching with his usual clatter and gayety.

"How-de-do, General," called out General Jackson to him before he had dismounted. "Get off and tell us about your trip. They tell me that from the time you crossed the Potomac into Maryland until you got back again you didn't sing a song or crack a joke, but that as soon as you got on Virginia soil you began to whistle "Home, sweet Home.""

Stuart came down from the saddle with a merry laugh and said it *was* a little uncomfortable. Those who were with him, however, said he was the only one in the party who was not at times a bit demoralized; and that at the time when it looked as if they might be cut off from the ford Stuart went galloping along the line whistling an opera air.

At this time General Stuart had his Headquarters at "The Bower," the beautiful and hospitable home of A. S. Dandridge, Esq., four or five miles from Bunker Hill, and a merry Headquarters it was. Mr. Dandridge and his delightful family seemed to turn over the house to the army, and vacant rooms were crowded with young lady visitors who never complained for want of room. The debonair Stuart and the gay cavaliers on his staff, and others of similar tastes, filled the house with a sound of revelry every evening. The sound of Sweeney's banjo and string band, the heavy step of martial heels drowning the soft sound of little feet lightly clad, the musical laughter of the dance, might be often heard late into the night. There had not been, there never was afterwards, another such

Headquarters in all the Virginias. Later on Moss Neck, below Fredericksburg, near which Jackson spent his last winter, became justly famous, but it differed from "The Bower" as Jackson differed from Stuart.

General Stuart visited General Jackson at Bunker Hill very often. The intimacy between these two officers, so dissimilar in every respect, was the cause of much comment—they seemed to have so little in common. How could Prince Rupert or Murat be on congenial terms with Cromwell? But Jackson was more free and familiar with Stuart than with any other officer in the army, and Stuart loved Jackson more than he did any living man.

This peerless Chief of Cavalry, never quiet, never depressed, whistling on the battlefield, singing in camp, laughing and dancing in the parlor, when he approached our Quarters was generally heard afar off. He scattered verses too, as occasion required, over the Valley or in East Virginia, or exchanged them for flowers and wreaths which the ladies sent him. But they were not always verses of gallantry. The Marylanders in his troop had given him a handsome bay horse, whom he named "My Maryland," and often in the watches of the night, through some wooded path might be heard the sound of horses' hoofs and then in a merry voice, as if to keep awake, his own verses.

> *"Your master's heel is in your flank,*
> > *Maryland, My Maryland.*
> *I hear his restless saber clank,*
> > *Maryland, My Maryland.*
> *He'll ride you hard and you may thank*
> *Your stars, if not left lean and lank,*
> *Without the rations due your rank*
> > *Maryland, My Maryland.*
>
> *I feel secure upon your back,*
> > *Maryland, My Maryland,*
> *When cannon roar and rifles crack,*
> > *Maryland, My Maryland.*

You bore me o'er the Po-to-mac,
You circumvented 'Little Mac,'
Oh, may I never know your lack—
      Maryland, My Maryland!"

Take him all in all—capacity, daring, skill, swiftness, *élan*—
America never produced Stuart's equal as a cavalry commander. I am not forgetful of Nathan Bedford Forrest, and
Philip Sheridan, and Wade Hampton, and others, but there
was but one Jeb Stuart!

Later on in the month of October I took another ride to
Shepherdstown to look across the river. I had not reached the
old town when I was advised there was more activity than
usual on the opposite side of the Potomac. I proceeded to the
cliffs, and along the river to different points to get such information and make such observations as I could, and I became
convinced the enemy were about to cross. I notified a cavalry
officer of my conclusion and as the day was nearly over I
started rapidly for Headquarters. I stopped at "The Bower,"
called General Stuart out of the parlor where he was otherwise engaged, and reported my apprehensions. He intimated
he had been expecting something of this sort, and very soon
orderlies and staff officers were departing in different directions and a very pretty girl was making a *moue* at me for
breaking up their party with some horrid news. I hastened on
to Bunker Hill and reported to the General what I had done
and that Stuart was already in the saddle. He sent orders for
infantry and artillery to be ready to move at early dawn and
for one brigade to move on Kearneysville to support Stuart.
By that hour we were on the march and I was off to the front
to join General Stuart and report developments. The enemy
did not disappoint us. They came, and came in such force of
three branches that quite a severe brush took place. There was
no serious attempt to drive them back. Our small infantry support fell back with the cavalry, and the enemy, having found
that Jackson was still hovering around, moved off in the evening toward Charlestown and Harper's Ferry. Very little
notice has ever been taken of this fight, although it was really

the opening of the autumn campaign and shortly thereafter Jackson and Stuart moved their Headquarters and their commands.

Before leaving Bunker Hill the difficulty between Generals Jackson and Hill was again opened and officially ended. It had not been passed over when Hill was restored to command at Harper's Ferry, for when in camp at Bunker, the trouble was revived. Between men of their nature it could not be otherwise. Jackson and Hill each preferred charges against the other, and they were forwarded to General Lee. This gave the Commanding General a great deal of anxiety and pain. One day he arrived at our Headquarters at Bunker Hill and was received by General Jackson. General A. P. Hill arrived about the same time and there was a feeling of military oppression—falling barometer—in the air. No one spoke of anything special, but everyone seemed to be under the influence of it. Generals Lee, Jackson, and Hill retired to General Jackson's tent and had an interview of some length. What transpired there was never reported; I do not remember that any staff officer was present to report it. It is likely the particulars of that interview died with the three parties to it. When it was over General Lee came out, spoke to all he recognized with his ever-gracious courtesy, mounted "Traveler" and rode away. Hill departed in a different direction, and Jackson returned to his tent.

How, I do not know, but it was rumored among the General's personal staff that for a time there was something of a sensation in that tent between Jackson and Hill, with hopeless indications, and that when the emergency came our grand Old Chieftain rose in his might. He impressed upon the other two their paramount duty to the army and their country; he told them his cares were heavy enough—almost more than he could carry—without the additional grief their disagreement gave him; and that they must not endanger all the public service. Everything went down before the majesty of his presence and his appeal. Jackson took his charges and tore them in two; those of Hill were never heard from again.[6]

Exactly how far this is the exact truth I do not know. Then

and there at least ended the public appearance of this unhappy feud between two willful men and heroic soldiers. But
it cannot be said that the cordiality of their personal relations
was ever restored. They seldom if ever met, except officially or
in the line of duty, and after Jackson was gone at Chancellorsville, it was grievous for me to notice that A. P. Hill had not
forgotten nor forgiven. It must be added that after Jackson
passed away Hill never added one cubit to the high military
reputation he had won as a Major General under the leader he
so cordially disliked.

One night, after the middle of it, General Stuart came riding into our Headquarters, accompanied by his artillery pet,
Captain John Pelham, the "boy Major," as he was afterwards
called, or "the gallant Pelham," as General Lee named him at
Fredericksburg.

> *He, who bore his banner to the very front*
> *Of our immortal youth.*

Everyone had gone to rest. Stuart went directly to General
Jackson's tent; Pelham came into mine. The General was
asleep and the cavalry chief threw himself down by his side,
taking off nothing but his sabre. As the night became chilly,
so did he, and unconsciously he began to take possession of
blankets and got between the sheets. There he discovered himself in the early morn in the full panoply of war, and he got
out of it. After a while, when a lot of us were standing by a
blazing log-fire before the General's tent, he came out for his
ablutions.

"Good morning, General Jackson," said Stuart, "how are
you?"

Old Jack passed his hands through his thin and uncombed
hair and then in tones as nearly comic as he could muster he
said, "General Stuart, I'm always glad to see you here. You
might select better hours sometimes, but I'm always glad to
have you. But, General"—as he stooped and rubbed himself
along the legs—"you must not get into my bed with your boots
and spurs on and ride me around like a cavalry horse all
night!"

Stuart made some facetious apology and begged for some breakfast.

During this rest at Bunker Hill great interest on the subject of religion was aroused throughout Jackson's camp, inaugurated by the earnest and indefatigable labors of the Reverend Dr. Stiles,[7] a most eloquent preacher from Georgia. Meetings were held in one of the camps nearly every night. Jackson often attended these meetings and took part in their exercises, offering a fervent prayer—*in forma pauperis*—to God in the midst of the camps. One night will illustrate.

He asked me to walk across the fields to the camp of the Stonewall Brigade to a prayer meeting, and we went striding over the rough soil. General Jackson's step at any time could hardly be called a walk; with his heavy army boots on he simply plodded along, talking as he went about sundry things, for he rarely spoke of war, he never "talked shop." As we approached camp—it was after night—he was recognized. A runner sprinted on before and gave the news. I noticed as we approached the tents, in many of them were sitting squads of fours, around a candle in an inverted bayonet stuck in the ground as a candlestick, absorbed in games of cards. As the General approached the light would go out, the cards would be put down in place just as they were held, the players would crawl out and fall in behind; and when he had reached the place of prayer, lo, the camp was there. Bowed heads, bent knees, hats off, silence! Stonewall Jackson was kneeling to the Lord of Hosts, in prayer for his people! Not a sound disturbed his voice as it ascended to Heaven in their behalf and, in their faith, the very stars seemed to move softly and make no noise. When he left, a line of soldiers followed him in escort to the edge of the camp and then, doubtless, returned to their cards. From a scene like this one, made vivid by the pencil of Vizetelly, came, I fancy, the engraving, "Prayer in Stonewall Jackson's Camp."

As we slowly journeyed back to Headquarters, the moon came out fully and lighted up our way. The General stopped in the middle of a field and planting his feet as if he intended to take root, looked up into the sky and said quickly, "Are you acquainted with the Man in the Moon?"

I confessed I never could make him out. At this he expressed astonishment and said he was as plain to him as a nose on a man's face. He stretched out his right arm and index finger and indicated exactly how he was engaged in picking up sticks. I wished for Vizetelly for I could make nothing out of it—my sense of astronomical perspective is wanting—and to this day that Man in the Moon is in the same jumbled condition.

When we reached our tents, having had enough of theology and astronomy to make me sleepy, I retired to my tent. The hour for tattoo came, and the rolling drums scattered it through the camps. Suddenly out upon the beautiful night there broke forth that wild and joyous yell for which the Stonewall Brigade was famous. Other brigades and divisions took it up and it sprang from camp to camp with increasing vigor, until the bright arch of Heaven seemed to resound with the thundering acclaim. The mingled roar was grand, peculiar, impressive in the extreme. When it was at its height I saw the General come out, bareheaded, from his tent, walk to the fence and lean his elbow upon the topmost rail. Resting his chin upon his hand he waited in silence the climax, fall, and conclusion of this strange serenade. The shouts decreased, the noise became fainter and fainter, and when it had almost ceased to be audible, he lifted his head to catch the last note and its last echo. When it was all over he returned slowly to his tent, and said in soliloquy as he entered,

"That was the sweetest music I ever heard."

Vizetelly's "Prayer in 'Stonewall' Jackson's Camp."
Drawn by F. Kramer, engraved by J. C. Buttre

FREDERICKSBURG AND MOSS NECK

THESE holiday days soon came to an end. Stuart disappeared from "The Bower." McClellan was crossing into Eastern Virginia, and Stuart was sent to keep an eye on him. Lee was over there, and Longstreet, and Jackson alone was in the Valley, with the Second Corps.

The pleasant Headquarters at Bunker Hill were broken up, and Jackson moved over nearer to the Shenandoah, for a day or two at Charlestown and Berryville, and then for some time longer at Millwood. On the day we left Charlestown, the General, with McGuire and one other member of his staff, went to Winchester to make some calls. This was the only day during the war he ever spent in social duties.

He dined at the house of his Medical Director's father, Dr. Hugh McGuire, and after dinner at the request of Miss McGuire went to Lupton's gallery to have his photograph taken for her. This is the best likeness that was ever taken of him during the war, and may be called his official photograph. Bendaun of Baltimore after the war made a pastel portrait, nearly life-size, from it. He presented that portrait to the Southern Relief Society of Baltimore. The Society raffled it off and it became the property of W. W. Corcoran of Washington. In the spring of 1867 Mr. Corcoran presented it to the Stonewall Cemetery of Winchester. On the 6th of June a committee, of which I was the chairman, raffled it again for the benefit of the Cemetery Association, and it is now the property of a lady in Winchester. Correct copies of it may easily be distinguished in a simple way. When the photograph was about to be taken, the artist called the attention of the General to the absence of a button and offered to sew it on. The General produced the button from his pocket, asked for a needle and thread, and said that as he was in a hurry he would put it on while the photographer was getting his camera ready. This he did, sitting in the chair without removing his coat. But the button is a little out of line—he did not get it as straight as he usually got things. It is the third button from the top on his left breast, and the little deflection is seen in all the copies of that picture.[1]

The General had one other photograph taken shortly before Chancellorsville. It was done by Minis of Richmond, who came to camp for the purpose. Having been warned that he could not hope to get General Jackson to sit for his picture, he resorted to strategy. He called upon the General and informed him that he had been sent from Richmond to get General Lee's photograph in camp, but that General Lee had surprised him by declining unless General Jackson would have his taken first. General Jackson hesitated and then, saying that General Lee ought to have his picture taken for the people and should not get out of it that way, he consented; and Minis got his photograph. For a while after Jackson's death it was the popular photograph, but it was not liked by his family or his troops;[2] it did not seem to represent the Jackson we knew, and it has given way for the Winchester picture taken for Miss Betty McGuire.

There never was a better country for Confederates to camp in than that rich and beautiful section of the Valley radiating from Berryville (Battletown was its long-ago name) toward Charlestown, Winchester, and Millwood. It was a region of beautiful old homes, where plenty did once abound, the home of brave men and fair women. Far toward the horizon had sunk the Confederacy when a plate could not be found at any table for one of her hungry soldiers. In 1862 every beautiful house proffered its hospitality for the General's Headquarters, but he rarely ever broke his rule of camping in his tents. He seemed to expect to be called upon daily to move through "Ashby's Gap" in the Blue Ridge to join Longstreet.

Before we left Millwood I had an interview which changed the course of events for me. I was visited by a Committee from my old Company B, Second Virginia Regiment—an officer, a sergeant, a private. They came to say that the company was so reduced that its aggregate was only nineteen present, that it was without hope, and that unless something was done it must be disbanded. After the record it had made this ought not to be. They believed I might restore it, bring back those who were absent, fit for duty, and bring others into its ranks. They had been sent to ask me to come back to them as their captain. They knew what they asked me to give up. But from the time I had gone in with them as a private the company had given me all it could, corporal, sergeant, second lieutenant, everything as it came, until I came away. Now they were in distress and asked me to go to their help. Would I go back to them? It was a test the like of which I had never then been put to. I felt the force of all they said, of their unhesitating friendship to me when I was the newest private in their ranks; and while they talked to me, full in those days of grateful sentiment and romance, there was ringing in my ears the words of the old song I had so often listened to girls lightly singing, "Won't you come back to me, Douglas?" I felt then and there that their wish must be a law to me.

I went over the matter with Pendleton and McGuire and Paxton, my most intimate friends of the staff, and then with the General and told him my inclination, but my apprehension of failure at last. He listened thoughtfully and finally said I had better decide for myself; the line was the place for promotion if I was ambitious for that, his staff had changed rapidly and now Paxton was to leave, perhaps I might do more lasting service if I went back to my old company who had made this unusual request. And if I did go and thereafter wished to come back to his staff, I would find a place for me, and a welcome. He said little and rightly made me take the responsibility.

So it was settled and I sent word to my old comrades in the ranks, that when we went into winter quarters, very shortly, I would become their captain and begin their reorganization.

But Paxton, being made a Brigadier General and placed in command of the Stonewall Brigade, said he would offer me the position of Brigade Inspector as soon as I took my company, as he believed I could attend to the duties of both, and I therefore would need my horse and equipments. The original General Order No. 120, November 11, 1862, now lies before me, by which "in consequence of promotion," I am relieved from duty as "Assistant Inspector General, Valley District, to take command of Co. B 2nd Va. Vols."

Pendleton handed me the original order when he signed it, saying, "Bring it back when you are tired of your new job and the General will revoke it." Before my place was filled, if he intended to fill it, General Jackson was dead.

Although I did not take command of Company B for a month, I began work on it at once. Men on detail from it, men on sick leave, convalescent, on duty at hospitals, and all men absent without good cause were sent for, and some new recruits came in. The men in camp were encouraged and took hold, and good results began to make their appearance before I did.

Matters were tending toward the Battle of Fredericksburg. General McClellan had been removed, and the country and both armies were startled by the appointment of General Burnside to succeed him. The attitude of our officers and men toward McClellan at that time was peculiar. We seemed to understand his limitations and defects of military character, and yet we were invariably relieved when he was relieved, for we unquestionably always believed him to be a stronger and more dangerous man than anyone who might be his successor. His great professional ability was never questioned. At this time the appointment of General Burnside created no apprehension with us. He was believed to be a frank, manly, modest, brave soldier, conscious of his own deficiencies, unwilling to supersede McClellan, but not possessed of capacity for an independent command. Burnside was never a pretender and, therefore, as soldier, Governor, or Senator,³ he was always popular and had many staunch friends. Had Burnside been a Democrat he never would have been McClellan's successor.

Had Franklin not been a Democrat, he in all probability would have been.

McClellan was removed because he did not do something. Burnside knew he must do something and do it quick. General Lee began promptly to make his arrangements to meet that something which he knew Burnside would be driven to. He began to assemble his forces for a fight, for his opponent this time would not be a man of strategy and would not need the watching McClellan did. Jackson had gone from Millwood up to the vicinity of Winchester and now he was ordered to hasten over the mountain. He left Winchester for another, and his last, trip over the Valley pike the last week in November. With long and rapid marches he passed Strasburg, Woodstock, to New Market, then turning to the east over the Massanutton and the Shenandoah to Luray Valley, then into the Blue Ridge and over it at Fisher's Gap to a different country of Virginia —to Madison Court House and Orange Court House. Here he had time to receive and digest the news that while he was making this forced march a daughter, his only child, had been born to him in Charlotte, North Carolina. Little Julia had come, but in his secrecy and his modesty he kept the news from his staff, and they learned it from other sources. I find from my diary I did not know of it until December 26th, the day after Christmas.

Jackson's corps gradually got up to the vicinity of Guinea Station and Fredericksburg in plenty of time for the battle, with some days to spare. There was some marching and countermarching, according as rumors of movements of the enemy made them necessary, but nothing came of them. I had not been well nor on duty, but was remaining at hospital quarters about five miles from Guinea Station. On the 11th of December, however, rumors and sound of artillery indicated that the enemy were crossing the Rappahannock and that there would soon be a collision. I joined my company, therefore, on the 12th and took command of it for action. The Second Regiment was under fire but a very short time, having no difficulty in repelling a slight attack against it. When General Paxton had placed his Brigade in position for further work, the Second Regiment

was the center of the five regiments and my company the center of the Second Regiment, but we did no work that day.

That night we were in bivouac. The men were in good spirits, jokes were told and songs were sung. "Annie Laurie"
seemed the best known and the favorite. Who *was* "Annie Laurie" to each one?

> *Each heart recalled a different name*
> *But* all *sang, Annie Laurie.*

So it seemed to me as I saw Captain Randolph, and Colston,
and Hunter, and Lieutenant Randolph, and others stretched
out on the ground in the firelight; and just that day I had received a letter from—Annie Laurie? The next day, the 13th,
was the Battle of Fredericksburg. Our regiment, fortunately
for me, took no part in it, for I was prostrated and carried off
the field, by the regimental surgeon's orders, with a high fever.
For the first time since Bull Run I was near enough to hear a
battle without being in it, and I was filled with anxiety. I met
General Jackson as I was taken off. He was in his new uniform,
stopped, shook hands, said a few words and rode on, evidently
in good spirits.

There was nothing interesting about the Battle of Fredericksburg, either in maneuver or action, in initiative or execution. Without strategy or tactics to speak of, it was a series
of gallant attacks with little hope, disastrous repulses with
little effort. In the deaths of General Maxcy Gregg and General T. R. R. Cobb, the army lost two of its most brilliant officers. No one made so much of a fight and so much of a name in
so short a time as Captain (hereafter Major) John Pelham
of Stuart's artillery, with his two guns resisting Franklin's advance. Handsome, charming, daring boy! General Lee has
spoken of him as "the gallant Pelham," and that settles it.

"Sandy" Pendleton of Jackson's staff, equally popular,
equally loved, was bruised by a musketball, striking a knife in
his trouser pocket after cutting both coats, but not enough
hurt to disable him. After this he was Major and Assistant
Adjutant General. Nine months after, he was struck in the
groin by the same kind of shot and killed.

The uniform which the General wore that day was, as to the coat, the one General Stuart had sent to him by Major von Borcke[4] of Stuart's staff, resplendent with gold lace and marks of rank; the trousers had been given to him in the Valley; the cap, the greyish blue one, with top falling to the front and a gilt band around it half an inch wide, had been sent to him from Richmond and was put on that morning for the first time; the boots, stout, useful, able-bodied, were a present from Staunton. Even the "Little Sorrel" was impressed with the display and looked rather better than usual, while the General was in his most serene and cheerful mood. Some of the boys, however, shook their heads and said it didn't look natural for "Old Jack to be dressed up as fine as a Lieutenant or a Quartermaster." In fact, it took some time for the old soldiers to get used to such fine feathers. A few days after, in passing through camp, he stopped to speak to Colonel Fry of Alabama. A seedy and patriotic son of that state approached and at a respectful distance took it all in (cap-a-pie), then beckoning to his chums he cried out *sotto voce,*

"Come here, boys. Stonewall has drawed his bounty and has bought himself some new clothes." They had just been paid fifty dollars apiece for re-enlistment.

The success at Fredericksburg was attained with so little effort and loss that Jeb Stuart was evidently the only one who appreciated its extent. He believed we should take the aggressive without delay. Naturally he looked first to Jackson for concurrence and assistance and he approached him first. That he satisfied Jackson of his correctness there can be little doubt, and it is not likely the impression that Jackson wanted to attack is erroneous. It was said that Lee held a council of war on the subject that night, that the majority thought Burnside would renew the attack the next day, that Stuart did not think so, that Jackson proffered no advice and, half asleep, said nothing until Stuart aroused him by name, when, raising for a moment "his tired eyelids from tired eyes," he simply said, "Drive 'em in the river," and relapsed into silence. I have no authority beyond current rumor for this story, and yet the remark that General Lee made to Mrs. Taylor of "Hayfield" during the winter, that General Jackson was cruel and inhuman "for he wanted after the recent battle of Fredericksburg to put bayonets on his guns and drive the enemy into the river," gives much color to the story.

When the General returned to his Headquarters he found his volunteer aide-de-camp, Colonel Boteler, in the same tent and asleep. Regardless of his new equipment, the General took off only his sword, hat, and boots and threw himself on the bed. In about an hour he quietly arose, thinking the Colonel was asleep, struck a light, took a box and fixed it so as to shade the eyes of the supposed sleeper, and prepared to write a note, or rather what seemed to be an order for the morrow. Just as it was finished a staff officer entered and said General Gregg was dying and would like to see the General, with whom he had had a difference a short time before. General Jackson at once ordered his horse and immediately rode off, unattended by staff officer or courier, having sent the officer on before with word that he was coming. Before Gregg, soldier, scholar, Christian, gentleman, passed away in the night, Jackson had been with him to soothe his dying pillow and join in his last prayer.

The army was now about to go into winter quarters, although it was not certain of it for several weeks. A word or two here about the General's war horses. General Jackson never had a handsome horse in the army, nothing to compare to General Lee's "Traveler," or Stuart's "My Maryland," or Ashby's white or black stallions. "Little Sorrel" was a plebeian-looking little beast, not a chestnut; he was stocky and well-made, round-barreled, close coupled, good shoulder, excellent legs and feet, not fourteen hands high, of boundless endurance, good appetite, good but heavy head and neck, a natural pacer with little action and no style. He was one of a dozen horses taken from a train of cars at Harper's Ferry in April, 1861, en route to Washington, and he was turned over to Colonel Jackson. It would have been impossible to have found another horse that would have suited his new owner so exactly—he was made for him. The General did not care to mount another horse, and never rode another one in battle except for a short time when the "Little Sorrel" was stolen. The endurance of the little animal was marvelous, and the General was apt to forget it was exceptional. He never seemed to change in looks or condition; his gait, except when the yells of the soldiers warmed him into a gallop, was always the same, an amble; he could eat a ton of hay or live on cobs. He survived the war for years. In 1884, I had him brought to the Hagerstown Agricultural Fair from Lexington, Virginia, in a private car. A picture lies before me, taken on the lawn outside of the window at which I write, and on its back is written,

"Stonewall Jackson's little sorrel 'Fancy,' Age 33, held by Napoleon Hull, age 85, the oldest survivor of the Stonewall Brigade—taken by Recher, Oct. 1884."

"Little Sorrel" lived for two or three years more, and Hull until he passed his ninety-second year.

The General had another horse, "Gaunt Sorrel," a large and useful chestnut given to him by Major Harman, a bay given him about this time by citizens of Staunton, and the gray "Trojan horse" from Maryland; but they made no historic record.[5]

On the 16th, feeling better, I determined to join my company, as it was reported that the enemy were crossing at Front Royal. When we reached the vicinity of Moss (Corbin's) Neck, we ascertained that Burnside had concluded not to try it and we were put into camp, and that vicinity became our camp for the rest of the winter. General Jackson established his Headquarters near Corbin Hall, which was one of the handsomest residences in Virginia, owned by Mr. Richard Corbin, then a private in the Ninth Virginia Cavalry. His family consisted of a young wife, a little daughter of five tender years (Jane Welford Corbin), and a sister, Miss Kate Corbin. The General declined all invitation to occupy any portion of the mansion, but established his Headquarters in tents. He soon consented, however, to occupy an attractive outbuilding known as "the office" for his official Headquarters. The surroundings of the room—which had been the library of the owner—were in strange contrast with the habits and tastes of the present military occupant. There were shelves of books of all kinds, except military, and of all ages and languages, legal, medical, scientific, and agricultural books, books for sportsmen and horsemen, ladies' magazines and black-letter books. There was fishing tackle, traps, skins of beasts and foxes, antlers of deer, plumage of birds and fowls; curious pictures, allegorical or sportive, engravings of "Boston" and other celebrated horses, gamecocks in bloody pictures, cats of fine breed and special dogs in frames. It was just the room to arouse the infinite amusement of Jeb Stuart the first time he saw it as the official den of Stonewall Jackson. While here, Jackson was a frequent visitor at the house socially, and his mess table was supplied with many necessaries and delicacies from that most hospitable mansion.

Active work was going on in camp, getting into comfortable winter quarters and taking steps to bring in the absent and improve the condition and effectiveness of the troops in every way. I gave much attention to the work that took me back to my old company and I soon began to see the good effects of it. The same kind of work was being done by other officers, working together harmoniously and in consultation. General Paxton soon indicated that his selection to command the Stonewall Brigade was an admirable one.

Christmas Day was a beautiful, warm day. Captain William Randolph of an adjacent company, I, and several other officers messed together. Randolph not only knew what good things to eat were, but he knew how to invent them from simple materials and how to have them cooked. He had been raised in the luxury of a gentleman's son, but he was full of endurance and expedients, tall, sinewy, manly, clever, courteous, daring. At least six times during that winter he disappeared, on leave, for several days. He had been across the Rappahannock, into the lines of the enemy, over in King George's County, sometimes as far as Alexandria, and he generally came back with a budget of information. But it did not take long to discover what he took little pains to conceal, that there was just as much of Hero and Leander adventure in those night trips across the Rappahannock as of patriotism. He did not go to Dr. Richard Steuart of Cedar Grove alone to get information such as he could give. In due time, a Miss Steuart became Mrs. Captain Randolph; and then, alas, before Appomattox came Major Randolph was killed, and she was left the widow of as gallant a soldier as ever drew a sword.

On this Christmas day, I paid my respects of the season to General Jackson and was again asked to remain to dinner—I had received the invitation before. I was anxious to do so, as Smith, aide-de-camp, was giving especial attention to that dinner. It was to be spread in that decorated office of which I have spoken, and Generals Lee, Stuart, Pendleton, and others were expected as guests. They came, it was said, and made it a lively dinner for the General. General Lee rallied him on his style in having a real dining room servant with a white apron on, and when Jeb Stuart discovered a fighting cock stamped on the "pat of butter" which Mrs. Corbin had sent him, he bemoaned such an indication of moral degeneracy. Randolph and I dined with Mr. and Mrs. Corbin and guests at the Hall and the evening was not slow.

On the 29th of December I was officially appointed Inspector General of the Stonewall Brigade and took upon myself that duty as well as that of captain of my company. I soon found I had my hands full. Then General Paxton was put under arrest by General Taliaferro, commanding division, for alleged disrespect, and that lasted about a week with Colonel Funk commanding the brigade. I was left to go my own way at this time. Colonel Charles James Faulkner, late Minister to France, came to General Jackson's Headquarters.

I find in my diary that during that winter I managed to do a great deal of reading. I read the New Testament through, and a greater part of the Old. *Army Regulations,* Vielé's *Handbook,* Lee on *Courts Martial,*[6] and other military books received my attention. Tennyson—much of Tennyson —Browning, Ossian, Shakespeare, Thackeray, Dickens, a cartload of novels, and Tucker's *Partisan Leader,* an apotheosis of the war.[7] The library of Mrs. Corbin in the mansion was large and of great variety, and it gave great comfort to many soldiers that winter. Then, too, we had a daily Richmond paper at twenty cents a copy—an indication that prices were advancing. When we began to pay $5.00 per gallon for oys-ters, $1.00 for a few thimbles full of bad new brandy, $1.00 for half dozen apples, small box blacking, $1.00, small cake honey soap, $1.25, it was an indication that our pay should be in-creased, but it wasn't. This was but the beginning of inflation in prices.

On the 8th I rode over to General Jackson's Headquarters where I met General Stuart and Major von Borcke of his staff and took dinner. I also had occasion to go there again at night. Faulkner had received his commission as Lieutenant Colonel and Assistant Adjutant General, and was appointed Chief of Staff to General Jackson. This was manifestly wrong. Colonel Faulkner had had no military experience whatever, and was not qualified for the place, especially as the senior Adjutant General over Pendleton, who had just been made Major and was and would continue to be the head of the General's staff. It is true Colonel Faulkner was appointed for the sole purpose of preparing General Jackson's neglected reports, and in-tended to leave all other official work as Assistant Adjutant General to Major Pendleton. But Pendleton was entitled in every way to the promotion and could have prepared Jackson's reports better than it was possible for Colonel Faulkner to do. Faulkner had never been in any of Jackson's battles, had never been in any battle, knew nothing about the engagements he was called upon to describe, and had put upon him a duty which even his ability and painstaking care could not satis-factorily accomplish. It was to him, at best, but a perfunctory business.

The reports, therefore, are very unsatisfactory and do both General Jackson and Colonel Faulkner great injustice.[8] The General had not prepared a report since Kernstown. His bat-tles had followed so rapidly, he had been so much occupied, that he had not time for the past. This was most unfortunate. Generals and other officers who had done brilliant services un-der him did not get the recognition their services were entitled to; they had good cause to complain and did complain. He had time and again spoken to members of his staff about collecting the material for his reports—for instance, I got together data for Cross Keys and in doing so had the helpful aid of General Trimble—but the reports were never written. No one suffered from this so much as his staff, at least those who did not survive him. The army never knew how much Jackson loved and was indebted to Sandy Pendleton, who now sleeps in the same graveyard with him, for he left small record of that regard. And as for Boswell, genial, energetic, ever-faithful, whose heart was pierced by the same volley which laid Jackson low, he is already forgotten.

These reports were not yet finished when Jackson died. Colonel Faulkner furnished a rough copy of the last one, without the usual perfunctory appendix with regard to the staff, and then hastened his own resignation from the army. In fact, after the war he very truthfully insisted that whatever part he had taken in "the late Rebellion" was a very little one. To those who were with Jackson in the battles thus reported and who knew how and under what circumstances the reports were written, they have much less weight than military men and historians will be apt to give them.

About this time the Stonewall Brigade spent a week on picket duty along the Rappahannock River. (During that time some Austrian rifles were distributed among the Second and Fifth Regiments.) Still we had some luxuries, for on the 15th General Paxton gave a dinner of wild goose, oysters, and scrambled eggs at which the President's message was read. I was also that evening given at Corbin Hall a silk and velvet tobacco bag, and an owl;[9] and I gave to Dr. McGuire a new laurel pipe which one of my company had carved for me. On the 20th General J. E. B. Stuart had a review of his Cavalry near Moss Neck mansion for the benefit of Generals Lee and Jackson. Everybody seemed to be working to get the army into effective condition and I may say here that it never was in better shape in discipline and morale than it was when the next campaign opened: witness Chancellorsville and Gettysburg.

I received a lady's little shoe from Corbin Hall to be mended —and a very little one it was. Wintermeyer [10] the cobbler first made a wee last and then he had no leather to patch the shoe.

The top of my boot furnished what was needed and the work was done in fine style and returned to the lady with the tiny last. Other little shoes came over from the same place for repairs.

About that time Burnside concluded he must do something again and he determined to advance against Lee by going up the river and coming across on his left. But fortune was against him. Rain and snow resented a winter campaign, and before his troops could get close enough to hit and be hit, they were buried in the mire, and the "Mud Campaign" came to an inglorious termination. But it was about time to change Commanders in the Army of the Potomac. Burnside made such sweeping recommendations for removal that it was evidently thought best to remove him and put "Fighting Joe" Hooker in his place. Brains seemed to be what the army needed rather than pluck, for there was no lack of fight among the generals of that army. Sumner was getting old and soon died. But why deprive it of the experience and ability of Franklin is a question for politicians rather than soldiers to answer.

Speaking of fighting, General Isaac R. Trimble took command of our old division, General W. B. Taliaferro departing. There was fight enough in old man Trimble to satisfy a herd of tigers.

On the 1st of February the Chapel of the Stonewall Brigade, built by the soldiers of pine logs, was dedicated, and on Sunday the 8th I took General Jackson to it to attend services. When we arrived the service had begun. When we dismounted, he told me to see if the church was full. I reported to him that it was very full, but that there would be no difficulty in getting him a seat. He knew that, too, but saying he did not wish to disturb the congregation, he rode off and we went elsewhere. But he came back in the afternoon to the services there at three o'clock.

At that time I received a letter from Lieutenant R. J. Nevin of General Amiel W. Whipple's staff, United States Army, asking me to find out from Richmond and let him know the fate of a fellow staff officer, Lieutenant Eddy, recently captured. I had some difficulty in getting the information, but got it through the Honorable A. R. Boteler and sent it through by flag of truce. Nevin was afterwards captain of artillery, and is now the Episcopal Rector at Rome, Italy.[11]

I notice about this time in my notes, "Papers full of anticipations of Peace"; they were not realized.

As I have said, discipline in the army was being strictly enforced, deserters brought back, tried speedily, sentenced and punished. The unusual penalty of flogging was restored. Early in February a court-martial in the Stonewall Brigade tried and sentenced six of its men as follows: one, six months labor, ball and chain, two to be flogged, three to be shot. By general order, the sentences were approved and ordered to be executed. Thereupon General Paxton prepared an application to General Lee, asking that only one of the three be shot, to be determined by lot. It is before me now, a long and able document in his own handwriting, and put with Paxton's unusual legal ability. Major General Trimble, in his own penmanship forwarded the application and approved General Paxton's recommendation that only one be shot. Following this, in General Jackson's handwriting comes an endorsement, beginning in these ominous words:

"With the exception of this application, General Paxton's management of his brigade has given me great satisfaction. One great difficulty in the army results from over lenient Courts and it appears to me that when a Court Martial faithfully discharges its duty that its decisions should be sustained. If this is not done, lax administration of justice and corresponding disregard for law must be the consequence. The Army Regulations define the duty of all who are in service and departures from its provisions lead to disorganization and inefficiency, etc."

Next is a long endorsement by General Lee, after two days consideration. He too has no amanuensis. He says the cases were carefully considered and the sentences confirmed, "however painful it may be to inflict the severe punishment which the good of the service requires." He adds that extenuating circumstances in an individual case will be considered, but refuses to interfere.

When Paxton received the paper, he handed it to me, saying, "The sentences must be executed; you must attend to it."

But some power, I know not what, intervened and on the 2nd of March, the day on which they were to be shot, they were pardoned by President Davis.

It will be noticed that in this case General Jackson was as hard as nails; in the performance of a duty he always was. I never knew him in such a case to temper justice with mercy; his very words were merciless. I can recall no case when he remitted or modified a punishment he believed to be just and according to law. Yet he was a gentleman of tender impulses and kind heart, he seemed to have a horror of cruelty. Why was this? Simply because in duty he was governed by his judgment alone, by a strict construction of his sense of justice, by the demands of the public service. There was no place for sentiment or pity. In the execution of the law he was inexorable, justice and mercy seemed out of place.

By contrast—little Janie Corbin, with her wealth of light golden hair, her large trustful, wistful eyes, "sweetest eyes were ever seen," and her perfect unspoiled ways, was to the General, as to everyone else, most attractve and appealing. He took a great fancy to her and asked her mother to permit the child to come to his office every day, in the afternoon. I went over to Corbin Hall to see her one day and found her in the General's quarters. She was standing between his knees and they had been having some conversation on the subject of writing, for he was showing her some paper that had been written on and she was listening very attentively. Her rich curling hair would fall over her face and she would throw it back with graceful gestures as she tried to look up to him. He asked her what had become of her comb which kept it back and she said it was broken. With a smile, as if a pleasing thought had occurred to him, he picked up the brilliant new cap of which I have spoken at Fredericksburg, looked at it and at her head for a moment and then proceeded to cut off the gilt band which encircled the cap. Having done this, he picked out the threads and then bound this golden band around her golden hair and, holding up her face in his hands, he asked her to wear that for him. Her face lighted up like a sunbeam and with a cry of delight she ran off to show it to her mother.

In a few weeks, the day the General moved his Headquarters from Moss Neck, Janie was ill with scarlet fever. Just before he rode away he went to the house to enquire for her and to leave a tender message. The next day he was told that his little friend was dead.

"He was much moved and wept freely," says Lieutenant Smith of his staff, whom he sent at once back to the Hall to express his sympathy and see if he could do anything.

General Jackson wrote tenderly to his wife of Mrs. Corbin's bereavement and spoke of the little girl as "one of the most attractive if not the most attractive" he had ever seen; and added, "there were two other little children, cousins of little Janie, who were staying at the same house and both of them died of the same disease in a few days." These were little Park Dickenson and her still younger brother, Gardner.

General Jackson showed the tenderest sorrow at the death of these three children. A few days before he would not consent to remit the death penalty incurred by three soldiers who had gone home, perhaps to see their little girls. Surely the ways of strong men in war are past finding out; and it must be so.

On the 11th of March General Jackson sent for me to ask if I remembered having carried any order from him to General A. P. Hill the day before the battle of Cedar Run. I did not remember. The feud between Jackson and Hill which I thought General Lee had put an end to at Bunker Hill was evidently still in existence and so were the charges they had preferred against each other. General Jackson was still at it, and Hill still of the same mood. Evidently only the death of Jackson prevented an outbreak; Hill never forgave.

On the 16th of March General Jackson removed his Headquarters from Moss Neck to Hamilton's Crossing, ten miles nearer Fredericksburg. Major Pendleton rode away with him, but not for good. Often I met him again in that hospitable and attractive Hall, and after months had passed away and we all had gone—in the following December, when the General was dead, and Boswell was dead, and I was a wounded prisoner of war off at Johnson's Island—he rode back again one day and carried away as his bride the fair and attractive sister of the house, Miss Kate Corbin, whose brother, Dick Corbin, the owner of the Hall, was then dead, too. Laurel and Cypress.

The following from my notes speaks for itself.

"March 19. It is snowing tonight and gloomy. Today I went to Guinea Station and could not attend Janie's funeral. And now comes the news. John Pelham is dead, killed in a cavalry fight at Kelly's Ford. 'Gallant Pelham,' 'the boy Major,' twenty-one years old! Harry Gilmor swore his body should not fall into the hands of the enemy and sweeping down with another cavalryman, picked it from the ground and carried it off. Stuart wept aloud over the body of his young hero —his fides Achates. It fills tonight with sadness for the 'wind is howling in turret and tree.'"

XIX

CHANCELLORSVILLE

W HILE at Hamilton's Crossing, the General established
his Headquarters in tents. His activity did not cease in
his efforts to get his corps in condition for the opening of the
campaign. After the middle of March we were time and again
annoyed and put in motion by rumors of the advance of the
enemy, but Hooker really seemed in no hurry.

While at Moss Neck the General began to grant a furlough to each of his staff who asked for it. He took no leave
himself, and this concession to them was something of a surprise. Once when I was with him I tentatively remarked that
I had not been out of the army since I entered it for a day.

"Very good," he broke in, "I hope you will be able to say
so after the war is over."

In camp we worked away, some of us to kill time as well
as to get the troops in fighting condition and *esprit*. The
winter was variable and disagreeable if not severe, and the
Stonewall Brigade changed its camp three times. I note that
on the 2nd of April I spent a good part of the night in my tent
reading Horace and proving the *pons asinorum*. And thus
another month passed away.

About the 20th of April Mrs. Jackson made a visit to the
General with her little daughter, Julia, about five months old,
and the General took quarters for them at Mr. Yerby's, perhaps a mile from his camp. This begat more or less social
gayety and everybody called on Mrs. Jackson and little Miss
Stonewall. Troops would be brought near for parade and re-

view, and the baby would be carried to where they could get a view of her. Mrs. Jackson's attractive looks, manners, and good sense did much to make these visits to her popular and pleasant, and the General was the model of a quiet, well-behaved first father. He was much in evidence, yet he did not seem to neglect any of his official duties.

On the 27th I accompanied the ladies from Corbin Hall, with Captain Stockton Heath, on horseback to call on Mrs. Jackson, and we found quite a gathering of officers and ladies doing the same. I do not forget my embarrassment when at the mischievous suggestion of one of the ladies Mrs. Jackson handed me little Julia to hold for a space. The General walked in and his amusement increased the surrounding merriment, but he made the nurse come to the rescue. Little Julia grew up in her beauty and was very fair to look upon. She married young and died young, and two children take her place with her mother.

But the storm was gathering. At breakfast on the 29th a message from General Early to Jackson told that the enemy were crossing just above Fredericksburg and Jackson's corps began to march toward and past Hamilton's Crossing. Mrs. Jackson and Julia were hurried off to Richmond, and all the decks were cleared for action. I met the General on the road that afternoon and he took me to his quarters to take supper with him. In reply to an enquiry for Mrs. Jackson, he said facetiously he had sent her "to the rear as extra baggage." He was in fine spirits and the prospects of a "scrimmage" seemed to put him in good humor.

It was raining at night and, as our brigade was in bivouac near Hamilton's Crossing, I slept in an ambulance with General Paxton. My old company being now in fair condition, I had turned it over to its other officers and was giving my attention to the brigade with Paxton.

General Hooker was putting into operation his plan. He threw Sedgwick directly across the Rappahannock in the front of Lee, and sent the main body of his troops higher up to cross at Kelly's and Germanna Fords, of which Stuart gave speedy notice. While General Lee made an imposing demon-

stration with his army along the heights of Fredericksburg in
the next afternoon, the 30th, his plans were doubtless determined upon. There was some artillery firing across the river.
Not having anything to do with the brigade at that time, I
was with General Jackson and was sent by him with instructions to Graham (Rockbridge Battery) to open with his guns
exactly at four o'clock. He gave no reason for the particulars
of this order. I delivered it, and immediately after my bridle
and halter reins were cut in twain and a letter from a young
lady knocked out of my hand by a piece of shell from the
enemy's guns.

During the night all orders were issued and preparations
made for an early movement the next morning. General
Hooker was moving with rapidity and skill. After leaving
Sedgwick with a large body of not less than 30,000 to threaten
Lee directly from Fredericksburg, the Federal general had
crossed some miles above and was concentrating the rest of
his large army on our extreme left. He seemed to have no
hesitation as to what he intended to do, nor as to the way he
was going to do it. He had altogether an army, well-equipped
and well-provided, of not less than 125,000 men of all arms,
and not less than 400 pieces of artillery. General Lee had
nothing like such a force to meet him. Longstreet and D. H.
Hill were absent with three divisions, led by such soldiers as
John B. Hood, George E. Pickett, and Matt W. Ransom.
Lee's command of all arms was not over 60,000, with less
than 200 guns. But it was observable that neither Lee nor
Jackson ever seemed more ready for a fight. Personally, I
gave more observation than ever before to the looks of things.
During the winter I had been among the ranks and close to
them and saw their daily improvement in condition and morale. I had also seen a deal of Lee, Jackson, Hill, Stuart, and
others and saw the interest with which they looked upon the
steady improvement throughout the army. And now it seemed
to me there never had been a better understanding between
officers and their troops.

The 1st of May, 1863, was spent principally in getting
into position and feeling the position of the enemy. We had

moved up to face the advance of Hooker, leaving Early to watch Sedgwick. There had been sufficient skirmishing during the day to indicate clearly that Hooker was on our front in great force and getting ready for a forward movement. But nothing of importance took place that day in the shape of fighting. Both armies spent much of the night throwing up intrenchments.

The night was clear and cold. The General had neither overcoat nor blanket, for his wagon was far in the rear. Lieutenant J. P. Smith, aide-de-camp, offered him his cape, which the General at first refused and then, not to appear inconsiderate of Smith's persistent politeness, accepted. But he did not use it long. Waking up after a short doze, he observed Smith asleep near a tree and went up to him and placed the cape on its owner so quietly that he was not aroused and slept on in comfort. When Smith awoke, the General was asleep in his old position. It was a sad as well as tender incident for the General caught a cold that night, which predisposed his system to that attack of pneumonia which ended in his death.

But neither Lee nor Jackson had any idea of knocking the head of their troops against the breastworks of General Hooker. Major Jed Hotchkiss, Jackson's topographical engineer, had been sent out in the night to ascertain whether there was not a feasible route around the right flank of the enemy. His report with a map satisfied General Lee that it was practicable, and naturally Jackson was selected to make the movement. He then began his last and greatest flank movement; the one that for all time established his reputation—as said by a Federal officer, wounded at Chancellorsville, who had served fifteen years in an European army—as the "supremest flanker and rearer" the world had ever seen.

With General R. E. Rodes's division in front, covered on the flank and rear by Fitz Lee's cavalry, the column moved silently and rapidly in a semicircle by Catherine Furnace and the Brock road, until it came out again on the Plank road, which it had left on the other side of the enemy. Up to this point Jackson had marched about fifteen miles. His first intention was to turn at this point and move down the road against the enemy. But after a brief consultation with General Fitz Lee, he left the Stonewall Brigade with him to prevent any movement down that road and crossing it with the head of his column moved on to the Old Turnpike. He directed me to remain with General Lee and bring in person any report General Lee might wish to send. Thus having completely gained the rear of the Federal right wing, he put his first division in line and moved quickly against the enemy.

From my position with Lee and Paxton on the Plank road in advance of their commands, I witnessed the exciting spectacle. The surprise was complete. There was not even a skirmish line to give General Howard warning that the Rebels were upon him. Having no time for a formation, the retreat became a stampede. It was about six o'clock when the bugles of Rodes—Blackford in charge of them—sounded the advance, while the Eleventh Corps was preparing its evening meal with the sound of whistling and song. Following the bugles were a few scattering shots, then from the opening in the road the whiz of a shell, and, following after the wild game escaping from the wood, "Jackson's Foot Cavalry" were upon them. The grey line moved on regularly with whoop and yell and the rattle of musketry. There was, there could be, no effective attempt at resistance.

The Stonewall Brigade was not engaged. It was enjoying the novel sensation of watching a running fight without taking part in it. But it moved on in line toward the enemy, when uncovered by Jackson's advance, so as to unite with the division, for General Fitz Lee had no further use for it. I hurried on to the division to report for orders and to give a message to General Jackson. But I did not see General Jackson at all. It was getting dark—in fact, was dark—and, my brigade not being up, I joined General A. P. Hill at his request. He was busy getting his division into position to take the place of Rodes and Colston, whose divisions had become intermixed in the confusion of the charge and of the darkness.

During the advance of Jackson, General Lee was pressing McLaws' and Anderson's divisions against Hooker's front from the other side, and Early was watching and occupying Sedgwick with his usual skill. General Jackson was most impatient to "push on" and urged every one to put forth his best efforts to that end. He wanted to get possession of the United States Ford road, which was the direct route from Hooker's rear.

Rumors came from the front that the enemy were massing and were getting ready to make a charge down the road from Chancellorsville. General Jackson, determined to investigate for himself, put aside all warnings and rode directly to the front with Boswell, Morrison, and Wilbourn, of his staff, and several couriers and others. Crutchfield was already in the front, locating and directing some artillery. It does not seem likely that the General went directly along the road, but evidently went through our lines at another position. It seems now an unnecessary as well as a fatal thing for him to do. He was soon fired upon by a squad of the enemy and several horses were shot. I believed from what I heard at the time that by that volley General Jackson was shot through the right hand. Warned that they were actually in the lines of the enemy, the little cavalcade galloped off to the left and rear, into the shelter of the wood. Suddenly from the rear came a cry of, "Yankee Cavalry!" and a sharp volley [from Confederate guns] rang out on the night air and sent death among its friends.

General Jackson was shot through the left arm below the shoulder, and in the left wrist. Boswell, gallant, chivalric Boswell, fell from his horse, shot through the heart. Morrison had his horse shot under him. Captain Howard, a staff officer with Hill, was also wounded. Captain Forbes was killed and Sergeant Cunliffe mortally wounded. The courier just behind the General was killed, and another wounded; a number of horses were killed or wounded. "Little Sorrel" became frantic with fright, rushed first toward the enemy, then, being turned by the General with his wounded hand, broke again to the rear. The General was struck in the face by a hanging limb, his cap was knocked from his head, and when he was reeling from his saddle his horse was stopped by Captain Wilbourn into whose arms he fell. Suddenly the enemy's artillery opened on the scene and added to the confusion and horror of it. Others of the party were killed or wounded, and verily, in the language of General Sherman, "war was hell" that night.

Pendleton came and rode rapidly away for a surgeon. McGuire soon came and found that Dr. Barr of Hill's command had been doing what he could for the General. Colonel Crutchfield, Jackson's chief of artillery, had been badly injured by a shot in the leg which disabled him for a year. Captain Benjamin Watkins Leigh, serving that day on Hill's staff, afterwards killed at Gettysburg, had his horse killed and was wounded slightly while helping Smith, who had come up, and Morrison to carry the General to the rear. It was a pandemonium of death and confusion, but above it all rose the iron purpose and commands of Jackson to General Pender and others to hold their positions.

And well was he seconded by Pendleton that night. At first, overcome by his personal grief and loss, as soon as he had seen McGuire and told him what had happened, he fell fainting from his horse. It was but a moment of weakness; he rallied, was soon in the saddle and during the night he remained there, knowing intuitively what should be done. A. P. Hill, having left Jackson when he was started for the hospital, was returning to his division to take command of Jackson's corps and issue orders when he, too, was wounded by a piece of a shell. I was with him at the time and a piece perhaps of the same shell cut through my boot and, cutting my stirrup leather, dropped the stirrup to the ground. He was temporarily disabled, and I immediately rode off to inform Pendleton. I met him on the road. He said General Rodes was next in command. At whose suggestion I do not know, but word was at once sent for General J. E. B. Stuart to come and take command of the Second Corps. When he arrived, both Hill and Rodes turned over the command to him. Everyone recognized at once that General Jackson would have suggested him as his choice to take command of the corps in that emergency. Certainly, as a matter of policy, for its effect upon the troops, the selection was a most judicious one. During the greater part of the night the troops were in great disorder, for in spite of the attempt to keep the wounding of Jackson from them it was very generally known throughout the corps. A gloom that was worse than night and disaster seemed to settle upon the army.

After rendering such assistance as I could to Pendleton in trying to communicate with the parts of the corps, I returned to General Paxton and the Stonewall Brigade, which had not been in the confusion that evening. I found General Paxton very much depressed; he had been so for several days. We had a long conversation late at night. At the conclusion, he repeated what he had stated to me in the beginning, that he was convinced he would not survive the next day's battle. He did not seem morbid or superstitious but he spoke with earnest conviction. He then told me exactly where certain private and personal papers were to be found in his desk, then in his headquarter's wagon, and told me what some of them were. He requested me to see to it that they were not lost but sent to Lexington. He had the picture of his wife and his Bible with him. He concluded by asking me to write to his wife as soon as he was killed and to see that his body was sent to Lexington by Cox, his faithful orderly, who had recently been made his aide-de-camp. I was never so impressed by a conversation in my life. Paxton was not an emotional man but one of strong mind, cool action, and great force of character. He was the last man to give way to a superstition. When he finished I had no doubt of his sincerity and of his awful prescience. Coming upon the horrors of the evening, I need not say my night was a sleepless, cheerless, vigil.

The next morning was Sunday and we were ordered to be ready to move forward at daylight. I had at that hour been along the line of the brigade, and the firing of artillery and of skirmishers had already begun in other parts of the line off to our right. I found General Paxton sitting some distance in rear of his line against a tree. He was reading his Bible. As I approached he closed it, greeted me cheerfully, and we conversed for a little while on indifferent subjects. In a short time the order came to get ready to move to the front. Paxton then recalled our conversation of the night before, asked if I remembered all he had said, and then added that when he fell, Colonel Funk would be the senior officer of the brigade and he would doubtless wish me to render him all the assistance I could in every way. He then said, "I will go to the right regiments of the Brigade — you look after the left," and we separated. We did not get into action for some little time.

After a while we became hotly engaged. For some time part of our brigade became separated and I feared Paxton was with it. We soon had some warm work and my time and attention were fully occupied. At the first lull, I was informed that General Paxton had been shot in the first movement and had died almost instantly. Very soon after, Captain R. J. Barton, Assistant Adjutant General, was wounded. I immediately sought Colonel Funk, directed him to take command, and briefly told him what General Paxton had said to me.

I will not go into the particulars of the battle. So far as our brigade was involved, it seemed to me I never saw a hotter one. While we were lying behind some logs hastily thrown together, just before the final charge on the Chancellor House, General Stuart came down the line. He sent for me and gave me some specific instructions to communicate to Funk and others. When the charge was made it seemed to be a whirlwind, but Hooker's center was broken. The fight of the day was over for us. Our brigade suffered greatly, losing about 600 killed and wounded—which was a heavy per cent —but the proportion of killed was unusually small.

When the charge was over my attention was called to the new cap Lieutenant Ray had brought me from Richmond. A ball had entered just above the visor and had made its exit, bending a little upwards; and although it cut a lock of my hair, which fell off as I removed my cap, the shot had

been such a clean one that I had not known it and had no
idea when I received it. But remembering Boonsboro, I swore
off from new hats in battle. I left that cap at home as a
souvenir, en route to Gettysburg, but I fared no better there.
I am indebted to both General Colston, commanding the division, and Colonel Funk for the special mention they made of
me in their official reports of that day's battle.

The attack upon Hooker had been generally successful,
except that Sedgwick's heavy column, moving from Fredericksburg, had driven Early's small force back and was following him toward Lee's right and rear. This made the
position of the Confederate army a very precarious one if
Sedgwick should be energetic and successful and if Hooker
did his part.

After this Sunday's fight I rode to the brigade hospital
and visited all the wounded. After doing that I went to see
General Jackson and was with him for an hour. I found him
not only cheerful but talkative—in fact, inquisitive. He
seemed to be in excellent condition. He expressed great gratification that General Stuart had handled his corps so admirably. He asked about the positions of the divisions and
even of the brigades and what news there was of Early. He
asked me to describe as well as I could the movements of the
several divisions during the battle and tell him what I knew
of the losses.

He then began to enquire about individuals, mentioning a
number of officers and asking if they were unhurt. He spoke
most feelingly of the deaths of Paxton and Boswell. Then,
saying he had heard I had been active with the Old Brigade
that day, he asked me to tell him all about its movements.
I described to him its different evolutions from the beginning: how Paxton was reading his Bible when the order came
to advance, how the brigade assisted in the assault and capture of the first line of the enemy's works, how Paxton was
mortally wounded, dying almost immediately, how the brigade then advanced and was repulsed, and how, when Stuart,
in person, started it in its last grand charge, it broke over
the field toward the enemy, shouting, louder than the din of

musketry, "Remember Jackson!" and swept everything like a tempest before it. For a moment his face flushed with excitement and pride and lighted up with the fire of battle. But at once, with moist eyes and quivering voice, he said,

"It was just like them, just like them. They are a noble set of men. The name of Stonewall belongs to that brigade, not to me." This latter sentence he repeated several times before he died.

May 4th was spent by General Lee in punishing Sedgwick, and Hooker gave him no help. Our division did no fighting. I was occupied during the day paroling wounded prisoners at the hospital at Mr. Hatch's house. I wrote to Mrs. Paxton as I promised to do.

May 5th Hooker retreated at night and did not wait for the attack which General Lee had planned. He went back to his old camp.

It rained hard during the day, causing, doubtless, the death of many wounded soldiers. I was at the hospital looking after our wounded.

General Jackson was removed to Mr. Chandler's at Guinea Station, where Mrs. Jackson and Julia joined him.

On the 6th General A. P. Hill took command of our corps, relieving General Stuart. Captain Moore, Divisional Assistant Inspector General, and myself spent the day in company with Dr. Thad S. Gardner, Sixty-second Pennsylvania Volunteers, paroling prisoners. (Under his medical advice I exchanged my pipe for the Doctor's gold pen and holder.) I joined my brigade on the 8th and found it in General Henry Heth's division, and on the next day I had an interview with General Hill in regard to a commander for it.

Sunday, the 10th, was a beautiful day. Service was held by the Reverend Dr. Lacy [1] at General Hill's Headquarters, and the text of his sermon was the hopeful one, "We know all things work together for good to them that fear God." It was an imposing service of the deepest solemnity.

Hope was expressed that the General was getting better, but private information gave no hope. I find this in my diary, "This afternoon my watch stopped at a quarter past three o'clock. At that moment the heart of Stonewall Jackson ceased to beat, and his soul departed for Heaven."

Stonewall Jackson had performed his greatest achievement and, from the hour he was struck down to the delirium of his last moments, his mind was upon it. He was virtually dying on the field, amid the trophies and ruins of his last victory. His spirit was riding on the whirlwind of the conflict.

"Order A. P. Hill to prepare for action!"

"Pass the infantry to the front——" and his soul seemed ready to go out upon the storm.

And then the light of the eternal future broke upon him and after a pause he said, "No, no, let us cross over the river and rest under the shade of the trees."

That evening the news went abroad, and a great sob swept over the Army of Northern Virginia; it was the heart-break of the Southern Confederacy.

On Monday, at the request of the officers of the Stonewall Brigade, I went to ask General Lee if in his judgment it was proper to permit that brigade or a part of it to escort the remains of General Jackson to Richmond. He received me kindly, listened patiently, and then in a voice gentle and sad replied:

"I am sure no one can feel the loss of General Jackson more deeply than I do, for no one has the same reason. I can appreciate the feelings of his old brigade; they have reason to mourn for him, for he was proud of them. I should be glad to grant any request they might make to show their regard for him, and I am sorry the situation of affairs will not justify me in letting them go to Richmond or even to Lexington. But it cannot be. Those people over the river are again showing signs of movement and I cannot leave my Headquarters long enough to ride to the depot and pay my dear friend the poor tribute of seeing his body placed upon the cars. His friends of the Stonewall Brigade may be assured their General will receive all the honor practicable. He never neglected a duty while living and he would not rest the easier in his grave if his old brigade had left the presence of the enemy to see him buried. Tell them, Captain, how I

Henry Kyd Douglas, taken while he was in Richmond to attend Jackson's funeral. Note the black arm band

sympathize with them. Tell them that deeply as we all lament the death of their General yet, if his spirit remains behind to inspire his corps and the whole army, perhaps in the end his death may be as great a gain to us as it is to himself."

I have given these remarks of General Lee as spoken, for I wrote them out in my diary and they are verbatim according to my fresh recollection.

Having reported to the brigade what General Lee had said, I at once went to the station and to Richmond with Mrs. Jackson and the staff. Colonel Sandy Pendleton and Dr. William H. Mayo, aide-de-camp to the Governor, had charge of the body. Dr. McGuire, Lieutenant Morrison, Lieutenant Smith, Major W. J. Hawks, Major Bridgeford, Dr. Smith, Dr. Tucker, Colonel Shiels, myself and others went with them, and several ladies accompanied Mrs. Jackson.

Crowds of people were at all the stations as the special train passed, and at Ashland a delegation of ladies placed fresh flowers and wreaths upon the coffin. At Richmond, where we arrived in the middle of the afternoon, a military and civic escort, under command of Major General Arnold Elzey, conveyed the remains, wrapped in the first new Confederate flag that had been made, to the Executive Mansion —the home of Jackson's staunch friend, Governor Letcher. During the night the body was embalmed and transferred to a neat metallic coffin.

The next day, the 12th, was a very warm one. There was an immense military and civic pageant, grand, solemn, mournful, to convey the body from the Governor's Mansion. President Davis and his Cabinet were there; Generals Longstreet, Ewell, Elzey, Pickett, Winder, Garnett, Kemper, Corse, and Commodore French Forrest were the pallbearers; and with all the pomp and circumstance of a warrior's funeral, the dead body of our modest and simple chieftain was borne through the crowds which lined the streets and deposited in stately repose in the Capitol of the new Republic. There the throng pressed through in continuous stream for a first and last view of the great general, whom they had learned to honor without seeing and love without knowing.

Late that night, after midnight when all was quiet, I went alone to the Capitol. The crowd had gone, the doors were closed, and several silent sentinels stood guard at the chamber of death. There was all that was left of the mortal man: a coffin on a low table, wrapped in a flag and buried in roses, a faint light of candles, a sentinel moving to and fro with unceasing tread, the high forehead and well-known face cold and white and firm as marble, the sharp nose and tightly closed lips. There was no voice to respond to a good-by. I picked up a few flowers and took my last leave of Stonewall Jackson:

> *He who cared not to be great*
> *But as he saved or served the State,*
> *Such was he; his work is done.*

On the 15th of May, General Jackson was laid to rest in the shade of the trees, at the spot he had chosen, "at Lexington in the Valley of Virginia."

His death was a shock alike to the South and the North, each believing, from different standpoints and with different sensations, that it was the first mortal wound the Southern Confederacy had received. Naturally it was no grief to the Army of the Potomac. To the people of the South it was simply unaccountable. It is said that a semi-lunatic was walking on the lawn of an asylum near Baltimore when someone announced to him the death of Stonewall Jackson. At the news he was dazed, disturbed, and his feeble mind seemed to be groping in the dark for some explanation for such a calamity. Deep sadness settled upon his face. Then suddenly a light broke over it and lifting his head and looking up into the sky he exclaimed,

"Oh, what a battle must have been raging in Heaven, when the Archangel of the Lord needed the services of Stonewall Jackson!"

Was a similar thought running through the mind of a venerable clergyman, who, at the unveiling of the Jackson monument at New Orleans years after the war, closed his prayer with these words:

"When in Thy inscrutable wisdom, Oh Lord, Thou didst ordain that the Confederacy should fall, then didst find it necessary to remove Thy servant Stonewall Jackson, Amen!"

STONEWALL JACKSON

And oft in dreams his fierce brigade
  Shall see the form they followed far—
Still leading in the farthest van—
  A landmark in the cloud of war.
And oft when white-haired grandsires tell
  Of bloody struggles past and gone,
The children at their knees will hear
  How Jackson led his columns on!

WE copy these words as the tribute of a generous Federal officer to the fame of his most dreaded foe. In this connection another one of a different kind may be mentioned. It is said that an affectionate friend brought from the grave of Napoleon a sprig of laurel and planted it upon the grave of Jackson at Lexington, as a tribute from the grandest warrior of the Old World to the most brilliant soldier of the New.

General Jackson was of sterling and respectable parentage, but he was virtually "his own ancestor." And it is well that Virginia who gave to the war Robert Edward Lee, of old and aristocratic lineage, should furnish Jackson as the representative of her people. On the 21st of January, 1824, in Clarksburg among the mountains of West Virginia, this boy, the youngest of four children, was born. And with no view to his future fame he was named Thomas Jonathan Jackson. It was a rugged, honest name, but it is no cause of regret that it is now merged in the more rugged and euphonious one he afterwards made for himself. No comet was seen at his birth, and there is little record of his boyhood, except that he was left an orphan when three years old and, being penniless, had a hard time of it in his youth.

At sixteen he was appointed a constable and two years afterwards entered West Point as a cadet. He graduated in 1846 and went to Mexico as a Lieutenant in the battery of Magruder, "Prince John," who afterwards served under him in Virginia. He was twice breveted for gallantry, and returned from Mexico at the age of twenty-four with the rank of Major. He served for a while in Florida, but, his health failing, he was obliged to quit the army.

In 1851 he was appointed a Professor in the Virginia Military Institute at Lexington. He there married Eleanor, daughter of the Reverend George Junkin, D.D., the President of Washington College. Dr. Junkin was an earnest Union man, and at the breaking out of the war resigned and went back to Pennsylvania. The loyalty of the old gentleman, however, could not subsequently resist the pride he felt in his famous son-in-law, and I recall that when I was wounded and in a hospital at Gettysburg he came to see me and exhibited with much pleasure a cane that General Jackson had given him and which bore on its silver head the initials of both of them.

Major Jackson's first wife soon died and he married the daughter of the Reverend Dr. Morrison [1] of Charlotte, North Carolina, another Presbyterian clergyman. He became a Presbyterian through marriage. In 1857 he went to Europe. While there he visited the field of Waterloo with some French officers and surprised them by his familiarity with the topography of the ground and the maneuvers of the two armies.

I saw him, first, when I was at Law School in Lexington in 1860. [2]

"Tell me something about Major Jackson—he's such an oddity!" I said to "Bath" Terrill, a classmate, who had once been a cadet.

"Old Jack is a character, genius or just a little crazy," he replied. "He lives quietly and don't meddle. He's as systematic as a multiplication table and as full of military as an arsenal.

Stiff, you see, never laughs, but as kind hearted as a woman—
and by Jupiter, he teaches a nigger Sunday-school. But,
mind, if this John Brown business leads to war, he'll be heard
from!"

Well, it did lead to war and Jackson was heard from, and
Colonel Terrill fell fighting under him.

In face and figure Jackson was not striking. Above the average height, with a frame angular, muscular, and fleshless,
he was, in all his movements from riding a horse to handling a
pen, the most awkward man in the army. His expression was
thoughtful, and, as a result I fancy of his long ill health, was
generally clouded with an air of fatigue. His eye was small,
blue, and in repose as gentle as a young girl's. With high,
broad, forehead, small sharp nose, thin, pallid lips generally
tightly shut, deep-set eyes, dark, rusty beard, he was certainly
not a handsome man. His face in tent or parlor, softened by his
sweet smile, was as different from itself on the battlefield as a
little lake in summer noon differs from the same lake when
frozen. Walking or riding the General was ungainly: his main
object was to get over the ground. He rode boldly and well, but
not with grace or ease; and "Little Sorrel" was as little like a
Pegasus as he was like an Apollo. He was not a man of style.
General Lee, on horseback or off, was the handsomest man I
ever saw. It was said of Wade Hampton that he looked as
knightly when mounted as if he had stepped out from an old
canvas, horse and all. John C. Breckinridge was a model of
manly beauty, John B. Gordon, a picture for the sculptor, and
Joe Johnston looked every inch a soldier. None of these things
could be said of Jackson.

The enemy believed he never slept. In fact he slept a great
deal. Give him five minutes to rest, he could sleep three of them.
Whenever he had nothing else to do he went to sleep, especially
in church. He could sleep in any position, in a chair, under
fire, or on horseback. Being a silent man, he gave to sleep many
moments which other men gave to conversation. And yet he
was never caught "napping."

He was quiet, not morose. He often smiled, rarely laughed.
He never told a joke but rather liked to hear one, now and

then. He did not live apart from his personal staff, although they were nearly all young; he liked to have them about, especially at table. He encouraged the liveliness of their conversation at meals, although he took little part in it. His own words seemed to embarrass him, unless he could follow his language by action. As he never told his plans, he never discussed them. He didn't offer advice to his superiors, nor ask it of his subordinates. Reticent and self-reliant he believed "he walks with speed who walks alone." The officer next in command often and very justly complained of this risky reticence; but Jackson is reported to have said, "If my coat knew what I intended to do, I'd take it off and throw it away." Such reticence at times was neither judicious nor defensible; but luck saved him from evil consequences.

Swiftness of execution was his most popular virtue: with him action kept pace with design. He was the most rapid mover in the South, and his old brigade got the name of "Jackson's Foot Cavalry" from the outstart of the war. He had no moments of deplorable indecision and no occasion to lament the loss of golden opportunities. From Carrick's Ford to Gettysburg the track of war was lined with the graves of soldiers who died while their generals were deliberating. Jackson had as little of this weakness as Napoleon, or the Archduke Charles, or Frederick the Great. This caused the mutual confidence between himself and his troops which was so marvelous. They believed he could do anything he wished, and he believed they could do anything he commanded.

Jackson was a man of strategy, and it is this quality of his mind that has attracted the admiration of military critics. It was his study as the best way of equalizing numbers and getting as even with the enemy as possible. He had not forgotten the lessons he learned in Mexico at Cerro Gordo and Contreras. Knowing the necessity of economizing in the slaughter of his men, he had rather maneuver his opponent out of a position than knock him out. Grant said, "I never maneuver." He did do it, however, and he did it well, although it was not his strong point—and greater generals than he have done it. But Grant had always so many troops to handle that he preferred to "hammer away." Jackson would have resorted to strategy if he had commanded a million men; he couldn't help it.

The question has been asked, what was the limit of Jackson's military capacity? It is not possible to answer it. In him there was exhibited no dangerous precociousness. He never sought promotion, but never expressed a doubt of his ability to manage any command given him. He put forth no useless strength. What was in him we shall never know for he went to the grave with the richness of the mine unexplored. He was equal to each new occasion as it arose, and in his movements there was no monotony, except in success. His development came as required, and he closed his career at Chancellorsville with his greatest stroke and died with fresh honors thick upon him. It has been said of his Valley Campaign and his movements around Pope that he violated all the established rules of war. So be it. So Count Wurmser and Beaulieu, the Austrian generals, said of the young Napoleon in his Mantuan Campaign. Rules of war are like piecrust, made to be broken at the right time. Both of these military culprits knew the rules and knew the right time to violate them; their success must be their apology.

I have already referred to an apparent inconsistency in Jackson's character: his gentleness and tenderness of heart and manner in his personal life, and on the other hand a hardness at times in exacting the performance of military duty which had the flavor of deliberate cruelty. Shortly after the First Manassas, when Jackson was Brigadier General, an officer in his command applied for a short furlough to visit his wife who was sick unto death. The General returned the application disapproved. Not dreaming of such a thing, so early in the war, the officer sought General Jackson and made a personal appeal to him. Seeing that his appeal was having no effect, he cried out, with great emotion,

"General, General, my wife is dying. I must see her!"

A shade of sadness and grief passed over the face of the General but for a moment, and then in cold, merciless tones, he replied, "Man, man, do you love your wife more than your country?" and turned away.

The wife died and that soldier never forgave Stonewall Jackson.

Yes, this was the man who was stopped on the highway by an old woman and raised his cap to her when asked innocently if he could tell her if her son would pass that way. Sharply directing his staff, who had thoughtlessly smiled at the interruption, to move on, except Dr. McGuire, he dismounted and began to question her. Having satisfied himself that her son was in the Fifth Virginia Regiment of his old brigade, he directed a courier to remain with her, find her son and give him leave to remain with her until next morning. Then, taking the old lady's hand, he said kind words to her, mounted his horse, and rode away.

This makes clear the distinction between his natural personal kindliness and his exacting, unyielding sense of public duty.

Thus it may be said of General Jackson that he was a normal human being, not a mythological creation. He was a soldier of great ability, activity, and daring, and not an irresponsible, erratic genius. In manner he was deferential, modest, and retiring, in the presence of women diffident to excess. He never blustered and even on the field of battle was rarely severe except to incompetency and neglect. He judged himself more harshly than anyone else did, but toward the weakness of others he had abundant charity. In religion he was a quiet Christian gentleman, absolutely liberal and nonsectarian: he was a Presbyterian but might just as easily have been a Methodist or an Episcopalian or, perchance, a Catholic. He was too liberal to be a bigot and had none of "the presumptuous fanaticism of Cromwell." Like many another great soldier, he was at first called "crazy," but it was soon found out he was always sober and in his right mind. Eccentric as many of his movements were, they were prompted—as Napoleon said of his own—"not by genius but by thought and meditation." He made war like a soldier of great brain and moral force, not as Blind Tom[3] makes music, guided by whispering no one hears but himself.

Many another great soldier has intoxicated his troops with

enthusiasm on the battlefield and led them to the performance of great deeds. No one, when he had gone, ever left behind him among the ranks greater reverence or a more tender memory. The morning after the unveiling of the Lee Statue in Richmond as the sun rose over the city, its first rays fell upon a row of figures, wrapped in gray blankets and sleeping on the grass around the Statue of Jackson in Capitol Square. One by one these sleepers began to unroll themselves—here a grey head, there a grey beard—got up, yawned and stretched themselves in the morning air. Just then a passing citizen said to them in kindly anxiety,

"Heavens, men, could you find no other beds in Richmond last night?"

"Oh, yes, there was plenty of places; all Richmond was open to us," said one, and turning his eyes toward the silent face of his immortal chief he added, "but we were his boys and we wanted to sleep with the old man just once more."

A few years afterwards I was present at Lexington when the Jackson Statue erected at his grave was unveiled. It was a day not to be forgotten. Old Confederates were there from far and near—men who had not seen each other since Appomattox. The Valley of Virginia gathered there, and East Virginia, and Maryland. Old soldiers in grey uniforms, all the old soldiers in grey hair or grey beards, crowded the streets of that historic town. The day was given up to memories, and Jubal Early, the oldest Confederate general living, spoke for us all on that occasion. I need not dwell upon the ceremonies, upon the pathetic scenes at this last reunion. The evening drew near and the departing day seemed to linger like a benediction over the sacred place of the dead. People were moving off and the order was given to the old soldiers to fall into line and march away. With trembling step the grey line moved on, but when it reached the gate one old Confederate turned his face for a last look at the monument and, waving his old grey hat toward the figure of his beloved General, he cried out in a voice, that choked itself with sobs,

"Good-by, old man, good-by! We've done all we can for you!"

GETTYSBURG

O N the 13th of May I left Richmond and returned to duty at camp. Major General Edward Johnson had taken command of Jackson's division. He offered me the position of Assistant Adjutant General on his staff, with the rank of Major, which I accepted, and in a few days left the Stonewall Brigade to assume my new duties. Captain R. W. Hunter was appointed Assistant Inspector General of the brigade, then put under the command of Brigadier General James A. Walker. Shortly afterwards upon the application of the field officers of the brigade the Secretary of War issued an order that thereafter that brigade should be officially known as the "Stonewall Brigade."

A committee had been appointed in the brigade to raise a fund to build a monument, or rather to erect a tomb, over the remains of General Jackson at Lexington. On the 21st of May that committee turned over to me the sum of $5,688 to take charge of as their treasurer. I sent it at once to the Honorable Daniel B. Lucus at Richmond, who deposited it in the Bank of the Commonwealth, except one dollar which he reported as not "bankable"! On the same day I wrote to Mrs. Jackson, in behalf of the committee, telling her of the desire of the members of the brigade to take charge of the General's grave so far as to erect a tomb or monument over it, and asking her consent. I also sent her a copy of the proceedings of the meeting held in the brigade. Her answer dated at Cottage Home, North Carolina, June 29, 1863, now lies before me, with its modest black border. In it she says,

"I think this tribute of love and respect from the noble old Brigade, which *he* regarded with so much affection and pride would have been very gratifying to their first Commander and for this reason I give my consent to their request to erect a tomb. With regard to any suggestion or recommendations as to the design for the monument, I would prefer the work should be entirely their own. I would advise them to regard *simplicity* in everything, *he* so loved it himself and it was one of his great characteristics."

But the campaign opened and such stirring events followed that the matter was postponed for the season; it could not be otherwise. Within a few weeks I was badly wounded at Gettysburg and became a prisoner of war. I returned from captivity in March, 1864, and as soon as I got established in camp I took the matter up again with the purpose of increasing the fund I had and of going on with the erection of the tomb before we all were killed. I wrote a number of letters and received replies. General Jackson had left no warmer friend in Virginia than Governor John Letcher of Lexington. His earnest, honest letter lies before me and I quote one paragraph of it.

"If it can be done in the present unsettled condition of public affairs, I think there is a propriety in erecting the proposed monument while his old brigade is in active service, as an organization. There is something striking and impressive in the idea, that amid the din of battle with the roar of artillery and musketry around them, the brigade can do their duty in the field and at the same time devise the means and make the preparation to pay an affectionate tribute to the memory of their great commander."

But this purpose was not to be accomplished. Again the roll of drums soon distracted the attention of the living soldiers from the dead: the campaign against Grant opened; the march to Lynchburg followed, and then the pursuit of Hunter to Lexington, past the grave of Jackson, on down the Valley to the Potomac and Washington; more marches, more battles, more dead; fewer of the old brigade left alive. And then followed Petersburg and the last retreat, and a squad of men staggering along with their guns to Appomattox; then came the surrender, when there was only a handful of the old line left and nothing left with them to build a tomb over Jackson's grave.

On the 27th of May, preparatory to movement, General Lee reviewed Early's and Johnson's divisions. On that day Captain B. W. Leigh, who had helped to carry General Jackson off the field when wounded, reported to General Edward Johnson for duty. The next day was election day and I voted for T. T. Munford (for Governor), Colonel A. R. Boteler (for Congress), Randolph Tucker (for Attorney General), Ned Moore (for State Senate), Claiborne Green and John Y. Beall (House of Delegates). On the 1st of June, Lieutenant General Ewell took command of the Second Corps, composed of Early's, Johnson's, and Rodes's divisions, Lieutenant General A. P. Hill took command of the Third (new) Corps.

Starting at four o'clock on the 5th our division moved off and marched for fifteen miles, through Spotsylvania. On the next day we were detained for a while by rumors that the enemy were making demonstrations at Fredericksburg, but we got off later and marched ten miles. The next day, being Sunday, we marched seventeen miles and crossed the Rapidan.

On the 9th we were kept under arms awaiting the result of a severe cavalry fight which lasted nearly all that day. Two cavalry divisions under General Alfred Pleasanton crossed the Rappahannock at two points and, advancing toward Culpeper Court House, met Stuart at Brandy Station and a battle followed. It was one of the few real cavalry fights of the war, with considerable loss on both sides. Toward evening General Pleasanton retired and Stuart claimed a victory for his sabres. The next day we only managed about ten miles; the day following we made eighteen, encamping at Gaines Cross Roads. Starting at 4:30 A.M. on the 12th, we marched eighteen miles and encamped near Cedarville. On the next morning Rodes's division moved toward Berryville, and Johnson and Early to Winchester. We found Winchester well fortified. The 14th was spent demonstrating against the town, Johnson in front and Early in rear, with some heavy cannonading in the evening. After dark our division drew off, and after marching about three miles on the Berryville pike we made a detour by way of Jordan Springs toward the Winchester and Martinsburg pike. We came to the pike about four miles from Winchester a little before daylight, and there we ran into General Milroy's army, retreating from Winchester. A sharp fight ensued and the enemy were routed and stampeded. Snowden Andrews with his battery got, as usual, into the most dangerous place and was again very severely wounded. The enemy scattered and were followed as vigorously as possible.

General Johnson, in his eagerness, pursued with his staff and bodyguard until he was far in advance of any organized troops and simply commanding skirmishers. In rushing across the Opequon Creek he rode into a deep hole, and both horse and rider were soon floundering in the depths. With assistance he reached the shore safely and one of the pursued Federals jumped into the creek, rescued the General's hat and brought it to him and surrendered. This called a halt to our part of the pursuit, and we returned to the troops.

An invitation which soon followed to go to the Springs and take breakfast with Mr. and Mrs. E. C. Jordan, was most welcome. Mr. Jordan had done us good service when awakened early in the morning to point out the roads; my first interview with his beautiful young wife was immediately after, when she rushed out of the house in terror, believing that the Yankees had carried off her husband. What battalions of Confederate soldiers both before and after that day found that there was no limit to the hospitality of the owners of "Jordan's White Sulphur"!

The defeat of Milroy was a most disastrous one; the victory of the Confederates, gained with little loss, correspondingly gratifying. Thirty pieces of artillery, thousands of small arms, stores and equipments of all kinds, and (including the captures by Rodes at Berryville) about four thousand prisoners were the spoils of that battle. My own share of it was a horse, afterward called "Dick Turpin." The most willful, but the toughest, beast I ever owned or rode, he proved invaluable. He was given me because he was so violent no one would have him. The movement of Ewell was quick, skillful and effective—

in fact, Jacksonian; the defense of Milroy was devoid of all military intelligence and actually discreditable. In the two days, the Federal troops were driven out of the Valley, without a battle.

I rode into Winchester and found that the great joy of the people of that faithful town at their release was clouded by their grief at the death of General Jackson: every citizen of the town mourned as for a great personal bereavement. When I left the town I wore a new Confederate cap which a lady had made for me, during the occupancy of the "Yankees." But a new hat for me always foreboded disaster in the next battle, and I was not mistaken in supposing it would be so again. Still I wore the cap until it came.

The next day we marched to Smithfield and encamped for the night, and on the 17th we encamped near Shepherdstown and I visited my home across the Potomac and saw the desolation of war. My beautiful home was a barren waste and a common, and the blackened walls of the burnt barn stood up against the sky as a monument of useless and barbarous destruction. I felt that it would be hard for me, going into Pennsylvania, to put aside all ideas of retaliation.

On the 18th our division crossed the Potomac at Shepherdstown, and were encamped for the night on my father's place. Johnson's Headquarters were at my home, and once more we were out of Virginia. We were waiting for Longstreet's and Hill's corps to come up from across the mountain. I could not get over the feeling that an invasion of the enemy's territory, however tempting, was the wrong policy for us; but at the same time I believed that General Lee must know better than I did. I was conscious of the fact that I was doubting everything since Jackson was gone and was rather ashamed of it. The wisdom of the policy of invasion when we were carrying on a defensive war has been much discussed; it is a subject for discussion and disagreement. The fact is, however, we brought nothing from Pennsylvania which can be considered even partial compensation for what we left at Gettysburg, while we aroused the weary and discouraged people of the North to renewed energy and animosity.

We moved on across Maryland toward Hagerstown, fifteen miles, and passed through. There, while visiting some friends, some ultraloyalist stole my pistols from my holsters, one of which was given me, as I said, by a Federal officer at Harper's Ferry, and the other was presented to me on the field of Second Manassas by General Jackson. If the thief had known what a good ransom these pistols would have brought, I might have heard of them again.

En route to Hagerstown that day, the head of the column was suddenly halted by a novel obstacle. At Tilghmanton, old John Bloom, the toll-gatherer, stepped out of his toll house, let down his gate, and stood by it to bar our passage. I was riding in front with General Johnson and staff, and as we approached the old man accosted us.

"Who is going to pay for all the horses and wagons I see coming?"

"I am, Mr. Bloom," I replied, "I'll give you an order on President Davis—take it to Richmond and get the money."

"Jeff Davis! I'll see him—— But look here! I'll swear! (recognizing me) you're running this crowd, are you? Go long (throwing up the gate). I wonder how long I could stop your army, with this old toll gate. I'll charge the toll to profit and loss."

John Bloom was not truly loyal, but he told me after the war that when he stopped our army on its way to Gettysburg, "it had better taken my advice and gone back into Virginny."

We moved and crossed Mason's and Dixon's Line with an army of about 65,000 of all arms, or about 54,000 infantry. There are various estimates of the strength of the Federal army. General Hooker said he had 105,000 *enlisted* men when he turned the command over to General Meade. It is safe to say the estimate was small enough.

The wheel at Washington was turned again, and "Fighting Joe" Hooker went down and General Meade rose to the top. General Hooker certainly had not made a success of it and did not justify the action of President Lincoln in placing him in command over Franklin and Sumner, who were removed from all command at the same time. We poor Confederates were compelled to struggle on with the same Commander in Chief and his chief lieutenants. We could not afford expensive experiments. We still held on to Lee and Longstreet and Ewell and Hill, and Death only had removed Jackson from command. General Meade was a man of high character and a soldier of excellent reputation; he never lost either.

When General Lee arrived at Chambersburg, a few days after we left, he issued on the 27th of June a general order to his troops. He commended them for their good conduct and impressed upon them with great force that private property of all kinds must be respected. He commanded them to remember that "we make war only on armed men," and must perpetrate no wrongs against the personal liberty of citizens. It had the ring of sincerity and determination. It calmed the fears of the people of the Cumberland Valley; but it is questionable whether one of them ever stopped to reflect that during the war no Federal commander invading the South ever seemed to think that the law of civilized warfare required him to issue such an order.

While we were near Chambersburg a little incident occurred which indicated what a tender memory and stern sense of duty General Jackson had left behind him. Captain Sandy Garber, Assistant Quartermaster of the Second Corps, had been spending the evening in Chambersburg and was returning late at night to his camp. He was halted at the outposts. Having neither pass nor countersign, in his dilemma he produced an old pass signed by General Jackson from his pocketbook and handed it with great confidence to the sentinel on post. The trusty fellow managed to read it by the light of a match and lingered over the signature. Then, as the light went out, he handed it back and looking toward the stars beyond, he said, sadly and firmly,

"Captain, *you can go to Heaven* on that paper, but you can't pass this post."

We stopped for a night near Shippensburg and our Headquarters were at the house of a clergyman who was extremely civil and gave us good entertainment. In the morning, before breakfast, I went to the stable to look after my horse and came upon a scene of merriment as the servants were busy taking out from the hay a new set of harness, saddles, bridles, and other things which had been hidden there. At breakfast I told our host that he was not as thrifty as the proverbial Yankee, or he would not let his valuable goods lie around in such places to give dyspepsia to horses. By that time he had found out that we were not on a plundering expedition and joined in our laughter at his feeble attempts at concealment.

I rode into Carlisle on Saturday to General Ewell's Headquarters. He had once been stationed for a while at the Barracks there—now an Indian School [1]—and being in a talkative mood, had much to say about it. While I was there, a committee waited on him to ascertain whether he had any objection to the prayer for the President of the United States.

"Certainly not," said Old Dick, bluntly, "pray for him. I'm sure he needs it." It was about this time he, himself, began to change. He entered the war a blunt, undevout soldier; he went out of it an earnest and humble Christian.

Soon an order came for concentration, and the faces of all three corps were turned toward Gettysburg. General Lee was satisfied that Meade, who had been showing more activity of movement than his predecessors, was marching toward that point. General Lee had been greatly embarrassed by the absence of Stuart and his cavalry and was compelled to make his combinations in the dark. Stuart had been overdoing the sensational. Much pain has been taken to explain his failure at Gettysburg, but it can hardly be said the explanation is satisfactory. For Stuart to fail at any time to do what was expected of him was a great surprise. Still there is much reason for the belief that the absence of the cavalry left General Lee in such uncertainty that the disaster at Gettysburg may be attributed in great part to it. One thing may be safely asserted: with Jackson alive and Stuart near and in his old form, the battle would not have been fought against Cemetery Hill.

Our corps moved down from Carlisle—except Early, who was at York—and crossed the South Mountain on the 30th of June at Cashtown, and Early moved on Gettysburg from York. Hearing that fighting was going on in the vicinity of

Gettysburg, Johnson pushed on with vigor in that direction; he seemed to be spoiling for a fight with his new division— Jackson's own. It is six miles from Cashtown to Gettysburg and before we had finished little more than half of the distance General Johnson directed me to ride rapidly to General Ewell and say to him that he was marching on Gettysburg rapidly, with his division in prime condition and was ready to put it in as soon as he got there.

I changed to "Dick Turpin," my Milroy horse, in a twinkling and with a courier was off. I reached General Ewell, without the courier, and found him with a group of officers on a hill, looking at Gettysburg and the surroundings. One of these officers was Brigadier General John B. Gordon, fresh from his part of the fight of the afternoon. I gave General Ewell my message and tried to express General Johnson's earnestness as well as I could. When I finished General Gordon seemed to second it, saying that he could join in the attack with his brigade and they could carry that hill—pointing to Cemetery Hill—before dark. Gordon seemed to be as earnest as Johnson in the matter. General Ewell hesitated, as if in thought, and then said quietly,

"General Lee told me to come to Gettysburg and gave me no orders to go further. I do not feel like advancing and making an attack without orders from him, and he is back at Cashtown." He then directed me to tell General Johnson that when he got well to the front, to halt and wait for orders. His remarks silenced all about him, and Gordon said nothing further; but Sandy Pendleton, his Chief of Staff, who was standing near, said to me quietly and with much feeling,

"Oh, for the presence and inspiration of Old Jack for just one hour!"

Yes, but it took the battle of Gettysburg to convince General Lee that General Jackson was really dead; but that did. Colonel Dick Taylor says General Lee sent him to Ewell with a suggestion to press the enemy and thinks it was before Johnson had received his orders to halt. But as General Ewell said to me that General Lee was back at Cashtown and I am sure General Lee, whom we left there, had not passed our column

when I left with Johnson's message to Ewell, I think Colonel
Taylor is mistaken as to the time of his message to Ewell.

The battle of the 1st of July was a spirited one, with something over 20,000 engaged in each side, and one of heavy loss
for its size and duration. It was fought between two corps of
Federal troops under General Reynolds, his own and How-
ards, and four divisions, Heth's and Pender's of Hill's corps,
Rodes' and Early's of Ewell's corps, on the part of the Confederates. That very able and distinguished officer, General
Reynolds was killed, and the gallant Harry Heth and General
Pender were wounded. The Confederates captured about
5,000 prisoners and the Federals claim to have captured 1,000.
The Confederates were entirely successful and the Federal
troops were driven from the field, in much apparent confusion.

After the fighting was over, our division was moved off to
the left around Gettysburg and placed in position in front of,
but some distance from, Culp's Hill for the night. After dark
I rode into town and was hailed by a college mate, who seemed
to have no difficulty in recognizing me at night and took me
into his house. He thought Meade's army had been routed and
ruined, and could not understand my expectations of rough
work ahead on the morrow.

It was the intention of General Lee to make a vigorous attack at all points early in the morning of the 2nd, and orders
were given with that view. Morning came, but General Longstreet did not, and afternoon came, and he was not at hand.
General Longstreet has given his explanation of this tardi-
ness; military critics will determine whether it is sufficient.
One thing is certain, it was a most calamitous delay; it ruined
General Lee's plans, and to it may be ascribed a fair share of
the disaster which overcame our army in the end. General
Longstreet arrived a little before four o'clock and his troops
were soon put in.

There was some severe fighting between that hour and dark.
At Round Top and Devil's Den some savage work was done
by Hood's division, commanded, after he was wounded, by
Law. McLaws had driven Sickles back from the Peach Or-
chard under the eye of General Meade, and Sickles was

wounded. Early attacked the front of Cemetery Hill with great vigor with two brigades and was repulsed. Johnson moved to the foot of Culp's Hill and led his troops into that second Devil's Den. They forced the enemy back up through the wood and rocks in spite of their breastworks, until the Marylanders and the Stonewall Brigade reached the crest at one point within a hundred yards of the Baltimore pike and inside the enemy's breastworks. Could a heavy column of our division have followed this opening and pushed on to the pike, the situation of the enemy would have been a critical one. But night came and the position of our few men in that advanced position was most perilous. The battle ended after a most unsatisfactory day's work. I had occasion to go to the Headquarters of Generals Lee and Ewell and I was not encouraged by any appearance of cheerfulness at either place. General Lee was not in good humor over the miscarriage of his plans and his orders.

The next morning the fight opened early. In front of our division was Culp's Hill, and it was necessary to press troops up that rocky height to the assistance of those who had been there all night, in that "imminent deadly breach." The Light Brigade, commanded by Brigadier General Smith, well known as "Extra-Billy Smith," who had just been elected Governor of Virginia and was anxious to be made a Major General before he retired from the service, was sent by Early to the support of Johnson. This was about 5:00 A.M. The firing had become very heavy and, fearing that General Smith was not aware of the necessity for haste, I galloped to meet and urge him to speed. He was cool and deliberate—too much so, just then, to my apprehension—and he began to question me about the situation.

In my impatience I perhaps forgot the proprieties and told him that, as I was familiar with the exact situation, I would, if he would permit me, lead his brigade in at the right place. To this he courteously assented. I lost no time in getting his column into line of battle and moved it to the rocky ascent. Artillery and musketry were filling the wood with the deadly din of battle and columns of smoke were spreading through the trees and rising into the air through their tops. Were we in time to prevent the destruction or capture of our men upon the crest?

I was riding in front of the line on "Ashby" and officers and men cried to me to dismount. I saw that I was alone on horseback. But I was about to turn the brigade over to its commander, and then it did not seem proper for a staff officer to dismount, although I knew I could not go far on horseback up that breakneck hill. I had given the order to throw some skirmishers to the front as we moved on, and was pointing with my sword, directing the line to the left oblique, when suddenly, from behind trees perhaps a couple of hundred yards up the heights, there sprang a dozen or more sharpshooters, and their muzzles seemed trained on me. I fancied I could look down the barrels and I fancied also they were large enough to crawl into. There came little puffs of smoke, a rattle of small arms, the sensation of a tremendous blow and I sank forward on my horse, who ceased his prancing when my hold was loosened on his bridle reins. The skirmishers sprang forward, up the rocks after those sharpshooters and several officers seized my horse and held me on him, taking my sword from my right hand.

The line passed on. General Smith stopped for a moment to express regret at my wound. I was taken from my horse, carried for half a mile to the rear on a litter and then put in an ambulance, with a surgeon. Before I was out of hearing I knew by the increased noise in the wood that the brigade was seriously engaged—the same brigade, by the way, which I commanded from Petersburg to the surrender at Appomattox.

I had a severe and ragged wound in the left shoulder, the ball having taken in with it a clipping from my coat, shirt, and undershirt, which it cut out in its haste and lodged with its accessories under the clavicle, cutting also some muscles and paralyzing for a time my left arm. My duty in that battle was over.

At the same hill, somewhat further to the left where it was less steep and rocky, Major B. W. Leigh, another member of Johnson's staff, whose name I have mentioned in connection with Jackson's wounding at Chancellorsville, was killed. He

was leading some troops in an attempt to capture the breastworks on the crest and, being also mounted, had forced his way
to within a few yards of the trenches when a volley at close
range laid him low. He was shot through the heart, and his
horse was instantly killed.

There also fell in that assault Wesley Culp, private, Company B, Second Virginia Regiment, Stonewall Brigade. The
Hill was named after his family and he was from Gettysburg.
He was twenty-four years old and very little, if any, over five
feet, and when captain of the company I procured a special
gun for him. When the war broke out he enlisted at Shepherdstown in Company B and was killed in the assault on
Culp's Hill, in sight of the house in which he was born. He
was buried there and sleeps there now.

Johnson's attack was premature, although he did as ordered, for the attack on the opposite side of the position was
not made as promptly as was expected. There was nothing to
prevent Meade from using all the troops he needed to meet
and repulse the attack on Culp's Hill, and he didn't fail to
do it.

On the front of Longstreet and Hill, there was one event on
that day which obscured all others and virtually closed the
battle of Gettysburg. The famous charge of Pickett's division
and its repulse. It was left unsupported and was slaughtered.
Much has been said of Longstreet's failure to do his duty in
that day and he has had his say. That there was a lamentable
failure of co-operation in the Confederate attacks, and that
somebody blundered there can be no question. General Longstreet saw proper, after the war, when both Lee and Jackson
were dead, to become their severest critic and to give signs that
he thought himself superior to either of them as commander.
He, therefore, cannot complain if his pretensions have been
punctured and the light thrown upon his own shortcomings.
"Old Pete" was a doughty fighter, a great soldier during all
the war; but it cannot be said that his course since has added
to his reputation.

General Lee's attacks at Gettysburg having failed, he
retired into Virginia by way of Hagerstown and Williamsport,

Maryland. He had lost about 15,000 killed and wounded and 5,000 prisoners. General Meade's loss was several thousand more in killed and wounded—a result, considering that General Lee made the attacks against strong positions, I am not able to understand—and a little more than 5,000 prisoners. General Meade pursued cautiously and deliberately, in which I think there was more wisdom than he is sometimes credited with.

When I was carried to the rear I was taken several miles on the Hunterstown road and placed in a house which seemed to be vacated, and quite a number of wounded soldiers were taken into the barn. I was laid on the floor of the parlor and during the day not less than half a dozen surgeons came to see and examine me. And among them entered with his long stride my friend, Dr. Hunter McGuire.

"I'm glad to see you're not going to die as I heard you were," he said bluntly, after examining me. "Our old crowd is getting too small. I'll leave Dr. Taney for you and the men in the barn, he's just the man."

And he was, bless his little body and bright brain and his great big heart!

During the day, I found the house was not vacated, for Mr. Henry Picking, the owner, entered and spoke a few kindly words. As the shades of evening fell, a tall, slender, young-looking woman, bearing the sweet likeness of her character upon her face, came softly into the room. It was Mrs. Picking, who with her little children, had gone off in the morning beyond the reach of battle, and had now returned. I began to express my regret at being such an unwelcome intruder and to ask her to remove me out of her parlor to some quiet place where I would be less in the way until I could be removed. She did not let me get far, but stooping down by me, she asked me not to worry, saying the room was less used than any one in the house and the most convenient one for her to look after. She disappeared and in a little while was back again with a bowl of the best chicken soup that culinary skill ever devised. A bed and mattress and equipment followed, and a large sick-chair, for it was painful for me to lie down. When night came I was established, and Mr. Picking made his appearance with his ruddy cheerful face, and bright children looked in at the door. God, every now and then, does make such people as Mr. and Mrs. Henry Picking and breathes into them his spirit of Christian charity, beneficence, and unpretentious nobility, to let the world know to what a high plane he could lift up mankind—if they would only let him. But he doesn't make such often.

Of course, as rapidly as it was possible for a badly wounded man to convalesce, I did in such hands. I was soon of the family and how they did feed me! Children ran in and out and, satisfied that the "big Rebel" was high in authority in the household, they did not hesitate to appeal to me for relief against parental denials, induced thereto by my nurse Smith Shepherd of my old Company B, who had remained behind, a prisoner, to look after me. Mr. Picking showed like kindness to the wounded in the barn, and it is no wonder that as soon as they were convalescent, a number of them took his wagon and horses, hauled in his wheat from the field and stacked it where he wished it. In a few days my mother and sister arrived, having driven from our home on the Potomac through both armies, by themselves, in a buggy to Gettysburg and then to where I was. It was a reckless thing to do, and yet, from the time they left home, during the several days they were on the journey, they met with no disagreeable incident, nor a discourteous word. They came and went in absolute safety and when blocked by artillery or cavalry or wagon trains they were helped on their way.

In spite of intimations from neighbors of a different stamp that such kindness toward the enemies of the Union was scarcely consistent with strict loyalty and that there might be a day of reckoning, Mr. and Mrs. Picking went their way. Good deeds rarely do harm, and it is pleasing to recall that soon after Mr. Picking was called from his farm by being elected surveyor of his county, and as such took an active part in laying out that wonderful battlefield. He lived a life of usefulness and integrity and died regretted by all his fellow citizens.

In a few days I was visited by a Federal Major, S. B. M,

Young of the Fourth Pennsylvania Cavalry, who admitted me to parole with the soldiers in the barn, by a paper which now lies before me, in his handwriting signed by both of us, in duplicate. I shall have something to say hereafter in regard to this parole. Major Young was a fine-looking man of soldierly courtesy, and it is gratifying to me that with years he has grown in rank and honors, until he is now Major General, United States Army, commanding the camp of volunteers at Augusta, Georgia; my old regiment, the First Maryland Infantry, U.S.V., is under his command.

Then came from York an ante-bellum friend of college days, Chauncey F. Black, son of Judge Jeremiah Black,[2] a new bridegroom rejoicing in his happiness and in a kindly frame of mind toward friends in any uniform. He brought with him a box of assorted wines and liquors, which he especially commended to my taste because with the assistance of his young wife he had confiscated them from the cellar of the Honorable John L. Dawson, his father-in-law. We took a sample, and greatly did his wit and humor add to the bouquet of the tipple. Then he brought me a note, too, from his good mother who offered to procure through Governor A. S. Curtin permission for me to be taken to her home for care and treatment. Of this offer I only considered the courtesy and the charity, for I knew it would not do. Judge Black, having been in Mr. Buchanan's Cabinet, was still under the ban of public suspicion in the North, and as he had started Edward M. Stanton in his national career by getting him into the same cabinet it was natural to a man of the type and ingratitude of Stanton that, when as Secretary of War he became military dictator, he should be as offensive as possible to his former patron. I, therefore, declined the kind invitation. People from Lancaster, Harrisburg, and Chambersburg came to view the field of battle and I had no lack of visits from old friends and acquaintances.

After the middle of July I was taken into Gettysburg and put in the Theological Seminary, which was used as a hospital. There I found General Trimble and General (afterwards Governor) Kemper [3] of Virginia, and other officers. It happened the first visitor I had the day I arrived was the Reverend Dr. Philip Schaff of Mercersburg Seminary, who, after shaking his cane at me because I had insulted his white horse by telling our cavalry not to take him as he was fifty years old and not within the age of conscription, said he was at least gratified to see me where he had hoped I would have come more willingly—in a Theological Seminary! This ecclesiastical sally got abroad and, needless to say, each clergyman who visited me repeated it in his individual style: clerical humor has always its own peculiar flavor.

WOUNDED AND IN PRISON

I REMAINED at Gettysburg for more than a month. I had nothing to complain of and no sympathy with those who looked for something unpleasant and found it. Dr. Ward, the surgeon in charge, was not only thoroughly qualified for his position, but he did not think it necessary to impress upon his captives that he had an eye on them and was incensed at their iniquity. He was a gentleman, from Indiana I believe. His assistant, who had immediate professional charge of me, was my personal friend, Dr. Harry Leaman of Lancaster, now of Philadelphia. I had known him at college: his brother was in the class before me, he in the one after me. His daily visits, often two or three a day, were a personal pleasure.

And then appeared upon the scene a little Sister from St. Joseph's at Emmittsburg. She looked very young and was very capable; she touched my room so as to make me forget I was in prison; she made me delicate things to eat until I thought peacocks brains would be no delicacy. She was from Mississippi and had a young brother in the Confederate army. Her beauty was her only tinge of mortality—how fresh and beautiful she was! But her devotion to duty, her self-forgetfulness, her gentle manner must have made every man she met her friend and guardian. And then, when no longer needed, she glided away—went to other duties, doubtless, never looking behind. There is no crown in Heaven too good for such an angel!

We had many visitors, some from curiosity, some in kindness. There was a comfortable chair which one man had sent me, and a lady brought the dainty curtains, which my "Little Catholic Sister" hung at the window, gracefully veiling with her deft white hands the blue sky beyond, to which she seemed to belong.

I was furnished with books, too, light and interesting, and one day a young gentleman, Mr. Samuel M. Smucker[1] brought me *Les Miserables*. It was just what I wanted in that place—plenty of reading for plenty of time, full of war and of love, full of wit, wisdom, everything; never before nor since have I ever enjoyed a book so much. It was translated, I remember, by a lady from Savannah, Georgia, during the war and, being admirably done, was reprinted in the North. Anyone who has read it can well understand what a treat it would be at such a time and in such a place.

Nearby lived two young ladies who were great favorites in the Hospital because their generous hearts did not, apparently, distinguish the color of uniforms—loyal as they were —and on occasional nights, when Dr. Ward was conveniently absent or not visible, I would stroll with them to make visits in the town, the marks on the sleeve of my uninjured arm being artfully concealed by some little female headgear which I was directed to carry just that way; and marching between the sisters—*in medio tutissimus ibis*—we generally landed at Duncan's and made an evening of it. It never seemed to occur to them that they were harboring a Rebel; and nothing occurred to me except their graciousness and attractiveness.

Before I left the Theological Seminary, I entrusted to Dr. Leaman a map which I valued, for it was one of the maps used by General Jackson in his Maryland and Valley campaign, which he had afterwards given to me. Dr. Leaman was to keep it until after the war, and then, if I were living, he was to return it to me, if not living, to keep it as a souvenir of our meeting at Gettysburg. When my imprisonment ended and I got back to Dixie, I was soon active in the army and forgot what had become of the map. After keeping it safely for twenty-nine years Leaman wrote to me that he had lost it twice and rediscovered it, and, in order to relieve himself of the trust, he sent it to me. It is among the few mementoes of the war I have not been persuaded to part with.

I left the ecclesiastical hospital with regrets for I did not again expect to be so well placed, and never was. I was taken to Baltimore and confined in West Buildings Hospital under stricter regulations. The surgeon in charge, Dr. George Rex, tried to make believe, by his growling and unsmiling countenance, that he was an old bear, but there were a lot of us he didn't deceive. He was simply an old gnarled oak with rough bark, sound and all right at the heart. I had a lot of friends in Baltimore who *would* send me things against the rules. The Doctor would publicly refuse to let me have them and turn them over to the female stewardess, or housekeeper, or whatever she was; and I got them. They were two of a kind, and she was just as much of a fraud in her generous way as he was.

"Douglas, you *must* write to your friend Johnston." (Henry E. Johnston, a banker, whose kindness had no bounds because I had been able to do his brother, Elliott, a small favor when he was wounded and lost a leg at Sharpsburg.) "He ought to know that I couldn't let you have that wine and bottles of brandy and whiskey he sent to you today. I turned it over to the stewardess."

"All right, Doctor, I'll do it"; and I did. I wrote to Johnston not to send me any more such forbidden fruit—until this was gone. When evening came, the stewardess sent for me and told me in the tones of a shrew that she must set her face against such donations—and then gave them to me as I wanted them.

Many a sick and wounded prisoner, who had no friends in Baltimore, found imprisonment and suffering more tolerable because of the good things to eat and drink that Johnston, his good mother and sister, and others of the same disposition lavished upon me at the West Buildings. Unless they believed I was a hydra-headed cormorant, they never expected me to devour such supplies of high-toned commissary stores. But it was all just like Baltimore in those days, and all days after, when suffering was abroad in the South. And Dr. Rex and

his female coadjutor were just like themselves and like no
other pair I ever met. As jailors they were trumps. I had
books and flowers sent me and a box of dominoes, a Yankee
puzzle, and a jewsharp. The last is the only musical instru-
ment I ever studied with any success. I wrestled with it valor-
ously but just as I began to understand its technique and
comprehend its expression and realize the beauty of its simplicity, it disappeared. Some people have no ear for music.

I have spoken of the parole given me at Gettysburg by
Major Young, Fourth Pennsylvania Cavalry. This is the
language of it, written by Major Young:

"Know all men that we the undersigned in consideration
of our release from capture by the military authorities of the
United States do hereby solemnly pledge our word of honor
not to do or undertake any act or to exert any influence for
the advantage of the Confederate army or against the Government of the United States during the continuance of the
present war or until regularly included in an authorized exchange of prisoners of war." (Here follows the signatures
of myself and the wounded in the barn of Mr. Picking.)

"Signed in presence of
          "HY. KYD DOUGLAS, Maj. and A. A. Genl.
          "S.B.M. YOUNG, Major 4 Penn. Cavl."

In Gettysburg, when well enough, I had sent the paper to
General D. N. Couch, United States Army, asking that I
be relieved from confinement. After some weeks he returned
it, saying he was without authority in the matter and I had
better apply to the War Department. On the 27th of September, while at West Buildings, I addressed a communication
to General Lorenzo Thomas, Adjutant General, enclosing a
copy of the foregoing paper and asking that under its terms
I be released from confinement on parole. I stated that I had
given my parole in good faith and believed that I was bound
by it, that I had strictly observed its provisions, that I had
supposed Major Young had a right to require such a parole
from me and to take it, that if he had not, I was in no fault,

that I had released Major J. H. Whittlesey, Fifth United States Cavalry, when captured, sick in Winchester in May, 1862, in the same way and he was allowed to return to his lines (enclosing a strong letter from Major Whittlesey confirming my statement as to his release and that of other officers),[2] that I had not doubted that I would be released, when sufficiently recovered, upon application, and that now I made the application in accordance with the written parole.

This communication was kindly delivered at the War Department by Captain Horatio C. King of General Samuel Heintzelman's staff. Being referred to Colonel William H. Hoffman, Commissary General of prisoners, it was returned by him to me through General R. C. Schenck's Headquarters with an endorsement: that my parole was "only a personal obligation" between myself and Major Young; that if I had made my "escape while under parole and had again been captured by the U. S. forces," I "could not have been held for break of parole"; that my parole "only remained in force until a superior authority thought proper to set it aside"; that I was simply like any "other prisoner of war." The petition was refused, and from this there was no appeal. While appreciating the grim irony of such reasoning, I knew perfectly well that if I had escaped, got into battle, killed some Union officer, and been recaptured, the same Colonel Hoffman would have given better reasons for shooting or hanging me.

It was then thought I was combative enough to get out of a hospital and should be removed hence. I was started northward, and celebrated my birthday on September 29, 1863, by landing at Johnson's Island military prison, out in Lake Erie, and off from Sandusky, Ohio. I soon found that I was in a much colder temperature, climatic and otherwise. But I had plenty of company, about 1,500 Confederate officers of all ranks, and several hundred privates. Still the 42° of Latitude, North, is hardly the place Southerners would select as a winter resort. Johnson's Island, however, was just the place to convert visitors to the theological belief of the Norwegian that Hell has torments of cold instead of heat.

To a newcomer the outlook was not hopeful. The prison

was an oblong, bare piece of ground enclosed by a high fence, and perched up on this fence, or barricade, at intervals, in sentry boxes, were armed sentinels. The barracks or prison houses were long buildings, hastily erected of wood and weatherboard, called wards. The weatherboarding was a single layer nailed to upright beams, and there was no plastering of any kind. The weatherboarding would sometimes warp, and in all rooms there were many knotholes, through which one lying in bed could look out upon the moon or the water; but when the weather got below zero, the scenery was scarcely compensation for the suffering. Bunks were ranged along the walls—if they can be called walls—in three tiers. In my room or ward, there were sixty of these. There was one stove in the middle of the room, which kept the room fairly comfortable within a certain range, except in very cold weather. It was about like living in a canvas tent. Of course out on that lake, the weather became excessively cold, below zero, and not infrequently drove the sentinels from their posts, knowing well enough that no prisoner could escape and live.

On the 9th and 21st of January, 1864—I am not so sure of one of the dates—the thermometer fell to 28° below zero. The former of the two nights I spent in the hospital, which was in the enclosure, nursing a very young fellow from Mobile, who, babbling in his delirium of flowers and fields and playing with his mother and sister in his sunny land, died before morning. During the night Captain Stagg of a Louisiana regiment was frozen so badly that when he was discovered in the morning he was speechless, and it required vigorous measures under a physician's directions to restore him. That same night, as often before or after, two men would squeeze into one bunk so as to double blankets, would wrap themselves up head and feet, and in the morning break through crackling ice, formed by the congealing of the breath that escaped, as one has seen on the blankets of horses in sleighing time.

Poor Captain Stagg had other troubles. His wife was in New Orleans, always used Creole French, and could neither read nor write English. She evidently regarded English with as much disfavor as some of the Pennsylvania Dutch. But as the letter censor could not read French—and all our letters were read—the Captain's letters to and from his wife could not pass that Cerberus. Stagg was in despair until my namesake, Major Henry Douglas, United States Army, whom I did not know, came to the rescue at my request and kindly took charge of that correspondence.

There has been much crimination and recrimination as to the relative treatment of prisoners at Andersonville and Johnson's Island, Libby Prison and Camp Douglas at Chicago. Into this I do not propose to enter. That there was a deal of suffering by those confined in Southern prisons I have no doubt; that the guards and managers of these prisons were often grossly negligent and careless of the health and comfort of their prisoners I do not question. Prisoners therein suffered from the same criminal neglect and ignorance that the Confederate soldiers in the field suffered from. But the conditions of the two peoples were entirely different. The North had everything it wanted and the world to draw from. With a large territory, exposed to invasion on only one border, it could place its prisons and hospitals where it preferred. The South was cut off from the world; was being invaded on all sides; scarcely knew where it could safely locate its prisons and hospitals; had little in itself and access to nothing it hadn't; medicine and drugs, especially such as are needed as a protection against fever, were contraband—that seems barbarous— and very scarce; and at last had so little food that the soldiers in the field became as emaciated and haggard as their prisoners.

With such a large, protected territory, I do not think any fair man in the North will attempt to defend the selection of Lake Erie as a winter prison for Southern soldiers, any more than he would have excused the selection of the malarial regions of southern Florida or Louisiana as a summer prison for Northern troops. Personally, I believe that the general suffering and ill treatment of prisoners on both sides have been grossly exaggerated, and I do not believe, with exceptions here and there, that there was intentional and willful cruelty on either side as a rule; there were hardships and suffering among prisoners on both sides from neglect, incompetency, and indifference.

If half the statements about the treatment of our soldiers in the Spanish war by their own government are true, its inhumanity exceeds anything that was ever charged against either government during the four terrible years of the Civil War. They were sometimes half-starved for want of food, but they were never poisoned with it.[3] At any rate, when it is known that out of 270,000 prisoners in the South 22,576 died, and out of 220,000 Southern prisoners in the North 26,246 died, it ought to stop a great deal of the wild talk about Libby Prison and Andersonville.

The food we received at Johnson's Island was not, except at times, such as a prisoner had a right to complain of. Then, too, we were allowed to receive boxes of provisions, under reasonable restrictions, from our friends, and we received many such contributions. It may be stated frankly that the Southern people never forgot their soldiers in prison and, however reduced in circumstances, never missed an opportunity to send them what they could; their many friends in the North acted much in the same way. On the contrary, Northern people were singularly indifferent to the fate of their own soldiers and took little pains, individually, to assist them. Of course there were many exceptions where there were sons or brothers in captivity, but I have heard the complaint made time and again by Union soldiers and bitter contrasts drawn. This may be because there were so many foreigners and substitutes in the Federal army and so many others who looked to the government for help; for some reason not much thought was given to the wants of those in captivity.

The hospital arrangements and the medical attendance were good. The officers and guards, with rare exceptions, were civil and considerate. There was a regulation that all lights must be out at 10:00 P.M. and no visiting was allowed between different buildings or wards after 9:00. On one or two occasions drunken sentinels on post fired into wards through the weatherboarding at candles that had been lighted because of the sudden sickness of a prisoner; on another, a man was shot in the thigh running to his ward, after he had overstayed the hour of 9:00 visiting friends.

The regulations limited the length of the letters we wrote or received to one page of note paper, because the censor could not get through such a mass of letters, daily, if there was not some limit to their length. This was plausible, but it was a nuisance all the same. General M. Jefferson Thompson sent for the censor, an excellent fellow, to whom I was indebted for many kindnesses afterwards, and made an arrangement by which he was to put aside all long letters until night and then examine them for the compensation of one-half cent for each and every page over the allowance, to be paid at the end of each week by an order on the Treasurer outside, who kept our money. It was a great scheme all around; the censor, a sergeant, quadrupled his soldier's pay, and we got bulky letters, which we were satisfied he never looked at, except to tear open and count the pages. I had bundles of letters of twenty and more pages, and wrote the same, and hours were spent reading and writing them.

There came a carload of boxes for the prisoners about Christmas which, after reasonable inspection, they were allowed to receive. My box from home contained more cause for merriment and speculation as to its contents than satisfaction. It had received rough treatment on its way, and a bottle of catsup had been broken and its contents very generally distributed through the box. Mince pie and fruit cake saturated with tomato catsup was about as palatable as "embalmed beef" of Cuban memory;[3] but there were other things. Then, too, a friend had sent me in a package a bottle of old brandy. On Christmas morning I quietly called several comrades up into my bunk to taste of the precious fluid—of disappointment. The bottle had been opened outside, the brandy taken and replaced with water, adroitly recorked, and sent in. I hope the Yankee who played that practical joke lived to repent it and was shot before the war ended. But then there came from my same friend, Johnston of Baltimore,[4] a box containing thirty pieces of clothing, for such disposition as I chose to

Ferry Hill Place as it is today

Nannie C. Douglas (Mrs. John M. Beckenbaugh), sister of Henry Kyd Douglas, in 1865 when she was twenty years old

Henry Kyd Douglas at Point Lookout, a prisoner. March, 1864

make of them, and another box of hams, chickens, biscuits and cigars for my own mess; and from Mrs. Mary T. Semmes —aunt of the "Alabama" Semmes—another wholesale box of coffee, whiskey, sugar, cigars, gloves, soap, worsted night-caps, Tennyson's poems, a spinning top (from her grandson), etc. She duplicated it afterwards.

There was nothing about Johnson's Island to resemble the one Robinson Crusoe was cast up on except the absence of the fair sex; but we heard from them. He didn't. News from home told of the death of my horse, "Prince," the one my mother had driven to Gettysburg. He was blind and had fallen over the cliffs into the canal and drowned. I sent my sister a dozen stanzas—in memoriam—which kept up my temperature for a while.

I was surprised about this time to receive a letter from Enoch, whom I have spoken of as my father's colored coach-man. He had gone off from home and was living in Harris-burg, Pennsylvania, working for his living, in freedom, but harder than he ever did in his life. He wrote to say that he heard I was wounded and in prison and was having a hard time, and that he had laid aside several hundred dollars and would send it to me, or as much as I wanted, if I were suffering or needed it. His letter was in his own untutored language, but its words were verily apples of gold. I did not need his money, but I hope I wrote him a letter that left no doubt of my ap-preciation and my gratitude. Poor Enoch, I never saw him again. I do not know that he survived the war; but our old "Aunt Hannah," his companion in slavery, said "he worked hisself to death for a lazy yaller free nigger gal he married up there." In his case, freedom brought him only bondage.

Early in February I was taken with chills which I was advised was a dangerous symptom in that climate at that sea-son of the year. About the middle of the month several hundred of the prisoners were to be taken farther south, but my name was not on the list. My friend the letter censor had become anxious as to the result of my chills, and he undertook upon his own motion to get my name on the list. I was not particu-larly informed of the method by which it was done, but years afterwards when I heard of men in cities casting their political ballots in dead men's names, I was not as surprised as I might have been. My faithful sergeant took, for humanity's sake, a double risk, for he not only was passing out of that prison one who was expected to remain, but he was perhaps saving the life of a Rebel soldier, who thus with his aid did "live to fight another day." General Jeff Thompson of Missouri was one of those sent out and may be said to have been the leader of that expedition. Arrayed in a black overcoat with a black cape, I looked more like a young clergyman than ever, and it pleased Thompson to refer to me as his chaplain.

We had a prisoners' ovation going through Baltimore and were hustled through that city at a quick step and put on board a steamer for Point Lookout, a point of land in southern Maryland on the west coast of the Chesapeake Bay, on which there was a prison and a hospital. I was rather startled to see the next day in a Philadelphia paper that after passing Harrisburg I had attempted to make my escape by jumping off the train, was thrown under the cars, and had my legs cut off. Some letters of enquiry followed hurriedly, and the rumor disarranged my correspondence for some time. I understood afterwards that some one had attempted that feat and was killed.

I was now in a much milder climate and the place was still different from any other I had seen. I began to look about me and adapt myself to the situation and soon found the change from Johnson's Island an agreeable one. I was soon on pleasant terms with Captain Patterson, the Provost Marshall, an excellent officer who managed to do his duty strictly, but with admirable suavity. His wife and his wife's sister, being Southern women, were not excessively loyal, although very discreet; and the sister saw no harm in furnishing me books and strolling along the beach at times within bounds: and neither did I. We fought over *Vanity Fair*—and I gave her the name of Becky Sharp—but we did not fight over the war, for I was fond of the little suppers I was invited to.

General E. B. Tyler, commanding, with Headquarters at

Baltimore, came once to the prison and called to deliver a letter entrusted to him from a friend of mine he knew. He was extremely courteous and then began an acquaintance and friendship which lasted until his death, years after the war. After he left, all my letters were sent to the care of Captain Patterson and I received them unopened. My replies went out with the same security—under the promise of course that I neither would send nor receive any letters not strictly personal. I was in Ward 15, Hammond General Hospital, and there was a surgeon of like civility to whom some of my letters were addressed. One is lying before me now, which contained a photograph I still have after these thirty-five years; and another, containing two pages of rhyme, clever, humorous and a bit satirical; and another accompanying some bottles of peach brandy and a bottle of quaker honey, that I might have "peach-and-honey" as a morning tipple. Although I never could take a breakfast appetizer I, at least, could enjoy the pleasure it gave my wardmates, Colonel Gibson of Georgia, Colonel Leventhrope of North Carolina, and our surgeon, the good Dr. M——.

After a month at Point Lookout, rumors of coming exchange were flying through the air. General B. F. Butler, Federal Commissioner of Exchange at Fortress Monroe, had visited the Hospital and inspected it. "Butcher" Weyler[5] was never more hated by the Cubans, than "Beast" Butler was, at that time, by Confederates. When he passed through our ward, there was death-like silence. He asked if there were any complaints of treatment; no one spoke. That they should be his prisoners added gall to their bitterness.

A few days after, on the 17th of March, a large vessel came steaming up to the Point, sent for prisoners. There was excitement and bustle through prison wards and hospital. Word was sent for those who were to leave to pack up and get ready at once and there was no delay. I slipped over to Captain Patterson's to tell the news of my departure and to get a last lunch in that lovely and hospitable household. When the time came everybody was at the boat and the soldiers quickly crowded aboard. I lingered to talk to those who had been so kind to me and among the last ascended the gang-plank with all my impedimenta.

Just as I touched the boat, a young officer hastily came up and took me off. Orders had come from Brigadier General Gilmon Marston, commanding the post, that I was not to be exchanged, and a private took my black hand trunk and bundle to carry them back to prison. I had met Major John E. Mulford, the Federal agent for exchange of prisoners, on the boat coming from Baltimore and he had been exceedingly civil to me. The young officer who had charge of me, evidently chagrined with his duty, offered his assistance in every way. He asked for Major Mulford; he was not on board. The Captain said he would take a note to him, and I hastily wrote him of what had happened and asked his intervention. The ropes were loosened, the whistle blown, and soon the boat, laden with rejoicing men, was churning the water into foam as it moved toward Dixie. Dejected, in spite of the cheerful attitude of "Becky Sharp" and others, I moved back to my old ward, nearly emptied out; and it did not add buoyancy to my spirits to be told, as I was, that it was rumored at Marston's Headquarters that I was to be put in irons and close confinement in retaliation for someone thus being punished in Richmond. I had a good, long, late supper that night at any rate. But when the Doctor came with me to the gloomy ward, I quickly got into my cot and was soon asleep.

About three o'clock at night there was a flash of light upon my face, and I awoke to see a group of officers standing near. Was it necessary to put a man in irons at this unseemly hour of night? I began to growl: why this infernal haste, etc.? My sleepy mutterings were broken by the cheery voice of Patterson,

"Hurry up, don't swear, dress yourself and get out of this quick if you want to go to Dixie!"

Enough said. I was dressed in a twinkling.

"This is Captain Puffer of General Butler's staff, and the General has sent for you."

In a few minutes we were on the boat and off for Old Point, and on the *Greyhound,* the General's famous dispatch boat, the fastest one afloat. Major Mulford had received my note, had seen General Butler, and this was the result, in spite of General Marston's order.

What a host on such a boat Captain A. T. Puffer was.

"Breakfast, there, a good one, at daylight and steaming hot," he cried out to a man below.

Upon the first invitation I reversed my decision not to take an "antifogmatic" so early in the morning. There were half a dozen in the party besides Captain Puffer, who was half a dozen more. We took "morning bitters" with one, "an eye-opener" with another, a "pre-prandial" with another, and then an "appetizer" all together, and when breakfast was ready at daylight, so were we.

The little boat ran through the water like a shark, and in the quickest possible time we were under the shadow of Fortress Monroe. A little off rocked the boat which had left me behind at Point Lookout, and in a little while, after saying my thanks and good-by to Captain Puffer and his delightful party, I was on board of her, shaking hands with Major Mulford.

I did not see General Butler, and had no opportunity to ascertain the cause of his extraordinary kindness in taking me out of the clutches of General Marston. Years afterwards, when he was Governor of Massachusetts, he came to Bar Harbor, where I was, for an outing on his yacht *American*, and invited me with several gentlemen to go out one day for some deep-sea fishing. Sitting on deck on our return, over a glass of rum and aerated water, I broached the subject, and ascertained what I wanted to know.

At the time I speak of, it will be remembered that he was in very bad odor with the Confederate government, and he and Judge Ould, the Confederate Commissioner of Exchange, had been carrying on a correspondence so acrid and so full of vituperative heat that their letters would doubtless have set fire to the mails, had they not been carried by water. This was all official and for public consumption and exasperation, whereas between themselves their mutual indignation and hurling of epithets were purely Pickwickian. War has its side lights and byplays. These two frowning officials, who had known each other well before the War and I think had been together in the National Democratic Convention in Charleston, South Carolina, in 1860,[6] when Butler voted fifty-seven ballots to nominate Jefferson Davis as the Democratic candidate for President, had a personal agreement that whatever be the obstacles in Exchange, they would each show courtesy enough to the other to send through any prisoners especially asked for.

It seems that Judge Ould had asked that Captain Cabell Breckinridge, a son of General John C. Breckinridge, Major Buckner, a brother, I think, of Major General Simon B. Buckner,[7] and myself be sent through for exchange, and perhaps others. Of course General Butler could not allow any little plans General Marston might have for my further incarceration to interfere with his promise to Judge Ould! Hence the proceedings I have related, which I could not explain until I saw Governor Butler. I asked him, then, after my convivial friend Captain Puffer and found he had gone to the other side of the inevitable river.

We left Fortress Monroe some time during the day and when we were well under way Major Mulford sent down into the vessel among the prisoners and directed that Buckner, Breckinridge and myself should join him on deck. He kindly took us into the salon of the boat and introduced us to his wife and sister, by whom we were received most graciously. After this both Breckinridge and Buckner vanish from my recollection, although they doubtless fared just as well. I was given comfortable quarters in a stateroom and the hold of that vessel knew me no more.

To add to the novelty of the situation and its fascinating excitement, I was introduced to Mrs. M. Todd White of Alabama, who was immediately given to my charge to escort to Richmond, which proved to be a most agreeable duty. Mrs. White was a sister, a half-sister, of Mrs. President Lincoln, and now that she is dead at an untimely age I may add, was young, handsome, and of great personal charm of manner.[8] Six weeks before she had gone through the lines, partially on a visit to her sister at the White House, and was now returning.

What she had in the thirteen trunks she now carried was of much curiosity to General Butler, when I saw him. He had not permitted them to be examined at Fortress Monroe, for he suspected there might be some things discovered that were contraband. This discovery would have involved the detention of Mrs. White and her trunks, a public disclosure, his own embarrassment and the especial embarrassment of President Lincoln, who would have released her and brought on himself bombardment from the Democratic press of the North. All this "Old Ben" took in when the Provost Marshall reported to him this mass of luggage, and he shrewdly adopted the wisest and most politic course by letting Mrs. White and her trunks go on their way.

I can account for one of the trunks, for it was turned over to me at Richmond for delivery: it contained the trousseau of Miss Hetty Carey of Baltimore, then in Richmond. She was the most beautiful woman of her day and generation; in January of the next year she became the bride of General John Pegram and was a widow within three weeks.[9] General John Morgan, having escaped from prison, arrived in Richmond just then, and he and his staff might have told the contents of another trunk which was intended for a hospital. But no hospital can successfully compete with a Kentucky woman's hospitality to a Kentucky hero.

At City Point on the 19th we took leave of Major John E. Mulford and his charming family. The name of this courteous and generous gentlemen should be held in lasting memory in every Southern household who had a prisoner of war pass through his hands; and it is pleasant to recall that when, after the war, he sought to make Richmond his home, he could have gone nowhere, where he would have been welcomed and received with more cordiality and good-will.

Not knowing the straits to which Richmond had been reduced in matters of luxury since Gettysburg, I telegraphed from City Point for a carriage and baggage wagon to meet me at the wharf on the arrival of our boat, in provision for Mrs. White and her luggage. I wish I had a photograph of the turnout which an old dilapidated Negro, with a burnished, napless silk hat, brought for us: a decaying carriage with two old condemned horses, leaning against each other for mutual support, and a baggage wagon and horses a few shades worse. But they managed to haul us to "The Spotswood," passing the Capitol grounds where President Davis was reviewing the returned prisoners, for which service I paid the polite old darkey, the modest compensation of one hundred dollars, in Confederate money.

The next night, upon invitation of the President, Mrs. White called upon him and Mrs. Davis. I took her in the same turnout, for the same compensation, and met the occupants of the Confederate White House. Mr. Davis who was one of the most dignified and accomplished men that ever occupied a public position, impressed me with the respect and admiration which all men had in his presence, Mrs. Davis with the entertaining cleverness and keen perception that always marked her conversations. Mrs. White, like all her sisters, was a Kentuckian, a Southerner, and a Confederate in every impulse of her nature. Mrs. Lincoln, herself, and Mrs. Grant were loyal to their great husbands and their husbands' cause, but their kindly feelings for their own Southern people were well-known.[10]

Confederate currency had long ceased to maintain any respectable commercial relation with gold; before long it fell below 16 to 1, and gave us warning that a government fiat cannot give value to money. I paid $30 per day for board at "The Spotswood," it cost a friend $300 to give half a dozen of us a night supper at an eating house, and a little later I gave $9.75 (why not $10.00?) for two mint juleps, $1,500 for a uniform, and was offered $5,800 for a horse worth, perhaps, $250. About this time a Confederate cavalryman, being offered $5,000 for a somewhat seedy-looking steed, proudly reined up his bony Bucephalus and explained,

"Five thousand dollars for this horse! Why, I gave a thousand dollars this morning for currying him!"

The Confederate soldier was then serving his country for less than forty cents a month in gold; he was virtually fighting without pay, without bounty, and with no expectation of a pension. Pay day became a sarcasm and a jest. The soldiers' money would buy nothing; it was only good to gamble with.

> *But our boys thought little of price or pay*
> *Or of bills that were over due;*
> *We knew if it bought our bread today*
> *'Twas the best our poor country could do.*
> *I'll keep it—it tells our history o'er*
> *From the birth of our dreams to its last,*
> *Modest and born of an Angel Hope,*
> *Like our hope of success,* it passed.

GRANT *VERSUS* LEE

AFTER a week spent at Richmond in expensive inactivity, I made a visit to the Headquarters of General Edward Johnson on the Rapidan. I was still on parole, unexchanged, and unable to go upon duty. I took note of the situation and the condition of the army; nothing seemed as satisfactory as upon the opening of the campaign of 1863. The troops were not in the same spirits and certainly not as well equipped, and yet they seemed ready for a fight, as they proved to be upon the first demonstration against them. I dined with General Lee and General Ewell and gathered such information as I could.

But being of no service, I left after a week's visit and went to the Valley of Virginia to see some friends at Woodstock. From there I went down one day through our lines to Strasburg. There Major Holmes Conrad [1]—afterwards Solicitor General under President Cleveland—made his appearance, and we moved further on. When night came on we started to penetrate the enemy's lines and enter Winchester, which was in their possession. This we did on foot, of course, and, passing through the field where the Confederate Cemetery now is and through an old graveyard, we entered upon the premises where Conrad's father lived and were admitted to the house through a back door by their faithful old slave, Esau. There we remained several days, enjoying the exciting hospitality of that always hospitable home. One night I went out, for we were about the center of the town, to make several visits and succeeded in passing small squads of Yankees on street corners unmolested. But when midnight had passed, we took our de-

parture and went as we came, passing through the lines in
safety. The next morning, a squadron of Federal cavalry
called at the house and politely enquired for us. They were
frankly told we had been there on a little visit but had taken
our departure. The squadron pursued with some vigor, but we
had too much start. Major Conrad had gone on his horse, and,
being informed in Strasburg that we were pursued by cavalry,
seen beyond Cedar Creek, I gave an old man thirty dollars to
take me to Woodstock in an old wagon with as much speed as
his dreary team was equal to. Riding along the road I wondered, if I had been captured, what view the Federal authorities would have taken then of Major S. B. M. Young's parole.
But in those days, one took little thought of risks, in which
there was a bit of romance.

After a stop of a week more at Dr. Murphy's, that home
of beauty, graciousness, and boundless hospitality in Woodstock, I went to Lexington, Virginia. I had nothing else to do;
and this kind of a furlough became something of an elephant
on my hands, with no home to go to. But I found bountiful
hospitality and kindness in Lexington at the house of General
F. H. Smith, Superintendent of the Virginia Military Institute, and his accomplished family. I wished also to consult
General Smith, Governor John Letcher, and others about the
project rarely out of my mind, then, of putting a tomb or
monument over the grave of General Jackson. My visit to it
while at Lexington and its appearance of melancholy loneli-
ness intensified my desire, and I worked at it that year until
work became hopeless.

Leaving Lexington, I became impatient for my exchange,
and after a brief stay of pleasure with the big-hearted family
of Colonel Mike Harman in Staunton, I went to Richmond
to see what I could do about it. I was quickly successful and
started at once for the army, for the air was filled with rumors
of coming movements. I went up on the train from Richmond
with Mrs. J.E.B. Stuart and her little son, the willfullest
and most unmanageable youngster that ever sprung from a
military sire to test the patience and affection of an amiable
mother. Mrs. Stuart was met at Gordonsville by Dr. Talcott

Eliason of General Stuart's staff, who had been sent to tell her that the General was on the move and bade her return to Ashland or Richmond. Anticipation gave way to sadness, and for a moment tears came into her eyes—ominous tears, for she never again saw her husband alive. This news hurried me off to the army and Dr. Eliason took charge of Mrs. Stuart.

Again the Army of the Potomac had changed commanders. General Grant—now Lieutenant General—had arrived and assumed complete control of the campaign, although General Meade remained in immediate command of the troops. General Grant's advent boded only evil for us. It was evident he intended to control the situation at Washington as well as the army in the field, and the days of dictation from the War Department were over. Everything he wanted was given him, troops, equipment, supplies, transportation. He assumed no mock modesty in taking command. On the contrary, notwithstanding the admirable simplicity of his nature and the unostentatious manliness of his character, there was a suggestion of egotism in his language and conduct at that time, that also crops out now and then in his *Personal Memoirs*. He more than intimated and unquestionably believed that the Army of the Potomac never had been fought to its limit, and this he proposed to do himself. He also believed that the ability of General Lee and his lieutenants had been overestimated by the North and its army. As this self-confidence took no such doubtful shape as that of General Pope, it may well be believed that it gave confidence and encouragement to the Army under him.

General Grant had no occasion to cry aloud, like some of his predecessors, for more troops. His rolls showed that at the opening of the campaign, he had in the Army of the Potomac 140,000 soldiers. It is therefore safe to say he opened the campaign of 1864 with 120,000 effectives in that army. He also had under his command, not far off, the Army of the James, under General B. F. Butler, with about 36,000 more troops. It is not probable that out of the 64,000 troops which composed the Army of Northern Virginia—including Longstreet's command which was absent when the campaign opened

—General Lee had more than 60,000 effectives; he also had, under the command of General Beauregard below Richmond, an army of about 30,000. In the Valley and its vicinity General Grant had 10,000 troops under Crook and 7,500 under Sigel; General Lee about 7,000 under Breckinridge. There were heavy odds against the South.

I joined General Edward Johnson as Assistant Adjutant General, and Chief of Staff, on the morning of the first day's fight, May 5th. Having no horses at hand, Major Douglas Mercer loaned me a large snow-white mule to ride for that day. For a turbulent, unmanageable war horse, he broke the record. With marvelous instinct he seemed to understand exactly what I wished him to do, and then straightway did the opposite. His color made his eccentricities the more conspicuous and ridicule did not improve his conduct. The danger in riding such a beast in battle made the ordinary risks less to be dreaded. My nine months' inaction and imprisonment had sapped my strength and, with this additional labor of training a mule, I was, when night came, completely exhausted.

General Grant with his grand army, splendidly equipped and boldly led, moved against Lee's veterans promptly in the morning of May the 5th, and "The Battle of the Wilderness" lasted two days. If he expected General Lee to meet his challenge with equal promptness, having, as he supposed, turned his right flank by crossing the Rapidan, he certainly did not expect the Confederate General to assume the offensive and, by throwing Hill against his left and Ewell against his right, to double back both wings of his army in turn; and yet that is just what Lee did. The battle was vigorous and bloody and General Grant had an opportunity to see the mettle of both armies tested, and to fight his own army up to his standard.

When the battle was over, Lee's army was still there and Grant's had been repulsed at all points. The loss to the Army of Northern Virginia was about 7,000, killed and wounded; in the Army of the Potomac about 14,000 killed and wounded. The wounding of General Longstreet, which disabled him for the rest of the campaign, was a severe loss to our army. Not far from where General Jackson had fallen he, too, was wounded by his own men, and while his wound was severer and more dangerous, the Commander of the First Corps escaped the sad fate of the Commander of the Second, and still lives,[2] although nearly every other general officer on that field is dead. General A. P. Hill was so ill as to be unable to remain with his corps, and General Early was on the 7th assigned to the command of it.

At the end of that battle General Grant must have modified his plan of campaign. His theory of "hammering away" was doubtless the right one—for him; but there are times when the anvil proves equal to the hammer. At any rate, after taking the 7th to consider, General Grant abandoned the front of General Lee and marched off toward Spotsylvania Court house. In view of this sudden pause to his plans, it must be interesting to the military and historical student to read the reasons he gives for his new movement, in his official Report.

"It was evident to my mind that the two days fighting had satisfied him (the enemy) of his inability to further maintain the contest in the open field, notwithstanding his advantage of position, and that he would wait an attack behind his works. Orders were at once issued for a movement by his right flank."

Remembering that Lee had from the first gone out to meet Grant and had taken the initiative in attack and that Grant, too, had thrown up works along his line, the language of the General's Report can hardly be regarded as frank.

At any rate General Grant moved off on something of an arc toward Spotsylvania Court House, and when his advance reached there on the morning of the 8th, Lee's advance was there, too, and stopped the way. The distance traveled by each was about the same. Again General Lee had been a mind reader and knew what was in General Grant's. When the troops met, a fight began of some sharpness. It was a contest for position and the Confederates obtained the one they were ordered to take and held it. The 9th was spent by the armies adjusting themselves. That very able officer and accomplished man, General Sedgwick, Commander of the Sixth Corps, was killed by a sharpshooter while making observations. Both armies threw up entrenchments and log works.

May the 10th was a continuous battle. The Army of the Potomac made not less than four violent assaults upon our army, the first about ten o'clock in the morning and the last about six in the afternoon. They were all gallant and determined and met by a resistance of the same character. They were destructive of human life and the one made at five o'clock was especially disastrous to the Federal assailants. Rarely during the war were so many killed in so short a time. In that assault the Confederate loss was comparatively small. In the last attack the Federal troops broke over the Confederate lines at one point, but their success was only temporary, and they were driven out by troops acting under the immediate eye of General Lee. The day was most disastrous to General Grant. He certainly had seen his troops fight up to his supposed standard, for they had made and repeated heroic attacks on our lines, yet he had seen them driven back at each assault. It is difficult, therefore, to understand how, on the next day, he could have written a dispatch to General Halleck, in which occurs this sentence:

"I am satisfied the enemy are very shaky and are only kept up to the mark by the greatest exertions on the part of their officers and by keeping them entrenched in every position they take."

Yet in the same dispatch he asks for reinforcements "as fast as possible and in as great numbers," although seven days before he had twice as many troops as Lee. Yet that dispatch, which is known as his "fight-it-out-all-summer" dispatch has been almost dramatized.

My portion of the spoils of the 10th was a handsome black horse with a bridle and saddle, belonging, it was said, to Lieutenant Colonel T. H. Higginbotham of the Sixty-fifth New York, who was captured. The horse and equipment were presented to me by the Louisiana troops who captured them. Colonel Higginbotham was killed at Cedar Creek on the 19th of October.

On the 9th of May General Sheridan, under orders from General Grant, had started on a cavalry raid around Lee's army and on to Richmond. With an overwhelming force he rode down everything in his way. At "Yellow Tavern," not far from Richmond, he was met and stopped by Stuart. A fight ensued and Stuart was defeated; what was worse, he was killed. Sheridan did not get into Richmond, but if he had accomplished nothing else, the death of Jeb Stuart justified his raid.

General Stuart was a great cavalry commander; taking him all in all, the greatest the war produced, unless Forrest was his equal. He was a great soldier but a born cavalryman, dashing, fearless, clearheaded, enterprising, brilliant. He held Lee in the greatest reverence; he admired and studied Jackson as no other man did; both of them had a personal affection for him. Fond of show and with much personal vanity, craving admiration in the parlor as well as on the field, with a taste for music and poetry and song, desiring as much the admiration of handsome women as of intelligent men, with full appreciation of his own well-won eminence—these personal foibles, if they may be called such, did not detract from his personal popularity or his great usefulness. He could not fail, in many things, to remind one of Murat. When Sheridan came to the front with his splendid corps of horsemen, picked men, well-mounted, fully equipped, the Confederate cavalry was sadly on the decline. It is no reflection on Phil Sheridan's reputation to say that he did not do anything which Jeb Stuart could not have done as well. Whether Sheridan could have done as well as Stuart, with what Stuart had, may well be doubted. General Stuart's loss was simply irreparable.

During the 11th of May, the armies about Spotsylvania watched each other and kept quiet. General Johnson's division occupied a "salient" in the line, a very sharp one—the necessity for which I never could understand—which after the next day was distinguished as the "Bloody Angle" or "Angle of Death." General Johnson and his officers were well aware of their danger, and the position and its approaches had been well examined. A second line in rear had been partially constructed, but it seemed necessary to occupy that salient. With troops on the alert and well-supplied with artillery, it would have been a dangerous place to attack. But in contemplation of some movement nearly all the artillery had been removed during the day. Late that night information reached General Johnson that the enemy were contemplating an attack on the salient. I had been out on the line and several soldiers who had crawled well to the front had returned with reports that satisfied me of their correctness. I rode to General Johnson and then to General Ewell and his chief of artillery with messages urging the immediate return of the guns to the salient. I was in the saddle all the night, helping as I could to speed the guns to their places.

Before daylight General Johnson and the majority of his staff had gone into the works, dismounted, and sent their horses to the rear. My duty with the guns kept me, fortunately, on horseback. The artillery began to arrive, to be moved to their places and their horses sent to the rear. But after all the labor the guns never got into position. Light streaks which heralded the coming dawn were appearing in the sky. I had just spoken to General Johnson who was in the trenches and was starting with a message for General Ewell when the storm burst. At the signal of a gun, a dark column broke from its cover and bore down in overwhelming mass upon that salient and soon made it a bloody angle indeed. Our artillery, not in place, was useless; our thin line of infantry could not resist the onset of Hancock's legions. A rattle of musketry made such a din in that early morning as I have rarely heard, bullets rattled like hail through the branches of the trees, for the attacking column was firing very high, rapid firing broke in from front and sides, seemingly in all directions, and the morning light broke upon a scene of blood and death, an indescribable pandemonium. Although mounted, I made my escape unhurt—the only mounted man I saw as I rode out of that rocky wood; but Hancock's corps swarmed over the breastworks, beating down all opposition, and capturing General Johnson and the staff who were with him and nearly 3,000 of his division.

A terrific contest followed during much of the day. The

Confederates determined to retake that salient, the Federal troops to hold it and advancing from it to break through our center. Reinforcements from both armies were rushed to that point, and tons of lead in the shape of cannon balls and rifle balls were poured into and from that angle of death. Destruction with a tornado of fire and iron swept over the limited field; the trees of the forest were shivered and shattered, and today, in Washington, may be seen the body of one tree nearly two feet in diameter which was perforated by musket balls ten feet at least above the ground, until it was almost gnawed in two. It has been preserved as a relic of that infernal fight.

On our side General Lee took command in person and for a while was in the front of the storm. But the soldiers rushing to the front cried out from the ranks, "General Lee to the rear!" and General Gordon, remonstrating with him in person, persuaded him to retire further from the front.

General Johnson captured, I at once attached myself to Gordon, who was commanding Early's division, and I was with him during that never to be forgotten day and saw the dauntless intrepidity with which he led his troops in that fight.

The battle ended only after night had fallen. The Federal troops held the salient, but could advance no further. The Confederates failed to retake that angle, but kept the enemy confined to it. The losses of the Army of the Potomac in the battles of the 10th and 12th were over 16,000 killed and wounded, and 2,200 prisoners. The casualties in the Army of Northern Virginia, in killed and wounded were much less, perhaps not over one-half of that of its adversary, but there were more than 3,000 prisoners captured. (It seems to me odd that while I know as a matter of record that the weather of the 11th and 12th was most disagreeable, cold, full of rain, doubly severe on fighting troops, I have no recollection of it; but the weather made no impression on me and I find I made no note of it.)

For the next five or six days, the armies were comparatively quiet and there was little excitement. General Grant says he spent the time maneuvering and "waiting for reinforcements." Lucky man to have reinforcements at his beck and call and plenty of them! But he called for them and they came until the gaps "horrid Mars" had made were filled up.

On the 21st of May, A. P. Hill returning to his corps, Early returned to his division, and Gordon, having been made a Major General, took command of Johnson's division and I became his Adjutant General—the beginning of an admiration and friendship for that brilliant soldier and gentleman which years of peace have not diminished.

General Grant on the 22nd moved on to the left, still attempting to get between Lee's army and Richmond, but the Confederate advance stopped the way at Hanover Junction. Here there was more fighting at intervals for three days, both armies entrenching. It is the habit of Northern writers to speak of the breastworks and entrenchments constantly constructed in this campaign by Lee's army. It is doubtful whether they did enough of it. The fact is, both armies began entrenching in this swinging campaign as soon as they met face to face; and as Grant had a larger army and more diggers and tools, there can be little doubt that the Army of the Potomac made more embankments, trenches, and breastworks than Lee's army. To do it, is war.

About this time I was put to personal embarrassment. General Early's Adjutant General, Major John W. Daniel, now Virginia's eloquent representative in the United States Senate,[3] had been disabled on the 6th by a wound which compels him to use a crutch to this day. General Early now applied to General Lee in writing to have me transferred to his staff as Adjutant General. General Gordon had brought his own staff to the division and, with the members of Johnson's staff, he had a larger one than he was entitled to. I was very unwilling to leave General Gordon and his congenial staff and to change such pleasant associations, and General Gordon expressed his unwillingness to have me leave. The officer who would take my place was then, as now, my warm personal friend, and General Early had not asked for him. In my dilemma General Lee sent for me and suggested that I comply with General Early's request, and that settled it. I took leave of General Gordon and became Adjutant General of Early's division.

On the 26th of May General Grant side-stepped again to
the left, pausing at the Pamunkey for a day or two; then
again to the Totopotomoy where Lee, at Atlee's Station,
again called "check"; then with another shuffle until the flanks
of both armies rested on the Chickahominy and on the old
battlefield of Cold Harbor, with positions reversed from those
of 1862. Here both armies entrenched. There had been fighting all along the line, with sad diminution and small reinforcements to Lee's army. But here again General Grant was reinforced by General "Baldy" Smith, with his fresh corps of
10,000, and compared with the dwindling forces of Lee his
army seemed like that of Xerxes. It was a fit weapon for his
inexorable will.

On the 1st of June there was a small conflict, but not what in
these days could be called a battle; and so on June 2nd. But
General Grant was impatient and ordered a general attack on
Lee for 4.30 A.M. on the morning of the 3rd. He wanted a full
day to make his success overwhelming, our defeat crushing.
The assault was made promptly, fiercely; and before breakfast time the battle of Cold Harbor was over. The real fighting
had not lasted an hour, but it was fearful while it lasted.
Grant's repulse was complete, the slaughter of his troops pitiable. For the time it occupied, the battle was the bloodiest of
the war. With rage and determination General Grant brought
his ponderous hammer down upon the little anvil, and the
hammer was shivered to pieces. It seemed incredible that such
disastrous results should come from such a brief contest, for
the battle was ended before the day had fairly begun. The
Army of the Potomac lost at Cold Harbor, chiefly, of course,
on the 3rd, in killed, wounded, and captured, nearly 13,000
men; the Army of Northern Virginia not one-sixth that
number.

While I was present and as much engaged in that battle
as any other, I had no idea until afterwards the extent of the
punishment inflicted upon the Union army. I was riding over
part of the field toward the close of the fight when I met a
party of prisoners being taken to the rear. A young officer—
but he was older than I—stepped out from the party and,

after remarking that his regiment had been terribly cut up, he took from his neck a pair of field glasses, like opera glasses, saying he had bought them in Washington a week before and, having no further use for them, would like to present them to me. They were of much service to me afterwards. Toward the close of the war, they were stolen, discovered, and returned to me ten years afterwards. I have them now; and often when using them at Bar Harbor, at Harper's Ferry, or in New York theatres I have wondered what was the fate of the handsome soldier who took them to war with him as a useful decoration.

With the battle of Cold Harbor General Grant's campaign of fighting on that line, if it took all summer, was virtually over, although the summer itself had scarcely begun. He certainly, as he determined to do, had fought the Army of the Potomac to its utmost capacity. In fact it may be said, remembering that on the 3rd of June a whole line had stood fast in protest against further slaughter, that he had "fought it to a standstill." With unexampled perseverance and tenacity he had waged a continuous fight for thirty days, over eighty miles of ground, and had, during its progress, sixty thousand men put *hors de combat*, an army in itself as large as that which Lee commanded when they first crossed swords on the Rapidan.

Grant had illustrated his theory of war to his satisfaction, and yet Lee was between him and Richmond and, as a matter of fact, Grant was no nearer to that coveted city, except geographically, than he was when the campaign opened. He was simply where Butler was, and where he might have been without the loss of a thousand men. In view of the criticisms upon McClellan, we must let military critics determine whether Grant's campaign of 1864 was a success or a failure. One thing is certain, however, General Grant was not dismayed and it was evident, if the Government at Washington and his people continued to support him and his policy, the outlook for the Confederacy was hopeless. It was the science of war reduced to a sum in mathematics; and after all he succeeded.

EARLY *VERSUS* HUNTER

WHEN Grant began his campaign against Lee, Major General Franz Sigel was in command of the Union forces in the Valley of Virginia, about 7,000, with his Headquarters at Winchester. He was supposed to be in communication and partial concert with Generals George Crook and W. W. Averell, who were operating in southwest Virginia. Brigadier General John B. Imboden, with about 1,500 troops, was stationed in the Valley at Staunton on observation.

About the time Grant moved, Sigel was instructed to move down the Valley and seek a fight. This he proceeded to do, slowly and cautiously. Imboden, aware of his movements, asked for reinforcements, and before Sigel got well under way General John C. Breckinridge arrived at Staunton with two small brigades and took command. Colonel Scott Shipp—now the Superintendent of the Virginia Military Institute—arrived from Lexington with his corps of 225 cadets and joined the little army.

Breckinridge marched out to meet Sigel and they met at New Market on the 15th of May. Sigel had about 6,500 men; he says 5,500 were engaged. Breckinridge's command was about 4,000—they not all engaged. Breckinridge took the initiative and forced the fight in his dashing style. The cadets, whom he tried to keep in reserve, forced their way into the battle and did good service, but lost 8 killed and 44 wounded.[1] The battle was sharp. The result, decisive, and Sigel was defeated and driven from the field, with the loss of about 650 killed and wounded, 186 prisoners, and 5 pieces of artillery. The Confederate loss was about 560 killed and wounded, and a dozen missing. Sigel continued his retreat until he was safe behind Cedar Creek. He reported to the Adjutant General,

"The retrograde movement was effected in perfect order. The troops are in very good spirits and will fight another battle if the enemy should advance against us."

This consoling dispatch evidently did not produce the desired effect in Washington. General Halleck telegraphed to General Grant,

"Sigel is in full retreat on Strasburg. He will do nothing but run; never did anything else."

Whereupon Sigel was removed from command and General David Hunter was put in his place.

Immediately after the battle of New Market General Breckinridge with his little force was ordered to join General Lee; the youthful cadets were moved here and there with no more casualties until they were furloughed on the 27th of June.

General Hunter took command at Cedar Creek on the 21st of May, and on the 1st of June began to advance much more rapidly than Sigel. General William E. Jones came from southwest Virginia bringing his troops with him and took command of the rather heterogeneous force collected, numbering between 5,000 and 6,000. General Hunter, it is officially stated, had 8,500. A battle was fought at Piedmont, not far from Staunton, June 5th, which resulted in a disastrous defeat of Jones. He was killed, and the loss in his command was very heavy. General Hunter places his loss at 500 killed and wounded. General Imboden puts the Confederate loss at 1,500, including 1,000 prisoners. Within the next two days General Hunter was joined by Crook and Averell at Staunton, raising his command to 18,000, and began to inaugurate that campaign of fire and vandalism, which has made it so infamous that Northern historians are glad to avoid mention of it.

When General Lee heard of the disaster at Piedmont, he detached General Breckinridge with 2,500 men and again

sent him to the Valley to do what he could to check and impede
Hunter. His first destination was Rockfish Gap in the Blue
Ridge. When he found, however, that Lynchburg was evidently the objective point of General Hunter, he moved with
his command to that place to await developments.

General Hunter entered Lexington, Virginia, on the 11th
of June, and the plundering began at once. On the 12th he
burned the Virginia Military Institute and everything connected with it.² The cadets had been there and had left: that
was enough for Hunter. But it was not enough to assuage his
thirst for destruction and he looked around for something
more to destroy. He found it in the quiet, simple home of ex-
Governor Letcher and he doomed that to the flames. He directed it to be done in the most brutal manner.

The officer and men sent by Hunter to do the work, writes
the Governor's son, Judge Letcher,³ "at once surrounded the
house and plundered it—while others of them were pouring
something inflammable over the furniture and setting fire to
it. They refused to allow my mother to have anything carried
out, not even a change of clothes; everything was destroyed
that was not stolen. One officer whose name we never knew
came in and offered to assist in saving valuables: he got a
trunk, but Captain Berry of a Pennsylvania Regiment who
was in charge of the burning, refused to let him carry it out;
an altercation followed when a soldier picked up the trunk and
carried it into the yard. Captain Berry ordered other things
that some persons were attempting to carry out to be seized
and thrown into the burning building. All the buildings were
burned. The roof of my grandmother's house caught fire and,
when a Negro servant tried to extinguish it, the soldiers threatened to shoot him if he did not come down; but a Captain
Downs rode up and ordered the fire to be put out. Captain
Berry and many of his soldiers were extremely rude and in-
sulting to my mother and sister. No reason, except the order
of General Hunter, was given for burning our house. Washington College was plundered, apparatus destroyed, books
torn up, etc."

General Hunter, in his report, mentions the burning of the

Governor's house by his order, but we find no mention of it in the reports of Crook, Averell, Rutherford B. Hayes, and others. They were doubtless willing that Hunter should monopolize all such glory. Having done with Lexington, Hunter, Crook, and Averell proceeded on their way, and on the 17th of June appeared before Lynchburg with their united force. McCausland with his small command of cavalry had impeded them as best he could, taking some lessons from them in the art of making the torch auxiliary to the sword, which, later, he put into practise in Chambersburg, Pennsylvania.

On the 7th of June General Grant had dispatched General Sheridan to make another raid, with a view to destroy the railroads at Trevillian Station and Charlottesville, and then to co-operate with Hunter in his advance. He started with two divisions of cavalry and sufficient artillery, to the number of 8,000, at his estimate. General Lee instructed General Wade Hampton (Stuart's successor) to meet Sheridan with his own and Fitz Lee's divisions, containing about 5,000 troopers. The two columns were commanded by officers, some of whom then and since were much distinguished. Sheridan had with him A. T. A. Torbert, David Gregg, Wesley Merritt, George A. Custer and others, while Hampton was aided by Fitzhugh Lee, M. C. Butler, T. L. Rosser, and L. Lomax. The first day's fight on the 11th, the brunt of which Butler (Hampton's division) bore alone—was a success for Sheridan, who drove our troopers beyond Trevillian and tore up the railroad there. The next day, when Lee was in it too, after some severe fighting, Sheridan was repulsed in all his assaults and charges. That night he retired and went back whence he came. The loss on each side was about equal and heavy for a cavalry fight.

On the 12th of June, General Early, commanding the Second Corps (General Ewell having been compelled by ill health to retire from the field and take charge of the defenses of Richmond) was directed by General Lee to move at once with his command to the Valley, in order to unite with Breckinridge and stop Hunter. Early left after midnight for Charlottesville and made a forced march of eighty miles to that place in four days. His corps had been greatly reduced in the campaign and numbered about 8,000 effective muskets.

At Charlottesville, hearing that Breckinridge had gone from Rockfish Gap to Lynchburg, toward which Hunter was marching, Early, by foot and rail, went to that city as speedily as possible. He was moving, *à la* Jackson, with Jackson's troops. He, with part of his advance division, reached Lynchburg after noon on the 17th, the same day Hunter appeared on the other side of it. He was surprised to find that he was in time, for had Hunter moved with half the speed, Lynchburg would then have been in his hands. Breckinridge, being in bed with an injury, D. H. Hill, who was in town, had prepared to defend the city as best he could. The two brigades of Early's division (now Ramseur's) were soon on the field, and in time to get a little taste of battle that afternoon, in repulsing a force that had driven in Imboden's cavalry. I had, therefore, a chance to be in the first of it. Nearly one-half of Early's command did not get up until the afternoon of the 18th; we were anxious, but General Hunter did not attack. When General Early's troops were all up, he had under his command, including Breckinridge and the Lexington cadets and convalescents, about 12,000 effectives. He determined to attack at daylight if Hunter didn't; but when daylight came, Hunter had gone and prompt pursuit was ordered. As Ramseur's division was in the advance, I was generally with the front, often with the cavalry.

It was a scene of desolation. Ransacked houses, crying women, clothes from the bed chambers and wardrobes of ladies, carried along on bayonets and draggled in the road, the garments of little children, and here and there a burning house marked the track of Hunter's retreat. I had never seen anything like this before and for the first time in the war I felt that vengeance ought not be left entirely to the Lord. The first day we pursued the "flying column" for twenty-five miles to Liberty, and just before night Ramseur drove Hunter's weary rear guard through the town.

Harry Gilmor of the cavalry and I were riding together and went through the village together. At the end of it **we** saw some young ladies run out of a house and come to the fence, one of them calling me by name. We rode up to the fence to speak to them, forgetting there was nothing in our front. The girls were full of excitement and semi-hysterical laughter.

"Look there, the Yankees!" cried one, and before they could run away we saw the white jet of several rifles, and a ball buried itself in the gate-post, tumbling from it a glass from which Gilmor had just quaffed the water. There was a rustle of feminine garments and a rush for the house, as we directed some skirmishers whom the firing brought up to clear the stable from which the shots came. But the Parthians had fled. Before the night was far spent I was back again for a more quiet visit. As for Gilmor, he was given something else to do.

The pursuit was kept up on the 20th and 21st to Salem and beyond, having done sixty miles at breakneck speed. Hunter had escaped into the mountains toward Lewisburg and his campaign in Virginia was over. General Early determined to rest his jaded troops during the 22nd. The troops had been so accustomed to forced marching, that this unwonted ease surprised them. Some of them spread a report that General Early, an ironclad old bachelor, had encountered a sweetheart of many years before near Big Lick (now Roanoke)— his Headquarters were at the Hollins Institute, a female Seminary ⁴—and that they both thought his troops would be better for a day's rest! But the next day we were off through Buchanan to Lexington.

En route I got permission to take some troops from the south several miles out of the way to see the Natural Bridge. I took several bands and have never forgotten the solemn effect of their music as it rose and swelled in volume, and filled the great arch and seemed to press against the sides of that cathedral dome, and then rolled along the high rocks that walled the ravine and died away in the widening wood. Years after when I took a military band into the Luray Caverns and, placing it in the "ballroom," went off into a distant gallery to get the weird effect of its softened music percolating through the rocks, its sharpness gone, its appealing melody left, I had a sensation akin to that at the Natural Bridge—a sensation of more tenderness but less majesty.

When we entered Lexington, Jackson's old division was marched past his grave. Not a man spoke, not a sound was uttered. Only the tramp, tramp of passing feet told that his surviving veterans were passing in review, while the drooping and tattered flags saluted his sacred dust. As I passed by I could not help paraphrasing the lines of Tennyson I had first read in Lexington,

> *They are here my own, my own;*
> *Were it ever so airy a tread,*
> *My heart would hear them and beat,*
> *Were it earth in an earthy bed:*
> *My dust would hear them and beat*
> *Had I lain for a century dead!*

Alas, how few of them were left.

We had parted company with General Hunter. The truth being known about this campaign, the historian of the war, in endeavoring to form an opinion of Hunter's military capacity and personal character, will be much enlightened by reading his official reports (June 8th and August 8th) of his operations: if not reliable, they are entertaining and certainly characteristic.

Leaving the cadets at Lexington, General Early stopped a day at Staunton to rearrange his command and to procure such equipments and supplies for it as were to be had. He left Staunton on the 28th of June, proceeded with rapid marches down the Valley pike, and reached Winchester the 2nd of July. Moving on without delay, he spread his little army, like a fan, from Martinsburg to Harper's Ferry, so as to dislodge forces of the enemy stationed at those places along the Potomac. This occupied a day or two, and on the 5th and 6th of July he crossed the river at Shepherdstown, to march through Maryland. This was a desperate thing to do, for with rapid marching and some losses, his effective force could not have been over eleven thousand muskets and forty pieces of artillery. It was so reckless that historians are still examining fig-

ures to see if it can be possible. Jackson being dead, it is safe
to say no other General in either army would have attempted
it against such odds. As Ramseur (Early's Division) was in
the advance, I only had a chance to take Early, Breckinridge,
Gordon, and Ramseur to my father's house for a brief call and
to get a glance at Sharpsburg and the battlefield as we passed
through. Several days' delay was caused by demonstrations
against Maryland Heights and waiting for shoes. The army
marched on different lines toward Frederick, and Ramseur's
division, going through Boonsboro and over South Mountain
by way of Turner's Gap, reached Frederick first, before noon
on the 9th. I took command of the skirmishers and was the first
horseman in the town, in recognition of which an enthusiastic
citizen—ever since my warm friend—Peter Zahm, presented
me with a handsome pair of spurs. I was appointed Provost
Marshal of the town for the day or until I was relieved, but
in the early afternoon I joined the division which had moved
toward Monocacy Junction on the Baltimore and Ohio Railroad. General Lew Wallace was strongly posted on the opposite side of Monocacy Creek waiting an attack. It soon came.

About four o'clock Breckinridge with Gordon's division,
half mile to our right, forded the stream in the wake of Mc-
Causland and attacked the enemy at once on his left flank. A
sharp fight ensued and the enemy were driven. Our front
being relieved, I took a body of skirmishers over on the railroad bridge, and Ramseur followed with the division in pursuit. But the retreat was so rapid that pursuit by infantry
was useless and it was soon stopped. While our division was
engaged in some skirmishing with small loss, the fighting was
done by Gordon and McCausland—not over 3,500—under
Breckinridge. Our loss of nearly 700 may be considered heavy
for the length of the battle. General Wallace had with him
6,000 troops, but Rickett's division did the principal fighting,
although E. B. Tyler's miscellaneous brigade also took part.
Wallace's loss was 700 killed and wounded, and about 700
prisoners, although he puts his missing at 1,300.

The audacity of Early's enterprise was its safety; no one

who might have taken steps to oppose or cut him off would believe his force was so small. General Wallace, in his official report, says Early attacked him with 18,000 and had two divisions not engaged. The newspapers and scouts represented "old Jubal" as moving on Washington with a veteran column of from 30,000 to 40,000 troops.

On the 10th the army moved on toward Washington. Ramseur was left for the rear, with instruction to destroy the iron railroad bridge. For want of sufficient powder the attempt was a failure. I noted a ludicrous attempt on the part of a battery of artillery to knock it to pieces with solid shot. This delay threw us much in rear of the rest of the column. We were annoyed also somewhat by the enemy's cavalry, and at the request of the officer commanding our rear brigade, I was ordered by General Ramseur to remain with him and take charge of the rear guard. McCausland's cavalry was in advance, skirmishing with bodies of the enemy and clearing the way.

We overtook the rest of the army after midnight and went into bivouac near Rockville. By noon of the 11th our extreme advance was near Fort Stevens, one of the fortifications of Washington. During the day the whole army got up and was put into line in front of the Capital of the Union. It then numbered, all told, certainly less than 10,000, and yet, had it been five times as strong, it could not have produced more consternation than it did.

As we were passing "Silver Spring," the residence of the venerable Francis P. Blair and afterwards of Montgomery Blair, his distinguished son, I was informed that the house had been abandoned and was being looted by soldiers. I immediately took a squad of soldiers and took possession of it. The family had gone, to Washington, probably, and not a servant was to be seen. A party of stragglers, hunting for booty and things to eat and drink, were found in the house and ordered out. I put a guard over it and left to report the situation to General Early. Afterwards Generals Early and Breckinridge took possession of it for a while, and it was there the conference between Early, Breckinridge, Gordon, and

Ramseur was held that night and a determination reached to assault the works the next morning. However considerate of private property these gentlemen and their staffs were, I feel compelled to say that the wine cellar of Mr. Blair was much depleted before they got away.

When the morning of the 12th came, the situation had changed. Wright had arrived with the Sixth Corps (Sedgwick's old Corps) except James B. Rickett's division, and Emory with the Nineteenth Corps (15,000 trained soldiers) and soon manned the works. The fact is, the fortifications had been admirably planned and constructed, were of maximum strength, and I think they could have been defended against Early's small force even with the "Veteran Reserves" and other local troops with their heavy artillery, before the arrival of Generals H. G. Wright and W. H. Emory. Their arrival made an assault out of the question. It has been said that if Early had moved more rapidly and assaulted at once (presuming, I suppose, that his men were all centaurs) he might have gone into Washington. I do not believe it. If he had I am sure he never would have gotten out again. In fact I am satisfied neither he nor any officer with him ever expected to take Washington.

Nothing was done on the 12th. Personally, I had felt very uncomfortable ever since I had seen the blue column of the Sixth Corps file into the breastworks that frowned upon us with such an array of heavy guns. Beyond a little skirmishing and picket firing, the day passed quietly until the afternoon, when a sortie was made from Fort Stevens. I saw it coming and thought we were "gone up." But the attack proved to be little more than a heavy skirmish and was easily repulsed. Our loss was small; General Grant says Wright's loss was 280 killed and wounded. Why the attack was made and, if made, not kept up, I cannot tell, unless it was to see if we were still there.

Some while after dark that night I was sent for by General Early. Generals Breckinridge and Gordon were with him. He seemed in a droll humor, perhaps one of relief, for he said to me in his falsetto drawl:

"Major, we haven't taken Washington, but we've scared Abe Lincoln like h——!"

"Yes, General," I replied, "but this afternoon when that Yankee line moved out against us, I think some other people were scared blue as ——'s brimstone!"

"How about that, General?" said Breckinridge with a laugh.

"That's true," piped General Early, "but it won't appear in history!"

Then he informed me that we were about to leave; that he had directed a detail of two hundred men, with proper officers, to be left on the picket line; that I should remain with them and keep them there until after midnight, unless driven in or ordered away before that time, and then march them as a rear guard until cavalry fell in behind me.

This I did. As I passed "Silver Spring" I sent a courier to relieve the guard at Mr. Blair's house and order them to follow; they soon appeared. A mile or two beyond, my attention was called to a bright light behind us, which proved to be the burning house of Mr. Blair. By whom it was burned is mere conjecture.[5] It was not destroyed by anyone's order. I feel confident the cavalry guard, in charge of a reliable officer did not do it; nor do I know what reliance is to be placed in the report that it was the work of one of Mr. Blair's neighbors. I know that it was burned, that its flames, seen at Fort Stevens, notified the enemy that we had gone, and that we were pursued and annoyed several hours before we otherwise would have been. I know also that a few days after, General Butler, in retaliation, sent a gunboat up the Rappahannock to the house of Mrs. Seddon, turned her and her children out of doors, and consigned house and contents to the flames.[6]

We crossed the Potomac River at White's Ford on the 14th, rested a day or two at Leesburg, then went on through Snicker's Gap in the Blue Ridge, over the Shenandoah River at Castleman's Ferry, and established a bivouac near Berryville on the 17th. The enemy followed and some fighting of no great importance took place on the 18th and 19th. On the 19th Ramseur was ordered to Winchester with his division.

Jubal A. Early some years after the War

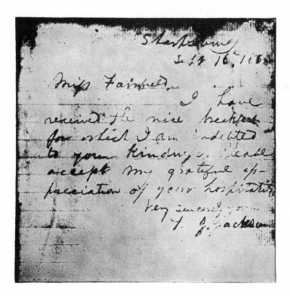

Jackson's Breakfast Thanks

We were about to enter on another stage of the eventful campaign.

When we look over the chapter of the campaign just ended and consider the small command General Early had, its long and continuous marches from Richmond to Washington, through Lynchburg, Lexington, Winchester, and Frederick, his contests with Hunter and Sigel and Wallace, his daring raid to the very gates of Washington, his rapidity, his audacity, his skill, he seems justified in saying that, in the particulars mentioned, "it is without parallel in this or any other modern war." For it, he never has and never will receive the credit he deserves, for the glories of that early and midsummer were overclouded and forgotten in the disasters of the autumn.

About this time General David Hunter again made his appearance in the lower Valley of Virginia at Martinsburg and Harper's Ferry. One will search the official records in vain for any evidence that he performed any military services other than sending Crook, Averell, and other soldiers to attack the enemy at different places. His personal attention was given to the congenial occupation of destroying private property and creating a vast amount of female suffering. He seemed to take special delight in torturing his old social acquaintances.

First he destroyed the house of his cousin, the Honorable Andrew Hunter of Charlestown, and had him arrested. Mr. Hunter was one of the most eminent lawyers in the country and his sin was that he had represented the Commonwealth of Virginia, by appointment of the Attorney General, in the prosecution of John Brown and his fellow criminals. I had been admitted to the Bar on motion of Mr. Hunter and I heard him say after the war that when his house was burned and he was taken before General Hunter at Harper's Ferry, he had on his finger a gold ring that years before had been given to him, as an evidence of affection, by his "cousin David."

Then was "Fountain Rock," the home of the Honorable Alexander R. Boteler, given to the flames. Colonel Boteler was an old-line Whig who fought earnestly against the secession of his State, being in Congress when the war broke out, was the author of the "Committee of Thirteen," the last effort to prevent the inevitable.[7] He was also in the Confederate Congress, and I have referred hereinbefore to his connection with General Jackson. For this his family was to suffer. His wife—née Miss Stockton of New Jersey—and his daughters and three little grandchildren were turned out of doors. One of his daughters, devoted to her piano, went back to it and, while the flames were roaring and crackling over her head, sang, until choked with tears, "Thy will be done, Oh Lord." Several soldiers stopped to listen and then, swearing a mighty oath that they would save that piano if shot for it, bore it and some other things out of the blazing house.

But the torch moved on and next reached "Bedford," the hospitable old home of Mrs. Edmund I. Lee, little more than a mile from "Fountain Rock." The circumstances attending the burning of this house were so infamous that there was raised a universal cry of horror. Mr. Lee, who was away from home, had several sons in the Confederate army. Mrs. Lee, a gentle, dignified, Christian woman was aroused to such an outburst by her grief, that on the next day, July 20th, she wrote General Hunter a letter, from which I make some extracts:

"Yesterday morning, your underling, Capt. Martindate of the First New York Veteran Cavalry, executed your infamous order and burned my house: the dwelling and outbuildings seven in number with all their contents being burned. I therefore, a helpless woman whom you have cruelly wronged, address you a Major General of the United States army and demand, why was this done? What was my offence?

"The house was built by my father, a Revolutionary patriot who served the whole seven years for your independence. There was I born. There the sacred dead repose. It was *my* house and *my* home: and there has *your* niece, who lived among us all this horrid war up to the present moment met with all kindness and hospitality at my hands. Was it for this you turned me, my little daughter and young son out upon the world without shelter? Or was it because my husband is the grandson of the Revolutionary patriot and rebel Richard Henry Lee, and the near kinsman of the noblest and greatest of Christian warriors, Robert E. Lee? Having failed to match him, your rage and malice find vent upon the helpless and inoffensive. Hyena-like you have torn my heart to pieces and demon-like you have done it without a pretext of revenge, for I never harmed you.

"Can I say 'God forgive you?' Were it possible for human lips to raise your name heavenward, angels would thrust the foul thing back. The curses of thousands, the scorn of the manly and upright and the hatred of the true and honorable will follow you and yours through all time."

Stanton knew his man when he selected General Hunter to preside over the trial of Mrs. Surratt. Two days before the foregoing letter (July 18th), General Hunter had sent an order to Frederick, Maryland, to seize all rebel sympathizers, "male secessionists and their families," and to send them to him at Harper's Ferry that the males might be sent to prison and their families south; and also to seize their houses for government purposes and sell their furniture at public auction. And yet we talk about Weyler in Cuba!

I have often wondered what the kindhearted Lincoln thought of this. Whatever he and Stanton may have thought of the ability of Hunter as an incendiary, they were not otherwise enamored of his military prowess, for before the month was out he was removed and General Philip H. Sheridan put in his place.

EARLY *VERSUS* SHERIDAN

WHEN General Ramseur moved to Winchester, Early, with the rest of his command, moved off via Millwood to Middletown and Strasburg. On the afternoon of July 20th General Stephen D. Ramseur, at Winchester, having received information that Averell was approaching on the Martinsburg pike with a body of cavalry, went four miles out to meet him, and soon found that he had been deceived as to Averell's force. A fight was soon on, and developed a strong line of infantry, making the column of the enemy too heavy for us. It is questionable whether, in any event, we could have held the field against the attack, but two regiments on our left flank—excellent regiments too—became demoralized and gave way in great disorder. Our flank was turned and we were driven in confusion from the field. The enemy pursued a very short distance and then retired from the battlefield and made no further demonstration. Averell's loss was about 200 killed and wounded. We lost about 250 killed and wounded, 4 guns, and perhaps 200 prisoners. Brigadier Generals R. D. Lilly and Edward P. C. Lewis were wounded.

General Ramseur was severely censured for making that fight. He felt the criticisms deeply and I do not think had recovered from their sting when killed two months later at Cedar Creek. It was such a mistake as an impetuous officer will make at times when too anxious for a fight. He was misled by information from a source usually reliable. If he had remained in the position he occupied after the retreat, Averell would not have attacked.

Some time in the early part of the summer I had been struck with the attractive appearance of a youth about eighteen years of age who had brought a message to General Early's Headquarters—a manly open-eyed, frank, compact, little fellow. Upon enquiry I found his name was Randolph Ridgeley; he was a private in the cavalry and a son of Captain Randolph Ridgeley, of fame in the Mexican War. I immediately had him detailed as a courier for Headquarters and, finding him prompt and reliable, had no difficulty in getting General Early, who knew the gallant Ridgeley in Mexico, to recommend him for a commission as Lieutenant and aide-de-camp. He soon obtained it and remained with me in Ramseur's division when General Early took command of Ewell's corps. He was gentle and quiet in camp, but in battle the hot blood of his father would show itself and he was often not only dashing but reckless. In the fight with Averell, when I saw the enemy was moving a column of infantry to our left, I told Ridgeley to ride over quickly and inform the officers of the movement. That was just to his liking, and he was off with a flash. He reached there just as our regiments were struck and stampeded and, still trying to deliver his message, was shot and fell from his horse. He was left on the field.

We abandoned Winchester that night but before I went out I called at the house of a friend and told the daughter of the house, Miss Matilda Russell, of the fate of Ridgeley and asked her to seek him, if living, in some hospital in the morning. I did not know the heroic mould in which the girl was fashioned. When our army was gone, she wrapped herself in a shawl and alone took her way through the night to the battlefield in search of young Ridgeley. It was a desperate thing to do. Through the wandering soldiers, through the night adding its horrors to war, with cries and groans of the wounded all about, this noble woman stepped her way, with a faith and courage that belittle all words of admiration. After a time she found young Ridgeley, fearfully wounded in the thigh and apparently dying. She took his head in her arms, bathed his face and wound and spoke bravely to him. A surgeon came, had no time for him until morning, promised to come then and see if he could be saved. And there upon that blood-stained field, through that long and fearful night and all its horrible surroundings, with now and then a prowling soldier stopping to wonder at the strange spectacle, sat this young woman, holding upon her arm this half unconscious youth and soothing his agony as best she could. She was fighting for his life and she won. Randolph Ridgeley was saved. But she—her trial then came. Stricken down with fever, she sank almost into the valley of the shadow of death, crying out with the pain of her swollen and injured arm. But an arm stronger than hers encompassed her about and she, too, was saved to her people.

That night on the battlefield is the subject of that well-known painting of Oregon Wilson called "Woman's Devotion" in the Corcoran Art Gallery at Washington.[1] Through John Esten Cooke, Wilson wrote to me about the incident, and that picture was the result of our correspondence. Randolph Ridgeley still lives, lame from his wound, and has a son in the United States Navy; but Miss Russell sleeps at Winchester, near the soldiers she loved so well. No Confederate ever passes her grave with covered head.

General Early went into camp near Middletown, about fifteen miles south of Winchester. General Crook came up with his forces from Berryville on the 22nd, joined Averell and Duffié, and took command. He moved out from Winchester a mile or two and encamped near Kernstown. His command consisted of three divisions of infantry, two divisions of cavalry, and five batteries. He was not settled in camp before Early determined to attack him. He moved against him promptly on the 24th. The battle was fought on the field from which Shields had driven Jackson. It was a short, decisive fight in which Breckinridge particularly displayed great skill and dash. Crook was driven from the field in great confusion and with great loss. But for the failure of our cavalry, the rout ought to have been ruinous to that army, especially as Crook's dismounted cavalry and some of his infantry behaved very badly. Early's loss was very small. Official reports make that of Crook, 100 killed, 606 wounded, and 479 captured or missing. The pursuit of the enemy was continued as rapidly as possible, until they had taken refuge on the other side of the Potomac or at Harper's Ferry under the shadow of Maryland Heights.

General Early moved to Martinsburg and tore up the Baltimore and Ohio Railroad again. The indignation and excitement in that part of the Valley over the persecutions and burnings of Hunter were so intense that it aroused Early to vengeance. He sent McCausland with two brigades of cavalry and a battery to Chambersburg, Pennsylvania, to demand $100,000 in gold or its equivalent in currency as partial compensation to Hunter's victims, or in default to burn the town. The money was not paid and the town was fired and many houses destroyed. Whether this kind of warfare, the destruction of private property, is excusable, when not necessary for the protection of an army, may be debatable. The provocation in this case was so great that it has not been questioned; but neither in principle nor policy can I see any good reason for such retaliation.

While this was going on, Hunter, heavily reinforced, was chasséing between Harper's Ferry and Monocacy Junction, as far from the enemy as he could well get. Early, therefore, concluded to make a trip into Maryland, and crossed the Potomac at Shepherdstown and Williamsport. Ramseur crossed at Williamsport on the 5th, and he and Rodes encamped near St. James College; Ramseur's headquarter camp was on the lawn, near its beautiful spring.

We were hardly settled for the evening, when one Benjamin Long, a neighboring farmer, was brought in, under guard of soldiers, he and the guard heavily laden with chickens, butter, and country produce. I at once began to enquire with some acerbity what this inexcusable indignity to a citizen meant, but Mr. Long took me aside to assure me that the arrest was by his own procurement, for his protection when we were gone. He only wished to contribute to our comfort in camp. I came to know Long well after the war, for he delighted in

litigation and I was often his attorney. On one occasion he
went as surety on the note of an indicted man to procure him
the services of counsel, although he was the chief witness for
the State and the man was convicted on his evidence.

In the evening the Reverend Dr. Kerfoot, President of the
College,[2] came to my tent and invited the General and staff
to supper. Knowing his intense loyalty to the Union and his
bitterness, I thought it best to decline. He returned in a short
while and saw General Ramseur in person. Impressed by the
suavity and cordiality of his manner, the General accepted
the kind invitation and asked me and several of the staff to
accompany him. We were treated with great civility by his
gracious wife and attractive daughter and had an excellent
supper. Toward its close a staff officer arrived with a message
and a written order from General Early to General Ramseur
to arrest Dr. Kerfoot and Professor Coit and put them under
close guard until further orders. Here was a pretty piece of
business.

I had gone out to receive the messenger, and that supper
now was causing worse than indigestion. I returned to the
table, conversed with the daughter blindly, and when we arose
I took a semi-malicious pleasure (for getting us into that fix)
in showing the order to the General. He communicated at
once with Dr. Kerfoot and, being an accomplished gentleman,
he did it with much consideration and tact. But he could not
avoid a scene. Dr. Kerfoot gave way to his alarm and, rather
bluntly informing his family, we were soon amid tears and
lamentations; it was a most trying scene all around. After
brief conference General Ramseur informed Dr. Kerfoot
(Professor Coit had also been sent for) that he would not put
them under personal arrest but would leave them in the house,
under such surveillance as he indicated. He and the staff left
for quarters leaving the details to me. I appointed a guard
for the house under an officer and made arrangements that
Dr. Kerfoot and his family were entirely satisfied with. In
fact, he says, "officers and guards were all tender and kind."
He spoke to me of my father, who had been arrested and car-

ried off with much less ceremony. My anger flared up at the allusion but in the presence of his family I simply said,

"Yes, my mother and sister have gone through all this, and General Early knows it."

Before I was in bed in my tent, Mr. John W. Breathed, father of Captain Jim Breathed, than whom no more gallant officer ever commanded a Confederate battery—whom Dr. Kerfoot had sent for—was at my tent, urging me to see General Early in behalf of the two prisoners.

At early dawn the next morning, General Early and Lieutenant Colonel Pendleton of his staff rode into our Headquarters and Mr. Breathed was at hand. I accompanied them to the Rectory and on the way made a personal appeal for the release of Dr. Kerfoot. Mr. Breathed was very earnest about it, but the General seemed to be inexorable. He called Dr. Kerfoot and Mr. Coit into the parlor and seated himself at a table. He then told the two gentlemen that he had ordered their arrest in retaliation for the arrest of the Reverend Dr. Andrew H. H. Boyd of Winchester, who was then sick in prison at Wheeling, Hunter's favorite Bastille.[3]

Calmly, at first, and with great force he told them of the outrages perpetrated by Hunter in Virginia and his cruel persecutions, and for fully half an hour laid their history bare. There were five or six persons in the room or at the door and everyone listened in silence to his eloquent and stinging arraignment of such needless cruelties. He concluded by saying that retaliation of the kind was against every feeling he had. He would release the prisoners, upon their parole in writing to go to Washington and obtain the release of Dr. Boyd in three weeks, and if they were not successful to report themselves as prisoners of war. He wrote the paper himself for them to sign and Pendleton wrote a duplicate, attested it, and gave it to them. It is a sad commentary upon the bitterness of the times that Bishop Whittingham[4] of Maryland endeavored to prevent Dr. Kerfoot from complying with his sacred parole. Would *he* not have burned a heretic or have thrown disbelievers to the lions?

As the interview ended a noise attracted our attention. The

two horses of Dr. Kerfoot and Mr. Coit had been hidden in
the Rectory cellar and their neighing betrayed them. Some
soldiers led them out with much merriment. General Early,
however, ordered them to be restored to their owners, and
gave them a safeguard for them. It is said they were taken
after we left.

The Reverend Dr. Kerfoot afterwards became Bishop of
Pittsburgh; but if, after that day at St. James College, he
ever indicated by any kindly act to an ex-Confederate any
remembrance of those who aided in his release, there is no
record of it.

On that day General Early's command moved back into
Virginia and continued slowly to Winchester. General Sheridan had superseded Hunter and was getting his large
well-equipped force in readiness to advance. There was skirmishing and shifting of position these days, and on the 12th
of August General Early was back at Fisher's Hill, in position. Sheridan was advancing, and Anderson with Kershaw's
infantry division and Fitz Lee with his cavalry divison had
arrived at Front Royal to aid Early. But Sheridan after
sundry demonstrations retired on the 17th toward Winchester, and was followed. Just before reaching Winchester we
had an affair with the enemy, Ramseur's division being in
front, and they were driven through the town with loss of 300
prisoners.

It was dark when we reached Winchester and General Early
directed me to take charge of the skirmish line and drive
through the town. It seemed a strange duty for a staff officer
and Harry Gilmor, predicting my immediate demise if I undertook it, galloped off to the right with some cavalry and,
soon after, made such a noisy demonstration on the Berryville pike, that the enemy's rear guard quickly abandoned the
town and my skirmishers had an easy time of it. Then "old
Jube" ordered me to report to him at the house of a friend
and managed to let it be understood—in the presence of the
daughter of the house [5]—that I was the first officer in town
and so impatient to get in that he had set me some dangerous
duty to give me the chance. For that little kindness he de-

served more gracious treatment than he received. He had taken a glass of fine old whiskey with the host and, when he was about to leave, Mrs. C—— had asked him to let her fill his canteen. She filled it and returned it to him. Riding to camp, the night felt a little cool, and when several miles from town the General proposed to take a drink. He handed his canteen to McGuire, who asked him to drink first. The General put it with a smile to his lips, tilted it and then,

"Milk. —————— —————— buttermilk!" he spluttered, and further quotation of his language may be omitted.

The army moved on the next day and its main body encamped in the vicinity of Bunker Hill. For a month this little body of soldiers was never at rest two days in succession. Sheridan was gathering a large army and Early was sending out excursions in every direction, toward Martinsburg, Charlestown, and Shepherdstown, continually skirmishing with infantry and cavalry, marching and countermarching. Our army was scattered piecemeal all over that section of the Valley, radiating from Bunker Hill. My diary of these days shows that Ramseur's division seemed nearly always in the front, had little or no rest, and nearly always happened to be where the skirmishing took place; and I noticed the same thing in the journal of Major Jed Hotchkiss. I think I was in every town of that section then, except Harper's Ferry, and going with a squadron of cavalry had a chance to ride into Shepherdstown and look over at my home in Maryland.

I never could understand why Sheridan permitted Early to play this reckless game under his nose. I apprehend when the historian studies this period and satisfies himself of the relative strength of the two armies, he will be forced to believe that the Federal General displayed a timid caution and want of enterprise that is not in keeping with the reputation he afterwards gained. McClellan was never guilty of greater prudence and hesitation.

After the 1st of September, the army was encamped in the vicinity of Stephenson's Depot and Winchester, but much scattered, and on the 4th we were marched hurriedly to the vicinity of Berryville to the aid of Kershaw, who had become involved with a large force of the enemy; but we returned to the neighborhood of Winchester. During two days of rest General Ramseur and Captain Don Halsey borrowed shotguns and went out to shoot partridges (quail). That does seem rather small game at such times, but they found the quail and they were a great luxury. I spent more than one afternoon on horseback, not like James' solitary horseman, but in an equestrian solitude *a deux*.

About the middle of the month General Anderson, with Kershaw's division, was called back to Richmond to join General Lee, and Ramseur's division took his position, about a mile from Winchester on the Berryville pike. Rodes, Gordon, and Wharton, with their divisions and battalions of artillery, were at Stephenson's Depot, five miles from Winchester on the Martinsburg pike. We felt that as soon as Sheridan knew of Anderson's departure, there would be a crisis. Early's army did not exceed 9,000 muskets, 3,000 cavalry, and a proportionate share of artillery. We must gather the strength of Sheridan's army from official reports. He had under his command at that time about 50,000 effective troops. Some of these were left at Harper's Ferry and other posts and did not follow up his campaign; but with three corps, nine divisions, and thirty brigades, it may be safely assumed that he moved against Early with more than 30,000 infantry, 9,000 cavalry, and a full quota of artillery.

On September 17th, leaving General Ramseur with his little division to protect Winchester and the line of communications, General Early moved off to Bunker Hill with Gordon and Rodes, Braxton's artillery and Lomax's cavalry. Such rashness seemed to invite disaster; it was simply bravado, and I have never seen any satisfactory defense of it. I remember well the anxiety felt at our Headquarters when we knew of this movement, and it would have been greater had we known that General Grant was then at Harper's Ferry in consultation with General Sheridan and giving him his orders. The air seemed to have a sulphurous smell.

My own anxiety is expressed, briefly, in these extracts from my diary:

"Sept 17. Genl Early, in these bold movements seems to rely too much upon the caution and timidity of Sheridan."

"Sept 18. A quiet, beautiful day. The Yankees to our satisfaction did not molest us. I shall be glad if tomorrow passes away as quietly."

But it didn't. General Sheridan knew at noon of the 18th that General Early was at Martinsburg with two divisions and he at once ordered a movement against Winchester by way of Berryville with a heavy force.

On the 19th at the earliest dawn a courier announced that the enemy were advancing. Ramseur had his division under arms at once and moved to meet them. It was soon developed that the advance was in great force of infantry, cavalry, and artillery. Checked for a short time at the Opequon, they were soon across it, and the duty devolved upon Ramseur with his little division of 2,100 muskets to resist and stay Sheridan's columns. Rodes and Gordon were not nearer than Stephenson's Depot. With determination and tenacity Ramseur, assisted by his artillery and what cavalry he had at hand, stopped the way. Never did that division or any other do better work. General Early was soon on hand, but it was not until after ten o'clock that Gordon, then Rodes, came to the relief, leaving Wharton and Fitz Lee's cavalry to oppose the enemy on the Bunker Hill road. The battle soon became general and severe. It was a hopeless fight, but a hot one.

The heavy columns of the enemy extended more to our left, and the fighting was severe all along the line. Time and again on both the Berryville and Bunker Hill roads, the enemy were repulsed with great loss, but they rallied and filled up the gaps with fresh troops and came on again. The Federal cavalry made daring charges and at times rode down upon our infantry lines, to be driven back. At last with the approach of night came the inevitable and our left flank on the Bunker Hill road was turned and routed. Early's army was driven from the field and retired through Winchester.

Ramseur's division, the first on the field, was the last to leave it; it had held its own during the long day, and when the army was defeated it was thrown across the rear and, that night, covered the retreat. The censure Ramseur had received for the battle of July 20th and the reflections which had been cast upon his division were splendidly retrieved in this battle. The Confederate troops, in the disasters which soon followed, failed to gain the credit which their heroic fight on the 19th September deserved; but Ramseur was unquestionably the hero of the day.

While it cannot be claimed that General Sheridan displayed either dash or dexterity in that battle, his losses show that he fought his men with a determination to win at any cost. He gives his loss at 697 killed, 3,983 wounded, 338 captured or missing. He reports a very heavy loss of officers. Early's loss was 259 killed, 1,794 wounded, and about 2,000 prisoners, and 3 pieces of artillery. The chivalric and heroic Rodes, after much brilliant service, fell on this field, and General Fitz Lee and Brigadier General York were severely wounded.

In the early afternoon I had been sent for some reason to our left to report to General Breckinridge who was in command. It is likely it was because I was familiar with that approach to Winchester. I witnessed and took part in the severe fighting for several hours before our retreat and watched the dashing charge of the enemy's cavalry. For the first time I saw a division of infantry, or what was left of one, form a hollow square to resist cavalry. It was evident our troops had more dread of Sheridan's cavalry than of his infantry and our cavalry was unequal to them. I was in the hollow square with General Breckinridge when the cavalry charge was made and repulsed. When the square deployed double time into line to fire after the retreating horsemen, I joined a body of our troopers and went with them. My horse, violently excited, ran off with me to the front and it required my utmost effort to keep him from taking me bodily over to the enemy. When I returned and General Breckinridge half complimented and half chided me for my rashness, I felt compelled to say to him,

"General, it was 'Dick Turpin,' not I, who deserves the reprimand."

On that day the General made me grateful for his soldierly

commendation, and months afterwards his approval took another form.

As we went through Winchester about sundown I borrowed from General Breckinridge his ambulance, and going to Mr. R. Y. Conrad's succeeded in getting Randolph Ridgeley and sent him out of town. Harry Gilmor, who had been badly shot, made his escape from the Riley's on horseback. Mrs. Gordon, the wife of General Gordon, who was at Mrs. E. I. Lee's, was compelled to wait for her ambulance. It was a critical moment. The last of our skirmishers, driven by the enemy, were coming in, much demoralized, on the Berryville road. Mrs. Gordon, on the pavement, grappled several of these and ordered them to stop and make a stand; but neither her example, her rank, nor her beauty stayed them, and they trotted on. Riding back for her, I saw from the corner the enemy coming, cautiously, not far off, and several shots advised me that I need not wait for them. Mrs. Gordon's ambulance arrived, I helped her into it, and she was taken out of town with great haste, followed by shots intended to speed the parting guest.

My couriers being sent on with Ridgeley, I stopped in front of Mr. Conrad's for a few seconds to warn the ladies on the walk to seek shelter, and then, for a minute, in front of York Hospital to speak with a surgeon who ran out to me with a message and an appeal to hurry on. The enemy's skirmishers were plainly in sight and the "zip" of their scattering shots uncomfortably distinct. I was enraged and mortified beyond words at being driven through Winchester with such unseemly haste. "Doing the bravado" was not my style, but I was young enough to be forgiven for it. I lifted up my sword in the presence of hospital windows and swore an oath that I would never shave my face clean until I returned to that beloved town, and then I galloped away. It was a foolish vow and gave much annoyance. My bearded face was soon reduced to a light moustache and an unimpressive goatee, but I kept my vow. I never saw Winchester again during the war. On my way homeward from Appomattox I stopped in the old town long enough to visit a barber. Never since that day have I worn a hair on my face, as I never had before that 19th of September, 1864.

We stopped for the night near Newtown and then the army moved on to Fisher's Hill. Ramseur was put in command of Rodes's division and General John Pegram in command of our (Early's) division. On the 21st we were in line at Fisher's Hill but there was no demonstration against us. General Breckinridge and his staff left us for southwest Virginia. Mrs. Breckinridge had just arrived and moved on with him.

On the morning of the 20th indications were ominous, for conscious impudence and confidence were displayed in the demonstrations of the enemy. They knew our exact force now, and caution would have looked like cowardice. The morning passed, but trouble came with the afternoon. We were vigorously attacked and about six o'clock Early's left was turned, driven back, and routed. No effort to stay the disaster succeeded. The confident enemy swarmed over us, pelted us, and we were driven from the field in great disorder. Night came on and saved us from any vigor of pursuit.

In the rear, on the retreat, I was directed to give special attention to the rear guard skirmish line, and remained with it in the dark and distressing march. Sandy Pendleton, General Early's Chief of Staff, came back to enquire into the situation and remained with me a short time. He was riding a white horse, and I warned him against riding such a beast on such a night. He made some light remark about the "deadly white horse," and rode along the skirmish line which was falling back very slowly. My orders were against unnecessary firing, but the enemy were practicing in the dark and at random. We had stopped for a minute, when Pendleton gave a groan and tottered forward on his horse. I dismounted, called a man or two; he fell gently into my arms and was taken from his horse. He tried to walk but could not get far and, just then, the man on the opposite side from me in assisting him was shot and he sank to the ground. Several strong men helped to carry him to the rear as the enemy's fire became more galling. I had sent for an ambulance and when it arrived he was placed in it. He was shot in the groin and through the body. He told me he was mortally wounded. He gave me his watch, pocketbook, prayer book, Bible, and haversack, and some letters from his wife, to be sent to her, and asked me to write and tell her of his death. He was taken to Dr. Murphy's of Woodstock—that home of all Confederates in need—and died the next day in the hands of the enemy.

The battle of Fisher's Hill (afterwards followed by Cedar Creek) made the Valley of Virginia, for us, what it had been during Jackson's day for the enemy, a "Valley of Humiliation." Early's loss in that battle, 250 killed and wounded, did not indicate much obstinacy of resistance, but we lost about 1,000 prisoners and about 15 pieces of artillery. Sheridan, attacking, lost about 500 killed and wounded and a handful of prisoners.

As these are personal memoirs I may speak, personally, of the death of Lieutenant Colonel A. S. Pendleton, as he was the dearest friend I had in the army. He was among the staff of the Second Corps what Jackson was among its leaders, the ablest of them all. I believe him to have been, in spite of his youth, the most brilliant staff officer in the Army of Northern Virginia and the most popular with officers and men. Brave, courteous, resolute, quick, and of high intelligence he was a model Adjutant General. Jackson loved him as a son and called him "Sandy." At Cold Harbor the General said to General Stuart,

"Sandy will not be killed in this war."

But Jackson, then Stuart, passed away in battle and Pendleton followed.[6] After Jackson's death he was invaluable to Ewell; to Early his loss was irreparable.

The next day we retired still further up the valley and the enemy followed leisurely. There was some skirmishing every day and at times the enemy seemed to enjoy themselves by firing volleys at us from their artillery. Sheridan's heavy cavalry, also, had a picnic now and then with our limited number of horsemen, and we soon found out that this branch of his army was more to be feared than his infantry—better soldiers all through. Our cavalry was feeble, badly mounted and badly equipped. Sheridan's cavalry in the Valley were picked men and his best; that could not be said of Early's.

"The laurel is a running vine," said old Jubal once with a grimace when he heard of the stampede of Rosser's "Laurel Brigade."

But whatever ridicule was heaped upon our cavalry in the Valley Campaign of 1864, it must be remembered that it was almost impossible, that late in the war, to keep a body of mounted men in even semi-serviceable condition.

We moved on day after day until the 25th of September we crossed the fork of the Shenandoah at Port Republic and took position in Brown's Gap of the Blue Ridge. This was the retreat to which Jackson had retired in 1862, when after having whipped Banks, Milroy, Shields, and Frémont he took a few days to get his breath before descending on McClellan at Richmond. The situation had changed, lamentably.

As Sheridan's cavalry had moved past us to Staunton and Waynesboro and was doing damage with the railroad, it was necessary to do something to stop this if possible. General K. B. Kershaw had again joined Early with his small division of about 3,000 muskets and Cutshaw's battalion of artillery, and we moved to Waynesboro and drove the enemy away from that place. We remained there several days and on the 1st of October were on the Valley pike again between Staunton and Harrisonburg. Here General Rosser with his small brigade of cavalry arrived and took command of Fitz Lee's division, and General Early endeavored to get his little army in condition to follow the retiring Federals.

Then, under instructions from Grant it is said, Sheridan set his cavalry to work on their campaign of arson, rapine, and starvation. General Wesley Merritt says, more in a tone of satisfaction than regret, that on its return his cavalry "was deployed across the Valley, burning, destroying or taking away everything of value or likely to become of value to the enemy," until, he adds, "the Valley from Staunton to Winchester was completely devastated." With an air of soldierly pride he reports officially, October 5th, that his division alone destroyed from Port Republic to Tom's Brook 630 barns, 47 mills, 410,742 bushels of wheat, 515 acres of corn, etc., etc., to the amount of $3,304,672. Sheridan reported to Grant 2,000 well-filled barns, 70 mills, wheat, grain, etc., destroyed. They both omit to mention the private dwellings which their troops, drunk with their license to burn, laid in ashes, and the unspeakable suffering and horrors they brought on innocent women and children. It is almost impossible to believe that a soldier with the reputation and distinction of General Wesley Merritt could have been an actor in such inhumanity. The reader may imagine what other officers and soldiers with less noblesse did and permitted to be done. For the decency of humanity it is well that a veil has been thrown over some of their fiendish acts. Official authority for much of the destruction has been denied; but when a General says to his soldiers, "Go forth and burn and destroy," what can he expect?

Lieutenant Meigs of Sheridan's staff was killed by a Confederate scout. As a holocaust upon his tomb, Sheridan ordered "all the houses within an area of five miles" to be burned. When General Grant told Sheridan he must make the Valley "so bare that a crow flying over it would be compelled to carry his rations," and Sheridan executed his order, did it not occur to either of them, after their smile over the sardonic joke had faded, that the women and children of Virginia were more to be pitied than crows, for with no rations to eat at home, they had no wings to fly away for food and refuge?

I try to restrain my bitterness at the recollection of the dreadful scenes I witnessed. I rode down the Valley with the advance after Sheridan's retreating cavalry beneath great columns of smoke which almost shut out the sun by day, and in the red glare of bonfires, which, all across that Valley, poured out flames and sparks heavenward and crackled mockingly in the night air; and I saw mothers and maidens tearing their hair and shrieking to Heaven in their fright and despair, and little children, voiceless and tearless in their pitiable terror. I saw a beautiful girl, the daughter of a clergyman, standing in the front door of her home while its stable and outbuildings were burning, tearing the yellow tresses from her head, taking up and repeating the oaths of passing skirmishers and shrieking with wild laughter, for the horrors of the night had driven her mad. It is little wonder that General Grant in his *Memoirs* passes over this work as if he could not bear to touch it, and that no reputable historian of the North has ventured to tell the truth about it and defend it, for it is an insult to civilization and to God to pretend that the Laws of War justify such warfare.

Moving on down the Valley, we reached Fisher's Hill on the 13th and went into camp. For several days there were movements to and fro and some skirmishing, but nothing of importance. I was out several times, beyond Strasburg, reconnoitering, as far as Hupp's Hill and got an accurate idea of the approaches to Strasburg, which was of service to me after the battle of the 19th. It being impossible to remain long in our position because of the scarcity of food and forage, General Early, after consultation with his generals, determined to attack the enemy, notwithstanding the great disparity in numbers. The movement to that effect was made during the night of the 18th, and the attack was on the left flank of the enemy at Cedar Creek before daylight on the 19th. Gordon, Ramseur, and Pegram (under Gordon) made a detour of some length from our right far to the enemy's left and, crossing Cedar Creek, surprised and attacked them. The surprise was complete and the enemy were driven back with little resistance. While this was being done, Early, with Kershaw and Wharton crossed near the center of the enemy and their attack completed the disaster. The Federals were driven in confusion from their camps, which fell into our hands with many wagons and many prisoners and eighteen pieces of artillery. Rosser was off on our left with his cavalry and Lomax off on our right, but they were not able to do much. The pursuit was continued to and beyond Middletown and then a line of battle formed. It was immediately evident that the enemy greatly outnumbered us.

Why we did not attack at once, before they got over the confusion and demoralization caused by the surprise and stampede, I do not know. We had much to gain by taking the offensive, everything to lose by delay. True, our infantry had been scattered and demoralized in stopping to plunder the camps they went through, and the temptation of food and the smell of cooking were too great for their famished stomachs to resist. At any rate *our* victory was over at ten o'clock. The enemy, knowing their strength and our precarious situation, took their time to get ready, and six hours passed away in virtual inactivity. Sheridan arrived an hour before noon and took command of his army. Whether he deserves all the credit that is claimed for him, and General H. G. Wright and his associates so little, we must leave for his own people to determine.

His line moved forward against us about 4:30. At first the resistance of our line was admirable, but being hopelessly overpowered, demoralization succeeded to defeat, and our army was driven from the field in confusion. Trying to hold his feeble line to its place, with grim determination, the dashing and fearless Ramseur was mortally wounded and left in the hands of the enemy. In the morning's onset he had cried out to me joyously as he rushed past on his bay,

"Douglas, I want to win this battle, for I must see my wife and baby."

General Ramseur had been married about a year and a few days before the battle had heard of the birth of a daughter. He lived only a few hours. General Merritt and General Custer called to enquire for him, and he was treated with much kindness. Aside from his ability and bravery he was one of the most attractive men in our army.

In the confused retreat from the field across Cedar Creek I was again directed to remain with the skirmish line which had been formed as a rear guard. Before reaching the Creek the enemy were very close to us and were firing at random and rapidly. My horse, "Dick Turpin," had been slightly wounded in the leg in the morning, and now a rifleman's bullet struck him in the center of the broad part of his jaw and, crushing through, came out on the other side. He gave a weird cry of pain and sprang into the air, then he reared straight up and, throwing his head back in his agony, struck me in the face and knocked me from the saddle. As I fell to the ground,

I heard a cheer from the advancing skirmishers. Bruised and stunned I jumped up. My horse was suffering too much to run off and one of our men had caught him. I climbed to the saddle and moved off. The blood was running out of his mouth over bit and reins, and constantly tossing his head in his pain he soon sprinkled me freely with it.

Driven across the Creek, we soon came to the narrow passage on Hupp's Hill where a small body of soldiers had collected to make a stand. We were almost immediately attacked by some of the enemy's cavalry, who were driven back. I ordered the men to get such things as they could lay their hands on to make a barricade; it was getting dark and I hoped to save the artillery and wagons that I knew were a short distance beyond. The enemy in the meantime was preparing for a more formidable attack of cavalry. General Pegram came and, believing we would be overrun, unfortunately ordered the line to retire. As it proceeded to do so, the enemy came at us with a rush. The few of us who remained could make little resistance and were virtually run over.

I found myself a mounted prisoner, but as it was now dark I was not noticed. I had on a black overcoat, buttoned up to my neck and top boots. I mingled with the cavalry and rode along with them, as with much noise and many oaths they captured wagons and guns and ambulances. It was a novel sensation, but didn't last long. Coming to a rocky and steep descent which led down to the ravine I had discovered a few days before, I determined to try it. My horse did not hesitate at the dark descent and was out of reach before my captors could stop me. "Dick's" activity and goat-like feet landed me safely in the path and I passed along parallel with the road and made my way out. I joined General Early at Fisher's Hill and reported to him what I had seen.

When I dismounted and took the saddle from my noble horse, he at once lay down. I took the bit gently from his mouth, and when he lifted up his head in pain and tried to rub it against me in mute appeal for help it seemed to me that tears were gathering in his eyes: it may be they were those in mine. Two days afterwards he died of lockjaw. His value was returned by the army appraisers at $2,000. I had been offered three times that for him. I sent to the Hospital at Staunton for my black horse, "Ashby," but reply came that the Yankees had captured him. I heard afterwards that he was doing duty with one of Sheridan's staff and I hoped he would break his neck.

Early fought the battle of Cedar Creek with about the same force he had at Winchester on the 19th of September. The arrival of Kershaw's small division about made up our losses at Winchester and Fisher's Hill, or nearly so. Sheridan's force was about the same as at Winchester. Early's attack was, therefore, the strategy of desperation.

Sheridan's loss at Cedar Creek was 644 killed, 3,430 wounded, 1,591 captured. Early's loss was 1,860 killed and wounded and about 1,000 captured. Early had captured 18 pieces of artillery in the morning, but in the evening they were recaptured, and about 30 pieces of ours taken. Some ambulances and ammunition wagons were captured, but the greater part of these taken at night were the wagons, ambulances, etc., our troops had captured in the morning.

"The Yankees got whipped; we got scared," was Early's comment on this battle.

One thing is certain: it was to us an irreparable disaster, the beginning of the end.

APPOMATTOX

THE next day we moved further up the Valley and went into camp near New Market. There we remained for some days. I sent to Brigadier General Edwin G. Lee $50 to pay for a coat which I had, in part, remade, and also a calf skin for which I had given $50 to be traded off for a pair of boots. He got me the boots for $200, the bootmaker allowing me $100 for the calf skin. The boots were not satisfactory, and I sent them back and gave something more for another pair. I had in some way come in possession of a new pair of trousers (which I call pants in my diary), but the first time I put them on and went to "Mt. Airy" to call my new horse fell with me and they were so badly wrecked—worthless shoddy—that I was obliged to remount and go back, seven miles, to camp, supperless. I changed that horse's name from "Jeb Stuart" to "Blunderer," but he afterwards did me such good service that I changed it back again.

One Sunday an impromptu fox chase was started in which I joined for a little while. It so happened that just about that time General Early issued an order for a stricter observance of Sabbath in camp, à la Jackson, and I generally observed it by going to "Mt. Airy," the home of Dr. Meem,[1] that open house where varied and boundless hospitality was dispensed with a graciousness and cheerfulness that one never forgets. A deer hunt from there was too great a temptation to resist. I took down my little black horse for the daughter of the house to ride, as she was to join the chase. Before day-

light the next morning we were off to the Massanutton, eight
men and eleven dogs. We had a day of sport, saw two deer,
but returned without any except the one we took with us, and
Harry Gilmor monopolized her.

On the 10th of November, General Early concluded to take
his command on a scouting expedition down the Valley. When
we got to Fisher's Hill the enemy retired from their position
on Cedar Creek, but when we reached Newtown they were in
line of battle at Kernstown. We loafed about leisurely and
returned to camp at New Market on the 14th and named it
Camp Ramseur. Here we remained inactive, because Sheridan was quiet, until the 1st of December. I managed to read
a great deal, rereading my old favorites, *Quits* and *Initials*,
and was much interested in a book sent me, with the suggestive
title *Not Dead Yet*.[2] On the 27th and 28th of November Rosser made a raid on Moorefield and New Creek, capturing 800
prisoners, 8 pieces of artillery, and a large quantity of cattle
and much needed military stores.

On the 6th of December we broke camp and moved to
Waynesboro, and thence Gordon's and Pegram's divisions
went at once by rail to Petersburg, General Gordon in command. I was left behind at Waynesboro to gather up stragglers, to organize troops that came in, and on the night of
the 10th I started for Petersburg with 600 men. We parted
with General Early, to whom with few troops, badly equipped,
was committed the hopeless duty of defending the Valley of
Virginia.

I reported with my troops to General Pegram on the 11th.
On the 21st General Gordon issued an order taking command
of the Second Corps. Mrs. A. P. Hill sent me a battle flag
to present to the Thirteenth Virginia Infantry—General
Hill's old regiment—now grown very slim. On Christmas Day
I went to dine at the most hospitable mansion of Mrs. Gilliam.
There I found General W. H. F. Lee, General R. D. Johnston
—a dinner party of eight gentlemen and five ladies, and a
most agreeable one. I remained all night and helped to make a
jolly bowl of eggnog before breakfast next morning.

Winter was upon us and for a time the war drums ceased

to throb. I took the opportunity to have a dentist in Petersburg look after several of my teeth for which I paid him the modest sum of $260. Social pleasures were abundant and, while the tenure of life was so uncertain, entertainments, dances, marriages were plentiful. The sound of parlor music and of "dancers dancing in tune" might be heard within cannon shot of the enemy. To go into a parlor for a call or for a waltz with sword and spurs, while orderlies outside held horses ready to mount at the first alarm was no unusual thing. To spend half the night in the saddle that the other half might be spent in social revelry was not strange enough to cause comment.

A letter lies before me written to my sister on New Year's Eve, where, after speaking of the engagements for the week, I notice the great New Year's dinner, which the people of Virginia and North Carolina had been for weeks preparing for Lee's army; the gathering of food, the arranging, the cooking, the work of hundreds of faithful women to spread this one, this last great feast for the Army of Northern Virginia on a table thirty miles long. It was the final, supreme evidence of their unselfish love and devotion.

Having waited during the winter until everyone else about Headquarters had a short furlough, I started off on the 9th of January upon a short leave of fifteen days, the only leave I ever had during my four years in the army. My first day was one of adventure. I had five ladies in charge who were en route to a wedding to which I had not been invited. But I knew the groom, William Francis Coleman, at law school and determined to go with them. When we left the train at the station not far from Charlottesville and it had departed, a little Negro arrived to tell us to go on to the next station as the "crick" was too high for carriages to cross and come for us. It was raining, as it had been all day. The station had no shelter but a shed, and in the only house near at hand was lying a dead man, with a mourning wife and children on the verge of starvation. We had nothing to eat; without food or shelter and night coming on, the situation was novel misery. Seeing an old engine on a switch, I was in a little while put in communication with a crippled engineer who lived within a mile. To bribe him sufficiently to induce him to fire up the engine; then, disobeying all orders and all propriety, to put it on the track; to take my precious burden in a caboose and run that "rickety" train at full speed to the next station, four miles above, crossing the stream on a railroad bridge, and whistling like fury as we flew; all this took some hours, made our engineer speechless with the risk, showed the pluck of my five girls, and added years to my age, for the time being.[3] After consternation and most merited reprimand on the part of Colonel Stuart of Chantilly at the next station, he obtained for me a covered two-horse wagon, in which I conveyed my bridal party over four miles of a villainous road, deep in mud, to their destination. I walked. Our unexpected arrival and greeting paid for the anxiety and labor; brandy, food, and bed made me all right next morning; I had my reward.

It rained on, but the wedding next night was a brilliant one, in that hospitable old mansion in the "Green Spring Valley." General Longstreet and many officers in uniform were there, and a band of music. I was the "best man"—there were thirteen groomsmen and as many bridesmaids—and my bridesmaid was the queen of the party, except the bride. It was a night of dance and merriment. When four o'clock came I was dancing with the bride, but my hour for departure had arrived. Hasty farewells and I was off to the train, riding a horse with a little darkey carrying my bag on a mule. I never saw the bride again; she died young, but left herself behind in a beautiful daughter.

With waiting and delay I did not reach Waynesboro until seven o'clock in the evening. But a glass of something, a bit of supper and a Confederate toilet, and I was ready for another wedding at eight o'clock. The groom was Captain Hugh McGuire, brother of Dr. Hunter McGuire, and a trooper who rode with Rosser. His bride was fair and worthy of him. My bridesmaid was, in beauty, compared with the bride, as a pink rose to a red. General Lomax and Dr. McGuire were others of the seven groomsmen and General Fitz Lee and staff were there. It was a merry, merry wedding until after midnight, when I took my bridesmaid to the house she was visiting, tremulous, pale, with a maddening headache. It was her first experience as a bridesmaid and the excitement, I told her, caused her headache; but on the next Sunday she was buried in the gown and the roses she wore at the wedding. A few days before the surrender Captain McGuire fell, leading a cavalry charge at Amelia Springs—generous, gallant, splendid Hugh —and a bridal wreath was exchanged for a widow's cap.

On the 14th to Staunton and stopped at General Early's Headquarters with Dr. Hunter McGuire. I intended to go down the Valley to Woodstock, to the wedding of Captain William Hull of Baltimore, but Colonel Harry Gilmor informed me that Sheridan had advanced his outposts and his cavalry had indicated an intention to be present at the wedding, unbidden. The bridal party had retreated, therefore, hastily in sections on parallel lines and had crossed the Massanutton and Blue Ridge. I went to church with General Early on Sunday, and that was almost as exciting. It was on that occasion as the story goes that the preacher, speaking of the dead of the centuries, asked his hearers with dramatic effect what they would do if the dead came marching back to earth by thousands and tens of thousands?

"I'd conscript every d—— one of them," was the semi-audible aside of old Jubal, thinking doubtless of his feeble little army and the hopelessness of reinforcements.

I wrote to Baltimore for some harp strings for the harp of my bridesmaid at Coleman's wedding, to be sent to Moorefield. Gilmor, who was to make a raid to that point, under orders from General Early, promised to get them for me.

He made the raid and tried to keep his promise, but was captured and confined in prison for the rest of the war, and thus ended Harry Gilmor's career. Big, kindly-hearted Harry was looked upon as a terror. Sheridan telegraphed to Halleck,

"He is an energetic, shrewd, unscrupulous scoundrel and dangerous man. He must be closely watched or he will escape."

Halleck replied, "A special guard should be selected to take him" to Fort Warren.

As for that harp, it continued to work mischief until the

last days of the Confederacy. When Sheridan and G. K. Warren broke our troops up at Five Forks, General "Rooney" Lee sent Captain Phil Dandridge of his staff with an ambulance and a squad of cavalry to remove Mrs. G—— and her family from their home to Petersburg. The daughter of the house refused to leave her harp behind. The big musical pet was brought out and tied upon the top of the ambulance. This took time, and before they were off the Federal cavalry were in sight. A spirited fight took place between Dandridge's escort and the pursuing cavalry, while the ambulance with its precious inmates took refuge in flight. As the escort holding the enemy in check were gradually driven back, the driver lashed his frantic horses and disappeared through the woods. As for the harp, the wind whistled through its tossing strings and played a melancholy dirge for the men who were being shot in defense of its fair mistress.

I did not get back to Richmond in time for General Pegram's wedding. He was married on the 19th in St. Paul's Church to Miss Hetty Carey of Baltimore. One of the handsomest and most lovable men I ever knew wed to the handsomest woman in the Southland—with her classic face, her pure complexion, her auburn hair, her perfect figure and her carriage, altogether the most beautiful woman I ever saw in any land. Ill omens attended her marriage. President and Mrs. Davis sent their carriage and horses—the only private turnout, I fancy, in Richmond—to take the happy pair to the church. The horses balked, became unruly and threatened a smashup. The bride's dress was rent going into church, and the veil nearly torn from her face as she approached the altar. A superstitious murmur passed through the immense congregation, but they went on to their fate.

I got back to Richmond on the 23rd with General and Mrs. Rosser. The General offered me the command of a regiment of cavalry. On the 25th I returned to our Headquarters at the Cross Roads near Hatcher's Run.

On the 2nd of February, General Gordon reviewed Pegram's division. I made it the occasion for a Review for the bride, and as Adjutant General invited Generals R. E. Lee,

Longstreet, Hill, Gordon, Anderson, Heth and others to be
present to meet the bride. They all came, and also a number
of ladies. As the division under General Pegram passed in
review before her—General Gordon abdicating in her favor
—General Lee was on her right and the other generals with
their glittering staff officers about her and in her train. Her
rich color emblazoned her face, a rare light illumined her eyes
and her soul was on fire with the triumph of the moment, the
horrors of war forgotten. I rode with her off the field, and as
we passed the troops returning to camp, she was sitting her
horse like the Maid of France and smiling upon them with
her marvelous beauty, their wild enthusiasm sought in vain
for fitting expression and vent. An excited "Tar Heel," whom
her horse struck and nearly knocked down, quickly sprang up
and, as she reined up her horse and began to apologize, he
broke in as he seized his old hat from his head. "Never mind,
Miss. You might have rid all over me, indeed you might!"

On the 5th, the enemy advanced early with cavalry and
some infantry across Hatcher's Run and toward Dinwiddie
Court House. Our division went out to meet them. We were
skirmishing all day with them. Gordon's division and one of
Hill's joined us in the afternoon and the enemy were driven
back across Hatcher's Run. Early on the 6th we were moving.
General Pegram, believing that only cavalry was demonstrating in our front, gave me two regiments, and directed me to
advance and develop them. Thinking he was mistaken, I did
it very cautiously, driving the cavalry, but I developed a
heavy column of infantry, forming a *tête-de-pont* on this side
the Run. I hastened to withdraw my line and had only time
to inform General Pegram before the enemy were upon us.
They struck our division. They were handsomely resisted but
we were gradually driven back. Gordon and Hill, each with a
division, then came to our assistance and repulsed the enemy
with severe loss. But it was now evident they were in heavy
force. Again they came forward and forced Hill and Gordon
to give way. General William Mahone of Hill's corps then
arrived, and Pegram joined him in the attack and the enemy
were driven across Hatcher's Run. In this attack General

Pegram was shot through the body near the heart. I jumped from my horse and caught him as he fell and with assistance took him from his horse. He died in my arms, almost as soon as he touched the ground. Colonel Hoffman commanding Pegram's brigade was also mortally wounded.

The battle was over and night had been upon us for an hour. Who would tell Mrs. Pegram?

"You must do it, Douglas," said General Gordon.

"Heavens! General—I'll lead a forlorn hope—do anything that is war—but not that. Send New. He's married and knows women; I don't."

Major New went on his unenviable duty and I took the General's body back to my room at Headquarters. An hour after, as the General lay, dead, on my bed, I heard the ambulance pass just outside the window, taking Mrs. Pegram back to their quarters. New had not seen her yet and she did not know; but her mother was with her. A fiancée of three years, a bride of three weeks, now a widow!

Our loss at Hatcher's Run is estimated at 1,000. I did not think it so much. Neither did I believe the loss of the enemy so heavy as they report, about 2,000.

General Lee on the 6th of February was assigned to the command of all the armies of the Confederacy: at least two years too late.

On the 16th we received orders to get the opinion of the soldiers on the subject of the appointment of volunteer Negro troops. There's a subject for reflection! Our division had become so small that General Lewis, commanding it, and I went to consult General Gordon about consolidating the regiments. I also, at the request of General Lewis wrote the report of the division's part in the battles of Hatcher's Run. In a few days General R. D. Johnston returned and took command of the division, and on February 27th Brigadier General James A. Walker was assigned to Pegram's brigade and took command of the division. I continued as Adjutant General with the understanding that as soon as General Walker was promoted, I was to be appointed Brigadier General and put in command of his (Pegram's) brigade—the same brigade I had taken into the fight at Gettysburg when I was wounded there.

After a little while our division was in Petersburg, in position at Colquit's salient and just opposite Fort Steadman. A boy with a strong arm could have thrown a stone from the works of one into the works of the other. To expose one's head an inch above the works was at the risk of a hole in it. In the salient the rifle pits were made into apartments and the approaches to them were covered for protection against mortar shells, etc. It was a dreadful line to hold. Petersburg was virtually surrounded; daily the inevitable was staring us closer in the face, but we never "let on." We held the lines, slept little, ate less, and at night went about the town calling and making visits with incredible gayety. We were waiting for something to explode, killing time, for time was killing us. For a long time before this a Confederate's outfit was "no haversack, all cartridge box."

General Lee determined to force a conclusion and ordered an assault on the enemy's line in front of Colquit's salient. Fort Steadman was opposite, and there were well-constructed works along the line, with abatis thrown up well to the front, where pickets were placed at night. The assault was to be made by Gordon's two divisions—about 4,000 muskets—to be followed and supported by other troops when the works were carried. On the night of the 24th I was put in temporary charge of the brigade I was to be placed in command of. Before dawn on March 25th the assault was made, my brigade —being nearest to the enemy's line—taking the initiative. There was a rush in the dark across 200 yards, capture of the pickets, tearing away of the abatis, a few sentinel shots, and we were over the fortifications and had Fort Steadman. Turning the captured guns to the right and left they swept the redoubt and drove the enemy from it. Other troops of the same command crossed the works and an advance was made inland. But where were the supports and reinforcements that were to follow Gordon? They had not arrived and we were left to go it alone. The enemy gathered on our front and about us in great force and Fort Haskell opened upon us with de-

structive effect. The return assault was made promptly and
vigorously, General John F. Hartranft especially distinguish-
ing himself on that occasion. We were overwhelmed and driven
from the enemy's enclosure under a galling fire, and many
surrendered rather than be shot. The loss was heavy for so
short an engagement. The enemy put their loss at about 600
killed and wounded and 500 prisoners: the killed and wounded
chiefly of Hartranft's Third Division, Ninth Corps. Our loss
was 1,900 prisoners and about 750 killed and wounded.

Immediately after the repulse I was directed by General
Gordon to open communication with the enemy at once, that
the wounded between the lines might be cared for. This I did,
and General Hartranft with some other officers met me between the lines. We agreed immediately to have the wounded
and the dead taken off, each by his own people. There was
not a moment wasted with red tape. Men ran over the field
from each side and gathered up their comrades, taking time,
when they could, to exchange pipes, tobacco, penknives, hard-
tack and anything that was tradable. General Hartranft and
I had gone to the same college, although we never had seen
each other. I gave him a letter to send to my home, which he
supplemented with a kindly one of his own in enclosing it. On
this day began a friendship between us which lasted during
his life and exhibited itself when he was Comptroller and
Governor of Pennsylvania,[4] and it was a great gratification to
me when his old division met after his death on the anniver-
sary of the battle of Fort Steadman at York, Pennsylvania,
that they should ask me to deliver a memorial on that gallant
soldier, faithful public officer, and honest, generous, incor-
ruptible man and citizen. When I left General Hartranft
that day, I gave him the following ghastly receipt which was
found afterwards among his papers.

"Received of Major [John D.] Bertolette 120 dead and 15
wounded in the engagement of the 25th March 1865.

"For Maj. Genl. Gordon

"HY. KYD DOUGLAS

"A. A. Genl."

I had received a letter from Captain Cabell Breckinridge, saying that General Breckinridge, then Secretary of War, had not forgotten his voluntary remark to me at Winchester on September 19th about recommending me for Brigadier General, and that my commission as such would go with General James A. Walker's commission as Major General. I was then, more formally, assigned to the command of "The Light Brigade"—a name given to it by A. P. Hill, and after Hill commanded by Early, "Extra-Billy" Smith, Pegram, Walker and others—and the two written orders making the assignment are lying before me now.

Events hurried to a finish. On the 29th Grant massed troops against our extreme left flank. Lee attacked his flank on the 31st and drove it in. The success was temporary and did not accomplish much. On the 1st of April Lee's army of all arms did not number 33,000 effectives at Petersburg. Grant had there 100,000 in good condition. On this day Sheridan attacked Five Forks and in the evening got possession of it. He renewed his attack on the morning of the 2nd and disastrously broke our lines. On that day Lieutenant General A. P. Hill, chivalric, dashing, distinguished on many hot fields, fought his last fight and was killed. Petersburg was to be evacuated and the retreat began after dark. There was no sleeping in Petersburg that night: no night except for the darkness. It was all commotion and bustle. While my brigade was waiting for its order to move, I rode to sundry houses to say good-by. Before we got away, shells were bursting at places over the town and the air was now and then illumined by the baleful light of mortars. The last person I spoke to in Petersburg was a young lady who afterwards became the wife of General W. H. F. Lee; she uttered not a word of fear or complaint: the infinite sadness of her silence was pathetic beyond words. Colonel Walter H. Taylor, General Lee's Adjutant General, started off for Richmond to get married and returned to the General on the retreat within forty-eight hours. General John B. Gordon, commander of our corps, marched off at the head of his command, leaving behind in that besieged and endangered city his beautiful and heroic wife, to whom just twenty-four hours before a son had been born. So with pangs and sorrows and memories of all kinds, we all marched away. The next morning when daylight came, I observed on my coat a faded red rose, a souvenir of a serenade a few nights before to Miss Agnes, daughter of General R. E. Lee, who died very young, shortly after the close of the war; it was an emblem of our drooping spirits. Shortly after I was directed by General Walker to fall back with my brigade and march it until relieved as the infantry rear guard of the army. This imposed on me a dreary and ceaseless vigil for more than twenty-four hours—sleepless, foodless, cheerless. At Amelia Court House another trial was added to our many: the rations for the army expected to be there had been run on to Richmond. We had nothing to eat; hunger became an ally of the enemy. Once I took some corn from my horse, beat it between stones and tried to swallow it. The little army was willing to march and fight, but starvation made stragglers of them; commands were reduced to skeletons, as their men had been some time before.

On the afternoon of the 6th in Gordon's fight, trying to hold the enemy in check as they moved against us from Amelia Court House, we were roughly handled and the loss in my brigade was very heavy for its size. We were driven back but I had held the hill assigned to me until the trains and artillery of the division had crossed the stream in my rear. Cutshaw, with his artillery battalion, armed with muskets (his guns being gone), reported to me for duty and was in that fight. His leg was torn off by a shell while we were watching the movements of the enemy, and I was shortly afterwards knocked from my horse by a spent musket-ball which struck a button on the breast of my coat. After this battle my brigade did not number over 500 men and we moved on to High Bridge. The next day I had a curious wound. I had been lying down near some artillery, asleep. The enemy's cavalry began demonstrating against my line and some men tried to awaken me. They got me on my feet, but I did not seem to be responding to their efforts when a shell exploded above me and a piece of it tore into my right shoulder. That awakened me. The wound was painful but not serious and after the doctor had dressed it and given me some brandy I was able to mount with assistance and travel with the brigade, with my right arm in a sling for that day and the next.

On the morning of April 9th, at Appomattox, but 8,000 Confederates stood to arms at the morning call: the rest of the Army of Northern Virginia was scattered, captured, demoralized, destroyed. On that morning General Lee directed General Fitz Lee to ascertain the situation in front of us and General Gordon to support him. My brigade was sent with Fitz Lee so far out that we were beyond the sight of the army, and General Fitz Lee, after giving me some instructions, moved further off to the right. There was some contest with Federal cavalry which was driven back, and there was moving and countermoving. After while I observed some infantry skirmishers in my front, apparently with no special desire to advance, and they were soon retired, a few harmless shots having passed between us. I moved cautiously until I became aware of a solid body of infantry across the front, but motionless— it was General E. O. C. Ord's corps. Puzzled by the situation which I could not understand, I remained quiet, and very soon I saw a horseman riding toward me with great speed who proved to be Major Robert W. Hunter of General Gordon's staff. With the good humor and facetiousness which never deserted him, he cried out,

"Douglas, what is this racket you are making? General Gordon wants to know whether you are in command of this army or General Lee; *he* has surrendered!"

This accounted for the peculiar conduct of the enemy. But my little brigade had fired the last shot from Lee's army, and I sadly moved it back to its place in the division.

I rode up to General Gordon's Headquarters and joined him and his staff on a visit to General Grant's Headquarters. I thus had an opportunity to see the uniform and tactful courtesy and consideration with which all the general, staff, and line officers there treated every Confederate officer who called. All communication was easy and without restraint. General Grant's soldierly and chivalric treatment of General Lee was an example which no one departed from on that occasion. What any one man could do to soften defeat, by quiet courtesy without effusiveness, General Grant did.

On my return I sent for my wagon and servant. The wagon came, with the information that my boy, Buck, with my other horse, bridle, saddle, my little black hand trunk and what of clothing I had worth anything, were gone. Early that morning I had put on my new uniform—wishing, if killed, to appear like Nelson at Trafalgar in my best clothes—and had told Buck if anything happened to me to save that little hand trunk if he could, for it contained papers very valuable to me.

"Gone to the Yankees, with your traps," was the brief comment of a by-stander.

"Buck? If there is one faithful creature in the world, never!" was my reply.

The gloom of the occasion was not made cheerful by a chilly rain the next day. For a time, in the morning, the clouds hung heavy everywhere. Seeing a horseman encircling a field off in front of my headquarters I sent a courier to bring him in. It was my friend, Colonel Charles Marshall of General Lee's staff. He was on his way to General Lee and, having dropped his eyeglasses, he was helpless and could not get along in the storm. I accompanied him to Lee's Headquarters. He had up to that time delayed preparing General Lee's final order to his troops, and being pricked to it by the General as soon as he arrived he climbed into an ambulance and went to work. He told me what he was to do and I left him undisturbed for the few minutes it took him to prepare that model of soldierly scholarship, deep feeling, self-repression, and devotion to his army, which is known as Lee's Farewell Address. He took it to General Lee and, coming out in a short time, he showed it to me with the few verbal changes the General had made, and I read it then with the admiration that has not lessened with the passing years.

When I returned to our camp, I was attracted by a crowd standing around a man on horseback and looking up at him intently. It was General John B. Gordon making a speech to his troops, in praise of their conduct in the past, in sorrow for their defeat and sadness then, with earnest and good counsel for their conduct in the future. I know no other General in the army who would have attempted to make a speech to the troops at that time,'or to whom they would have listened with as much patience and pleasure.

When the time came to march out and give up our guns and flags, in surrender, I asked General Gordon to let my brigade—as it had fired the last shot—be the last to stack arms. This he readily granted. In a little while my time came. A heavy line of Union soldiers stood opposite us in absolute silence. As my decimated and ragged band with their bullet-torn banner marched to its place, someone in the blue line broke the silence and called for three cheers for the last brigade to surrender. It was taken up all about him by those who knew what it meant. But for us this soldierly generosity was more than we could bear. Many of the grizzled veterans wept like women, and my own eyes were as blind as my voice was dumb. Years have passed since then and time mellows memories, and now I almost forget the keen agony of that bitter day when I recall how that line of blue broke its respectful silence to pay such tribute, at Appomattox, to the little line in grey that had fought them to the finish and only surrendered because it was destroyed.

AFTERMATH

O<small>N</small> the 11th of May, carrying with me a parole saying that I had permission to go to my home and there remain undisturbed, and to take with me two private horses, I left Appomattox on my horse, "Jeb Stuart." I had a servant with me, who rode a mule I had obtained leave to take, as Buck had gone off with my other horse. My first purpose was to go in search of my man and my properties. I had, as finances, a fifty-cent Confederate note. I traveled leisurely—in company for several days with Colonel H. B. Latrobe and Colonel John W. Fairfax of General Longstreet's staff— stopping for the night where we could get lodging and something to eat. I went to Charlottesville, Waynesboro, and then to Lexington.

As I rode through the latter place late one afternoon, I was halted with a shout, and Buck stood in the street by my side; he began a rapid explanation of what he had done. Fearing that I would be sent to prison and remembering my injunction as to the hand trunk and papers, he had determined to escape through the lines with my spare horse, my hand trunk, and all he could carry. He swam the James River at night near Amherst Court House, crossed the mountain and arrived safely in Lexington. There he intended to wait awhile for me. If he could hear nothing from me and the war went on, he intended, as he said, to "cut his way through to General Johnston"—which it was supposed General Lee was trying to do. My horse was at pasture out in the country and my hand trunk was hidden in a hole in the cellar under the wood-pile and everything in it was safe. The next day Buck appeared with the horse and hand trunk and the papers in it (else these recollections had never been written) and said he wanted to go with me without pay. I had hard work to make him understand that I must learn to do without a servant. I gave him the horse to help him start in life and I departed with the hand trunk. General Pendleton's black man, "Mr. Snow," went with me to Shepherdstown and drove an ambulance I obtained, drawn by "Jeb Stuart" and my mule. In Lexington I heard of the assassination of President Lincoln; and it gave me an unaccountable foreboding of evils to come. I moved on down the Valley, stopping at Staunton, "Mt. Airy," Winchester, and in due time reached Shepherdstown.

For some reason I never understood—pure cussedness I think it was—I was told my parole would not permit me to go to my home across the Potomac and that I must stop south of that river. I had no money to pay boarding, but fortunately a bachelor friend, James H. Shepherd, took me into his comfortable home. I was informed that I must get out of that rebel uniform. I had some time-eaten clothes at my home, and I had also a mule. I sold that animal for $125 in Greenbacks, bought a few clothes and began life.

Then the stay-at-home loyalists began to make it warm for me. It was soon understood at all neighboring posts that I was a dangerous character to be unconfined. The ball I received at Gettysburg was giving me much annoyance and pain—having gravitated to the region of my heart—and I had it cut out. This was in some way a matter of suspicion. Of course, I desired the ball out of me because it was a Union ball, and not really because I objected to balls in my person. But their espionage soon accomplished results. One day a lady suggested that I go with her to Darnell, the photographer, and have my picture taken in uniform with her. It seemed a harmless suggestion and I adopted it. Not wishing to attract attention I carried my uniform coat on my arm. The photograph was taken and I returned to my room. But this act of

disloyalty did not escape observation and that very afternoon it was reported to the military authorities at Martinsburg. The next morning Captain Seidenstricker was sent with
a company of cavalry to Shepherdstown with orders for my
arrest and the confiscation of the objectionable negative. He
came with much of the pomp of war, raided the photographer's and carried off the picture, and then demanded my
surrender. I was lying on the bed, a little sore from the effect
of my operation, but this had a taste of pleasing excitement,
for life was already getting very monotonous. I got my horse
"Jeb Stuart" and was soon off with my military escort. It is
fair to say that the Captain acted most courteously and I do
not think he relished such unsoldierly duty. Several years
after he returned me the negative of the photograph which
he had kept.

At Martinsburg I was committed to solitary confinement.
The Catholic Church had been taken and its basement was
being used as a stable for cavalry horses. At the rear end was
a small, narrow room, ten feet by eight feet, damp and
gloomy, with one small window, and chiefly underground—
this was my prison. I was not permitted to see friends and
was made the more uncomfortable because my fresh wound
was not benefited by such treatment. It seemed that everything was done to magnify my importance and my crime, and
as rumors were constantly started that old Confederates were
determined to rescue me, the guards made it very unpleasant
for me, especially when, as was often the case, one or more of
them were drunk. My horse had been taken with a promise of
safekeeping. A few days after I was informed he was stolen. I
learned he was confiscated by an officer who took a fancy to
him and was sent away. I never saw "Jeb Stuart" again.
There were officers in the Army of the Valley as well as men
who never got over the example set them by Hunter and
Sheridan.

General William H. Seward, Jr., a son of the Secretary of
State, was the commanding officer at that post and, in his
absence, Colonel Roger E. Cook. I had gone to school to
Colonel Cook when a boy. He was a kindhearted man and

visited me surreptitiously now and then and was as courteous as he dared to be.

But it was evident that such an offense as mine was not to pass without serious consequences. A Military Commission of five officers and a Judge Advocate was ordered for my trial, and charges were preferred. An improvised court house was erected of boards in the public square of Martinsburg, and there, on the 8th of May, sat that august tribunal. Major O. A. Horner, First Maryland P.H.B.C., was president and one Captain S. F. Adams preferred the charges and was Judge Advocate. The charges were:

First, *Violation of Parole: Specification.* That the prisoner H. K. Douglas did appear in the streets of Shepherdstown in Confederate uniform—"a badge of treason and rebellion, intended and designed to encourage and incite rebellion, against the government," etc.

Second, *Violation of Military Orders: Specification.* That the said Douglas, did appear, etc. (same as above) and in violation of military orders No. 28 issued at Harper's Ferry.

Third, *Treason: Specification.* That the said Douglas "did take up arms and attempt to overthrow the government of the United States" *and* "did appear in the streets of Shepherdstown, etc." as in first specification.

An official copy of this Quixotic paper lies before me now. If Artemus Ward had been around I would have suspected him of it. Upon it I was solemnly arraigned and called upon to plead, before this grave Court. Impressed with the seriousness of the proceeding and the oppressive gravity around me, I asked for leave to employ counsel. This was denied, the Court saying it would assign me a loyal member of the bar of Martinsburg, if I desired it. This I declined, preferring to defend myself. The next day, testimony was taken, not lasting long, and the Court again graciously adjourned to give me time to prepare my brief in defense. Having one's picture taken for a handsome girl was such a novel crime to me that I am afraid my brief was more satirical than weighty. Then the Court took time to deliberate, and I was remanded to my cell.

When the finding of the Court was made known, it was:

Of the first charge, *Violation of Parole,* "not guilty."

Of the second charge, *Violation of Military Orders,* "guilty," except the words, "designing and intending to incite treason and rebellion."

Of the third charge, *Treason,* "not guilty."

The Commission sentenced me to confinement in Fort Delaware for two months! Most lame and impotent conclusion. It will be observed that I am the only Confederate who, after the war, was tried for treason.[1] This Court judicially determined that taking up arms against the United States Government, to overthrow it, in the late war, was not treason. The humor of this farce will not be fully appreciated without quoting from the order of General John D. Stevenson, approving the finding and sentence. It was much after the fashion of Dogberry:

"The wearing or display of any badge of treason, proceeds from a spirit of hostility to the established government. The purposes of the Government and the whole purposes of the war, are (sic) to utterly eradicate such feeling in the country. Acts savoring of treason, of themselves, cannot be palliated— this is one of them!"

I defy Mark Twain to equal that.

After a few days I was marched to the train, to the tap of martial music, and guarded by an imposing file of soldiers, to be sent on my way; but the only half-suppressed ridicule of the citizens along the streets seemed to deprive the denouement of the impressiveness the proceeding contemplated.

I was stopped at Harper's Ferry for the night and thrown into a "guard-pen" with horse thieves, bounty jumpers, deserters, etc.—all drawing pensions now, doubtless. Two of my guard offered to remain with me to keep me from being robbed and did so.

The next day I had a diversion of excitement. Instead of being taken to Fort Delaware I was hurried off to Washington. En route it was intimated I was supposed to know something of the assassination of President Lincoln. The situation was getting complicated and perplexing. In Washington I was taken to the Provost Marshal's office where I met that distinguished and unsavory Maryland patriot, Lafayette C. Baker, and was sent, to my relief, to the Penitentiary. It was the day of General Sherman's grand entry into Washington, and my guard permitted me to go to a restaurant on Pennsylvania Avenue to get a long-drawn-out breakfast, that he might view the parade. At the Penitentiary I was turned over, as I anticipated, to General Hartranft and soon felt more at ease. He was military Governor of the District and had full charge of the Penitentiary, in which Mrs. Mary E. Surratt and her fellow prisoners were confined. I was assigned to a so-called cell, a comfortable room, next to that of Mrs. Surratt, but entirely cut off from communication with it.

I now learned the cause of this new complication. An adventurous little German, one H. von Steinacker, had deserted from Blenker's division of the Union army in the spring of 1863, had joined a regiment in the Stonewall Brigade, had been detailed as draftsman to Captain Heinricks at our Headquarters, had been used by me on the march to Gettysburg as a courier and forager, had got into trouble for stealing and abuse of prisoners, had been put in the guardhouse, had made his escape and deserted to the enemy. Having landed in the command he deserted from, he had been arrested, tried for desertion, and sentenced to three years' imprisonment. In the trial of the Conspirators came his opportunity. Seeing the effort to implicate the Confederacy in the assassination of President Lincoln, he gave notice to the prosecution that he could give testimony implicating officers of the Stonewall division in the assassination. He was sent for and put on the stand as a witness. His testimony, or part of it, is found in the garbled official record of that trial. He had seen John Wilkes Booth, he swore, in our camp in the summer of 1863, in Virginia, and dragged in the names of General Edward Johnson, Heinricks, myself, and others.

It was such an absurd tissue of lies and so transparent that the wonder is that even that Court could listen to it with patience. Nothing better illustrates the insanity of the times than the fact that witness after witness, no better than this convicted deserter, should have been put upon the stand to testify, and thus be accredited to the world by that Military Commission as persons entitled to credence. But the Commission seemed determined to omit nothing that would discredit them and their verdict in the eyes of history.

General Johnson, Heinricks, myself, and others were sent for and taken to the Penitentiary, semi-witnesses, semi-accused. As soon as I arrived I asked General Hartranft to have von Steinacker apprehended that he might face us, and sent the same request to General Hancock by Captain Ike Parker of his staff. But von Steinacker, being released, had disappeared and in spite of efforts to track him was never again heard from.

After a conversation with me, General Hartranft introduced his staff, and during my stay in the Penitentiary—although at night in my comfortable cell—I was treated as a guest by them at their table and in daily intercourse. I walked about as I pleased within the limits of the prison, and being in citizen's clothes no one knew me.

The trial was held in the Penitentiary. My room opened into the courtroom and was used as a witness room during the day. The day after I arrived I looked in upon the Court; it was a strange scene. There was General David Hunter in the congenial occupation of presiding over a Court of Death with evident pride and satisfaction. There were eight others, but no one of them has ever been known to mention, in the record of his life, that he was a member of that Commission: the fact is a skeleton in each one's closet. It was the most severely solemn tribunal I ever faced. I never saw a smile upon the face of judge, counsel, or spectator; and with the exception of General John G. Foster, who now and then gave a semblance of fairness and justice to the proceedings by intervening on behalf of prisoner or witness, there was never any attempt on the part of the Commission to curb or question the arbitrary insolence and injustice of the Judge Advocates. An examination of the "official" record of the proceedings, cooked, mangled, and distorted as they are for publication, will convince any fair critic, that for willful disregard of every principle of law and justice this tribunal has no rival since the days of the "infamous Jeffreys." [2] And why cannot even that important publication be had in any bookstore— why is it so rare that few people have ever seen it? Perhaps Reverdy Johnson was right when he wrote me that it could not be had because the Government had bought up and destroyed every copy it could get. I have one, sent to me from Southern Maryland.

If Justice ever sat with unbandaged, blood-shot eyes, she did on this occasion. The temper, the expressions, the manners, the atmosphere pervading the Court made it an unprecedented spectacle. The Commission illustrated the very spirit and body of the times; and passion decided everything. Of judicial decorum, fairness, calmness, there was absolutely none. Even the Judge Advocates, of whom it can be said, their quality of mercy was not strained, were sometimes compelled to interfere for the appearance of judicial decency. Counsel for the prisoners must have had a hard time to submit in patience to their daily trials. I suppose there is no case on record, where a distinguished attorney was compelled to submit to such indignities as General Hunter and several of his Court put upon the venerable Reverdy Johnson. Although the Court was organized to convict, the trial need not have been such a shameless farce. As Judge Elbert H. Gary, before whom the Chicago anarchists were tried in 1886, said, "The end, however desirable its attainment, excuses no irregular means in the administration of Justice." Lewis Payne, and all the men in the conspiracy with Booth, merited death, and they would have been convicted in any court in the land. The Majesty of the Law would have avenged a President's death —as it did in the case of Charles J. Guiteau, the assassin of President Garfield; and the record of the trial would have been open for the inspection of the world. The grief of the nation at the death of the gentle and merciful Lincoln would have had no touch of shame. It was due to his memory that in avenging his death passion should not depose reason, the administration of justice should not be degraded, and no unnecessary blood should be spilled at his grave.

The range of the investigation indicated why a military commission and not a civil court was selected to try the murderers, and also that another object, scarcely secondary, was to connect the Confederate army, in some way, with the assassination and conspiracy. In fact this latter seemed the main object of the investigation, although at this day no reputable man would risk his reputation for intelligence by saying there was ever the slightest ground for such a charge. Evidence was admitted of "Jacob Thomson's bank account," "Booth's oil speculations," "Jefferson Davis and the assassination," "Burning of steamboats," "Plot to burn New York," "Mining of Libby Prison," "Commissions for raiders," "Introduction of pestilence," "Starvation of Union prisoners," "Papers from Rebel archives," etc., etc.

It reads like the headings of a dime novel and detective story. The Commission had been ordered by President Johnson to proceed in a manner "to avoid unnecessary delay and conduce to the ends of public justice"; and that is the way they did it. When I stood at the door, looking in at the proceedings, I saw another scene which reminded me of the French Revolution. Ladies of position, culture and influence enough to be admitted sat about the Court, near the Judges, talked to the prosecutors, and with scowls and scorn, white teeth and scorching eyes, augmented the general horror. I never felt as wicked in my life as when, on the stand an unwilling witness, I saw the gaze of their wrathful eyes upon me; they glared at me as if they thought I had taken a hand in a murder which I thought the direst calamity that could have befallen the South. Still fuller of vengeance were the glances they cast at poor Annie Surratt, when on the stand as a witness for her mother. No wonder Mrs. Surratt was offered up as a burnt sacrifice to the wrath of her sex. I confess I do not judge these women harshly nor think they were without excuse, for everything about them cried out for vengeance, but it taught me to regard with more leniency the women who excited the bloody excesses of the French Revolution.

The prisoners, with the exception of Mrs. Surratt, were not a comely-looking set, and with the exception of Payne the men were generally a sorry lot, low enough to be capable of any crime. Mrs. Surratt was rather an attractive and amiable looking woman, a widow, "fair, fat and forty." No woman was ever more unlike Dickens' Madame Lafarge than she was. She sat nearest my door and the other seven, David E. Herold, Lewis T. Powell alias Payne, George E. Atzerodt, Samuel Arnold, Edward Spangler, Dr. Samuel A. Mudd, and Michael O'Laughlin, sat in a row on her left, an armed sentinel being seated between each one. Mrs. Surratt was not ironed during the trial as the others were, although so represented in the pictorial papers. General Hartranft would not permit it. She was supposed to be fed on prisoners' rations, like the others, but, in fact, Hartranft sent her daily from his table not only the substantials but the delicacies with which it was abundantly supplied.

Payne was a remarkable and desperate man. One day I observed that he seemed to recognize me. I asked General Hartranft to find out in his next visit to his cell who he was. He reported that Payne's name was Powell, that he was the son of an Episcopal or Baptist clergyman; that he had been a private in the Second Florida regiment, wounded at Gettysburg as I was; a prisoner in West Buildings Hospital at Baltimore when I was, and that he had seen me there; that he subsequently had escaped and never returned to the army. I saw that Hartranft had taken great interest in him as a character study. He said Payne seemed to him a man of iron will, cool and fearless, a typical desperado and singularly truthful. He told me one day that Payne had said he had taken his life in his hands when he agreed to go into the affair with Booth; that he had lost and expected to die; that he asked neither pardon nor mercy; and then, he said, Payne paused and solemnly concluded,

"In the presence of Almighty God I swear Mrs. Surratt is innocent of the crime charged against her."

General Hartranft unquestionably believed Payne spoke the truth, as the world believes now. Payne was assigned to the assassination of Secretary Seward, but failed in the attempt.

One night during my sojourn in this Bastille, ex-Governor

Letcher of Virginia was brought in about midnight and put
in the room next to mine. The next morning the General sent
for him to be brought to the dining room, gave him a goodly
sample of morning bitters and then an excellent breakfast.
The next midnight he disappeared as silently as he came, back
again to the Old Capitol Prison, and it never transpired what
he was sent for. The life of a prisoner in such a mysterious
gaol was more or less exciting and interesting after it was
over, an experience one was glad to have had but not anxious
to repeat.

I was put on the stand as a witness on May 30th. Von Steinacker having been summarily disposed of by previous wit-
nesses, my examination was brief. I then asked permission to
make a statement.

General Howe: "I object to the *prisoner* making any statement."

General Foster: "I hope the *witness* will be allowed to make
his statement."

General Hunter looked at the Judge Advocate, who consented, unless I wanted to talk about von Steinacker, and I
was permitted.

I said I had noticed the effort to connect the Confederate
army, especially the Stonewall Brigade, with the assassination of President Lincoln; that no one knew better than this
Court the material of which that brigade was composed, the
bone and sinew and best blood of the Valley of Virginia; and
in the name of their dead and their living I protested against
the attempt to associate their fame and memory with such a
cowardly and unsoldierly act as that midnight assassination.
None of them knew anything about it and had no sympathy
with it.

Then came down with violence the indignant gavel of General Hunter, but I had said nearly all I wanted to say. He directed that the statement be omitted from the official record
and ordered me from the stand. The papers, however, had my
statement next day. Some commented on my impudent arraignment of the Court and the comment of the Philadelphia
Inquirer indicates the temper of the ultraloyal:

"A rebel officer who voluntarily expressed the abhorrence felt by officers of the rebel Stonewall Brigade at the assassination of Lincoln is a tall, slender young man of Virginia type, who professes to be governed by the Code of Virginia chivalry; but as Booth used the motto of the Old Dominion, at the moment of executing his infernal deed, these professions do not amount to much."

And thus I ran the gantlet of that historic Court and had a new experience; but I cannot say I learned much law from it.

On the same day Miss Annie E. Surratt was put upon the stand as witness for her mother. It was a pitiable scene. She was tall, slender, fair, handsome; for her to stand the stare of the cruel, stony eyes riveted upon her was a trying ordeal. She must have known that her testimony made no impression on that tribunal, and toward the close of it she began to show signs of a collapse. The veins and muscles of her neck seemed swollen and she gave evidence of great suffering. General Hartranft was about to go to her, but knowing her horror of him as her mother's jailor, he, with delicate consideration, asked me to bring her from the stand. I brought her out, passing just in front of her mother, and as she reached my room she fell forward and fainted. The door was shut quickly, a doctor called, and at his instance General Hartranft and I carried her below, to his room. There she had a spasm and began to tear out her beautiful hair and to rend her dress. Women arriving, she was left with them and the Doctor, who succeeded after a while in quieting and putting her to sleep.

The visit of Miss Surratt to President Johnson, after the conviction of her mother, with a petition for her life and, it is said, a letter from General Hartranft; the refusal of Preston King and Senator Lane to let her see the President; her prostration on the stone steps of the White House, waiting, weeping, pleading, nearly all the day; her hopeless mission; all this is part of the pathetic history of those bloody days. Mrs. Surratt—now conceded to have been unjustly convicted —was hanged, and so were the guilty Payne, Herold, and Atzerodt; Arnold Mudd and O'Laughlin were imprisoned for life at hard labor and Spangler for six years. Such is the record.

The Honorable Reverdy Johnson and General Thomas Ewing made conclusive arguments to show that, under our Constitution, a military commission had no jurisdiction or right to try Mrs. Surratt and that their sentence would be void. If that tribunal listened to the argument at all, it gave no consideration to it. Johnson would not appear before the Commission after his treatment in the beginning of the trial and his argument was read by another attorney.

After Mrs. Surratt was executed, the Supreme Court of the United States decided, in the Milligan case, that such commissions had no jurisdiction to try citizens on such charges, when the civil courts were open. It is impossible, therefore, to escape the conclusion that the hanging of Mrs. Surratt was judicial and deliberate murder. The perpetrators soon became aware of this and began to blame each other. President Johnson declared Mrs. Surratt would not have been hanged if he had seen a recommendation for mercy signed by some of the Court; he charged Judge Advocate Joseph Holt and Secretary of War Stanton with fraud in concealing it. This they denied, charging him with drunkenness, and the controversy became loud and bitter.

Nemesis at once began to avenge the wrong. President Johnson got into trouble and was impeached. Holt struggled to the end of his life to vindicate himself but never succeeded. Stanton suffered with remorse and on his death bed said, "The Surratt woman haunts me": whether he died a natural death has been much questioned. Both Lane and King, who stood between Anna Surratt and mercy that fateful day at the White House, committed suicide; and so did General Foster, the gentlest man of all that Court. General Butler charged John A. Bingham in the House of Representatives with hanging an innocent woman. Sanford Conover, the principal witness against Mrs. Surratt, was afterwards convicted of perjury. Weichman, the most notorious witness, confessed his own perjury, then recanted his confession and died in shame. Since then there has been a struggle for forgetfulness. The Peniten-

tiary in which Mrs. Surratt was tried has been torn down and
its very foundation torn up. Not one stone was left standing
to tell a tale; where it stood the sod has been planted and no
one can point out where that dread tribunal sat.

After about three weeks of exciting and interesting confinement I was released. I claimed attendance as a witness. This
claim was disputed upon the ground that I was a prisoner in
custody, but with the assistance of General Hartranft and a
jolly member of his staff, I got it. The Captain reported to
the General that the first thing I did was to go into a store
on Pennsylvania Avenue and buy a fine soft hat of Confederate grey. But there was an incident which the Captain, being on the outside, did not know. The merchant, finding out
that I had worn my old grey slouch in the war, wanted it for
his disloyal daughter and said he would trade me any hat in
his store for it. The bargain was struck and as I went out he
hid my old hat under the counter.

I went home but was not left in peace. About once a week I
was arrested and taken to Harper's Ferry that I might be
sent to Fort Delaware, and each time I was released by General Egan, by order of General W. S. Hancock. About the
fourth or fifth time I was arrested, on Sunday, coming out of
church with a lady and again carried off to Harper's Ferry.
General Egan expressed himself very freely about this continuous annoyance and asked me to dine with him and his
staff. He said General W. H. Emory at Cumberland had ordered my arrest this time and I had better go to Baltimore and
see General Hancock. He sent an officer and sergeant with
me the next day. Unfortunately General Hancock had gone
to New York to the wedding of Ike Parker's brother, and I
had no friend at Headquarters. Colonel Adam E. King, his
Adjutant General, declined to let me await his return and ordered me to be taken to Fort Delaware; I landed there that
evening.

During my sojourn at Fort Delaware, there were but two
prisoners, Colonel Burton H. Harrison, President Davis' con-
fidential staff officer, and myself. There were the usual guards,
and the morning and evening guns, and we were well taken

care of. Harrison and I were not permitted to speak to nor communicate with each other. We saw each other at a distance but that was all, for he was kept aloft in his bastion apartment. I had liberty enough, but he was the suspect. General Schoeff, the commandant of the Fort, was simply obeying orders. To me, personally, he was full of courtesy and consideration. I was soon allowed all the liberty I wanted: called on the General's family, was often called upon by them; drove with them around the Island and took pleasure in teaching the General how to handle the reins over his new horses—a matter in which he had little experience; was given free access to the Fort library, in which I read many books and where I studied Napoleon's campaigns and wrote my first lecture on Stonewall Jackson.

Colonel Harrison was there when I went and remained after I had gone. I believe that General Schoeff and his family became so attached to him that they afterwards named a son for him. His punishment was vicarious, suffering for and with Mr. Davis; mine was for my own sins.

In some respects Fort Delaware was not, for me, an uncomfortable summer resort. But on the 23rd of August, the General issued Special Order No. 328 saying that as my sentence had expired—I think I had only been there about a month or a little over—I would be discharged and furnished transportation to my home at Shepherdstown. On that day, accompanied by his wife and daughter and staff, he took me to Wilmington on his boat and gave an excellent dinner on board. At Wilmington I took my leave of them, with sincere expressions of thanks for their uniform courtesy, one and all, while I was the unwilling guest of the Government at Fort Delaware.

For me, the War was over, at last!

THE AUTHOR AND HIS BOOK

BY

FLETCHER M. GREEN

THESE hitherto unpublished recollections of Henry Kyd Douglas, youngest member of Stonewall Jackson's staff, are based upon his contemporary writings. Among the Douglas papers are a three-volume war diary, letters, and miscellaneous papers written between 1862 and 1866. The recollections cover the period from John Brown's Raid at Harper's Ferry in 1859 to the hanging in 1865 of Mrs. Mary Surratt as an accomplice in the assassination of President Abraham Lincoln. As a boy Douglas had unwittingly assisted Brown in smuggling arms to his stronghold in Maryland, and as a Confederate veteran, awaiting imprisonment in Fort Delaware, he was a witness in the Surratt trial.

Henry Kyd Douglas, son of the Reverend Robert and Mary (Robertson) Douglas, was born at Shepherdstown, West Virginia (then Virginia), on September 29, 1840. In his early childhood his parents moved to Ferry Hill Place in Maryland directly across the Potomac River from Shepherdstown. Here in this red brick plantation house, erected in 1812 and still standing, Henry grew to manhood. Henry had a sister and two younger brothers with whom he roamed the countryside with dog and gun. The family ties were very close and later, when Henry was in the Confederate service, his mother and sister not only sent him letters through the lines but his brother John spent some time in camp with him.

Douglas attended Franklin and Marshall College, Lancaster, Pennsylvania, from which he was graduated in 1859. Among his college mates were Chauncey H. Black, son of Attorney General Jeremiah S. Black, later Lieutenant Governor of Pennsylvania; Robert J. Nevin, later Major in the United States army and Rector of St. Paul's Church in Rome, Italy; and John F. Hartranft, later Major General and Governor of Pennsylvania. These and several other college friends were to be met as friendly enemies during the war, 1861-1865. After graduation from college Douglas studied law at the private school of Judge John Brockenbrough in Lexington, Virginia, and in the office of Judge Weisel of Charles Town. He was admitted to the bar in 1860.

Shortly after the election of Abraham Lincoln to the presidency in November of 1860, Douglas moved to St. Louis, Missouri, and began the practice of his profession. Surprised and stunned at the news that Virginia had adopted the Ordinance of Secession on April 17, 1861, Douglas nevertheless determined to offer his services to his native state. Within a week the young attorney, not yet twenty-one years of age, was in Shepherdstown to enlist in the army.

Douglas served as a Private, Lieutenant, and Captain in Company B, Second Virginia Infantry. He then joined the staff of General Thomas J. Jackson and served as Assistant Inspector General and Assistant Adjutant General until Jackson's death. He was selected by the staff to notify Mrs. Jackson of the Brigade's determination to erect a suitable monument to the memory of her husband and served as treasurer of the committee that raised more than $6,000 for that purpose. He was also a member of the committee that petitioned the Secretary of War to designate officially the First Virginia as the Stonewall Brigade. Douglas later served as Chief of Staff and Assistant Adjutant General to Generals Edward Johnson, John B. Gordon, Jubal A. Early, J. H. Pegram, and John A. Walker.

As a Colonel Douglas led the Thirteenth and the Forty-ninth Virginia Regiments. He was six times wounded and on more than one occasion cited for bravery. Severely wounded at Gettysburg on July 3, 1863, he was captured and taken to a hospital at the Gettysburg Theological Seminary. After a month there, he was sent to the West Buildings Hospital in Baltimore, where he remained until September 29. He was then transferred to Johnson's Island Prison, where he spent the winter of 1863-1864. From there he was taken to Point Lookout and spent a month at the Hammond General Hospital. He was finally paroled and exchanged on March 18, 1864.

Returning to his old command Douglas was cited for conspicuous bravery and distinguished service at Winchester, and General John C. Breckinridge voluntarily offered to recommend him for promotion as a brigade commander. He was then transferred to General Walker's staff with the understanding that he would be given command of the Light Brigade as soon as Walker received his promotion. At Petersburg Douglas was notified by Captain Cabell Breckinridge that General Breckinridge, then Secretary of War, had forwarded the two commissions, and Douglas took command of the Light Brigade. The commission was lost, however, and Douglas was never officially promoted, but he continued to command the Light Brigade until the close of the war. His troops fired the last shot at Appomattox and were, by order of General Gordon, permitted to be the last brigade to stack arms upon General Lee's surrender.

Douglas had kept a diary for two years as a college student and, when the army left Winchester in 1862, he promised his friend Miss Sallie H. Conrad, daughter of Robert Y. and sister of Colonel Holmes Conrad of the Confederate army, that he "would keep a... journal, such as camp life would permit, and in my letters to that friend write down so much of the journal as I thought proper." This entry, dated December 11, 1862, in Camp, five miles from Guinea Station, Spotsylvania County, Virginia, opens the "Diary" that is the backbone of these recollections. There are no entries for the eight months during which Douglas was a prisoner of war.

The "Diary" closes with the entry for February 28, 1865.

Among Douglas' manuscripts is a bundle of war letters written to and by him. There are also a few letters written after the war which bear directly on various points of the recollections, most important of which are by General Jubal A. Early and Colonel S. Bassett French. Douglas mentions many other letters which he used in the preparation of his manuscript.

As a member of the staff Douglas wrote many unofficial as well as official papers which he used in writing the recollections. Some of these are now among his manuscripts, others are mentioned by him. Among these should be noted the speech which General Jackson delivered to his Brigade upon being transferred to the command of the Army of the Valley, the only one he ever made to his troops. Douglas went immediately to his tent, wrote out the speech, and then called in others who had heard it to check the thought and words. He sent a copy to the Richmond *Dispatch* which published the speech on November 8, 1861. Another important paper was the memoir of Colonel A. S. "Sandy" Pendleton, one of the most popular and capable of Jackson's officers. A copy of this paper is preserved in the manuscripts.

While Douglas was in the West Buildings Hospital in 1863 he first conceived the idea of using his "Diary," letters, and other papers in writing a series of "Papers" on Stonewall Jackson and the Civil War. The work was begun at that time but unfortunately only fragments of these first "Papers" are now extant. Writing to his sister Nannie on September 20, 1863, Douglas said: "I am preparing notes for a book of my recollections of the General while I was on his staff. I have nothing else to do and this occupies my time pleasantly. I have been at it several weeks and have written about one third enough. It is to contain anecdotes of the General, which I know to be true and also a description of his conduct on different battle fields. I find my memory on the subject better than I supposed it would be. Of course I do not want this to be known in Shepherdstown, or otherwhere as the book may never be published." December 5, 1864, the Reverend R. L. Dabney, formerly a Major and Adjutant General on Jackson's staff, called on Douglas and asked him "to furnish him [Dabney] some personal recollections of the General for his life." Douglas consented and generously supplied him a considerable volume of notes which Dabney used in his *Life and Campaigns of Lieut.-Gen. Thomas J. Jackson,* published in 1866. Dabney's request seems to have spurred Douglas to renewed activity, for on January 6, 1865, he notes in his "Diary" that he is "writing some in my notes and Recollections."

After the war ended and Douglas had been released from Fort Delaware he took up his pen anew and "the greater portion of it [the book, was] written immediately after the war from diaries I had kept and notes I had made and when my recollection was fresh and youthful." The work, which he entitled "Stonewall Papers," was finished in 1866, but for some reason Douglas made no attempt to publish it. He drew heavily upon it, however, for several articles and essays which were published in newspapers and magazines. Douglas wielded a facile pen and, with his intimate knowledge of the subject, wrote interestingly of Jackson and the Civil War. In 1898-1899, Douglas reworked his "Papers" into the present form. As he himself says, he has "added somewhat and taken away more freely; and time has mellowed the acerbity of the more youthful days."

I have carefully read the original "Diary," letters, papers, and other manuscripts left by Douglas, together with fragments of the original Stonewall "Papers," and have checked the 1899 version of his recollections against them. I find very little in the present form which does not appear in the contemporary manuscripts. The most noticeable differences appear in those passages in which Douglas expresses resentment and hostility toward the North. These passages are modified and the feelings expressed in the last are less severe than in the "Diary." This is especially true when Douglas writes of Hunter's raids in the Valley and of his own arrest for treason, his trial, and imprisonment after the war had closed.

For the spelling of names and places, I have checked the manuscript against published works and the official sources. Where errors appear I have corrected them. I have made some few changes in phraseology in order to make clear the meaning of passages that might otherwise be obscure. I have left the work, however, that of Douglas a participant in and an observer of all that is here reported. Where errors are such that they could not be corrected without drastically changing what Douglas wrote, a note has been added. Some additional information on some points has also been added in the notes to be found at the end of the book.

Douglas' range of interests was remarkably broad for a young man and his mind was keen and elastic. Even during the stress of war he read widely from history, poetry, fiction, the Latin classics, philosophy, the Bible, military science, and the periodical and daily press. What is more significant, he took time to record his views of and reactions to many books he read. His views of contemporary fiction and his philosophy of poetry as expressed in his "Diary" denote rare critical faculties and great maturity of mind in a man only twenty-four years of age.

As a member of the staff of several of the most colorful and important Confederate generals, Douglas had the rare privilege and stimulating experience of seeing the great and near-great in undress. The serious Jackson, the fun-loving Stuart, the courtly Gordon, the beloved Lee, "Old Pete," and many others are introduced as intensely interesting human personalities. He had also the privilege of meeting many interesting foreigners who served in the armies or visited the camps. Among those introduced are Sir Percy Wyndham, Heros von Borcke, Garnet Wolseley, Francis Lawley, and Frank Vizetelly. Because of his good family connections and his important status as a staff officer, Douglas is able to present intimate views of the best of Virginia society at Richmond as well as at such famous plantations as Moss Neck and Mt. Airy. Finally, Douglas tells of the life of the soldier and of the civilian during war times—life as it really was.

Always Douglas writes from the vantage point of one "in the know." He was of the inner circle—close to those high up in the councils of war. He had his own opinions, too, and if they differed from those of Jackson or Stuart he did not hesitate to make them known. If, at times, he seems to claim for himself prophetic vision and knowledge of coming events, as for instance in predicting defeat on the invasion of Maryland, do not doubt his word. His "Diary" of the days just preceding Gettysburg is full of foreboding and prophecies of defeat for Lee's army. But Douglas had an explanation for his view, perfectly simple and logical. The incomparable Jackson was no more!

When the war was over, Douglas resumed the practice of law at Winchester and then at Hagerstown, Maryland. He became a prominent figure in the legal, political, and military circles of Maryland. He was a successful lawyer and an able jurist and served several years as judge of the Fourth Judicial Circuit of Maryland. A forceful and an effective orator, he was often called upon to speak on public occasions. He delivered the memorial address of his friend Brigadier General and Governor John F. Hartranft at York, Pennsylvania, in 1889. He was the Democratic candidate for Congress from the Sixth District in 1888 and a leader of the Gold Democrats of Maryland in 1896.

Douglas retained his interest in military affairs to his old age. He took an active part in Confederate Memorial Associations and was especially interested in the Maryland State Confederate and the Stonewall Jackson Cemeteries. He served as Captain, Colonel, and Adjutant General of the Maryland Volunteers and, as Major General, commanded the Maryland troops at the time of the General Strike in 1894. He was appointed a Brigadier General of Volunteers in the Spanish American War but his health did not permit his acceptance.

Henry Kyd Douglas was a tall, stately, but kindly figure, who won the affection and admiration of all those who came to know him. Even his former enemies of Civil War days visited him in his home and gladly entertained him in theirs.

Charles King, a Union soldier, who had come to know Douglas intimately, said that he "never knew a man who more deserved the too-often used words, 'a soldier and a gentleman.'" For many years Douglas suffered from tuberculosis. He died at his home in Hagerstown, Maryland, in 1903.

Fletcher M. Green
Chapel Hill, N. C.
August 8, 1940

NOTES

BY

FLETCHER M. GREEN

CHAPTER I

1. This statement is in conflict with the view expressed by Oswald Garrison Villard in *John Brown, 1800-1859: A Biography Fifty Years After* (Boston and New York, 1910). He says (pp. 407-408) that the people "gradually grew suspicious," often stopped members of Brown's party "to ask questions," and that "the conspirators were soon face to face with another danger besides the inquisitiveness of their neighbors." And, "After the occupation [of the Kennedy Farm] it became apparent that the farm was, after all, too near the highway, and that the neighbors were too inquisitive for comfort. They were constantly 'dropping in,' after the friendly Southern fashion, and could not understand why they were not asked into the house" (p. 404). Villard cites the letters of Brown's daughter, Annie Brown Adams.

2. Douglas is not strictly accurate as regards the number killed. There were four whites and one Negro killed. These were Thomas Boerley, an Irishman; George W. Turner, a slaveholder and farmer of means and prominence; Fontaine Beckham, Mayor of Harper's Ferry; Private Luke Quin of the United States Marines; and Shephard Hayward (Heyward Shepherd), a free Negro baggagemaster at the railway station. Another Negro was found dead in the river but it was not known how he met his death.—Villard, *op. cit.*, pp. 433, 435, 440, 441, and 454.

3. According to statements of Judge Richard Parker who presided at the trial of the conspirators, and of Andrew Hunter, a special state's prosecutor, John Anthony Copeland, Jr., not John E. Cook, aroused most interest and sympathy. Copeland, a free Negro, born in Raleigh, North Carolina, was educated at Oberlin College. His dignity and good behavior were especially noted by both Parker and Hunter.—See Villard, *op. cit.*, p. 684, for their statements.

4. Douglas falls into a common but egregious error in this statement. If the Democratic party had not divided but had nominated only one candidate and this one candidate had received the entire popular vote cast for Stephen A. Douglas, John C. Breckinridge, and John Bell, Abraham Lincoln would still have won the election. The combined popular vote of the three men would have caused a shift of the electoral vote in only two states, California and Oregon, and Lincoln's electoral vote would have been 173 against the 130 of his opponent. It is not correct therefore to say that Lincoln was elected by the division of the Democratic party.

5. Douglas was graduated from Franklin and Marshall College at Lancaster, Pennsylvania, in 1859 and then attended Judge John Brockenbrough's Law School in Lexington, Virginia.

6. Douglas gives some additional data on the murder of his friend, Rench, *infra*, pp. 155-156.

7. Douglas uses military titles rather loosely in that he does not always take time into account. Thus he may refer to one officer as colonel when the said officer has already been commissioned brigadier general, or, vice versa, he may refer to an officer as general when at the particular time the officer is only a colonel.

Jackson was appointed Colonel of volunteers by Governor John Letcher on April 27, 1861, and stationed at Harper's Ferry; in July, 1861, the Virginia troops were merged with those of the Confederacy and, on July 3, Jackson was promoted Brigadier General in command of the First Brigade; October 7, 1861, he was promoted Major General and placed in command of the Army of the Valley; and October 11, 1862, he became Lieutenant General in command of the Second Army Corps.

Chapter II

1. This was Lieutenant Colonel William Allan, Chief Ordnance Officer of the Second Army Corps, and the author of a *History of the Campaign of Gen. T. J. (Stonewall) Jackson in the Shenandoah Valley of Virginia* (1880).

2. It should be borne in mind that this brigade was officially the First Virginia Brigade until the Secretary of War gave it the name "Stonewall" after Jackson's death.

3. Douglas' figures are at variance with those taken from the official sources by James Ford Rhodes, who places the Federal troops at 29,000, the Confederate troops at 28,000, Federal losses at 460, and Confederate losses at 378.—*History of the United States from the Compromise of 1850* (9 vols., New York, 1928), III, 448, 450. Douglas seems to follow G. F. R. Henderson who, in his *Stonewall Jackson and the American Civil War* (London and New York, 1898), I, 168, gives the number of troops engaged on Henry Hill as 18,000 in each army.

4. This reference is evidently to Major William Gilman (not Gilham), *Manual of Instruction for the Volunteers and Militia of the United States* (Philadelphia, 1861). It was reissued by West and Johnston of Richmond in 1861 as *Manual of Instruction for the Volunteers and Militia of the Confederate States.* Douglas was doubtless using the Confederate edition.

5. Reverend William S. White was an intimate friend and correspondent of General Jackson. He was the father of Captain Hugh A. White of Jackson's army who was killed at Second Manassas. Dr. White was the pastor from 1848 to 1867 of the Lexington Presbyterian Church, of which Jackson was a member.

6. Had Douglas only known the liberties which other writers were to take, and had taken, he would not have said that the verbiage of Jackson's speech had never been changed. R. L. Dabney in his *Life and Campaigns of Lieut.-Gen. Thomas J. Jackson* (1866), Mrs. Mary Anna Jackson in *Memoirs of Stonewall Jackson* (1895), and Colonel G.F.R. Henderson in *Stonewall Jackson and the American Civil War* (1898), all quote the speech. All differ among themselves, and all have made numerous changes from the version reported by Douglas. None of the changes are serious, but none of the authors explain that they are making changes. Henderson is the greatest offender in

that he not only makes many more changes than either of the other two but also adds to the speech. There are thirty-one differences in the Douglas and Henderson versions. Henderson not only changes words, tense, capitalization, punctuation, and paragraphing, but he also omits and adds words. Dabney, who secured data from Douglas for his *Life of Jackson*, is more nearly in accord with Douglas than either Henderson or Mrs. Jackson.

CHAPTER III

1. Alexander S. Pendleton, familiarly known as "Sandy," was the son of Dr. William N. Pendleton, rector of Grace Episcopal Church of Lexington, Virginia. The elder Pendleton, a graduate of the United States Military Academy, led the famous Rockbridge Battery and became a Brigadier General in command of Lee's artillery. Sandy Pendleton was a member of Jackson's staff and a great favorite of the General's. Promoted to Lieutenant Colonel for bravery at Gettysburg, he became Adjutant General and Chief of Staff to General Early. He was only twenty-four years of age when killed at Fisher's Hill on September 22, 1864.

2. Douglas was exceedingly proud of his "George Washington Sword." He speaks of it by name on several occasions in his "Diary" and letters. It was given to him by George Washington, who was killed at Gettysburg in 1863.

3. Douglas penned a note in the margin of his manuscript to the effect that "In the original manuscript, the General had written the word 'followers' but rubbing it out with his finger, he wrote over it, the more modest word 'soldiers.' "

CHAPTER IV

1. Turner Ashby, son of Colonel Turner Ashby of the War of 1812, was born at "Rose Bank" in Fauquier County, Virginia, in 1828. Educated at a private school, he entered upon a career as a planter and businessman and amassed a considerable fortune before the war. He recruited the Ashby Rangers of which he was Colonel and had the distinction, also, of employing the first battery of horse artillery used in the war. He was promoted to Brigadier General in May, 1862, and was one of Jackson's most famous officers. Jackson said that he "never knew his

superior as a partisan leader." Ashby was killed at Harrison-burg, June 6, 1862.

2. Lieutenant R. Kidder Meade was Ordnance Officer on General Jackson's staff during the Valley Campaign. He later served as Major of Engineers with Longstreet's Division, and was Adjutant General to Brigadier General William B. Talia-ferro. While in camp near Fredericksburg, Meade often visited and dined with Douglas.

CHAPTER V

1. For Belle Boyd's account of this episode, differing some-what in detail see Chapter VI of her *Belle Boyd in Camp and Prison* (New York, 1865).

CHAPTER VI

1. For conflicting views of Jackson's plans in regard to Harper's Ferry see Bradley T. Johnson, "Stonewall Jackson's Intentions at Harper's Ferry," *Battles and Leaders of the Civil War*, II, 615-616; and Henry Kyd Douglas, "Stonewall Jackson's Intentions at Harper's Ferry," *ibid.*, 617-618. Both these articles are in reply to John G. Walker, "Harper's Ferry and Sharpsburg," *Century*, X (New Series, 1886), 296-308.

CHAPTER VIII

1. These lines come from "Dirge for Ashby" written by Mrs. Margaret Junkin Preston, wife of Professor J. T. L. Preston of the Virginia Military Institute. She was the daughter of Dr. George Junkin and sister-in-law to Jackson by his first mar-riage. She was born in 1820 and died in Baltimore in 1897.

2. Percy Wyndham (1833-1879) was one of the most in-teresting foreign adventurers who entered the Union military service. The son of Colonel Charles Wyndham of the British army, he enlisted in the Students' Corps at Paris in 1848. He served in the Revolutions of 1848-1849 and then transferred to the French navy as an Ensign. In 1851 he was in the British artillery and in 1852 in the Eighth Austrian Lancers as a Cap-tain and commander of a squadron. In 1860 he enlisted in the Italian army and, for bravery at Capua, Garibaldi made him a

Colonel and bestowed upon him the title of Chevalier of the Military Order of Savoy. In 1862 he entered the United States army as Colonel of the First New Jersey Cavalry. After conspicuous service he retired in 1864. He went to India where he founded a successful comic paper, was impressario of the opera in Calcutta, and commander-in-chief of the army of the King of Burma. He lost his life in 1879 when a balloon which he constructed fell in Royal Lake in Rangoon.

3. These lines are from the poem "Turner Ashby," written by John R. Thompson of Richmond, Virginia, editor of the *Southern Literary Messenger* from 1847 to 1862. He became literary editor of the New York *Evening Post* in 1866 and died in New York City in 1873.

CHAPTER IX

1. Erastus B. Tyler was born in New York but moved to Granville, Ohio, as a youth. With only an elementary education he entered on a business career with the American Fur Company of which he became part owner. He entered the Federal service as Colonel of the Seventh Ohio Infantry and because of his knowledge of the region, gained as a representative of the American Fur Company, was sent to the Valley of Virginia. Promoted a Brigadier General at Winchester in 1862, he was later called to Washington and placed in command of a Pennsylvania brigade. Still later he was placed in command of the defenses of Baltimore and it was here that he befriended Douglas. After the war he re-entered business.

2. Samuel Sprigg Carroll, of the Charles Carroll line, was born in Washington, D. C., in 1832. He was graduated from the United States Military Academy and was a Brigadier General during the war. He retired from the army as a Major General in 1869. Douglas was the Democratic candidate for Congress in 1888. Carroll died in 1893.

3. Claude Crozet, born in France in 1790, was educated at the École Polytechnique and served under Napoleon in the Russian campaign, being captured at Moscow. After Napoleon's overthrow, Crozet came to the United States, was a professor at West Point, 1816-1823, state engineer of Virginia, 1823-1832, and was influential in founding the Virginia Military Institute in 1839. He died January 29, 1864.

Chapter X

1. Hunter Holmes McGuire, who appears so often in this work, was a Major and Surgeon in the First Virginia Brigade under Jackson and in the Second Army Corps under General Richard S. Ewell. He became Medical Director for the Army of the Valley. He also organized the Reserve Corps Hospitals of the Confederacy. Born at Winchester, Virginia, in 1835, he was educated at the Winchester Medical College, the University of Pennsylvania, and the Jefferson Medical College. After the war, he founded the University College of Medicine and was Professor of Surgery at the Virginia Medical College, 1865-1878. He served as President of both the American Medical and the American Surgical Associations. He died in 1900.

2. Robert Lewis Dabney, born in Louisa County, Virginia, in 1820, was educated at Hampden Sidney, the University of Virginia, and the Virginia Union Theological Seminary. He was a professor at the latter from 1853 to 1860. He was a chaplain during the war and a Major on Jackson's staff as Adjutant General. He published a *Life and Campaigns of Lieut.-Gen. Thomas J. Jackson* (1866), and *A Defense of Virginia and the South* (New York, 1867). He never became reconciled to the defeat of the Confederacy and advocated emigration of the whites to other countries. He was professor at the University of Texas, 1883-1894, and died in 1898.

Chapter XI

1. The Parrott gun was invented by Robert Parker Parrott (1824-1877), who was graduated from the United States Military Academy in 1824. After some years spent as a professor at that institution and as a member of the Ordnance Bureau, he became superintendent of an iron foundry at Cold Springs, New York. Here he perfected his gun, a muzzle-loading, cast-iron rifle. Cast hollow, it was strengthened by shrinking wrought-iron bands over the reinforced section.

2. Jim was Jackson's personal servant and cook.—See *infra* pp. 154-55.

3. Major Dabney tells this story with a greater wealth of detail, but casts himself and Douglas in reverse roles to those they play here.—See Henderson, *Stonewall Jackson*, II, 71-72.

4. Mark Tapley is a droll, whimsical character in Charles Dickens, *Martin Chuzzlewit*. Tapley seeks to find enjoyment and pleasure in even the most unpleasant tasks and circumstances.

5. John Stevens Cabot Abbott, minister and historian, did much to popularize history and biography in the United States. His *History of Napoleon Bonaparte* (2 vols., New York, 1855), was one of his most popular works. Douglas read it during the war.

CHAPTER XII

1. Moses Drury Hoge (1819-1899) was educated at Hampden Sidney and the Union Theological Seminary. A noted Presbyterian preacher, he volunteered his services to the Confederacy as a chaplain. In 1862 he ran the blockade to England and returned with a cargo of 10,000 Bibles, 50,000 Testaments, and 250,000 miscellaneous publications. He was chosen by the Virginia legislature in 1875 to deliver the oration at the unveiling of the Jackson Statue given by admirers in England.

CHAPTER XIII

1. R. Snowden Andrews was promoted to a colonelcy for bravery in action. After the war he practiced law in Baltimore. He died in 1903.

CHAPTER XIV

1. Though only a Colonel, Baylor had been given command of the First Brigade. He had been recommended for promotion to Brigadier General but the commission did not reach him before his death.

CHAPTER XV

1. Richmond Pearson Hobson, born at Greensboro, Alabama, August 17, 1870, was educated at Southern University and the United States Naval Academy. He became a national hero for his attempt to bottle up the Spanish fleet at Santiago in 1898 by sinking the collier *Merrimac* in the entrance of the harbor.

2. General Jackson wrote Mrs. Jackson of hearing Dr. Zacharias, whom he called a "gifted minister." He confessed that

he went to sleep but explained that fact by saying that he was so far in the rear of the church that he could not hear the sermon.—Mary Anna Jackson, *Memoirs of Stonewall Jackson*, p. 332.

3. Charles Marshall was born in Warrenton, Virginia, in 1849. He was educated at the University of Virginia and was a professor at Indiana University from 1849 to 1852. He removed to Baltimore and began the practice of law in 1853. During the war he was Major and Assistant Adjutant General and Inspector General on Lee's staff. After the war he returned to his legal practice in Baltimore, where he died in 1902.

4. Whittier continued to believe the Frietchie story to the end of his life. For his statement of the case see *The Complete Works of John Greenleaf Whittier* (University Edition), III, 245. However, Valerius Ebert, a nephew of Barbara Frietchie, gives the facts almost as Douglas does. He says that his aunt, almost ninety-six years old, was confined to her bed at the time. He disagrees with Douglas, however, as to the disloyalty of Mrs. Frietchie.—Ebert's letter in Jackson, *Memoirs of Stonewall Jackson*, p. 334. For an exhaustive discussion of the problem see George O. Seilheimer, "The Historical Basis of Whittier's 'Barbara Frietchie,'" in *Battles and Leaders of the Civil War*, II, 618-619, where Whittier's letters of 1888 are cited.

5. Douglas recounted this Boonsboro incident in his article, "Stonewall Jackson in Maryland," *Century Magazine*, X (1886), 285-295. M. M. Green replied to the article in the Baltimore *Sun*, quoting a contemporary account of the engagement written by B. P. Green, a Private in the Black Horse Cavalry. Green claimed more credit for Lieutenant A. D. Payne in saving Jackson than Douglas gives in this account. Douglas wrote Colonel (then Judge) S. Bassett French for his view. French's letter, dated June 28, 1886, agrees in general with Douglas and concludes as follows: "two things are certain beyond dispute— 1. The black Horse did gallantly charge the enemy, and pursued them out of the village, down the road up which they came into the village. 2. That you did with knightly chivalry cover the retreat of your chief with your own person. Both were gallant actions, and whether the one or the other saved Jackson from capture, that fact, be it as it may, neither adds to nor detracts from the gallantry of either. Both the B. H.

and yourself during the whole of that unhappy war won glory enough, for a whole staff and a dozen troops." (The clipping from the Baltimore *Sun* and French's lengthy, seven-page letter are in the Douglas papers.)

6. At Ecouen, a small town in France, was a famous chateau that, during the French Revolution, was used as a military prison, then as a hospital, and finally as a political prison. In 1807 Napoleon established a school for the daughters of the members of the Legion of Honor in this chateau. It was this school which he visited. He had won his great victory over the Austrians at Marengo in 1800.—Pierre Larousse, *Grand Dictionnaire Universel du XIX Siècle*, VII (Paris, 1865), 155-156.

Chapter XVI

1. Alexander Robert Lawton, born at Beaufort, South Carolina, November 4, 1818, was graduated from the United States Military Academy and studied law at Harvard University. He practiced law in Savannah, Georgia, and was active in railway building and state politics. After a distinguished career as a Brigadier General during the war, he returned to the practice of law, was president of the American Bar Association in 1882, and Minister to Austria 1887-1889. He died in 1896.

2. George Brinton McClellan, Jr., born in Dresden, Saxony, November 23, 1865, was graduated from Princeton in 1886. He was elected a Democratic member of Congress in 1895 and served until 1903 when he resigned to become Mayor of New York City, a post he held until 1910. He was a professor of history at Union Seminary from 1912 to 1931 and served overseas in the World War as a Lieutenant Colonel. He is still living.

3. William Thomas Hamilton (1820-1888) was educated at Jefferson College. He was a Democratic member of Congress 1849 to 1855. During the war he belonged to the peace party of Maryland and he and his law partner were known as "Jeff Davis' Masked Battery." He was a United States Senator, 1869-1875, and Governor of Maryland, 1879-1883.

4. Randolph B. Marcy led a famous exploring party on the Red River of the South in 1852. George B. McClellan assisted him on the expedition and married Mary Ellen Marcy in 1860. Marcy became McClellan's Chief of Staff during the war.

Chapter XVII

1. Henry W. Slocum (1827-1894) was elected to Congress four times 1868, 1870, 1882, and 1884. He resigned before his last term expired.

2. On the margin of a fragment of the original "Papers" Douglas penned the following note: "In August, 1901, I met an old Union soldier who said he was of the Fifth New York Cavalry and present at the incident mentioned. Having heard I was at Paul Smith's in the Adirondacks he had told the story about it—mentioned my father's house on the Hill and seemed intensely anxious to meet me. I met him. He told all about the reckless things I was supposed to have done and made me a great curiosity with the old Union soldiers and their friends."

3. Garnet Joseph Wolseley, first Viscount, was born June 4, 1833, and died March 25, 1913. With only a day school education he entered the army and won rapid promotion. Colonel Wolseley was sent to Canada with a detachment of British troops when it appeared that the Trent Affair might cause war with the United States. He then visited the South and spent some time with both Lee and Jackson. He wrote an article in *Blackwood's Magazine* in which he expressed unbounded admiration for both. He served in many campaigns and wrote much on military affairs. He was promoted General and Commander-in-Chief of the British army in 1890 and was largely responsible for the reorganization and reforms which made the British army the great fighting force it was in 1914.

4. Francis Charles Lawley (1825-1901) was a graduate of Rugby and Balliol College. A Liberal in politics, he was elected to Parliament in 1852 and later served as private secretary to William E. Gladstone, who secured him an appointment as Governor of South Australia. The appointment was canceled and Lawley came to the United States in 1856. During the war he acted as correspondent of the London *Times*. He was an ardent admirer of both Lee and Jackson and wrote an *Account of the Battle of Fredericksburg*, and *Sport in the Southern States*.

5. Douglas confuses Henry and Frank Vizetelly. Henry Vizetelly, born in London in 1820, came of a long line of journalists. Trained in wood engraving, Vizetelly worked on the *Illustrated London News*. He then established the *Pictorial*

Times and also reprinted *Uncle Tom's Cabin.* In 1855 he established the *Illustrated Times,* which was suppressed in 1865, and Vizetelly returned to the *News.* He died in 1894. Henry's brother Frank represented the *Illustrated London News* "in . . . America during the Civil War," and sent a vast number of sketches to that paper. He was killed at the battle of Kashgil in the Soudan in 1883.—See the *Dictionary of National Biography,* XX (1909), 384-386.

6. For the beginning of the Jackson-Hill dispute see *supra,* pp. 146-147, 158. The conference described here did not settle the controversy.—See *infra,* p. 215.

7. The Reverend Joseph C. Stiles was not a Georgian, as Douglas supposed, but a Virginian. He served Grace Presbyterian Church in Richmond for a time and then became pastor at the Mercer Street Church in New York City. Upon the outbreak of the war he returned to the South and at seventy years of age was a chaplain in General Ewell's division. He died in 1875.

Chapter XVIII

1. General Bradley T. Johnson quotes Dr. Hunter McGuire to the effect that his fourteen-year-old sister Betty persuaded Jackson to sit for the photograph at Winchester. Before doing so, however, Jackson took time to get his hair trimmed. The picture was made by Rontzahn, not Lupton, according to Johnson.—Jackson, *Memoirs of Stonewall Jackson,* p. 533.

2. Mrs. Jackson says that she persuaded the General to sit for the Minis photograph, not for the reason Douglas gives but because he had never presented a finer appearance of health and also, womanlike, because he was wearing the new uniform given him by Jeb Stuart. The artist went to Mr. Yerby's, where Mrs. Jackson was staying, to do the work. Since the General's hair was unusually long, Mrs. Jackson curled it in large ringlets. Jackson sat in the hall of the house, where a strong wind blew in his face causing him to frown and giving him an unnatural sternness. Mrs. Jackson says that she liked the Winchester photograph best but that the soldiers liked the Minis one because of its stern soldierly look.—Jackson, *op cit.,* pp. 413-414.

3. Ambrose Everett Burnside, known chiefly as a soldier, was prominent also in industrial and political circles. He invented a breech-loading gun and served as director and president

of several railroad, steamship, and locomotive companies. He was three times Governor of Rhode Island, 1866, 1867, and 1868, and was a United States Senator from 1874 to his death in 1881.

4. Big, fun-loving Heros von Borcke, an officer in the Third Dragoon Guards of the Royal Prussian army, successfully ran the blockade, landed at Charleston, South Carolina, and made his way to Richmond in 1862. Jeb Stuart gave him a place on his staff and recommended him for a commission. He became a Major and Adjutant and Inspector General despite his broken English. Incapacitated by wounds at Gettysburg, he went abroad on a Confederate mission. Later, restored to health, he re-entered the Prussian army and served in the Wars of German Unification. He left an interesting account of his Confederate service in his *Memoirs of the Confederate War for Independence* (2 vols., Edinburgh and London, 1866; reprint New York, 1938).

5. "Little Sorrel's" original name was "Fancy," and Mrs. Jackson says he was a favorite of her father's family as "Old Fancy" for many years after the war. She mentions other horses used by General Jackson in the army, one of which, "Superior" by name, was often ridden by him. For an interesting account of the problem of horses in the Confederate army see Charles W. Ramsdell, "Lee's Horse Supply, 1861-1865," *American Historical Review*, XXX (1929-1930), 758-777.

6. These three books were essential for staff officers. Full titles are as follows: *Regulations for the Army of the Confederate States, and for the Quartermaster's and Pay Departments. The Uniform and Dress of the Army. Published by Authority of the Secretary of War* (New Orleans, 1861); Egbert L. Vielé, *Handbook for Active Service; Containing Practical Instructions in Campaign Duties* (Richmond, 1861); and Charles Henry Lee, *The Judge Advocate's Vade Mecum: Embracing a General View of Military Law, and the Practice Before the Courts Martial, With an Epitome of the Law of Evidence, as Applicable to Military Trials* (Richmond, 1863). The *Regulations* and Vielé's *Handbook* were both revisions of United States Army regulations. Lee's book was the standard authority on his subject.

7. *The Partisan Leader; A Tale of the Future*, by Edward William Sidney [pseud.], was first published in Washington in

1836. Written by Nathaniel Beverly Tucker, it is said to have been suppressed by Tucker and Duff Green, the publisher. It was reprinted in the North at the outbreak of the war as a key to disunion. It is a romantic prophecy of what was to, but did not, happen in the South.

The reading done by Douglas during the period covered by his "Diary," December 1862 to April 1865, is astounding both as to quantity and range. In addition to the authors mentioned here he read from J. S. C. Abbott, Charles Lamb, Leigh Hunt, Bulwer-Lytton, Nathaniel Hawthorne, Walter Scott, James Fenimore Cooper, Thomas Moore, Edgar Allan Poe, Augusta Evans Wilson, Victor Hugo, Mrs. Ann Radcliffe, John C. Jeaffreson, Baroness J. Tautphoeus, H. Blair, Horace, the Bible, *Harper's Weekly*, as well as many others, long since forgotten. His "Diary" lists by name more than three hundred volumes which he read.

8. Charles James Faulkner (1806-1884) was graduated from Georgetown College. He served in the Mexican War, was a member of the Virginia Constitutional Convention of 1850 and of the United States House of Representatives from 1851 to 1859, and Minister to France 1859 to 1861. At Jackson's request he was appointed Colonel and Adjutant General of his staff. Colonel G. F. R. Henderson thinks that Faulkner did a good job in collecting and combining the reports of the coördinate commanders into a general report for General Jackson (see *Stonewall Jackson*, II, 379). More than once Douglas complains that Jackson's staff did not receive due credit for its services. This feeling may explain his harsh criticism of Faulkner.

9. The young screech owl was given to Douglas by Miss Kate Corbin, sister of Richard Corbin, the owner of Moss Neck. Douglas kept the owl in his quarters for some time but it later sickened and died, grieving him greatly. Diary entries of January 23, 24, and 25, 1863, tell the story of the owl.

10. The cobbler was the same William Wintermeyer who entertained Douglas and the other soldiers with his jokes and droll stories when in camp at Winchester.—See *supra*, pp. 190-191.

11. Robert Jenkins Nevin, born in Allegheny, Pennsylvania, November 24, 1839, was a classmate of Douglas at Franklin and Marshall College. He served in the army as Lieutenant, Cap-

tain, and Major. After the war, he studied theology at the General Theological College in New York and, after a short pastorate in Bethlehem, Pennsylvania, went to Rome, Italy, as Rector of St. Paul's Episcopal Church where he remained until his death in 1907. He erected the present St. Paul's Church in 1870-1876 and was President of the American Churches in Europe.

Chapter XIX

1. Beverley T. Lacy, a Presbyterian minister in whom Jackson had great confidence, was appointed general chaplain at Jackson's Headquarters to have supervision over all the chaplains in the army. Lacy was to supply chaplains for destitute regiments, to serve as a channel of intercourse between the army and the clergy of different churches, and to give the labors of chaplains and ministers the unity and impulse of an ecclesiastical organization. He succeeded surprisingly well in this task and a revival of religion swept through the army as a result of his work.

Chapter XX

1. Jackson's second wife was Mary Anna, daughter of Reverend Robert H. Morrison, a Presbyterian preacher and President of Davidson College. It should be noted, however, that Jackson's first wife, Eleanor Junkin, had led Jackson into the Presbyterian Church before her death.

2. This was the Law School conducted by John Brockenbrough, a graduate of the University of Virginia and Federal Judge of the Western District of Virginia. The School was opened in 1849. It was later to become the Law School of Washington and Lee University.

3. Blind Tom, a musical prodigy, was born near Columbus, Georgia, May 25, 1849. He was the slave of Thomas Green Bethune, whose name he took. Almost entirely blind and a low-grade moron if not an idiot, he early began to imitate the sounds of birds and animals. He loved best, however, to imitate the music of the pianoforte. He could repeat from one hearing the performances of such artists as Herz and could reproduce Bach or Chopin once he had heard them. He appeared in New York in 1861 and later toured the United States and Europe, playing before large and appreciative audiences.

Chapter XXI

1. This was the United States Industrial and Training School, better known, because of its football team, as Carlisle Indians. It grew out of the experiment conducted by Captain R. H. Pratt in 1879 of placing Indian boys and girls in white homes during their vacations from school so that they might more easily learn white man's civilization. The school was discontinued in 1917.

2. Chauncey Forwood Black was Lieutenant-Governor of Pennsylvania, 1882-1886, candidate for Governor in 1886, and President of the National Association of Democratic Clubs. His father, Jeremiah Sullivan Black, was Chief Justice of the Supreme Court of Pennsylvania and Attorney General in President James Buchanan's cabinet. He was appointed to the United States Supreme Court, but the Senate failed to confirm him. He opposed the Lincoln policy on confiscation of property and on interfering with civil rights and defended President Andrew Johnson in the impeachment trial.

3. James Lawson Kemper was elected Governor of Virginia on the Conservative or Democratic ticket in 1873. The legislature elected him to the United States Senate, but he refused to accept the office.

Chapter XXII

1. Samuel M. Smucker was born at Gettysburg, Pennsylvania, February 26, 1844. He was educated at Pennsylvania College and at the College of the City of New York. He was a Sergeant in the Twenty-sixth Pennsylvania Regiment. After the war he practiced law and served as Judge of the Court of Appeals of Maryland from 1898 to his death in 1911.

2. Major Whittlesey's letter is as follows:

Concord, N. H.
Sept. 10—1863

Sir.

Your note of the 4th Inst. has just reached me, and I hasten to reply.

While I regret your personal misfortune—I take pleasure in the opportunity it affords me to bear testimony to the high courtesy you exhibited toward myself and others—on the occasion of my capture by the Southern troops under General Jackson, last summer in the town of Winchester, Va. While I was confined to my bed by sickness—you kindly interested yourself in having the privilege of parole granted me—and on the evacuation of that town by Gen. Jackson—you being a member of his Staff—at the expense of much personal trouble—courteously called at my residence—to receive my parole—and to hand me the order of your General permitting me to "go at large." All this you were kind enough to do for me, without any personal acquaintance—and at a time when, unfortunately, like the present, the paroling of prisoners of war was not general.

You are at liberty to use this communication in any application you may see fit to make to the Hon. Secretary of War of the United States—for the privilege of being admitted to parole—and I have no doubt that the courtesy you have shown in the past to our prisoners of war—will be regarded by him as a sufficient reason for making an exception in your case at this time.

      I am Sir

             Very resp'y

                     Yr obdt Servt

                     J. H. Whittlesey

To   Maj. 5 U. S. Cav.

   Maj. H. K. Douglas,

      Prisoner of War

         West's Hospital

         Baltimore, Md.

3. During the Spanish American War considerable scandal developed in regard to the meat sold to the United States army by the "beef trust." It was required to be refrigerated so as to be ready for use in seventy-two hours. Treated with a preservative fluid, much of the beef was putrid when it reached its destination. It had a terrible stench and often made the soldiers sick. Because of the preservative fluid and the stench, the soldiers called it "embalmed beef." Theodore Roosevelt claimed that fully one-tenth of the beef bought by the army was not fit to eat. These charges led to an effort to impeach Secretary of War Russell A. Alger. He was investigated but "whitewashed." See Ellis Paxson Oberholtzer, *History of the United States Since the Civil War* (5 vols., New York, 1926-1937), V, 558-561.

4. Johnston notified Douglas of the shipment of food and clothing in the following letter:

Office of Johnston Brothers & Co.

Bankers.

Baltimore, Dec. 23, *1863*.

H. Kyd Douglas, Esq
   Prisoner of war
      Johnson's Island

Dear Sir,

Enclosed you will find the receipt of Harnden Express Co. for two boxes, addressed to you and containing the following articles—

2 overcoats	2 roast hams
3 pants	1 pr. roast chickens
1 vest	1 bag of biscuit
4 drawers	1 box of cigars
2 sack coats	
2 doz. collars	
7 pr. socks	
2 hats	
2 cravats	
2 pr. sheets	
6 linen sheets	

I have written to Lieut. F. Cage to call upon you for a suit of clothing which please give to him—he writes to me poor fellow that he has not had a change for six mos. So I hope he will not object to wearing some clothes partially (but not much) worn by myself—the claims and applications are so numerous that I could not afford to send him a new outfit and as he is entirely a stranger to me, thought he would have to take the best I could send him.

I think perhaps the partially worn overcoat is warmer than the new one which I was advised *not* to send of grey cloth and to be as plain as possible. Of course take your choice and if there is anything else you fancy, keep it—if there is not anything of use to you, please give the articles to any of the prisoners who may require them. I hope you will enjoy the cigars—the edibles were gotten together in such a hurry that I fear they will not be nice.

Truly yrs

Henry E. Johnston

My sister Emily requested me a long time ago to say to you that your letter addressed to her was not received—several of your letters to me have miscarried. I will see Mrs. Carr and P. and report.

Address
    The name of the party is
        Lieut. *Fielding Cage*
          P of w
            Johnson's Island
            Sandusky Ohio

5. Captain General Weyler was in command of the Spanish troops in Cuba in 1896 and 1897. Notorious for harsh and relentless measures, he was bitterly assailed by the warmongers in the United States, especially by William Randolph Hearst of the New York *Journal* and Joseph Pulitzer of the *World*. Representative William Sulzer of New York, in a speech in Congress, called Weyler the greatest thief, coward, brute, liar, and murderer the world had ever seen.

6. Robert Ould (1820-1881) was born at Georgetown, D. C., and educated at Columbian College and the College of William and Mary. A noted lawyer and United States Attorney, he prosecuted Daniel Sickles in one of the famous murder trials of Washington. He was Assistant Secretary of War and Chief of the Bureau of Exchange of Prisoners for the Confederacy. According to the records, Judge Ould was not a delegate to the National Democratic Convention at Charleston, South Carolina, in 1860.

7. Douglas is mistaken here. Simon B. Buckner did not have a brother in the Confederate army.

8. Mrs. M. Todd White, sister of Mrs. Lincoln, had married Dr. White of Selma, Alabama, before the organization of the Confederacy. She and her sister, Ella Todd, who was visiting in Selma at the beginning of the Civil War, made and presented to

Captain N. H. R. Dawson a silk flag which was carried by the first regiment of Alabama troops. Mrs. White and Mrs. Dawson (for Ella Todd married Captain Dawson) were noted for their support and loyalty to the Confederate cause.

9. The marriage of General John Pegram and Miss Hetty Carey of Baltimore was one of the oustanding social events of Richmond during the war. The wedding took place at St. Paul's Church on January 19. General Pegram was killed at Hatcher's Run on February 6, and his funeral service was conducted at the same church in which he had been so happily married.

10. Mary Todd Lincoln (1818-1882) was never sympathetic to her husband's family but she was a devoted wife. She was much criticized, as a Southern lady in the White House, during the war, but most of the criticism was mere gossip and malicious slander, and the imputations of disloyalty were unfounded. In addition to Mrs. White two of Mrs. Lincoln's sisters married officers in the Confederate army and three of her brothers were Confederate soldiers.

Mrs. Julia Dent Grant was the daughter of Colonel Frederick Dent, a slaveholder and an ardent Southerner. Colonel Dent gave Mrs. Grant two slaves and made Grant an overseer on his farm. When the war came on Dent looked with much disfavor on his Federal son-in-law whom he regarded as a traitor and a renegade. Mrs. Grant, while loyal to her father, nevertheless clung to her husband. When his son Frederick T. entered the Union army the father began to soften toward Grant but he continued to criticize the Yankees even when living at the White House with his daughter.

CHAPTER XXIII

1. Holmes Conrad (January 31, 1840-September 4, 1916) was the brother of Miss Sallie Conrad for whom Douglas kept his wartime diary. Conrad was educated at the Virginia Military Institute and the University of Virginia. He was Major and Assistant Inspector General in Rosser's Cavalry. After the war he studied law, was a member of the state legislature, Assistant Attorney General of the United States in 1893, and Solicitor General in 1895. He then became Professor of Law at Georgetown University.

2. James Longstreet lost caste with the Southern people

when he accepted reconstruction, turned Republican, and accepted office under Republican Presidents. He died in Gainesville, Georgia, on January 2, 1904.

3. John Warwick Daniel (September 5, 1842-June 29, 1910) went from Harrison's Classical School in Lynchburg into the Confederate army and became a Major at the age of twenty. Wounded in the Wilderness in 1864 he was a cripple for life. He was a member of the United States House of Representatives, 1884-1886, and of the Senate from 1887 until his death. The "Lame Lion," as he was called, led the free silver group in Virginia and the fight to disfranchise the Negro in 1902.

Chapter XXIV

1. The Virginia Military Institute made notable contributions to the Confederate cause. In addition to the services and losses of the cadet corps, the school gave from its faculty and alumni to the Confederate army: 1 lieutenant general, 3 major generals, 18 brigadier generals, 160 colonels, 110 majors, 306 captains, and 221 lieutenants.

2. The residence of General G. F Smith, in which his daughter was ill, was spared through the kind intervention of Colonel Du Pont when told by the physician that her removal would result in the girl's death. All other buildings were burned. In later years the Federal government appropriated funds to recompense the state of Virginia for its losses in the burning of the buildings of the Virginia Military Institute.

3. Sam Houston Letcher was born at Lexington, Virginia, in 1848. He attended the Virginia Military Institute and saw service as a cadet at New Market. He then enlisted in the Confederate army and was commissioned a lieutenant in December, 1864. After the war he returned to the Institute and was graduated in 1869. He practiced law for a number of years and was appointed to an unexpired term as Judge of the Circuit Court of Virginia in 1898 and was re-elected successively until he voluntarily retired in 1912. He died in Lexington in 1914.

4. This school was to become the first college of higher education for women in Virginia. Founded in 1842 as the Valley Union Seminary, it became a coeducational school in 1852 but in 1855 as Hollins Institute it became again a girls' school. In 1911 it became Hollins College.

5. Douglas is in error here. "Silver Spring," the home of Francis P. Blair, Sr., was not burned. It is, in fact, standing today. Gideon Welles, Secretary of the Navy in Lincoln's cabinet, visited the place immediately after the Confederates left and was amazed that so little damage had been done. The place was damaged, said he, little if any more than it would have been if occupied by Union troops. John C. Breckinridge had taken care to protect the place because of his friendship for Blair.

The Confederates did burn "Falkland," home of Montgomery Blair, Postmaster General in Lincoln's cabinet. This was done in retaliation for the burning of Governor John Letcher's home by General Hunter's troops. General Early denies that he ordered the burning of "Falkland" but holds that it was a justified act.—See William E. Smith, *The Francis Preston Blair Family in Politics* (2 vols., New York, 1933), II, 273; *Diary of Gideon Welles* (3 vols., Boston and New York, 1911), II, 76-80; Jubal A. Early, *Autobiographical Sketch and Narrative of the War Between the States*, p. 395.

6. This was the home of James A. Seddon, Secretary of War in Jefferson Davis' cabinet. General Butler wrote General Grant and Montgomery Blair that he had sent General C. K. Graham with the army gunboats up the river to burn Seddon's place in retaliation for the burning of "Falkland."—See Benjamin F. Butler, *Private and Official Correspondence* (5 vols., Norwood, Mass., 1917), V, 6.

7. Douglas was somewhat confused on this point. Alexander Robinson Boteler (May 16, 1815-May 8, 1892) was not a member of the Senate Committee of Thirteen. He was a member of the House of Representatives and introduced a resolution that resulted in the appointment by the House of a Committee of Thirty-three that proposed an amendment to the United States Constitution which, if adopted, might have stayed the dissolution of the Union.

CHAPTER XXV

1. Douglas was mistaken as to the location of this painting. It is not, nor has it been, in the Corcoran Gallery of Art in Washington, D. C. (Letter of Robert L. Parsons, Assistant Director of the Corcoran Gallery of Art, to Fletcher M. Green, February 5, 1940.) Oregon Wilson was a native of the Valley of Virginia and painted "Woman's Devotion" shortly after the war.

2. John Barrett Kerfoot, born in Ireland in 1816, settled in Lancaster, Pennsylvania. Educated at St. Paul's College, he was President of St. James College in Maryland (1842-1864) where, because of his strong Unionist sentiment, he was bitterly criticized by Confederate sympathizers. He was President of Trinity College (Connecticut) from 1864 to 1867. Consecrated Episcopal Bishop of Pittsburgh in 1866, he played an important role in the reunion of the Episcopal Church. He died in Meyerdale, Pennsylvania, in 1881.

3. Douglas added the following note in explanation of the arrest of Dr. Kerfoot:

"In the statements of Professor Coit and Dr. Kerfoot in Mr. Hall's *Life of Bishop Kerfoot* there is confusion as to some of the facts. There was no Colonel Peyton on Early's staff. Major Peyton was on Rodes's staff, but Rodes had gone. Peyton was not there at all; and they have evidently in places used Rodes's name for Ramseur's and Peyton's name for mine. There are some other small errors. But as they were in much confusion at the time and both Dr. Kerfoot's diary and Professor Coit's account were written some time after, little inaccuracies are not surprising."

4. William Rollinson Whittingham (December 2, 1805-October 17, 1879) was born in New York City. He was graduated from the General Theological Seminary of that city and served the institution for several years as professor and librarian. Elected fourth Protestant Episcopal Bishop of Maryland in 1840, he served that diocese until his death. It is estimated that two-thirds of the Bishop's clergy and laity were Confederate sympathizers during the war; hence the bitter criticism of the pro-Northern Bishop in contemporary Southern writings.

5. This was Douglas' dear friend Miss Sallie Conrad for whom he kept his war diary upon which this work is based. She was the daughter of Robert Y. Conrad and sister of Holmes Conrad. According to this diary, they were engaged, but for some unknown reason they were never married.

6. At the request of members of the staff, Douglas wrote a beautiful appreciation of the brilliant Pendleton, which he sent to John Moncure Daniel, editor of the Richmond *Examiner*, to be published as an obituary. (The original of this tribute together with Douglas' note to Daniel are preserved in the Douglas manuscripts.)

Chapter XXVI

1. Mt. Airy was the home of Dr. Andrew Russell Meem, a noted agricultural reformer and a Surgeon in the Confederate army. He died in 1865. Dr. Meem had three brothers who saw service in the Confederate army: Gilbert S. and John G., both Brigadier Generals, and Captain James L. who was killed at Seven Pines. Because of their personal interests and sacrifice, Mr. and Mrs. John G. Meem, Sr., kept open house at Mt. Airy for Confederate soldiers, and here Douglas spent many hours when free from military duty.

2. *Quits* and *Initials* were written by Baroness J. Tautphoeus; *Not Dead Yet*, by John Cardy Jeaffreson. Both were popular authors of their day. Douglas read many volumes from the large and well-selected library at Mt. Airy.

3. In a marginal note Douglas wrote, "An account of this adventure in full and others on that trip may be seen in my article, 'Cupid Under Fire.' " This was probably published in a daily newspaper of either Philadelphia or Baltimore. Douglas wrote many short articles for both.

4. John Frederich Hartranft (1830-1889) won Douglas' affection when the latter was a prisoner in the Penitentiary at Washington. Hartranft was in command of the Penitentiary and not only showed him every courtesy possible but also introduced Douglas to his family socially and fed him delicacies from his table. Hartranft is best known for his suppression of strikes by armed force when Governor of Pennsylvania, 1872-1876.

Chapter XXVII

1. Douglas is in error here. Robert Ould was tried for treason but was acquitted. General Sickles pushed the case against Ould in revenge for Ould's prosecution of the charge of murder against Sickles for the killing of Philip Barton Key in 1859.

2. Lord George Jeffreys (1648-1689), Chief Justice of England from 1683 until the overthrow of James II in the Glorious Revolution of 1688-1689, was notorious for the Bloody Assizes in which he condemned hundreds to death without the semblance of a fair trial. Sir Thomas Armstrong was condemned without a trial. Jeffreys died a prisoner in the Tower of London.

BIBLIOGRAPHICAL NOTE

IN ADDITION to his manuscripts Douglas left the following published articles bearing on his services and experiences in the Civil War:

"A Ride for Stonewall," *Southern Historical Society Papers*, XXI (1893), 206-212.

"Stonewall Jackson, Between His Death-bed and His Grave," *Southern Magazine*, XIV (1874), 370-372.

"Stonewall Jackson in the Maryland Campaign," *Century Magazine*, X (New Series, 1886), 285-295.

"Stonewall Jackson's Intentions at Harper's Ferry," *Battles and Leaders of the Civil War*, 4 vols. (New York, 1888), II, 615-616.

"Stonewall Jackson in Maryland," *Battles and Leaders of the Civil War*, II, 620-629.

"Stonewall Jackson and His Men," *Annals of the War* (Philadelphia, 1879), pp. 642-653.

"Stonewall Jackson and the American Civil War," a review of Colonel G. F. R. Henderson's book of the same title, *American Historical Review*, IV (1898), 371-377.

Short biographical sketches of Henry Kyd Douglas are found in *The Confederate Veteran*, XII (1904), 125; and in *Who's Who in America* (1903-1905), 409-410.

Of the biographies of General Jackson the following throw light on Douglas' military career:

Dabney, R. L., *Life and Campaigns of Lieut.-Gen. Thomas J. Jackson* (New York, 1866).

Henderson, Colonel G. F. R., *Stonewall Jackson and the American Civil War*, 2 vols. (New York, 1898).

Jackson, Mary Anna, *Memoirs of Stonewall Jackson* (Louisville, 1895).

Other works of value are:

Allan, William, *History of the Campaign of Gen. T. J. (Stonewall) Jackson in the Shenandoah Valley of Virginia* (Philadelphia, 1880).

Avirett, J. B., *The Memoirs of General Turner Ashby and his Compeers* (Baltimore, 1867).

Early, Jubal A., *Autobiographical Sketch and Narrative of the War Between the States: with Notes by R. H. Early* (Philadelphia and London, 1912).

Freeman, Douglas Southall, *R. E. Lee, A Biography*, 4 vols. (New York and London, 1934-1935).

Thomason, John W., Jr., *Jeb Stuart* (New York and London, 1930).

The monumental but poorly indexed *War of the Rebellion Official Records of the Union and Confederate Armies*, 228 vols. (1881-1900), is an essential work for the study of any soldier of the Civil War.

INDEX

DATE DUE

NOV 10 76			
NOV 22 76			